The Wilsons of Tranby Croft

by

Gertrude M. Attwood

HUTTON PRESS

1988

Published by the Hutton Press Limited
130 Canada Drive, Cherry Burton, Beverley
East Yorkshire HU17 7SB

Phototypeset, printed and bound by
The Walkergate Press Limited
Lewis House, Springfield Way
Anlaby, Hull HU10 6RX

ISBN 0 907033 71 7

*This book is dedicated to Raymond Wilson
and Thetis Malcolmson, descendants of Arthur and Mary Wilson,
and to the children of Hull High School for Girls
who, in a different sense, are also their descendants.*

CONTENTS

ACKNOWLEDGEMENTS

It would be impossible to acknowledge all the help and support from so many good people during the lengthy research and compilation of this book. Wherever possible, acknowledgement has been made in footnotes to the text and photographs; but I would like to express my gratitude here to everyone who has helped. In particular, my thanks go to Mr. Raymond Wilson and Mrs. Thetis Malcolmson, grandchildren of Arthur and Mary Wilson, for their continued support throughout the project, and to Mr. Malcolm Strachan who brought us face to face, and has himself helped in so many different ways. I should also like to thank my three headmistresses at Hull High School for Girls – Miss H. W. Thompson, who gave me the incentive to start the research, Miss C. M. B. Radcliffe, the present headmistress, and the late Miss L. M. Jefferson; also the present deputy headmistress, Mrs. M. P. Grady; the Parents' Association; and the staff and girls whose unfailing interest did so much to improve my morale on many occasions. I am grateful to Mr. R. Fewlass and Mr. M. M. Webster, late of Ellerman's Wilson Line, and to Mr. N. Higson who enabled me to study their archives in the Brynmor Jones Library of the University of Hull. I would also mention Mr. R. Allen, sometime Postmaster of Hull, who established contact with St. Martin le Grand; Miss J. Hobbins, the late Professor T. E. Hope and Mrs. M. Hope for allowing me to view the property in Grosvenor Terrace, Leeds; Mrs. J. Pressling, who gave to the school most of the beautiful old photographs in memory of her aunt, former housekeeper at Tranby Croft, Mrs. Frances Woolrich, and the photographers Mr. I. Innes, Mr. K. Jackson and the late Mr. K. Hickey for their reproductions of these and other original prints.

Above all, my thanks go to my late husband, James, and my daughter, Elspeth, who had to live with this project for so long and did so with such helpfulness and goodwill; and to Miss J. Crowther and her willing band of helpers at the Local History Library, Albion Street, Hull who also gave me support over a long period. Without their help, this book might never have been written.

Finally I would like to thank Mr. and Mrs. Charles Brook of the Hutton Press, who with great skill and kindness have steered me through the final process of bringing the book before the public.

Gertrude M. Attwood
Hull
September 1988

Gertrude M. Attwood
Photograph by courtesy of Paul Anderson

PREFACE

I first saw Hull High School for Girls, Tranby Croft on a glorious summer afternoon in 1947. Later that year I was made responsible for the teaching of history in the school, and was immediately intrigued by the continuous hints – they were never more than that – concerning the Baccarat Scandal. It was pointed out to me however, and with some force, that this was a subject which should remain buried, and research would not be welcomed. Thus, my interest lay dormant for a generation, which was a pity because during that time many people died who could have helped a lot.

In the Summer Term of 1971 the headmistress of the school, Miss H. W. Thompson, asked me to write a short, illustrated account of the house and the family. This would be distributed to members of the Council of the Church Schools' Company (to which the High School belongs) and to heads of the Company schools, who were to visit Tranby Croft a fortnight later. During that short time I realised how little information on the subject was readily available, and how very much more there must be, hidden away. Baccarat became one of many issues. From that moment I could never let go. I still cannot.

This book was originally part of a much longer work, but I hope that it will give an insight into the life and times of a Hull family which, for a long period, involved itself socially, commercially, and philanthropically in the local community, who made it what it was, and for whom it had a great regard.

CHAPTER ONE

The Emergence of the Wilson Empire

In the latter part of the eighteenth century the old town of Hull, set squarely between the Humber to the south, the River Hull to the east, and the lines of the old moat to the north and west, continued to remain the nerve centre of trade and commerce in that area of Yorkshire. Along the High Street, running parallel to the Hull on its western bank, the merchants still lived with wharves at their own back doors; and off High Street to the west was George's Yard, where lived David Wilson, lighterman, the first member of his clan of whom we have any knowledge. His was an exacting job, dependent on tides and the appearance of shipping in the Humber, and David, using a boat which was virtually an empty shell, took cargo from the wharf side to load up the ships in the river, and brought their cargo back again. He made a reasonable living, and could bring up his family in something like comfort.

He had married Elizabeth Gray, by whom he had at least ten children.(1) Eight were girls, and if they survived to womanhood their dowries would pose a problem, if not a downright headache to their father. The two sons were named David and Thomas. Of the younger David we know nothing, so far, except the fact of his birth in 1786. He may well have died in childhood. Hull, like most towns, was both dirty and insanitary, and the frequent and regular outbreaks of infection carried off the more vulnerable inhabitants. Thomas, however, born on 12th February 1792 and christened two days later at Dagger Lane Independent Church, not only survived but became relatively famous in his own area and beyond.

Young David, if he lived, would have inherited his father's business. Thomas would have to make his own way in the world. His father was wise enough to ensure that he was adequately educated. Both father and son were ambitious, and turned their attention to the developing trade of Hull, particularly in Swedish iron ore. So, the starting point would undoubtedly be the admission of Thomas into the counting house of a Hull merchant, and the usual approach would be to answer a local advertisement:

"An Apprentice wanted: For a *Mercantile house* in Hull, where a *young man* will have an opportunity of acquiring a general knowledge of Business. A handsome Premium will not only be required, but the same diligent attitude to Business that is expected from a hired Servant".(2)

The most venerable school where Thomas could have been educated was the ancient local Grammar School, with its emphasis on classical learning. This would not be so useful in a commercial career as a sound grounding in English, French and Mathematics, and it is probable, therefore, that Thomas was schooled in one of the private academies, of which there were several.

David's job would bring him into regular contact with the Hull merchants. He knew

7

their difficulties and, truth to tell, they were a somewhat nervous little lot. The journey across the North Sea, sometimes treacherous in summer, was impossible in winter. A merchant trading by himself could lose everything he possessed if a single ship foundered. The Hull merchants, therefore, normally traded in groups, two, three or even four together. David Wilson became increasingly interested in one of these groups where a merchant, strangely enough, bore the same surname as he did himself.

John Wilson, merchant of Hull, had learned his trade in the counting house of the brothers William and Joseph Williamson who were in the forefront of the iron ore trade at Gothenburg. When Joseph Williamson died, he left no less than £1000 to John Wilson. This was to be paid on John's 21st birthday, 28th August 1789, and to this sum would be added any interest accruing after Joseph's death. This was a considerable help to the young man in setting up as a merchant in his own right.(3) John also made a very successful and profitable marriage, for his wife, Ann, was an heiress, and the daughter of Caius Thompson, merchant and iron master, who had been sheriff of Hull in the year 1773. With such good fortune and his own determination, it was hardly surprising that John Wilson was successful. By the time young Thomas, David's son, was ready for work, John was trading in company with Charles Whitaker and Anthony Wilkinson as well as with the Williamson family, and he had a counting house at 47, High Street. All this David Wilson knew. He also knew that one blessing had been denied to John Wilson — he had no children. David must have wondered whether, if his son Thomas could be introduced into the Wilson counting house, John might be prepared to do for his lad, should the boy prove worthy, what, a generation earlier, Joseph Williamson had done for him.

It is very likely that this happened, although David did not live long enough to see it, for he died when Thomas was in his eighteenth year. He would have been proud of his son. Thomas learned quickly. At first he was a clerk. Then he was sent as a traveller in the Sheffield area, where he was able not only to increase his knowledge of the iron and steel business, but to make several new business acquaintances which would certainly come in handy in the future. Thomas also took a leaf out of John Wilson's book when he married, on 1st September 1814, at Drypool Church, Hull, Susannah, daughter of John West, a wine and spirit merchant of Summergangs, east of the town. True, there was also a son, Charles, but he died in 1846. His will had provided that his young son, Charles Matthew, could be taken on as a merchant's clerk by the three trustees (one of whom was Thomas Wilson), and that when he reached the age of 21, he should be entitled to a quarter share in the profits of the business. However, if it should be desirable to direct the business in any other way in order to safeguard the interests of Charles' family, this was to be done. Since the other two trustees were Charles' widow, Rhoda, and a relative, Charles Turner West, who was a doctor, it is not surprising to find that Thomas' eldest boy, David, was given the task of running this business, which he did, with typical Wilson efficiency, so that it prospered. So, although Thomas had to wait longer than John Wilson, his marriage also was financially and commercially fruitful.

John Wilson was wealthy enough to retire early, and he and his wife, Ann, settled in a small country house at Melton Hill, some half dozen miles to the west of Hull. By 1817 Thomas Wilson was operating in his own right from the High Street counting house. Certainly his wife's dowry would have helped him, and it looks likely that John Wilson had used his influence, if not also his charity. John's retirement did not last long. On 11th January 1822 the *Hull Advertiser* mournfully reported "On Sunday evening last, at his seat at Melton Hill (died) John Wilson Esq, aged 58, a man of great generosity and feeling.

Integrity and candour marked all his actions. He was a most excellent husband, a faithful friend, a kind hospitable companion, a benefactor to the poor and obtained the regard and confidence of his friends by cultivating harmony and amiable intercourse amongst them." His wife must have been grateful for such a proud memorial. She had 33 years in which to remember him before her turn came.

Thomas Wilson had now successfully negotiated the first rung of the ladder. At first he concentrated on what he knew. Consignments of iron left his yard on Garrison-side for the West Riding, and a steady stream of trade developed, particularly with the Sheffield area. By 1826, and possibly some years before that, he had begun an association with a Mr. J. Beckinton (or Beckington), a Hull merchant who hailed from Newcastle, and he now operated from Beckinton's counting house at 14, Salthouse Lane. He was also developing an interest in shipowning, which would seem to imply that, financially, he was at least keeping his head above water. This he certainly needed to do, for his family was growing at what we would call an alarming rate. Eventually there were 15 of them, nine boys and six girls, and Thomas and Susannah managed to rear all but one boy and one girl. Still, ships were bought. The earliest of which we have any knowledge was a "billy boy", the "Thomas and Ann", 51 tons and registered to Thomas Wilson in 1825. A "billy boy" was a seagoing vessel, a derivative of the Humber keel. It had high bulwarks and rounded lines, and carried coal "in one bottom", as the inelegant phrase has it, anywhere between Barnsley and Louth or Barton.(4) By 1831 Thomas and his partner certainly owned the "Swift", of 100 tons, and were negotiating with Whitby for a second ship. What both partners needed was an injection of money from an interested business man, and this they received from John Leech Hudson, a Hull druggist and importer of leeches, who operated from a shop at 28, Waterworks Street, Hull and also had premises at 26, Hosier Lane, West Smithfield, London. Thomas Hudson, gentleman, of Newcastle, possibly a relative of John, was also an investor.(5)

In 1834 the chance came for Beckinton and Wilson to extend their sphere of operation. Thomas Wilson had been born during the time of the French Revolution. While he was growing up, Napoleon was first securing France and then rampaging through Europe, meeting his most persistent opposition from England, a country which he would have to invade, if it were to be brought to heel. This Napoleon, with his tremendous continental commitments was unable to do, and he therefore sought to accomplish the same purpose by blocking England's trade. Parts of Scandinavia had not been directly involved, and so the mail had, therefore, been sent by packet boats from Harwich to Gothenburg every Wednesday and Saturday. The service had continued with the backing of the English and Swedish Post Offices until April 1834, when Sweden finally gave up its support. Any replacement service would now have to compare with the standard of the land mail through Western Europe which, since the end of the war had proved more reliable. The St. George's Steam Ship Company from Liverpool, supported by the British government (still hoping that the Swedes would renew their interest) undertook to sail once a week to Gothenburg. Sweden, however, did not grant a subsidy, Stockholm tending to regard the new service as a venture between Gothenburg business men, and in spite of repeated efforts by the British company, they refused to chip in. Therefore, in March, 1835 the ships involved, "The Superb" and "Cornubia", were removed to more lucrative trading routes.(6)

Here was the opportunity for Beckinton and Wilson. They decided to run a packet service between Gothenburg and Hull using one brig and two schooners.(7) It was a purely

GENEAOLOGY OF THE WILSONS OF TRANBY CROFT

David Wilson, lighterman of Hull 1737/8 – 25.4.1810
=
Elizabeth Gray

Mary b.1772	Elizabeth b.1773	Hannah b.1775	Margaret b.1776	Elizabeth b.1777	Martha b.1781	Sarah b.1786	David b.1787	Elizabeth b.1791 = Edward Brown	Thomas 12.2.1792 – 21.6.1869 Founder of the Shipping Line = Susannah West 19.11.1794 – 25.11.1879 daughter of John West of Summergangs, wine merchant		

David 1815-93

John West 1816-89

Edward Brown 1818-74
=
M. J. Buckton d.1900

Thomas 1819-1901
1. S. E. Collinson
2. M. P. Dawson
3. L. A. Patrick

Susannah 1820-1902 H. Garbutt b.1819

Elizabeth Gray 1822-1903 E. R. Sanderson d.1855

Hannah 1823-4

Harriet West 1824-79 = W. E. Bott

William Burton 1825-64 = M. E. Hill

Frederick 1828-1908 = M. L. Musette

Charles 1830-2

Rachel 1831-1911 = Joseph Lambert J.P.

Charles Henry 1st Baron Nunburnholme of Warter Priory 22.4.1833 – 27.10.1907 = F. J. H. Wellesley 8.10.1853 – 8.12.1932

Continued bottom left with Emily Howa...

Susannah West (Tottie) 1864 – 15.12.1943
=
1. John Graham Menzies (Freddie) d.15.5.1911

2. Lt./Col. Sir George Lindsay Holford

Ethel Mary 1865 – 10.4.1934
=
Sir Edward Lycett Green IInd Bart. 25.5.1860 – 16.1.1940

Keith 1888-15.12.1952	Maj. Gen. Sir Stewart Graham 30.1.1890– 28.5.1968 = 2. P. T. Beckett	Ian Graham b.5.11.1897 ?	Edward Arthur Lycett IIIrd Bart. 1.4.1886-4.3.1941 = Elizabeth Williams	Nancy Lycett 20.2.1888-6.5.1970 = 1. Capt. Adrian Rose 2. George. IVth Lord Vivian b.1878	Phyllis Mary Lycett 22.2.1890-7.9.1954 = G. F. Milner	David Cecil Lycett 4.6.1892-1.5.1960 = 1. ? 2. ?	Francis Denis Lycett (Peter) 2.11.1893-14.7.1959

GENEAOLOGY OF THE WILSONS OF TRANBY CROFT – *continued*

Continued from Charles Henry, top right, previous page

Emily Howard
25.4.1835 – 3.5.1921
=
Arthur Harrison

Arthur, M.F.H. of Tranby Croft
14.12.1836 – 21.10.1909
=
Mary Emma Smith
9.8.1843 – 22.11.1927
daughter of E. J. Smith of London.
Constantinople and Leeds

Arthur Stanley (Jack) 30.7.1868 – 12.4.1938
of Raywell House: M.P. for Holderness
=
Alice Cecil Agnes Filmer (Queenie)
daughter of Sir Edmund Filmer. IXth Bart
of Sutton Park. Kent

Edward Kenneth
9.11.1869 – 1.2.1947
of Roehampton Court
and Cannizaro
=
Adele Mary (Molly) Hacket
d.23.8.1946 daughter of
G. A. B. D. Hacket of Moor Hall,
Warwickshire

Thomas Raymond
chr. 10.11.1872
– 9.12.1885

Muriel Thetis
24.3.1875 –
19.10.1964
=
Capt. Richard
Edward Warde
(later Major)
M.C. d.29.5.1932

Clive Harry Adolphus,
D.S.O. 12.6.1878 –
18.1.1921
=
Elvira Maria Ercilia
Magherini of Florence
d.12.4.1962

Arthur Thomas Filmer (Wilson Filmer after 1917)
(Tommy) 29.9.1895 – 17.4.1968
=
1. Hon. Olive C. Wynn
dissolved 1931
2. Lettice M. Ward
dissolved 1947

Robert (Robin) Filmer
26.4.1903 – 14.8.1944
died of wounds in Italy
=
Patricia Kenneth Richards

Hilary 9.3.1903 – 29.10.1979
=
Geoffrey. Vth Earl of Munster
17.2.1906 – 1975

Thetis Mary b.3.2.1908
=
Ian D. Malcolmson

Raymond Clive b.23.5.1909
=
Aileen Amelia Horstmann

private venture, and there was no scheduled timetable. When sufficient passengers and goods were collected, the ship would sail. The citizens of Gothenburg were not satisfied. They wanted something better. They petitioned their Chamber of Commerce, the Handels-Societeten, to ask that the mail should be carried by steam ship. They felt sure that in a couple of years the service would become self supporting. They also approached the Treasury Lords in Britain who said "Yes", although the Swedes did not. The people of Gothenburg disliked the long route taken by the Hull ships — Beckinton and Wilson were, admittedly, self interested and were proceeding via Hamburg. However, as before, the people of Gothenburg were opposed by the people of Stockholm, who were engaged in steam traffic with Germany and wanted to keep things as they were. Aware that no fewer than 60 firms in Gothenburg were petitioning, Thomas Wilson let it be known that he was prepared to risk a steam ship service in the hope that the British government would contribute. Beckinton, initially, agreed, and since Hudson continued to be loyal, the firm engaged to run the service with two steamships each of which would make one passage a week in each direction. A yearly subsidy of £5,000 was agreed, and since Norway also showed interest and was willing to contribute, the service was extended to Christiania.

This had not been a blind venture. The firm had learned a certain amount about steamships when they had chartered the "Cornubia", from the St. George's Steam Ship Company at the beginning of 1835, with the idea of establishing a new line of steam communication between Hull and Dunkirk. The "Cornubia" had sailed weekly, leaving Hull on Wednesday and returning there on Saturday. The service only operated until the end of July of the same year, but it taught Thomas Wilson a good deal, and very quickly, about the merits and present imperfections of the new invention, and it probably led to a parting of the ways with Beckinton, whose health was deteriorating and who was soon to die.[8]

So, when the new service opened in May 1840, Beckinton had gone and Thomas Wilson would have to prove that he could stand alone. The Hudsons were still behind him, but the major decisions would now be his. At first all went well. The "Glen Albyn", a ship owned by the Berwick Steam Packet Company and taking passengers but not goods, made the maiden crossing including the stop at Christiania, and did it in the fastest time ever — 64 hours. Passengers paid three guineas for a first class ticket, and the cabin class cost £2. 3s. 0d. The ship would leave Hull every Saturday at 4 o'clock in the afternoon, and the return journey would start from Gothenburg at a similar time the following Friday. The "Innisfail" a ship belonging to the St. George's Company alternated with the "Glen Albyn", which, after the winter break, was replaced by the Dublin Steam Packet Company's "Scotia". In 1842 the "Innisfail" was teamed with the "Empress" also from the Dublin Company.

Suddenly, in the Autumn of 1842 the Swedish Post Office withdrew its support. It was said the steamships did not come up to their requirements, and indeed this was almost certainly true. The troubles of the steamship were hardly over, although they already had a fairly long history in Hull, since, as early as 1796 a steam packet had been built on the River Hull in a yard off Wincolmlee. By the 1830s steamships were becoming a fairly regular sight on the Humber, but they were still far from dependable, as the accident to the small steam packet "Union" in 1837 shows. She was getting up steam in the Hull dock, preparatory to sailing round the coast of Lincolnshire when she blew up, killing all her crew of 13. But time and experience would right these deficiencies, and Thomas Wilson knew that once the teething troubles were over, the steamship would outclass the sailing

12

ship in every respect. If he could change over to steam at the right time, he would be way ahead of his Hull rivals.

At the moment he was hedging his bets. He now owned four sailing ships and all his captains had shares in the vessels in which they sailed. By now Thomas Wilson was dealing with practically all the iron from certain Swedish mines, and, not surprisingly, was a staunch supporter of the repeal of the import duty on Swedish iron ore (then at £1 a ton), which would make such a difference to his Sheffield customers, who took something like 10,000 tons a year. He was also trading regularly with Dunkirk.

Just before the Swedish Post Office pulled out there was a further change in Thomas Wilson's fortunes. The Minutes of the Hull Banking Company on the 22nd November 1841 stated "Wilson, Hudson and Co. announce the withdrawal from their firm of John Hudson and Thomas Hudson stating that the business would in future be carried on as Thomas Wilson Sons and Company".(9) Thomas had now four strapping sons actually working in the business. David, born in 1815, was already experienced. So was John West, a year his junior. Edward Brown, the third brother, was shaping well, and although the fourth son, Thomas, showed no interest at all, having already set his sights on becoming a doctor, the fifth boy, William Burton, appeared able and willing. This was enough for Thomas. The new firm was said to have a capital of £20,000, its discount account with the Bank of England being £3,000 (Thomas was an early customer of the branch of the Bank of England in Hull). Eventually two other sons joined the firm, the two youngest and eventually the most famous, Charles Henry and Arthur. The remaining brother Fred, an artist, went to live in Florence and remained there. Thomas insisted that the boys should all learn the hard way, working through every department, and in later years Charles Henry would recall his experiences as an office boy, sticking on stamps and coming back to the family home at 14, Salthouse Lane well after midnight, when he had had to wait for a tide. To begin with, there was some animosity between David, the eldest, and John, the second son; and before David was sent off to run his mother's family business and thereby become a wine and spirit merchant, Thomas found it expedient as well as practical to send John out to Gothenburg, to act as a family agent and run the business from that end. This was entirely successful. John relished his new independence, and he came to love his adopted country. He became a naturalised Swede and though, like David, he never married, he was worth more than half a million pounds when he died in 1889.

After the withdrawal of support from the Swedish post office, eight years passed before a steamship service was resumed between Gothenburg and Hull, but trade in Hull was booming. There were now three docks. The original, known as the Old Dock but later renamed Queen's, was entered from the River Hull. The building of the Humber and then the Junction Docks, roughly along the line of the old moat, meant that shipping could enter direct from the Humber. The situation was still very unsatisfactory; ten acres of docks (or thereabouts) were simply not enough. On 9th February 1844 the Hull Dock Company was instrumental in introducing a bill into Parliament to extend. An influential committee of ship owners, which included Thomas Wilson, opposed it, not because the bill was trying to extend the dock area, but because it was not proposing to extend far enough. During that year Humber Dock became so crowded that ships waited in the river day after day to get in. There was an instance in November where a ship had to wait for a whole week. With the rapid development of English railways just around the corner, such a dilatory attitude would seem to be suicide.

Between 1842 and 1850 there had been endless negotiations between the Gothenburg

13

merchants and the Swedish, Norwegian and British governments, but nothing had been accomplished. In June 1850 Thomas Wilson Sons and Company, by now dedicated to steam, produced their new and powerful paddle steamer "Courier" and offered to trade with Christiania and Gothenburg, leaving Hull and Gothenburg on alternate Saturdays. The offer was accepted and the new steamship, built by Barclay of Glasgow, proved itself to be fast and efficient, and arrived in Gothenburg the following week, to be received in some style by John West Wilson. (She was, incidentally, the only sea going paddle steamer that Wilsons ever owned — the superiority of the screw propeller was soon recognised). The service proved to be of value, and continued regularly until the end of the year. Hull was a convenient landing place, even for London, for it had rail links with the capital long before Harwich and Tilbury did. By 1860 there were express trains, and it was possible for a business man to leave Gothenburg on Friday at one o'clock in the afternoon, and be in London at ten o'clock on Sunday evening. For service of this quality he would pay three guineas for a single ticket and five guineas for a return.

The Wilson firm played its part in an unusual set of circumstances in early July 1853. Carl Winberg, a Swedish citizen, had absconded from Gothenburg, carrying with him £600 which belonged to his employers, Messrs. Witterding. He came aboard the Wilson screw steamship "Scandinavian" and travelled on it to Hull, which was reached on Monday, 4th July. The passengers had to wait until the next morning before being landed, as there were a considerable number of them who were emigrating, and therefore had to be sent on to Liverpool. Winberg joined these people and went too. Meanwhile, his employers had discovered their loss, and their agents in Hamburg had promptly telegraphed Wilsons via Ostend. The message arrived very late on Tuesday night, but the following morning Wilsons went into action. They not only telegraphed a report to the Liverpool police, but they also dispatched one of their own clerks to Liverpool on a morning train. Much later in the day, a Hull constable, P.C. Greaves, and a clerk to Messrs. Clay and Squires, the Swedish Consular Office, also went off in pursuit. Since they did not leave Hull until seven o'clock in the evening, it was early on Thursday morning when they arrived in Liverpool and hurried to the Swedish Consular Office. When they got there, they found the man Winberg already in custody, with a Liverpool detective and a Wilson clerk, who could hardly contain his delight at being there first, in close attendance. They were about to return the prisoner to Hull, that being the first stage of his journey back. The Hull constable and the consular clerk were told that within ten minutes of Wilson's telegraphed information Winberg had been apprehended, and the £600 removed from his person. It was one of the earlier examples of the efficiency of the electric telegraph. Winberg and his captors reached Hull at half past six that Thursday evening, and Wilsons sailed him back to Gothenburg on the usual run the following Saturday — on the "Scandinavian".(10)

The Wilson Empire continued to expand. The girls were growing up and marrying. Harriet, the third surviving daughter, joined hands with William Eagle Bott of Hyde Park, then in Middlesex, a merchant, who became the Wilson agent at 1, East India Dock Avenue, London. Harriet's elder sister, Elizabeth, married Edward Rheam Sanderson, whose family were operating from Liverpool and later America and St. Petersburg. Members of this family also became Wilson agents. By 1880 there were 12 agents in England and 49 abroad. Soon after this, and for the second time, trade with India was opened up, and the Wilsons were now known commercially in most areas of the world.

The 1850s were years of war, disruptive to trade, and requiring courage and ingenuity if merchants were to acquire fresh markets. From 1854 to 1855 the Crimean War was waged, a war which would add a new dimension to the life of young Arthur Wilson's future father in law. Hard on its heels came the 2nd and 3rd Chinese Wars and the Indian Mutiny. At the beginning of the decade Thomas Wilson was concentrating on building up his fleet. In 1852 he ordered his biggest ship so far, the 500 ton "Scandinavian" (on which the malefactor Winberg later sailed). She was built by Thomas Wingate of Glasgow, could carry 40 first class and 12 second class passengers, and was registered solely to the 19 year old Charles Henry Wilson, who would later on become, with his brother Arthur, the effective owner of his father's Empire. The following year, however, the firm of William Earle opened up a yard in Wincolmlee on the River Hull, and from that time onwards most of the Wilson ships were built there — a real Humberside partnership, if ever there was one. During the Crimean War Thomas Wilson ordered three of the new, more stable screw steamers with their iron hulls. They were called the "Baltic" the "North Sea" and the "Humber". As soon as the war ended, the "Baltic" and the "Humber" opened up and established a new service to St. Petersburg (Russia had been our enemy during the recent struggle). The firm continued to do well. In 1853 its discount account with the Bank of England was raised to £10,000, and its capital had risen to £40,000. Later in the year, the discount limit was extended to £15,000. By the end of the decade the firm's capital had reached £70,000.(11)

All six brothers were now working for the firm, and Edward Brown had been given a chance to move away from Hull, first to Leeds (where the Wilsons had had an office since the 1830s) and then to Tunbridge Wells (from which there was reasonable access to London). When the North of Europe Steam Navigation Company dissolved in 1860, Thomas Wilson Sons and Company were in a position to take part of their business and several of their ships. Just before this time they adopted the practice of calling their ships by names ending in O. One of the first was the "Flamingo" built in 1858, and the first to be built by Earles was the "Dido" in 1862.(12) They had green hulls and red funnels, and flew a triangular flag which was white with a red circle near the thick end by the mast. Local people called them "Wilson's parrots".

The firm was doing well, but old Thomas was becoming an increasing embarrassment; he had now reached the time of life when it was easier to look back than to look forward. His health was indifferent and he was deaf, but would make few allowances for it. No doubt the untimely death of his son William, a day before his 39th birthday in 1864, saddened him. He seemed to be more ruthless. At least one of his sons complained that he was a martinet. Thomas, the doctor, said it was almost impossible to get him to pay his medical bills. He must have felt the pressure of youth and opportunism, and reacted in the only way an aging man could. A photograph exists of Thomas, Susannah and their five daughters in the garden of their house in Cottingham. It is as fierce an array of womanhood as one is ever likely to contemplate. Firm jawed, all of them, upright, rigid and implacable, they stare out at the camera with what seems to be haughty reserve if not downright hostility. Old Thomas himself only escapes because of a trompe d'oeil, which turns his jutting underlip into a hearty guffaw, incongruous in these Amazonian surroundings.

The private life of the family was all that might have been expected from good and loyal servants of the established church. They lived in a solid, substantial and fairly commodious dwelling with a portico at the front at 14, Salthouse Lane. At the time of writing it still stands. For some years it was used as a counting house as well as a home, but with a family of this size it must soon have become uncomfortably full. Thomas and Susannah

Thomas and Susannah Wilson and their five daughters in the garden at Park House, Cottingham. Photo by courtesy of Hull City Museums, Town Docks Museum, from the original in the possession of the Eagle Bott family.

were devout church goers and trailed their brood around the corner to St. Mary Lowgate every Sunday. At one time, the family must have filled at least three pews. Cooper Scott, the young son of the vicar (who was a personal friend of old Thomas) found them fascinating. He later described the parents as a "noble looking couple", Susannah "calm — looking, dignified", and the well scrubbed children "as handsome a family as could be found".(13) It was the vicar, John Scott, who advised his church-warden to send Charlie and Arthur to the new secondary school, Kingston College, off the Beverley Road, after they had attended the little national school associated with St. Mary's during their first few years of instruction. This was a privilege the elder brothers probably did not get.

As the family became more prosperous, Thomas began to spend more time in his quiet, gracious house in North Street, Cottingham. It was not a pretentious house, and not even very large considering how big a family might have to be squeezed into it on a celebratory occasion. The only unusual thing about it seems to have been a large powlonia in the garden, (these were very popular in Victorian times) but Thomas' unfortunately died. The house probably did not cost him very much, but it was within easy reach of Hull, and was therefore very handy for a man who insisted on keeping a close watch on his business. Cottingham was not, in some ways, an ideal place to retire. It was described by a reporter from the "Criterion" in 1874 as "a maloderous little village — I came expecting a scent of honeysuckle and jasmine and lo! I was greeted, and my nose has ever since been clogged, with the vapours of sewers and cesspools".(14) It has to be admitted that the night soil carts from Hull were emptied here!

Sometime later Thomas decided to try the sweeter breezes of the Yorkshire coast and he certainly spent the summer of 1867 at Ravine Villa, Filey (of which no trace remains),

16

while his sons sweated away in the office, no doubt thanking providence that they were, at the moment, left on their own.

Thomas had always been a philanthropist by inclination, and he continued to give generously for the welfare of his native town. In 1861 a scheme was afoot to provide at least a temporary home for fallen women. A local shipowner, Mr. J.A. Wade, headed the list of subscribers with a donation of £100. The erratic and greatly respected Sir Tatton Sykes of Sledmere and the Hull shipowner Zachariah C. Pearson (who had just been mayor of Hull, during which period he had presented his native town with its first public park, appropriately named after himself) followed up with £50 each. Thomas, like many more, contributed £10, and the £525, which was the eventual total, enabled the committee to purchase a house in Nile Street, where 61 girls were admitted during the first twelve months, although by then the total cost had reached £1,105.[15]

Two years later a subscription list was set up in order to build a Hull Seamen's and General Orphan Asylum - a necessary, timely and laudable aspiration. John Torr, a Baltic merchant hailing from Liverpool, but now for some years resident in Hull gave £2,000, whereupon Frederick William Hudson (soon to become sheriff) offered £500, providing that his figure could be matched by three further similar contributions. Thomas Wilson and his son David promptly paid up, and the last contribution was given by the Hull shipowner William Brownlow. In February 1864 Trinity House offered a suitable site of nearly an acre of land in Spring Bank, and the foundation stone was laid on 29th March 1864 by Torr. In a cavity behind the stone a bottle was placed, containing coin of the realm and a parchment giving names of the officers of the institution, among whom were listed Thomas, David, Charles and Arthur Wilson. Almost immediately Thomas, recognising the grand old Yorkshire principle that it would be a pity to spoil the ship for a ha'p'orth of tar, donated a further £1,000, thus giving the orphanage a promising start.[16]

The dock area of Hull was now extending rapidly, and in 1865 the Dock Company obtained powers to build an extension to Albert Dock (it was finally opened in 1885 as William Wright Dock). Thomas was a member of the reorganised board of directors, but the death of his son at Bridlington Quay the previous Christmas had been a bitter blow to him, and he was now seriously considering the possibility of handing over to his two youngest sons.

In his old age it must have been pleasing to Thomas to observe the way in which the rigorous moral and social training instilled into the children by Susannah and himself was bearing fruit. His three most famous sons, David, Charles and Arthur were all devout churchgoers, as he was himself. On Wednesday, 1st January 1868 the churchwardens of Cottingham (David Wilson and his sister Emily's husband, Arthur Harrison) gave a tea for the poor people of Cottingham, some 400 in all. The catering lists survive, and the generosity of the donors is self evident. There were 10 tongues weighing 40 lbs., two hams weighing 60 lbs., 150 lbs. of boiling beef, six pork pies weighing 50 lbs., four legs of mutton weighing 40 lbs., 100 dozen tarts and cheesecakes, 8 dozen buns (presumably for those with an exceptionally large capacity for eating), and four chests of oranges. The churchwardens had prevailed upon the ladies of Cottingham to serve the guests, who rolled in from the neighbouring villages to share in this munificence.[17] When Thomas had given, he had done so gladly and with thanksgiving. It seemed that the next generation would maintain the tradition.

On 15th June 1869 Thomas, as Chairman of the Committee, presided over a general meeting of the Seamen's and General Orphan Asylum. He did it with his usual attention

Thomas Wilson. Photo by courtesy of Hull City Museums, Town Docks Museum.

to detail, and few who said "Goodbye" to him that day would realise that they had received from him a last farewell. A week later he was dead. The 19th June was a Saturday. Thomas pronounced himself ready to get up as usual, round about seven o'clock — he was ever an early riser — when suddenly he could not speak. A severe stroke put him back in bed immediately, and he never showed signs of recovery. Mercifully for him and his devoted family he died on the following Monday morning. The circumstances of his funeral show that he had become one of the great men of Victorian Hull. As the reporter from the local newspaper pointed out:

> "Our humble task is merely to place on record outward manifestations of grief which were today to be seen on every hand throughout the long route by which the funeral cortege passed from the residence of the deceased at Cottingham to the narrower and more abiding tenement in Hull Cemetery."[18]

Cottingham was a silent village. All blinds were drawn, and it was said that the village people spoke to each other in whispers. John came home from Sweden, but not Fred, who remained in Florence. The preliminary service was read in a crowded Cottingham church, the police having been called in to maintain order among the crowd and keep them out, so that it was possible for the mourners to get in. After this, the cortege made its slow and stately progress towards the big new Hull cemetery in Spring Bank West, collecting more and more followers at every turn in the road. At Rose Cottage on the Beverley Road a contingent of Wilson employees joined the procession. Later on, a detachment from Earles' shipyard arrived. Then the orphans from Park Street joined in, and after them the orphans from the Seamen's and General. (The latter sang at the graveside "When our

18

heads are bowed in woe.") At the cemetery gates the procession was still growing, for here directors and officials of the Hull Dock Company were waiting. By now there were 57 carriages, and it was reckoned that at least 1,500 had witnessed or had taken part in the funeral.

Thomas was gone, but his work had been a secure foundation on which his sons could safely build. In one sense, his career is only preparatory to the brilliant careers which followed, but neither Charles Henry nor Arthur, in spite of all their wealth and achievements, were ever to know the depth of feeling and support from their own sons which they had been able to give to their father. If that had not been so, this story might never have been written.

(1) I am indebted to Penelope Pattinson for this information.
(2) *Hull Advertiser* 21st April 1810 p.3 (advertisement).
(3) Will of Joseph Williamson DDHB/28/91 (Harrison Broadley Papers, County Record Office Beverley). Quoted Gordon Jackson: *Hull in the Eighteenth Century.* Oxford, 1972, p.102.
(4) *Hull Daily Mail* Friday, 5.1.1973 p.14. Article "Humber Keel Models on Display".
(5) Mentioned E.W.L. HU 4/1 Brynmor Jones Library, University of Hull.
(6) E.W.L. HU 4/1 Brynmor Jones Library, University of Hull. Article by Claes Krautz.
(7) *Journal of Commerce and Shipping Telegraph* 11.10.1934. Article by Clement Jones C.B.
(8) F. H. Pearson: *The Early History of Steam Shipping.* Paper for Hull and District Institution of Engineers and Naval Architects (Hull. Goddard & Sons 1896) p.28.
(9) See Dr. J. M. Bellamy: "Some Aspects of the Economy of Hull in the Nineteenth Century with special reference to business history." Unpublished thesis 1965, for University of Hull.
(10) *Hull News* 23.7.1903 p.10 column b. (Events of 50 years ago).
(11) See Dr. J. M. Bellamy: "Some Aspects of the Economy of Hull in the Nineteenth Century with special reference to business history." (Unpublished thesis, Hull University Library, 1965) p.158.
(12) *The Humber Light* March/April Vol. 4 No. 2 Article by J. H. Kerman.
(13) S.C. Scott: *Things That Were* (Christophers 1923) p.86.
(14) *Criterion* Vol. 1 No. 22 p.5 (30.5.1874).
(15) J. J. Sheahan: *A History of the Town and Port of Kingston upon Hull* (2nd edition 1867) p.611.
(16) Ibid p.615 See also J.D. Hicks: *Our orphans* (Lockington Publishing Co. 1983) Chapter 3.
(17) *Hull News* 4.1.1868 p.4 column c.
(18) *Hull News* 26.1.1869 p.8.

CHAPTER TWO

The Smiths of Greenwich

The earliest mention of Mary Wilson's family relies entirely on oral memory. Her great great grandfather, Dr. Henry Smith, studied at Leyden, gained an enviable reputation, and was one of the physicians attending the Empress Catherine II of Russia, when she chose to show her devotion to the progress of medical studies by allowing herself to be inoculated against small-pox.(1) Catherine's, husband, who became Peter III in 1762, was mentally unstable and an unpopular king, inspiring little confidence. After a palace coup, Catherine had him confined and might well have been responsible for his murder shortly afterwards. Dr. Smith's problem arose when he was asked to sign the death certificate, which he, in all honesty, could not do. He therefore left St. Petersburg in a hurry, and, according to family tradition, turned up in London and was appointed physician to that idiosyncratic personage Frederick, Prince of Wales who achieved fame posthumously through a less than friendly poem which ended:-

"But since 'tis only Fred,
Who was alive and is dead, —
There's no more to be said".(2)

The only problem about this part of the story is that "Fred" died in 1751, so if the tradition is substantially correct, the events must have taken place in reverse order. The problem about the other part of the story is that Catherine founded a College of Medicine in 1763, but was not inoculated against small-pox herself until five years later, long after Dr. Henry was supposed to have quitted Russia.

The Greenwich connection really begins with his eldest son, also called Henry, who joined the navy, seeing some action, presumably during the Seven Years' War. He was wounded and therefore retired from the service, finding employment as a Lieutenant at the Royal Greenwich Hospital which existed to relieve and support seamen belonging to the Royal Navy who, because of wounds or age, were unable to maintain themselves. It also helped widows of seamen "happening to be slain or disabled",(3) educated their children, furthered the relief and encouragement of seamen, and improved navigation. A man like Henry Smith, who had been fortunate enough to attain high office, had potentially a good and lucrative job, which could become a sinecure. Henry did, in fact spend much of his time on art, for he loved painting and produced a fair number of pictures.(4) It was a talent he seems to have passed on to his sons.

In the early 1770s he married Maria Short, a woman some fourteen years his junior. Their four children were born in their apartments at Greenwich Hospital, and their second child and elder son received the somewhat unusual names Lord Henry. He grew up to enter the Navy Pay Office where he did well and, if not affluent, lived on a comfortable salary. Being so much older than his wife, great grandfather Henry purchased two houses on

SMITHS OF GREENWICH

Dr. Henry Smith of St. Petersburg and London

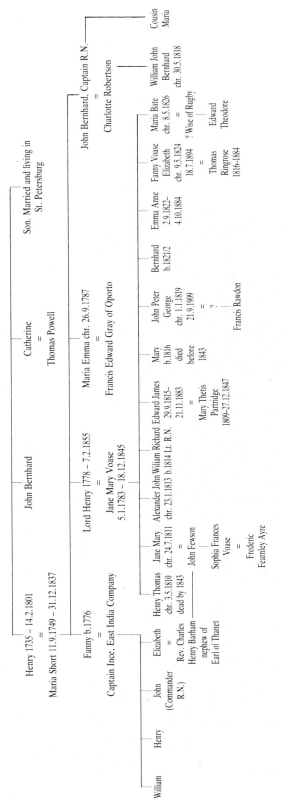

Croom's Hill, overlooking Greenwich Park, and when he died in 1801, great grandmother went to live in one of them, and took with her those children, including Lord Henry, who were not yet married.

Shortly after this, a young woman came from the north of England to visit friends of her family in Greenwich, Dr. and Mrs. Carnarvon. The Carnarvons introduced their guest to Betsy Smith, who was about her own age, and the two young women would often go together to drink the waters of the well at Lewisham. It was not long before Lord Henry Smith became aware of the attractiveness of the young visitor, and it often happened that he would be exercising his pointer dog just at the very time when the girls were taking their long walk. What could be more natural than that he should join them! In October 1805 Lord Henry Smith and the visitor, Jane Mary Voase, became engaged.

Jane Mary came from Anlaby, near Hull. Her father, John Voase, when a young man made his way from Howden to Hull to become apprenticed to a cooper. He did well, eventually sending his ships to Oporto, and becoming involved with the Greenland whale fishing. He owned a large house at No. 23 High Street, Hull in the merchant quarter, and a mansion, Anlaby House, where Jane Mary was born on 5th January 1783, as well as other property in several parts of the East Riding. The year after Jane's birth he became Sheriff of Hull. John Voase was an irascible man, and had many of the characteristics to be found in Thomas Wilson a generation later. His nature was redeemed by a sense of humour — if one could fine it — but this was a quality sadly lacking in his only son William, ten years older than Jane Mary, and this caused her much grief later on and even, I believe, influenced her grand-daughter Mary Wilson.

John Voase had brought up his children in fine style, and was not particularly pleased when Lord Henry Smith asked to marry Jane. In spite of all his wife's urging, he refused to come to the wedding, which took place at Holy Trinity Church on New Year's Day 1806. Eventually he came to accept his son in law, and when he died in 1810 he left Lord Henry £5,000 and settled an annuity on Jane which brought in a further £400 a year, so that the family was comfortably off.

The young couple had gone to live at Flint House, Greenwich, a rambling old place actually built of flint and red brick, and believed by all the Smiths to have been a part of the old palace in which Edward VI, that unfortunate young and only legitimate son of Henry VIII, had died. The house stood back from the main street, near the corner of Royal Hill. It had a spacious courtyard in front and, to give privacy, a row of tall lime trees which had to be clipped every year. In the coach house stood an old fashioned and very large "family chariot". It had belonged to Jane Mary's mother, and after the death of her husband, John, she used to travel from Yorkshire down to Greenwich in it. At the old lady's death the coach remained at Flint House, where it was seldom, if ever, used and was regarded with awe by the children.

The house had a big garden divided longitudinally by a wall, which had vines growing up its west side. Vines also grew along the south wall of the house itself, and Emma Anne, one of the children and later the author of the family memoirs, remembered seeing clusters of purple grapes below her mother's bedroom window, where she went early every morning to learn her lesson. There were fine pear trees in the garden and a walnut and a mulberry tree. The last was a special favourite and during the hot summers the children would sit in its shade to read or work. Lord Henry had an elder sister, Fanny, whose husband had been employed at one time by the East India Company. When he died she turned up every day at Flint House, and had been given her own patch of ground to cultivate as she wished. She had filled it very full of all kinds of flowers, and threatened the Smith children (who were terrified of her) with dire punishment and worse if they dared to touch the flowers or damage the borders.

Both grandmothers visited regularly, and both were dearly loved. Grandmother Smith had the warmer nature, and was still a handsome woman in extreme old age. She would sit in the dining room window looking out at the children playing in the garden. She wore lavender coloured dresses in satin or silk with a black silk apron over the top, and a white net cap. In her pocket was a little horn box which was always filled with sugar plums. She would stop one of the children and ask how a word should be spelled, and the child knew that the reward for a correct answer was a sugar plum. Grandmother would also carefully peel an apple in a single long swirl, which, before the admiring eyes of her grandchildren, immediately became a swan. Paper hats and boats were always being created from sheets of newspaper. Grandmother Smith was never idle, and when she visited, would always ask Jane Mary to let her have some sewing, and she was perfectly happy if she could sit turning old sheets. She taught the children to love all living things, and never to inflict pain.

Grandmother Smith always came into her own at Christmas time. There was a large playroom opening out from the dining room. Here, it was the custom on Christmas night for the whole family to gather and Grandmother Smith at over eighty years of age would lead off in "Thread the Needle" and "Puss in the Corner". Then it was father's turn. On special occasions like this Lord Henry would bring out his magic lantern and show to the children pictures of the Eddystone lighthouse with a ship sailing by, and the Grand Turk "with a stupendous beard, and opening a mouth full of truculent looking teeth".(5)

On ordinary days one of the children's main sources of pleasure was to walk. On Sunday their parents would take them in the park or on Shooters Hill Road. Their favourite walk, however, was down the river bank towards Woolwich. This had its disadvantages. There was a stench from the river, and decaying carcases of drowned dogs could always be seen floating along. There were also the Gibbets. Here, bodies of men who had been executed for piracy hung for months and even years. They swung and rattled in any light breeze, and shed tarsal and metatarsal bones, which the young John Peter used to find and pick up. There were still shreds of clothing attached to the skeletons of these poor creatures, and as the children stood and looked up at them, they seemed to be longer than any human being they had ever seen. One day the Duke of Clarence, shortly after he had become Lord High Admiral in 1826, saw the Gibbets as he sailed down river. They must have given him a shock, because he ordered their removal, and thereafter John Peter found no more bones.

The children's father, Lord Henry Smith, dominated the family in Greenwich just as surely as his wife, Jane Mary, was to dominate it after they moved away. He was an attractive man, handsome and dignified; he had had a good grounding at Westminster School, and he acted and looked like a gentleman. He was a voracious reader, and since he remembered what he read, his general knowledge was wide. He adored his wife, but, since they both had hot tempers, the children heard more than the occasional row. He was kind hearted, and very proud of his eleven children, but when they were little he found it hard to relax with them, and often spoke sharply if they interfered with what he was doing, or if their inconsequential chatter upset him. As he grew older, he enjoyed a nap after the five o'clock dinner. The servant would put out the lamp, and the family would draw their chairs into a half circle round the fire, father and mother opposite to each other, and nearest

23

the blaze. The children had to whisper together, and if one of them laughed aloud, their father would always wake up and admonish the offender. This they feared. After his nap the bell would be rung and the lamp relit. Lord Henry ate and drank in moderation, but he would lose his temper if the food came in ill prepared or incorrectly served. He would say "God Almighty sends good meat, but the Devil sends cooks".

As in Thomas Wilson's family, the custom at Flint House was that Sunday mornings were spent at St. Alphage's Church. Lord Henry was insistent that the behaviour of his children should be exemplary, but he himself seems to have been somewhat of an exhibitionist. If the sermon dragged — and Lord Henry had an antipathy for long sermons — he would look at his watch and proclaim in an audible voice by how many minutes the preacher had exceeded his schedule. Not only this, but he would begin to shake and rattle his seal and chain, in the hope that it would attract the attention of the priest. As the family sat well to one side of the church, this did not always happen. In the middle, under the pulpit, sat the school children. On some occasions their behaviour became unacceptable to Lord Henry, who would then threaten a wrong doer by pointing his finger at the child. The mistress in charge would then attempt to mend matters, but she could be by no means certain which child he meant. If she admonished the wrong one, he would exclaim aloud "No, no, not that one, it's the other" which would send his own brood into silent paroxysms of mirth.

He had no business sense at all. When he married, he had had a well paid job in the Navy Pay Office, but soon afterwards, probably at the time when John Voase's legacy reached him, he resigned it. The reason for his retirement was foolish. He did not get on with the head man where he worked, believing him to be pompous, opinionated and very unpopular. With his talent for drawing, and with the connivance and possibly the assistance of a fellow clerk, Henry Wardle, Lord Henry drew a caricature of his obnoxious superior, and was found out. The subject of the drawing himself complained to his head of department, and the two artists were suspended from their work for a week. However, when quarter day came, they both discovered that a week's salary had been deducted from what they received, and this incensed them so much, that they both resigned. John Voase had made a fortune in the wine trade, so Lord Henry now proposed to do likewise. He was soon disillusioned, and pulled out before he had lost everything. Even so, he refused to be careful, and shortly afterwards was foolish enough to stand surety for a Mr. Whitelock, a clergyman and post master of Bath whom he did not even know, but who was a friend of his friend. He stood for £4,000, which was all he now had. When Mr. Whitelock disappeared, Lord Henry was declared bankrupt in 1828. There was now only Jane Mary's £400 a year between the family and starvation, and Jane Mary realised that this, too, could soon go the same way as the rest. It was Fanny Voase, the second wife of Jane Mary's brother, who found a way out of their difficulties. William Voase's first wife had not long survived her marriage, leaving behind her a young daughter who sadly died at the age of seventeen, some two years before Lord Henry's bankruptcy. There were no children of the second marriage, and, at the time of the bereavement, Fanny Voase seems to have asked the family in Greenwich if they could spare Jane, their eldest daughter, then fifteen years old, to come to Anlaby. Perhaps the Voases even thought of an adoption. Jane stayed with them for several months and received kindly treatment, her aunt taking great trouble with her lessons, but in the end, it was Jane's youngest sister, Fanny Voase Elizabeth who became the heiress.

When Fanny Voase of Anlaby became aware of the financial difficulties of her sister in law and brother in law, she immediately suggested that they should leave Greenwich and come north. This made good sense. Flint House was now far too expensive to run, and a move, especially into the neighbourhood of the wealthy Voases, had plenty to recommend it. Fanny assured Jane Mary of her brother William's sympathy, but apart from advancing £500 to redeem the furniture he gave no help at all. Nevertheless, the family packed up, and moved themselves and their belongings to the East Riding, travelling on Friday, 8th August 1828 on the Brown and Pearson steamer Prince Frederic, one of the pioneer steamers to engage in a regular service between Hull and London. It was a stormy passage, and they all felt very sick when the ship finally entered the Humber on the following Sunday afternoon, but it was the only way to go. By land, they might have got to Yorkshire within days, but their baggage certainly would not have done so.

A house had been made available for the Smiths in Beck Bank, Cottingham, some three or four miles away from their rich relatives, and for it, they would be expected to pay £30 a year. It was a pleasant house, with a big green lawn in front of the windows, and some fine elm trees at the further end. Lord Henry's recent troubles seemed to have sapped all his confidence. He sadly admitted to himself that his family would now be dependent on the Voases and not himself if any further calamity should happen. Jane Mary was left to organise everything. She shouldered the responsibility with courage and dedication, but in the end, it proved to be too great a burden. One of the first things which she was determined to resolve concerned the education of her children. Eight of them had come to Cottingham. The three eldest boys had already entered the navy and were away at sea, but the ages of the others varied from seventeen years at the top, down to the toddler, Maria, at two and a half years, and for these children, provision would have to be made.

The Pearson & Co. ship, "Prince Frederick". Photo by courtesy of Hull City Museums, Town Docks Museum.

The Smiths were not, of course, penniless. They had come to Cottingham where they could be genteel without being rich, but there was not enough money for any unnecessary expense. Therefore Jane Mary, Lord Henry and their eldest daughter, Jane, became schoolteachers. Jane Mary would rise at six o'clock in the morning in summer, and as soon as it was light in winter. Breakfast was not until eight o'clock, but for an hour before this she would have Emma Anne in her room, to repeat her last lesson, and to read aloud. Fortunately the child was an avid learner, and the time was enjoyed by both of them, which is somewhat surprising as the readings were nearly always from English history, an ambitious choice for so small a girl.

After breakfast, lessons went on throughout the morning. Jane Mary taught all the girls to play the piano. Young Jane, instructed by her mother, was responsible for Mary's progress. Fanny, now five years old, was completely in Jane's charge. Baby Maria was still in the nursery. The boys were a more difficult proposition. Edward, later Mary Wilson's father, was thirteen when his father's troubles came upon him. At that age any ambitious boy, and Edward was ambitious, would feel the change in circumstances very deeply. At some sacrifice they sent him to the best of the three schools in Cottingham. It was in Northgate, and was run by an elderly teacher named Green, and here Edward remained for three years, until he entered Post Office service, and moved back to London. The two younger boys, John and Bernhard, did learn at home. Their father taught them Latin and Greek as well as the arithmetic, French and writing which he taught to all his children. It is possible that the younger boys in their turn went on to Green's school. If so, it may have helped to fire the enthusiasm of young Bernhard towards a career in art and sculpture. Green's son was George Pycock Green, who went to London to study with Henry Perronet Briggs R.A.(6) John seems to have left Yorkshire as a young man. There are indications that he, like Edward, entered the Post Office, but in Liverpool. There are also indications that he married a Liverpool bride.

Lessons for the younger Smith children were over by noon, at which time they were allowed to play in the garden. Each child had a plot of land and could cultivate it according to inclination. Lunch, a fairly substantial meal, was at one o'clock, and after this, if the weather were fine, the younger children would go for a walk with their nursemaid, who was so tiny that it was sometimes difficult to see her over the waving grasses. Whenever she could, Jane Mary would accompany the little cavalcade, and they explored all the lanes and fields around Cottingham, though in winter they were ordered to keep to the high roads. Evenings, as in Greenwich, were spent sewing and modelling while the children's mother read to them from "an instructive book".

It was necessary for Jane Mary to be a good organiser. She had to run the house and her large family with the minimum of help — a cook, a housemaid and the little nursery maid. There was also a young boy, a jack of all trades, who waited at table, cleaned boots, fetched, carried and swept, and, when there was any time left, worked in the garden and the yard. The family found the villagers easy going and sociable. Emma Anne thought that several, like themselves, were in reduced circumstances. Soon Lord Henry and Jane Mary were entertaining in the evenings in a small way. Jane Mary was an excellent hostess (a trait she passed down to her grand-daughter Mary Wilson who also inherited her bright brown eyes and intelligent expression). She was always cheerful, interested, welcoming, and able to put strangers immediately at their ease, since she never stood on ceremony herself. To the child Emma Anne, her mother was the driving force that kept the family together in Cottingham, her aim being, so far as she could, to ensure that they continued to receive the upbringing of the children of a gentleman. Young Jane alone could understand the difficulties of the situation, and in Jane alone could her mother confide, on the many occasions when she was anxious and troubled. Jane not only helped to teach the younger children, but, with her mother, helped to make all their clothes. The Victorian gospel of self help seldom had a more shining example than this Cottingham family. The children thrived and were happy, and, what is more remarkable, they valued what their mother was doing for them, and did not hesitate to tell her so.

From Emma Anne we have a clear picture of Cottingham society in the 1830s. She tells her story with clarity and wit. There were only two families with closed carriages. Apart from a Mr. Hentrey who kept a pony phaeton, and three old Quaker maiden ladies called Travis who had a little donkey carriage (which they later changed for a little carriage pulled by a pair of Norwegian ponies) everybody else in Cottingham walked. There were two stage coaches running a daily service into Hull at the cost of a shilling inside and sixpence outside, but there were no cabs yet. This meant careful organisation when an evening party was to take place. If it rained, the usual procedure was for the host to contact Billy Atkinson, who kept the William IV Inn, and who, for five shillings, might be persuaded to go round the houses of the invited guests, blowing his horn as he reached each one, and convey the party goers forwards and backwards. He was, however, likely to be truculent if the party went on very late, and on many occasions refused to get out of his bed to convey them all home. When this happened, the deserted ones, cloaked, booted, and, in the case of the girls pattened also, walked each other home carrying lanterns. Emma Anne thought this an excellent solution to the problem, especially when she grew a little older and her escorts were handsome.

The post from Hull was brought late in the evening by a simple soul called Tommy Paterson. He, too, used to sound a horn as he approached Cottingham, and would tell the people, what he honestly believed himself, that he had walked the distance quicker than the mail coach could do it. The job of delivering the parcels which had been brought by the coach was done by "Whistling Dick". He was an old soldier with only one arm and one leg. He would tell anyone who would listen how he had lost them at Waterloo, but since he imagined this to be in Spain, it would seem likely that he was with Wellington in the Peninsula earlier in the war. He would stump along, his good arm wielding his stick, while the parcel to be delivered hung from a hook suspended from the end of his wooden arm. Dick was fond of drink and was apt to indulge freely on the night when his pension was paid out. After these drinking sessions he was known to beat his wife with the wooden leg, but she got very wise, and usually managed to hide it.

The village tailor, Tommy Ion, was a timid and obsequious little man, who did his job, as was the custom, seated crosslegged on his table. He must have made a poor living, for much of the work he did was patching and repairing well worn clothes for this careful community. There was a hairdresser, Mr. Lythe, who described himself as a coiffeur. The Smith girls visited him regularly, for the current fashion was for girls to wear their hair short. Mr. Lythe, too, had military experience, but it was earlier in the French Wars than that of "Whistling Dick".

As in any village the parson and the doctor were individuals to be reckoned with. The Rev. James Dean did not appeal to Emma Anne. He was old, his brown wig was invariably askew, he was near sighted and often singed his coat tails by standing too near the fire. Once he nearly sat down on it by mistake. His sermons were painful. They always lasted an hour, and had to be borne in dreadful discomfort as there was no heating in the church even in winter. The walls showed patches of green mould, and the pews in which the children sat were lined with baize which was moth eaten. Dr. Watson, or Mr. Watson as Emma Anne called him, was more interesting. He was an elderly bachelor, who loved both ladies and gossip. His professional visits seemed much more like news exchanging sessions. The old maids loved him. The young girls were attracted to his nephew, who acted as his assistant, and in addition to his youth, had a personal charm as great as that of his uncle.

Among her father's acquaintances, Emma Anne thought highly of Tommy Ringrose, who became a great friend of the whole family. He was a land agent, had only one eye which had sight, was tall, thin and wiry, and would sit nursing his leg on his knee as he talked, or would twist and twine one of his legs round the other. The girl would watch this rigmarole with fascination, and, when she was little, used to think that the man had no bones at all. Tommy Ringrose always wore pepper and salt suits, and looked what he was "a shrewd, humorous, long headed Yorkshireman — a Don Quixote in appearance".(7) He wrote poetry, and liked to hear it read. Unlike the Smith family, he was a dissenter, but this was no cause for concern in Cottingham, where villagers often went to church in the morning and chapel in the afternoon, whether for comparison or good measure is conjectural.

The three excellent Misses Travis (the ladies with the donkey carriage) were very kind to the Smiths, and to Jane Mary in particular. She had worked so hard that she had made herself ill, and was suffering recurrent bouts of bilious headaches, which made her life a misery. When the ladies exchanged their donkey carriage for a pony phaeton, one of the first things they did was to take Jane Mary to Hornsea for ten days. What a blessed relief that must have been! She so seldom got a change of scenery, expense being a major problem, but she loved the sea and was so happy to go with her friends. Perhaps this kindly action reminded the Voases of Anlaby of their moral obligation, for shortly afterwards, in the autumn, they invited Jane Mary to their cliff top cottage at fashionable Filey, and she was able to stay here for several weeks.

The three Misses Travis were maiden ladies of character, being full of fun and, like most villagers, lovers of gossip. Where they saw a need for a kindly act, they did it, without ostentation and with no expectation of recognition. They were never idle, and spent much of their time making clothes for the poor, creating odd little toys, working in embroidery and painting. Every year they put all their creations together and held a sale, every halfpenny they received going straight to charity. Fanny, the clever one, had a stout heart. One night, just after one of their bazaars, while the money they had collected was still in the house, she woke up hearing a noise in her room. It was made by a burglar. The man roughly told her that he wanted her money, and meant to have it. Fanny got up. She told him to stand aside to allow her to get what he wanted, but asked him politely to lower his voice as sister Bessie was ill, and would be frightened. Then she talked to him in such a way that he became ashamed of his own conduct. He not only left the money where it was, but he also took off his heavy boots and tiptoed downstairs, helping Fanny to put back the shutters (which he had forced open when he came in) before he left. Fanny calmly went back to bed.

After five years at Beck Bank the Smiths moved to a house in the centre of the village. It looks as if the family circumstances may have altered slightly for the better. A further indication is that, in the following year, 1834, Grandmother Smith now nearly eighty six years old came to visit them, accompanied by Edward, whose service with the Post Office had now begun. They came up by steamer, and Grandmother Smith's pleasure at being with her family again was a joy to see. There was a farmyard and a paddock attached to the house, and the old lady would pat and try to tame the chickens, then sit for hours on a rustic seat which had been placed near the duck pond at the bottom of the paddock. This time she had barley in her pocket, and the ducks soon got to know her. Her family inherited her love of animals, and this came out passionately in her great granddaughter, Muriel Wilson.

Edward's career in the Post Office had begun on 7th February 1832, when he was sixteen years of age. He was employed as a clerk at the very nerve centre of that institution, St. Martin le Grand. His salary initially was £80 a year, but it rose with reasonable rapidity to £200 a year and later £300 a year.(8) He lodged round the corner from his work, at No. 1 Pancras Lane, which was useful, because he was ambitious and a hard worker. He came into this work at a vital time in the history of the Post Office. In 1840 Rowland Hill's revolutionary Penny Post heralded a new, efficient and effective era in literary transport. By the time he was twenty six years old, Edward was in a position to marry, and on 17th August 1842, in the parish church of St. Mary le Bow, he married Mary Thetis Partridge, daughter of Arthur Partridge Gentleman, whose address was given as 1 Pancras Lane also. Mary Thetis was a full six years older than her husband. Perhaps she brought him a good dowry! Their first child, Mary Emma, the future Mrs. Wilson of Tranby Croft, was born on 9th August 1843, and in the autumn of 1845 a son and heir, Edward Francis Partridge appeared. Shortly after this, the family moved away from central London. It may have been due to the indifferent health of Mary Thetis, but it might also have been caused by events which had taken place up in Yorkshire.

Lord Henry and his family had remained in Cottingham certainly until late 1840. Jane Mary's health had worsened, and she must have felt lonely after her eldest daughter, Jane, married John Fewson. The burden of domestic administration now fell onto the shoulders of Emma Anne, where it remained. Sometime between 1841 and 1845 the family moved to Paull, a quiet little village on the north bank of the Humber, some ten miles east of Hull. In the late eighteenth century the Blaydes family lived at High Paull House, described later by the historian Poulson as delightfully situated on an eminence facing the west, and sheltered, at its rear, by the clay, sand and gravel cliffs, which rose between twenty and forty feet — an outstanding feature in such a low lying area.(9) When the young Hugh Blaydes died in 1836, his brother Charles Benjamin decided to let the house, and it was occupied in 1841 by a Mr. C. Robinson. When he left, Lord Henry Smith took it, and it was here that Jane Mary's last days on earth were spent. She died at High Paull House on Saturday, 13th December 1845. It is difficult to understand why Lord Henry took an ailing wife to live so near to the river with its fogs and floods. It is also surprising that he could afford to live in such style, but it was surely Jane Mary's due that she should die in circumstances befitting the wife of a gentleman. Perhaps William and Frances Voase had helped once again.

William Voase died in August 1844, comfortably off and childless, leaving a generous annuity and much property and furnishings to his wife. Frances survived him for fifteen years. On her death, the heir was to be the young Fanny Voase Elizabeth Smith, Lord Henry and Jane Mary's tenth child. She would inherit, but only if within the space of one year after her entitlement she would change her surname to Voase only, and no other surname, and would get a proper licence from the Crown to authorise her to do so. Meanwhile, the executors administered the property on behalf of her aunt. Fanny did inherit. When her uncle died she was already married to Thomas Ringrose, nephew of her father's friend, and was living in Cottingham. The couple immediately became known as Ringrose-Voase. In 1860, after the death of her aunt Frances, and by which time there were five children of her marriage including two sons, they changed their name to Voase only. So one of Lord Henry's children was certainly well settled.

William Voase, however, remembered all the others. The four surviving sons Alexander, William, Edward and Bernhard and the three surviving daughters were each given a small legacy. Edward found his very necessary. The sadness of his uncle's death followed by that of his mother proved to be an unhappy preamble to an even more personal tragedy. After the birth of their son, Edward and Mary Thetis moved their household to No. 8, Brixton Villas, on the south side of the River Thames, a far more salubrious locality then. At the new house, on 12th February 1847 a second son, Henry Wilson Ringrose was born. He was called after his Cottingham uncle, the husband of the heiress Fanny, as, up to that point, there were no children of that marriage. Mary Thetis had no sooner recovered from Henry's birth than she found herself pregnant again. It was more than her indifferent health could stand. Late in November there was cerebral congestion. On 27th December 1847 she went into a coma, and after six hours she died. She was thirty eight years old, and she left behind her a five year old girl, a four year old boy, and a baby not yet on his feet. Edward's household included two maidservants and a manservant, but it needed a mistress.

Since the improvement of his fortunes, Edward had been able to acquire a house which was big enough to accommodate his father's family as well as his own. It would make good sense to invite them to come. After the death of Jane Mary, Lord Henry had returned

Henry Wilson Ringrose Smith, brother of Mary Wilson (from the Ayre Collection).

30

to Hull and by 1848 was living at No.1 Bond Street. By 1851 he and the remainder of his family had joined Edward in Brixton. He did not long survive the move, and on 7th February 1855 he died. Emma Anne, who might possibly have been looking forward to her freedom when she had completed her filial obligations to him, was now saddled with a lifetime's work, bringing up and trying to be a mother to her brother's young family. With her came Bernhard, now twenty eight years old. He would have described himself as an artist, painter and sculptor, but his contribution to the financial stability of the family was probably scanty.(10) Edward was now able to relax. His children were being cared for by someone he could trust and who would, in the acceptable fashion of the Victorian spinster, subjugate her own ambitions to the well being of her niece and nephews. Being his sister, she would be unable to make the demands on his time and attention which were inevitable while his ailing wife was alive. Edward flourished, and in 1854 his devotion, drive and industry secured for him a post of great responsibility in the service of his country during the Crimean War.

In 1854 the British government, led by the pacifist Lord Aberdeen, lurched tentatively into war against Russia. The growth of Russian influence in the Black Sea area had been a headache for every British Prime Minister since the Younger Pitt, but the great Palmerston had usually managed to cope with the problems which had occurred by means of diplomacy. In the early 1850s the new French Emperor, Napoleon III was seeking military success. Unlike his famous uncle he was prepared to cooperate with Britain and both countries realised the need to keep the weak and indolent Turkey in the north eastern corner of the Mediterranean. Russia, after some provocation, invaded the Danubian provinces early in the year 1854, and was fairly promptly pushed back over the River Pruth by the fighting Turks. But the western allies, afraid for Constantinople and determined to keep tabs on one another, had already moved troops out to the mouth of the Danube. Having got them there, they determined to use them, and so shipped them out to the Crimea, with the object of attacking the great Russian naval base of Sebastapol from the north. So began the tragedy of the Crimean War, rightly described by the politician, John Bright, as a "crime". This was a war in which the troops proved to be excellent, the generals wrong headed and uncooperative with each other, and in which the supply of food and ammunition was abysmal. Florence Nightingale, the only bright star in the murderous heavens (until Palmerston took over from the nerveless Aberdeen in January 1855) asked for underwear for her sick and shivering soldiers, and was told there were some teapots and coffee pots. Boots arrived for the left foot only, and supplies of flour turned up in the shape of fodder for horses.

As early as June 1854 the Postmaster General had authorised the appointment of an Army Postmaster "with a view of relieving Officers of Her Majesty's Forces in Turkey from the irksome business of arrangement and distribution of the large mass of correspondence of which the Mails between this country and the Army were likely to be composed."(11) The man who got the job was Edward James Smith. On arrival at Constantinople, he was to contact immediately the General Commanding in Chief and Her Majesty's Ambassador (the famous Stratford de Redcliffe), both of whom would give him every assistance to set up his Post Office. There is no suggestion that the Turkish authorities were consulted at all.

Then followed instructions concerning the actual handling of the mail. It was not Edward's job to deliver letters to individuals. He was to separate the correspondence for each regiment or detachment, and then send them on in bulk to the appropriate persons to receive them, or forward them to where the regiment or detachment was stationed, the army providing the means. Naval correspondence was necessarily difficult, and about this Edward was simply told to do his best.

The first Post Office would be set up in Constantinople, but if the General Commanding in Chief advised and the Post Master General agreed, it might be necessary later on to set up other offices in the area. This did become necessary, and Edward soon found himself on the Crimean peninsula, while his second in command, Thomas Angell, had to leave Constantinople also and start up a new office in Varna, Bulgaria, near the mouth of the Danube. While in Constantinople Edward, where not specifically instructed, would obey the General Commanding in Chief, who would liaise with Lord Raglan in the field. Both Edward James Smith and his deputy, Thomas Angell, received £100 to help them with their initial expenditure.

Poor Edward James! Right from the start he had trouble with unpaid mail, and he addressed an urgent but respectful letter to Rowland Hill, Secretary to the Post Office, from Constantinople on 25th June 1854 to say:

"... on my arrival here I found a large accumulation of unpaid letters for Offices both in the Army and Fleet in the French Post Office which the Director Mons. Ferrier had no means of forwarding to their destination unless the payment of postage was made. This I did, from my private means and forwarded them on to Varna but a great many have again arrived by this day's mail."

He persevered. An article in *The Times* of Saturday, 19th August 1854 highlighted the problem, mentioning both Smith and Angell by name. Edward cut it out and sent it to Rowland Hill on 7th September, with a note to say that having paid out £40 already, he could not afford to go on doing it, especially since Angell at Varna was doing rather better than himself, General Raglan having given him £50 to sort himself out.[12] Both men were overworking, and more help was obviously needed, and swiftly. Two more clerks were therefore dispatched, but Henry Mellersh, Edward's new second in command, arrived at the Constantinople office to find that his superior was already with the army at Balaclava, in the Crimean peninsula.

Organisation of the mail was no easier here. On 23rd November 1854 Edward saw fit to write to Lord Raglan, the Commander in Chief of the Army. He had met obstruction head on, in every direction. He wrote a second letter to inform Rowland Hill, as a result of which the War Office was alerted to the difficulty. *The Times* had already done its best on 18th November 1854, complimenting Smith and Angell as being indefatigable in the discharging of their duties and "most zealous and energetic in their exertions for the good of the public services", but revealing that there was gross inefficiency.

On 27th November 1854 Edward again wrote to Rowland Hill.[13] This time he spared no feelings, and because of this we have a thorough and detailed diary of his war experience up to the time of his writing. It is an unhappy catalogue of events which show how a man, attempting to be efficient, was faced by impossible odds. When the mail had arrived from England on 6th September at Constantinople, Edward had had it sorted and sent on to Angell at Varna, which was what he was supposed to do. The expedition, however, had already sailed, so Angell followed by Edward had to catch up the fleet. Edward went ashore to see the Adjutant General, Estcourt. Walking back along the shore he noticed some unattended sacks. He went closer, and found, what he had suspected when he first spotted them, that they contained the mail from England. The sacks had been left there on the beach without any protection, nor, when he enquired, had anyone been told of their arrival, least of all Edward himself.

On 19th September the mobile Post Office had "moved House" from the "Sovereign" to No.3 transport "Her Majesty", which was a commissariat store ship. The following day they had weighed anchor and sailed to the mouth of the River Alma, arriving just as the English and French routed the Russian forces and sent them scuttling towards Sebastapol, which could be fortified more strongly than it already was. Unfortunately, the allies gave the Russian, Todleben, time enough to do a good job.

On 27th September notice was given at noon that the Post Office was to proceed to Balaclava. This was to the south of the now heavily fortified Sebastapol, but attack from the north would have had to contend with the Tchernaya estuary. At half past two in the afternoon the "Golden Fleece" took them in tow, and by seven o'clock in the evening they were in Balaclava Bay, at which point the tow rope snapped. As the weather was unsettled and threatening, the captain decided that the best thing to be done was to stand out to sea, so the night was spent in the teeth of a gale. Fortunately it soon moderated, and No.3 transport came into harbour at mid afternoon the next day.

On the day after that, 29th September, Edward was told that there was not room for No.3 transport in the harbour, and that therefore the Post Office must move to another ship. He objected strongly to all this moving about, and, as a result was allocated a little house with two rooms which could be used for an office. Things ought now to have been very much better, but relations with General Estcourt were poor, for Edward was convinced that the General was disturbing arrangements which, left alone, were perfectly adequate for the collection and distribution of the mail. Angell and Mellersh now kept a journal, so that in future all deliveries and dispatches of mail would be documented. Confirmation of Edward's facts can be found in the letters of the soldiers themselves. Captain Jasper Hall of the 4th (King's Own) Regiment of Foot stationed at Scutari wrote to his sister, Jane, on 18th November 1854 "A day or two ago (13th) I received two letters from you one dated *11th July!!* the other dated 2nd August."[14]

There was one other, and this time a rather pathetic communication to the base from the Postmaster to the Forces before the end of the year. On 18th December Edward wrote:

"Sir,
The prospect of passing the winter in this country being no longer a matter of doubt I am enboldened by the liberality already displayed by His Lordship the Postmaster General to solicit that the undermentioned articles of winter clothing may be supplied to me.

Viz 1 Pilot Cloth coat, lined
1 Fur Cap (with ear lappets)
1 Pair Fur Gloves
6 Pairs of Lambswool Stockings
2 Guernsey Shirts
3 Pairs Flannel Drawers
1 Pair of Knee waterproof boots

I am Sir,
Your obedient humble servant
E.J. Smith"

We can only hope that he had more luck than Florence Nightingale.

Early next year Field Marshal Raglan was writing to the Duke of Newcastle complaining that Mr. Smith's independent attitude was causing trouble. The Post Office had by this time been moved to Army Head Quarters before Sebastapol, but Mr. Smith had gone off to Constantinople without letting Lord Raglan know. However, on Saturday, 3rd February 1855, the *Daily News* printed a report from its correspondent in Balaclava, which had been written on 13th January and which had come down whole-heartedly on the side of Messieurs Smith and Angell.

The article ended with a plea for sympathy from those sitting at home, for those doing their jobs to the best of their ability at the front.

When the fighting was finally over, and Edward had survived not only it but disease, which had polished off both Raglan (of dysentery) and Estcourt (of cholera) the Postmaster General suggested to the Treasury that since there was no national Post Office in Turkey, it might be a charitable as well as a useful suggestion that Mr. Smith and one or more of his assistants should be placed at the disposal of the Turkish government to organise one for them, based on our own system, but adapted to the habits and wants of the Turkish people. The Treasury and Foreign Office agreed, and the British Ambassador, Lord Stratford de Redcliffe, approached the Turkish government and received their consent. Edward was pleased by the appointment "as it proves that my exertions out here have met with your approbation".(15) He was, however, sceptical about their chances of success, and complained of the "inertness" of the Turkish officials, of whom he had now had plenty of experience. The authorization for this new venture came through on 31st August 1856.

By the beginning of November 1856, the Turkish government had still made no move to enable Edward to establish his Post Office, so the Postmaster General decided to bring him back to London, to be asked for his personal opinion as to whether the project was still feasible. There was much for him to do in England. His father had died the previous year. His sister and children were to be provided for. He was now in a peace time appointment, so it would keep the family together if they came out with him, or to him. He was back in Constantinople in early March and continued to wait to begin his work. He was still waiting in November 1858 when he was told abruptly and informally that he was sacked. This was confirmed through the British Ambassador on 5th December 1858, and Edward wrote, in some heat, to Rowland Hill:

> "what a mockery had been made of the intentions of the British government in its desire to ameliorate the state of the Turkish Post Office by accepting my services, keeping me in idleness for upwards of a year and a half, and now dismissing me in a most insulting manner treating me in fact worse than a menial servant".(16)

He proposed to return to England as soon as possible.

The Foreign Office took the matter up, and the British Ambassador had an interview with Aali Pasha, as a result of which Edward's services were retained, and the Turkish government promised to make provision for his work, but it did not honour the new agreement. Edward wrote again to Rowland Hill from Constantinople on 13th September 1859 to say that he had just received a dispatch from Sir Henry Bulwer at the Foreign Office:

> "informing me that the Ottoman Government do not *now* intend to carry that engagement into effect.

"Grieved as I am in being thus trifled with I consider it will be useless to make any further remonstrance on the matter, but it will prove to His Lordship the Post Master General how utterly foolish any attempts are to instil ... ideas of civilization into a people still in a semi barbarous state and who really are at heart opposed to all innovations."[17]

Although he wished to come home at once, Edward was quite unable to do so since he had not been paid for ten months and was quite without funds. However, Fuad Pasha informed Sir Henry Bulmer that although the Turkish government would not put Edward's plans into operation, they would give him a gratuity amounting to a year's salary — £1,000. Bulmer said he would tell the Turks that he thought they were wrong not to accept a good offer, and also agreed to press for the gratuity to be paid. Fuad Pasha admitted that "Monsieur Smith a rempli consciencieusement son devoir et les plans qu'il nous a fournis ont recontre notre approbation", but there were other powers to be considered and the organisational problems were, at the moment, too great. It was an excuse and Bulmer knew it. Then followed a miserable period for Edward, during which the arrears of money owing to him were hotly debated. The matter was not finally settled (by a somewhat complicated compromise) when Edward was appointed to a new post.

The Postmastership of Leeds had recently become vacant. Fifty one candidates applied for the job, twenty eight of whom were considered to be suitable. These were arranged in order of seniority, and Edward stood at No.3. He was, however, the best qualified for the job, and he had received a glowing "character" from his superior officers, who would no doubt heave a sigh of relief to get him resettled. On 6th January 1860 he was recommended

Edward James Smith, father of Mary Wilson (from the Ayre Collection).

35

for the post, and on 21st January, the *Leeds Intelligencer* reported:

> "Lord Elgin, Post Master General has appointed Edward James Smith of the General Post Office, London ... to be Postmaster of Leeds."

In some ways Edward was lucky. The new job was worth over £700 a year and enabled him to live like a gentleman. His head quarters were in Park Row in central Leeds, but he took a delightful house, No.1 Grosvenor Terrace, Headingley, in which to live.(18) It was just over a mile from the Post Office, across Woodhouse Moor and off the north side of the main road. Even today the house, and indeed the terrace, has a quiet, dignified and private charm of its own. When the Smiths came to live there, it was practically in the country. No.1 was at the west end. It was not a large house, but was double fronted, stone built, and possessed two cellars and an attic storey. It was a small household consisting of Edward himself, Emma Anne and the young Mary — soon to become Mrs Arthur Wilson. The boys do not seem to have come to Leeds. Francis had already disappeared from the scene, and may have died young, perhaps while the family was in Turkey. Henry, now fourteen years old, was to be apprenticed to Earle's shipyard when he had finished with school. He had long wished to be an engineer, and would now work at the yard where many of the Wilson ships would be built.

At the time when Edward James Smith moved to Leeds, his sister Fanny Voase Elizabeth and her husband Thomas Ringrose moved into Anlaby House on the death of Frances Voase. The *Hull News* of 21st January 1860 reported from the *Gazette* of 6th January:

> "Her Majesty has granted Thomas Ringrose of Cottingham Esq. and Mrs Ringrose her royal license that they may in compliance with a clause in the will of the late William Voase of Anlaby House Esq. (the uncle of Mrs Ringrose) take the surname of Voase only."(19)

With his sister firmly established at Anlaby House, it was in the best interests of Edward, now only 50 miles away, to keep up a close acquaintance. It may well have been at a Voase reception that the young Mary Emma met Arthur Wilson. Both were certainly present at the end of January that year at a Grand Charity ball in aid of the Hull General Infirmary, where 130 of the Hull élite disported themselves. Meet they did, and very soon affection was exchanged for love, and on a Wednesday morning, 1st July 1863, the two were married in Leeds Parish Church. The Wilson employees were given a holiday, and some of them went off to Withernsea in a bus drawn by six grey horses. Ships in the Humber were decked with flags. The *Hull News* described the bride very simply as the daughter of "a humble post master of Leeds".(20) They did Edward less than justice.

(1) Much of the information in this chapter is taken from a transcript of a manuscript written for the family by Emma Anne Smith at Mentone 1882-1884, and edited by her brother John Peter George. It is in the Brynmor Jones Library, University of Hull, and I am indebted to the Archivist who allowed me to use it.
(2) Anonymous. Quoted *Horace Walpole: Memoirs of George II* (1847) vol.I p.436.
(3) Quoted Christopher C. Lloyd: Greenwich (1961) Pamphlet (Spottiswoode, Ballantyne and Co. Ltd.) p.11.
(4) He was listed as Clerk of the Cheque in 1773. I am indebted to Judith M. Blacklaw, Librarian Royal Naval College, Greenwich for this information.
(5) Quoted from the M/S of Emma Anne Smith op. cit.
(6) The most famous painting by Pycock Green still in Hull is a full length portrait of Queen Victoria as a comparatively young woman (she visited Hull in 1854). This portrait stands at the head of the main staircase in the City Hall.

(7) That part of Emma Anne Smith's memoirs which refers to Cottingham was transcribed by Mr. Norman Higson and printed in the Journal of the *Cottingham Local History Society* June - July 1974 pp 174-8 and December 1974 - January 1975 pp 199-201.

(8) Post 59/50 p.55. Archives St. Martin le Grand.

(9) *George Poulson: The History of Antiquities of the Seigniory of Holderness Vol.2* (Thomas Topping, Hull 1841) p.487.

(10) From the Census returns 1851. I am grateful to the Archives Department, Minet Library, Knatchbull Road SE5 9DY for this information.

Some time later Bernhard left the country. Emma Anne Smith, in 1880, said he was in Australia, and there is some indication that he may have married out there, and produced a family. Little is known of his artistic progress while he remained in England, but *Benedict Read: Victorian Sculpture* (Yale University Press 1982) shows a photograph of a little medallion dated 1849. It is a right profile of Miss (or Mrs) M. E. Gray, and is engraved Bernhard Smith P.R.B. (Pre Raphaelite Brotherhood). His aunt, Maria Emma was married to Francis Gray of Oporto, and Francis is a Smith family name.

More positive evidence comes from *Algernon Graves F.S.A.: The Royal Academy of Arts Exhibitors 1769-1909* (S. R. Publishers Ltd. and Kingsmead Reprints 1970: from the original edition edited Henry Graves and Co. Ltd. and George Bell and Sons, London 1905). There are entries under Smith B. Sculptor, and Smith Bryce, Miniature Painter pp.166-7. The commentary indicates that the two are hopelessly mixed in the catalogues, but there are at least five which can be identified as Bernhard's work. These are:

    1844 Lieutenant Henry Thomas Smith (Bernhard's eldest brother).

    1845 Rowland Hill (his father's chief).

    1847 Christopher Rawdon Esq. (the father in law of his uncle, William Voase).

    1848 Medallion of Mrs Thomas Ringrose

        L. H. Smith (his father)

Listed in the year 1842 is a medallion portrait, unidentified, which may be the one referred to by Benedict Read.

(11) G.P.O. Min 511 (G/1856) Quoted Post 45 4 c.1854-1910 Levant and Ottoman Empire, British Post Office Official History (J. P. Alexander) p.1.

(12) Post Office File 24 Packet 802 G/56 33.235/56 802G/56.

(13) Post Office Packet 511G56.

(14) *Letters from the Crimea: Captain Jasper Hall of the 4th Regiment of Foot to his sister and father.* Transcribed and annotated by Edith Tyson F.M.A. (Lancaster Museum Monagraph). p.7.

(15) Post Office, St. Martin le Grand 51.562/61 28.883/56.

(16) G.P.O. Packet 1, 141 1/58 op. cit.

(17) G.P.O. File IX.

(18) I am indebted to Miss J. Hobbins of Harrogate, who lived at the present No.1, for much of this information, and for allowing me to photograph her house. She also alerted me to the fact that the houses have now been renumbered from the opposite end. I am also indebted to the late Professor and to Mrs T. E. Hope, who live at the present No.5 (originally No.1 and therefore where Edward James Smith and his family lived) for permission to photograph the exterior and interior of the house. I have also received considerable help from Mrs. J. Slater of Hull, who used to live at No.3 Grosvenor Terrace.

(19) p.6 column d.

(20) *Hull News* 4.7.1863 p.7 column a.

CHAPTER THREE

Early married life, and the building and occupation of Tranby Croft

Arthur Wilson brought his young wife to live at No. 5 Charlotte Street, in the very centre of commercial Hull, and close to the new dock. Although it was one of the three main residential streets of the town, and the houses in it were commodious, Charlotte Street was not exactly what an aspiring hostess would have wished for. For the first five years, however, Mary did her Victorian duty by her husband, and busily presented him with a family. Susannah West, usually called Tottie, was born in the late summer of 1864; Ethel Mary followed just over a year later; the son and heir Arthur Stanley, always called Jack by the family but Stanley everywhere else, was born in July 1868; and Edward Kenneth appeared late in 1869.

The firm of Thomas Wilson, Sons and Company had now come into the hands of the two brothers on the spot, the two who, on the face of it, would have seemed most unlikely to get hold of it. Charles and Arthur had always worked extremely hard, but they now continued to do so with added incentive, for they were ambitious men. Within twenty years they had transformed their father's firm from one which had a European reputation to one which had a world wide one, and they themselves were two of the richest men in the land. So the first few years were busy enough. Mary, however, was restless. She may have resigned herself to bearing children with Victorian regularity, but she was ill content to surround herself with domesticity, and she wanted a social outlet. She was married to a wealthy man, soon to become very wealthy indeed, but, as she well knew, society would never come into central Hull. Her Voase relatives for the last three generations had been a part of the society of the East Riding. Her own father had written letters to Rowland Hill, the gist if not the whole of which had been submitted to two of England's prime ministers, Lord Aberdeen and Lord Palmerston. Mary would not be content with riches without prestige. She had already agreed with Arthur that their sons should go to Eton. The local college which had been good enough for their father would not do for them.

The chance came in 1867. The lessee of Wolfreton Grange, Kirkella, decided not to renew. The lessors were Rachel Whitaker of Melton Hill, widow of Thomas Wilson's old partner, and her son, Charles.(1) The property was commodious and consisted of a house with stables, coach-houses and outbuildings, gardens and shrubberies, and extensive grassland. Arthur Wilson took it from 4th April 1867. He was to paint and care for all the property, and keep the garden in good trim. He was not allowed to break up or till the grassland, but must stock it "with sheep or neat cattle not grazing more than 5 horses in the said closes at one time and not keeping a bull thereon". He must also spread on every acre of grassland not less than 40 shillingsworth of "good manure to be well rotted". All timber was to be carefully preserved, and within six months Arthur must lay out at least £400.0.0d on the property, painting and decorating as required. Captain Palmer, the previous lessee, had built a greenhouse which Arthur and Mary considered was too small.

They were told that they might take it down and erect a more elaborate one, but plans and the final result had to be shown to the Whitakers and Mr. Foale, their surveyor.

At Wolfreton Arthur and Mary began a new life. One of Arthur's less characteristic passions was for horses. Now he could indulge his pleasure. The family continued to increase. Another son was born at Wolfreton in the late autumn of 1872. They called him Thomas Raymond. By the time of his birth Arthur's brother Charlie, slower at the matrimonial stakes, had finally married in 1871, and his bride, Florence Wellesley, was a member of the family of the Duke of Wellington. Charlie took Florence to live with old Susannah at Park House in Cottingham, but this did not last long, and they moved to nearby Thwaite House. Soon Charlie let it be known that he was going to enter politics, and that he intended to acquire a country house and estate and move into the Riding. This he finally did in 1878, taking over Warter Priory with its 300 acre estate from Joslyn Francis, 5th Baron Muncaster. By this time he was launched politically. He had been Sheriff of Hull in 1870, and was elected Liberal M.P. for Hull in the 1874 election. (He sat continuously in the Commons until 1906 when Sir Henry Campbell-Bannerman, needing younger blood in the lower house, made him a peer). Charlie had also entered the London clubs — a far cry from old Thomas' attitude this. When he had had to visit the capital, he had always stayed quietly and substantially at Morley's Hotel, just off Trafalgar Square; but it was a sign of the times, and Arthur would need to follow his brother.

The family was beginning to move socially in the Riding. On Tuesday, 23rd January 1872 the Mayor and Mayoress of Hull, Alderman and Mrs. Jameson, had sent out 500 invitations to a ball in the Town Hall to celebrate the return to good health of the Prince of Wales, and Arthur and Mary had attended with their Ringrose-Voase relations and the Sandersons of Cottingham.(2) At the beginning of April they had also been present at the Bachelors' Ball, held in the Public Rooms, with sister Harriet Eagle Bott and her husband (who had come up from London), an assortment of Harrisons and Ringroses, and Mary's young brother Henry Wilson Ringrose Smith, now a fully fledged engineer at Earle's, and shortly to join with Charles Amos and manage his own firm.(3) Arthur felt he might be trailing, though he could rely on his Mary to give a thumping great push in the desired direction. He had no wish to emulate brother Charlie in the political field. (Arthur's politics, incidentally, were conservative). He did not like public speaking, and had, so far, done as little as possible, but he felt that if Charlie, his alter ego, was going to live like the county families in a big country house, he could hardly deny to his own brood a similar life pattern.

In fact, he got in first, and in Spring 1873 told his solicitor to acquire 34 acres of land at Tranby Croft. The site of the proposed new estate gives rise to speculation. Why did he want this particular land? One likely reason was that Mary was keen to have it. Here would be her opportunity to rehabilitate her grandfather Smith. Tranby Croft stands immediately to the west of the Voases' house at Anlaby, but it stands on rising ground. It would look down on the earlier foundation. It would be much bigger. Its entrance gate, immediately across the road from the Voase house, would be more ornamental, and more impressive. Mary could probably imagine the social traffic turning west off the Beverley Road, not east. If this was so, the estate would be a perpetual reminder to the mistress of Tranby that the Smiths had made good.

The purchase of the estate was done piecemeal, field by field, through William Hodgson of Hull, who got it together during April and May 1873. At the end of the eighteenth century Anlaby, like nearly all other English villages, had been enclosed, since when, the fields which Arthur Wilson wished to acquire had changed hands on several occasions.(4)

On one part of the land stood the only dwelling house on the property — Tranby Cottage. This was a small, attractive two storey cottage with a steeply ridged tiled roof into which were set five dormer windows, the outermost set slightly further forward because the rooms at either end were deeper than the rest. It was half covered in creeper, and in front was a sunken lawn. To the south was a summer house, and to the east, an orchard. The house had probably been built in 1816 and was owned by Jane Stork Holden in 1853.(5) If Mary Wilson is to be believed, negotiations for the property were first made with Jane's husband. The Wilsons decided to keep it, and later it became very useful for housing laundry and dairy people, and for putting up any "stray" valets who could not be accommodated at the big house.(6)

From a small lodge at the eastern end of the estate and, incidentally, right opposite the Voase family home at Anlaby House, a gravel path gently curved upwards to the west through woodland to the parkland ahead. Less than half way to the house the trees gave way to grass, and to the south could be seen a large tree shaded boating lake and a cricket ground. To the north were the rose gardens and conservatories. The grass land continued almost to the house itself, but since this was well elevated, two sets of balustraded stone steps climbed two grass covered banks to the front terrace, the carriage way sweeping round from the north to enter also.

The formal gardens, of which there were many, lay mainly to the south of the house. Arthur Wilson got into the habit of asking his captains to bring home specimens of trees

The Lodge gates — from a sketch by "Gus" in an unidentified newspaper, and copied here by Douglas Potter.

from whatever part of the world they were visiting, and these small plants and cuttings were introduced into the estate. On occasions, important visitors might be invited to make a planting, and an iron plaque on the site, would bear the name of the planter, the date of the planting, and would register the type of tree. King Edward VII was asked to do this, and the plaque still exists, but the excellent head gardener, Mr. Leadbetter, made careful records of all that was done, and Canadian maple, Australian fire bush, cedars of Lebanon and magnolias all found their way into the gardens. His plaques still turn up.(7)

Among the formal gardens was a lily pond, on the north side of which was a beautiful double bank of rhododendrons, of which Arthur, and later his second son Kenneth, was very fond. White, pink, purple, orange and deep red, they continued to bloom for over a century before most of them fell to make way for further rebuilding long after the house became a school. Close to the lily pond was a rock garden, steep, rugged and plentifully watered — Tranby Croft abounded in natural springs. There was an arbour with a sundial and, right away from the house, a field with a summerhouse in it; where the children could play.

The gardens began to take shape before builders started to lay the foundations of the mansion. By May 1874, when the laying of the foundation stone took place, the visitors could get a very fair idea of the demesne. The two vineries were already planted with young vines, and the vineries, peach houses and nectarine houses were an imposing structure some 200 feet long. There was room for a corridor of figs and 2,000 forced strawberry plants.(8) Behind the greenhouses were an undergardener's room, a boiler house, potting shed and mushroom house. A substantial detached cottage for the head gardener stood nearby, and there was a kitchen garden, some 280 feet square, with a 12 foot high wall around it. About ten years later, Arthur installed an open air swimming pool on the west side of the kitchen gardens near the little cottage. He allowed all who worked on the estate to use it, provided that they did not interfere with the requirements of the family.

Across a narrow track on the west side of the greenhouses, and on the north west corner of the estate, the stable court had already been started, and to this day the high entrance arch bears the monogram A.W. and the date 1874. The block forms a hollow square 100 feet each way, and provided stabling for 19 horses — 8 stalls and 11 loose boxes. The blue tiling at the back of each stall remains — the horses would have nibbled at wood — and the door handles are metal rings depressed into the thickness of the doors, to prevent the horses from nudging them open. A trophy room was on the ground floor opposite the main point of entry, and on top of this central, two storey block was an ornate stable clock, topped by a weather vane in the form of a fox. In front of this was a deep well, and the drain piping from the roof went straight into the ground, as it still does. Later on, when the house was sold, this well was filled in, and because, at the same time, the presence of no fewer than fifty brass carriage lamps had become an embarrassment (who, in the 1930s could have foreseen the future market for such items) they were all pitched into the hole which was then filled in and a layer of concrete put on top.(9) There, to the best of my belief, they still are.

To the left of the high entrance arch, as one approached, was accommodation for the head groom, with a tiny flat above the arch itself for the under groom. To the right was a huge and high room with space in it for three big coaches. In the heyday of life at Tranby Croft the job of one man was to take a small carriage down to Paragon Station, Hull early every morning to collect mail and packages. After his return, for the rest of the day, he

The rose walk, photographed in the 1920's (from the Pressling/Woolrich bequest).

polished the carriages and brasses.(9) At the north east corner of the square, a high water tower supplied the whole of the estate with water. The tower is still there, although the water tanks and the electric dynamos have gone, but, pushed under the shelving at the base of the tower are several cube shaped wooden boxes, very like tea chests. They are baize lined, and were used to hold the silver when the family travelled each year to their house in London or to their villa in the south of France.

At the south western corner of the stable block two long, narrow rooms were used as the laundry. The laundry maid's section of the organization of a nineteenth century country house was one of four, the other three being ruled over by the butler, the cook and the house keeper. In some houses the laundry maid came under the jurisdiction of the house keeper, but more often, and traditionally, she was independent. The organization at Tranby Croft would lead to the assumption that the laundry section was self-contained, out there in the stable block, and probably Mary Wilson's visits would be far less regular than those she paid daily to the kitchens.

The three storeyed mansion itself was to stand some 200 yards to the south east of the stables, across a dirt track suitable for horses and farm waggons. It would be a house in the Italianate style, and when it was first built, one half of it was almost a mirror image of the other, and drew the eye horizontally rather than vertically. The main entrance was almost at the south east corner, and rising to 72 feet 6 inches above it there would be a thick, solid square tower, which, from the ground would look squat, but which would add dignity to what otherwise would have appeared to be a plain low structure, halfway up our insignificant East Riding hill.

From the top of the tower, an excellent vantage point, one could expect to see the

Lincolnshire farm lands across the Humber to the south; to the east the town, not yet the city, of Hull; and to the west, the rising ground of Swanland hill would appear almost flat until it met the skyline. To the north was Kirkella church, and when, a quarter of a century later, Arthur Wilson was laid to rest in Kirkella cemetery, half way between his great house and the church, it was said that the celtic cross erected above the vault was in a bee line between the house and St. Andrew's Church, with which he had been associated for so long.

The architect of the new building was C. R. Chorley of Leeds. Nelson and Sons, also of Leeds, fitted up the hot water pipe system connected with the greenhouses, while Lindley of Leeds did the plumbers' and glaziers' work. Lindley was one of the oldest tradesmen in the city, having been in business at that time for forty years, during which time he was responsible for work on several important local buildings.[10] The house was built in yellow brick, supplied by Cockings of Walkeringham, because the raw materials used in that area produced an unusual quality of cream coloured brick. The bricks were first shipped down the canal, which ran alongside the brickyard, in narrow boats. At West Stockwith they were transferred to keels belonging to William Newton, and were then sailed down the Trent and Humber, finishing their journey for the last couple of miles by horse and cart.[11] The brick, masonry and joiners' work were all done by Wilsons' own workmen directed by their foreman joiner Mr Gibson. The clerk of the works was Mr Eckles of Hull. Arthur Wilson appointed the paymasters and did his own supervision. There were, apparently, several strikes during the construction of the house, but of short duration, yet Arthur was glad when, after two years, the house was finished and habitable, and he was heard to say that he would not like to repeat the experience.

Tranby Croft: view from west. Photo by courtesy of Local Studies Library, Hull City Libraries.

The laying of the foundation stone took place early in May 1874, and was performed by a six year old. This was the son and heir, Arthur Stanley, usually called Jack. Visitors streamed in from Hull and the surrounding villages to look at the estate and to admire the flowers, already flourishing in profusion. It was not until two o'clock in the afternoon that the Wilson party arrived with their friends, to be cheered by the workmen and the visitors. With Arthur and Mary came old Susannah, the little girls Tottie and Ethel, and Jack, who was wearing a sailor suit and was at once presented with a ceremonial trowel of silver parcel gilt with a pierced blade and pearl handle, on which was inscribed "Presented to Master Arthur Stanley Wilson by the contractors and workmen, on his laying the foundation stone of the mansion at Tranby, 2nd May 1874". Behind the commemorative stone onto which a plaque was fixed, and which Jack was now about to lay, a cavity had been left, and into this were placed bottles containing newspapers, and a photograph of Arthur and Mary Wilson. With much more cheering, the contractors now handed to Jack a silver mounted carved mallet, so that the stone could be well and truly tapped into place. Young Jack even made a short speech in which, according to the *Hull News* he "expressed a wish that prosperity might attend the undertaking".(12) The formal part of the proceedings was completed when the crowd gave three cheers for Arthur, for Mary, for old Susannah, for Jack and for the Wilson Line. Then the workmen moved off to a marquee, which had been specially erected for the occasion, where a large meal had been provided for them, Jack, Tottie and Ethel joining in as waiter and waitresses. When the meal was over, the grounds of the mansion remained open for games and walks, and it was not until dusk that the last visitors left.

Arthur and his family moved in during the late summer of 1876, at which time the employees of Thomas Wilson Sons and Company collected £124.8.6d to buy him a present, though we no longer know what form the gift took. There were sixty rooms in the mansion on three storeys, but before many years had passed it was necessary for the house to be extended. At the time Tranby Croft was completed, the local hunt, the Holderness, was in the doldrums financially, and needed a master with a deep pocket to set it upon its feet. Arthur fitted the bill admirably. He accepted the position, and was immediately taken into local society and became a part of it. Thus it was that before he became sheriff in 1888 he needed to have built a whole new wing to the west of the house, and add to it - that necessity to a late Victorian country house — a well equipped billiard room jutting out at its north western corner. This brought the number of rooms up to just over a hundred, and the Wilsons could entertain on a very vast scale indeed.

Tranby Croft - a Victorian Country House

To many people Tranby Croft was just another example of a nouveau riche mansion. England was now a well developed, industrialised country, and the financial status of some of her industrialists and commercial magnates — like Arthur Wilson — was very enviable. The aristocracy found it increasingly difficult to keep up financially, although more than a few of them were industrialists in their own right. So a situation was evolving in which the newcomers were eager to learn, to join and to adopt the standards of the aristocracy; and the latter were becoming more prepared to let them in.

Arthur Wilson never had any illusions as to what his critics thought about his lovely new house. To him it was modern and comfortable, utilitarian and safe, lit throughout by electricity, and very well heated. (So he honestly believed, but generations of school children and teachers in the three decades after the Second World War might have begged to differ). He would also remind his critics of the excellent fire extinguishing appliances, both inside and out, a precaution which turned out to be very wise.

At the main entrance near the south east corner four shallow steps led to a plain oak double door, rounded at the top. This in turn opened into a small, square outer hall, plaster panelled and heavily decorated, including a flamboyant monogram of the founder carved in two of the interior panels of the door. Surrounding it is a square pediment with matching decoration, and the heavy frieze above the wall panels matches too. In the two outside corners of the room are two heaters, marble topped and iron grill fronted. A high, shallow alcove leads to the inner door, and to the south side of this is a second door leading to a small room for steward or butler which, tiny though it is, also has direct access to the main hall. The inner door matches the outer one in general shape, although it is only a single one, with four panels of purple, yellow and green stained glass above hip height.

On the far side is the main hall, which appears almost square. An area 20' square at the north western end is the site of a fine oak staircase, mounting by two right angled turns to a gallery above, the first flight leading directly to a huge triple window. This window let in very little light, since it overlooked a small, and apparently useless central well, and was, in any case, glassed in green, yellow and purple like the entrance door. Above and to the south of the staircase, a balcony with stout oak posts, brass rails and knobs ran along the edges of the main area of the hall; and above it the roof curved into a shallow, flat topped dome, the whole of the centre of which was filled with the same coloured glass. Looking up from the floor of the hall some 50 feet, it was a subdued light at the best of times, and artificial light must have been used constantly when the family first moved in.

The "Sheriff" dog. Photo by courtesy of Margaret Wood.

The "Fish" pillar. Photo by courtesy of Margaret Wood.

45

Propping up the balcony, or at least appearing to do so, were four, and later six pillars heavily carved to waist height, and thereafter pinfolded to the capital at the top. The carvings are superimposed on a metal cylinder, and the pillars are therefore quite light in weight. Each portrays a different aspect of family life. One shows intertwined fish (it must be remembered that the Wilson money came from the sea) and hunting dogs (which was a reminder of their entry into local society). Another shows flowers and fruit (the big greenhouses bore witness to the Wilson interest here, and earlier at Wolfreton they had pulled down the existing greenhouse to build a bigger one). A third pillar has a cherub playing pan pipes while a second cherub pours good things into a cornucopia (Mary Wilson, Tottie, Ethel and Clive all sang well). On a fourth pillar are two artists' palettes and brushes (Mary's uncle Bernhard was a painter and sculptor, and Arthur's brother Fred was an artist in Florence). The other two pillars were placed on either side of the west wall at its southern end when the area was opened up to give direct access to the conservatories and the drawing room. One pillar has a cornucopia and two crossed hunting horns (a happy coincidence this, since Arthur Wilson's entry into local society came about because of his election as master of the local hunt). The other is more unusual. On one side were carved the smiling and mournful masks associated with the Thespians (Mary, Clive and the girls, particularly Muriel, were very fond of acting — as befitted society ladies and gentlemen in late Victorian England); on the other side two swallows with outstretched wings fly away from each other. It has often been said that when the swallows desert a family home, that home will cease to be. Arthur had created his family seat: was he now attempting to ensure its continuance with this wooden subterfuge!

The carvings around the balcony depict flowers and fruit and, over the staircase, a fox hunt.(13) Also, above the staircase at its western end, are two particularly attractive bosses in the form of reptiles, though it would be surprising if they were much admired as that part of the hall was, and still is, poorly lit. The staircase itself has five heraldic beasts on top of its corner posts. At its foot, on the left as one stands looking out across the hall, a lion carries a shield bearing the intertwined initials of Arthur himself. On the right, a dog supports a similar shield bearing Mary's initials (a sure proof, that "M" and "W" do not do this successfully). Behind Mary's dog, at the top of the first short flight, a fox bears a shield carrying the initials of the Holderness Hunt; while opposite, a dog supports a shield with the date 1889, the year when Arthur Wilson was Sheriff of Hull. At the second turn in the staircase yet another dog, on its shield, carries the legend "S of H", whether shipowner or Sheriff of Hull we must decide for ourselves. Just below the staircase, and to the left as one descended it, is an area some ten feet square, which was an excellent place to put a small orchestra when the family entertained. So, just as the stair gave practical details of Arthur Wilson's progress, the ground space gave more heed to the arts, and Arthur and Mary were often saddened when they heard (at second hand, naturally) that it was being said that their family had little to recommend it apart from money. If such a claim could be levelled against them when they first came to Tranby Croft, they had certainly dispelled it within a generation.

Opposite the staircase stood the fireplace with an overmantel and several large urns on its mantelpiece. Later on, Cope's picture of Arthur in hunting pink hung nearby. There were several small tables, and later on, busts of the Prince and Princess of Wales and of Prince Albert Victor (their elder, unfortunate son) stood here. Sometimes the grand piano was brought in, and occupied a position in the centre of the hall, though not too close to the fire. As was usual at this period, the hall was meant to be used and lived in, and magazines such as "Tatler", "Strand", "Punch" and the new "Country Life" were left around. There were huge palms and aspidistras, and one palm, standing in an immense bowl near the fire, was tall enough to reach the gallery above. Extra light came from many lanterns, suspended from balcony and walls, and there were many screens, door height, for this room led to doors and corridors all over the house. One screen at least was glass panelled, and this was usually placed to the west side of the staircase, between it and Mary Wilson's morning room, thus stopping the draught from the west corridor.

The morning room, perhaps the most beautifully proportioned of all the reception rooms, was Mary's domain. Her escritoire stood by the bigger of the two west windows, which overlooked the croquet lawn. At the southern end of the room three graceful, round headed arches ornament the wall, and on the north side a semi-circular aperture with shell-like decoration arching back into the recess is very reminiscent of Palladian design. Below waist height the arch is filled by a shelf and cupboard. When John Singer Sargent drew Muriel's portrait in 1907, Mary placed it in this alcove, where it had pride of place among the other family portraits. Above the fireplace on the east wall was an ornate mirror, reaching almost to the ceiling; and next to it, on the south side was a huge portrait probably of Tottie wearing a white dress, and holding a rose. A round headed arch leading into a shallow alcove opposite the fireplace brought one to the full length, triple window with its wooden pelmet, and two slim and elegant round wooden pillars taking the stress of the pelmet to the floor of the room. In this alcove was the escritoire, which Mary used constantly. At this period the well mannered female guest was expected to spend her morning in her room writing letters, but it was here, in the morning room, that most of the family correspondence was done.

Walls and ceiling were decorated like a Wedgwood vase, and when the house became a school, the room was known for some time as the Wedgwood room. The ceiling was a pale blue with silver stars painted all over it, and Mr Hazelhurst of Hessle remembered being told by his grandfather, one of the decorators, that the wall panels were done in French art silk. The white stucco motifs at the top of each panel were a simple and effective frieze. There were chintzes and palms, and the room was lit by a magnificent crystal chandelier with globes like tulip heads. This was a room of taste and distinction, of memories and present commitments, and Mary loved it more than any other.

On the south side of the hall were two rooms, but these could easily be thrown into one, when parties were held, by pulling back the sliding panels which normally separated them. The first room, nearer to the steward's office, was at various times a business room, a smoking room, and, much later, Muriel's boudoir. Half panelled, with much pinfold work, it was, and still remains, a dignified room, high and alsmost square. The fireplace is one of the most delightful in the whole of the house. Ceiling height, with a large plain mirror above the mantelpiece, it has splendid tiling of the Burne Jones style. The designs were probably worked out specially for this particular fireplace, and both panels and borders are hand done. Each panel is an eight inch square, rather than the more usual twelve by six.(14) On the left side there is a border of leaves, and flowers. The leaves are ivy; the flowers, sunflowers. This pattern borders the panels except at each corner where there is a square, geometric design. Within this framework are four square tiles, one below the other. Those nearest the top and the bottom each have designs of fruit and leaves. The two middle panels depict a beautiful young woman dressed in Greek fashion in a long white robe gathered in at the waist. Her hair is golden, and there is a wreath of flowers around the top of her head. She carries kindling over one bare shoulder, and a small bunch of

The Morning Room, looking north (from the Pressling/Woolrich bequest).

daffodils in her free hand, so the year is at the spring. Behind her the trees blossom thickly. The wind blows her draperies and she seems to float along the path. On the right side of the fireplace as one faces it, the pattern is the same in all but the two middle panels. The beautiful girl is again represented, but in very different circumstances. It appears to be winter: the sky is black and the girl is huddled into her robe with the shawl over her head. She holds a long stick, and warms her bare feet at a small fire, the smoke from which curls behind her in the same way that her shawl, blown by the spring wind, curled in front of her in the other picture. Whereas in spring the girl was inside a town's walls with fields and orchards beyond, she is now outside the walls. We can see the towers and turrets and, beyond them, a sky which is black as ink with no stars. The Victorians, where there was a double room, as there is here, would sometimes have two fireplaces which between them depicted the four seasons. This is not so at Tranby Croft. As will be shown, the fireplace at the other end is much inferior. Perhaps these two pictures tell a story. One cannot help feeling some curiosity and pity for the unfortunate young woman who, in the second picture seems to have been rejected by her society.

Opposite the fireplace are the sliding doors, and beyond them the most spectacular reception room in the house. Called by its owners the "drawing room", the "music room" or the "library", it has a magnificent painted ceiling (still intact), a beautiful gilded mirror of the type displayed at the Great Exhibition in Hyde Park in 1851, and what Mary Wilson used to call with pride her "Limoges panels". The ceiling is a geometrical pattern in stucco and paint, mainly gold, blue and rust on a beige background. Artificial light makes the prolific gold paint sparkle with life, and more than one visitor has referred to the room as an "Aladdin's cave". The ceiling is even more spectacular in a semi circular alcove on the

The Drawing Room, looking south west (from the Pressling/Woolrich bequest).

south side of the room, where the full length windows are. Here, the ornate character of the ceiling, frieze and hangings is emphasised by the comparatively small space, and by the glitter thrown back from the semi circular bay windows with their curved glass and ornamental brass handles which, according to local tradition, were so admired by the Prince of Wales, later Edward VII, that he had them copied for Osbourne.

The door was to the right as one stood at the sliding doors looking in. This much smaller door, which had an ornate semi circular pediment above it with delicate swirls of decoration in stucco, was divided into eight panels. These Limoges panels were black, and on them, painted with great delicacy, mainly in white were, from the top, two severely classical female heads; ornamental medallions of a Greek youth and maiden, who appear to be scattering good things on the land; the sun in splendour; and decorated lamps. Mary would be glad to know that since her house became a school, every painter of doors has been asked to work carefully round these panels, but, unobtrusive as they are, it is by no means unusual for them to remain unnoticed by those who use the room.

Also on the north side was the gilded mirror, which has an eagle with outspread wings at the top, two birds of prey sitting one at each side on the shoulders, and a little animal leaping at a small tree in the middle at the base. Garlands of flowers wreath the top and sides, and ornate shell-like fronds are at either end of the base. On the same wall, but further to the west, was a huge arch opening directly into the main hall. This Mary Wilson would curtain off when necessary, and she often added a screen for warmth. The presence of the arch made it possible to roll up the carpets (Persian, Oriental and Aubusson at Tranby Croft) and use the interconnected rooms as an additional dance floor if a hunt ball were in progress and the main hall crowded. At the far end of the room was a fireplace with

49

a round topped mirror, which, like the one opposite, reached to the frieze. The tiles of this fireplace are not so unusual as those at the other end of the double room. They are machine made and printed from an original artist's design, and are glazed at the back. The main interest lies in the central panels, which are the normal size for that era — 6" x 12" — and in one piece. On the left, as one faces the fireplace, is a picture of a modest young woman in flowing robes carrying a hand organ, which is slung over her left shoulder. On the right side is a graceful young hunter; he walks away from the viewer, and has a sheathed sword at his left side, a bow (which looks rather like a crossbow) in his left hand, and a quiver full of arrows on his right hip. When the folding doors are back, the mirrors at either end of the two rooms reflect each other, to give an impression of endless depth.

In this room the grand piano was normally to be found, near the smaller window. There were several display cabinets along the walls, and in a corner between the fireplace and the big arch, and behind a low angled settee, there were rows of small portraits. At first the lighting came from many branched silver candlesticks. Later, wall brackets were fixed at intervals, two by two. Three palms reached almost to ceiling height in different parts of the room, but there were, too, bowls of smaller flowers and plants on every flat surface. Furniture was surprisingly small and dainty, and included a Louis Quinze settee.

It had become the custom, in late Victorian England, for country houses to possess a billiard room. The game had been played for a long time, but usually in the main hall of the house, which was almost certainly where it was first played at Tranby Croft. With the entry of the Arthur Wilsons into society, and the prospect that Arthur would become the Sheriff of Hull, the time had come to rectify the omission of a special room for the game. In any case, much building and rebuilding was going on in the mid-eighties. The perfect

The Billiard Room, (from the Pressling/Woolrich bequest).

symmetry of the house was spoiled by the addition of a new wing, and sticking out from the north west corner of this, like a massive pan handle, was the new billiard room. To get to it, one left the main hall by the west corridor, whose oak door was leather padded and studded at the back. After passing the schoolroom, the butler's pantry and storerooms, a left turn brought a guest into the smoking room and the new wing. This new smoking room was half panelled, but unremarkable apart from the fact that Arthur Wilson's monogram appeared over its door — the only door in the house, apart from the entrance, to have this distinction thrust upon it. At the far corner of the room a carved oak door led to the billiard room, and this door was the only contact between the billiard room and the rest of the house. It was not a large room, but was beautifully equipped with roof lighting as well as windows along the south wall, which included a shallow, rectangular bay. At the western end was an elaborate and ornate fireplace alcove with many carved heads, made even more heavy by the deep and equally ornate frieze above the panelling. A casual glance at the alcove shows that the Wilsons had become aware of heraldry. Back in 1882, when Mary had produced several performances of Gilbert and Sullivan's *Patience*, she had had printed, in the top left hand corner of the programmes, the crest of a demi-wolf and the motto "Semper vigilans". Similar carvings appear in the top corners at the entrance to the alcove, while high up, in the middle of the fireplace itself, is what looks more like a demi-unicorn. Arthur Wilson had a ring made, which incorporates this crest, and his grandson, Raymond, still wears it.

On the mantelpiece the Wilsons placed hunting cups and trophies, and over it hung what appears to be a panoramic school photograph. These often appeared in billiard rooms, and this one may well have recorded some aspect of the boys' life at Eton, where they belonged to Everard's house. In the very centre of the room, hanging low from a shallow dome of glass in the roof, was an ornate brass chandelier, its six lamps, in two rows of three, spotlighting the billiard table immediately below. Around the table, but not underneath it, and filling up practically the whole of the floor was a flowered carpet. Settees were placed against the walls. A clock on a wall bracket ticked away in one corner, and on a small table leaning against the wall there, was a painting of a race horse. At right angles round the sides of the room, suspended from small ornate iron brackets, the wall fitting of each having the letters "AW" intertwined, were further lights. This room was the scene of one of the two famous games of baccarat, which involved the Wilson family in so much trouble.

A door in the north east corner of the main hall led into the dining room, another example of an adaptation of Palladian design. The room is rectangular, about twice as long as it is wide. On the far side, on the north western corner, is the door through which the food was brought; and in the middle of the north wall is a high, shallow recess with rounded top, and a canopy above it reaching the frieze. This recess was completely filled with a heavily carved, dark oak dresser. At either end of the canopy, where it touches the ceiling, are two ugly and unusual little bosses. The one nearer to the door is in the shape of a gnome who clutches the sides of his face below the ears. Perhaps he has eaten so much of Arthur Wilson's good dinner that he has toothache. On the other side, a similar creature clutches his stomach. Arthur was far more abstemious than many of his guests. He may even have asked for these queer little people to be carved because he was aware that some guests came to his house to gorge their fill, after which they would go away and ridicule his nouveau riche image in the Riding. Practically all the interior carving was done by workmen from the Wilson firm under the direction of their foreman joiner, Mr. Gibson,

The Wilson crest (Semper Vigilans) in the Billiard Room. Drawn by Barbara Newby.

Detail from the old fireplace in the Dining Room. Photo by courtesy of Margaret Wood.

and it would be a simple matter for Arthur to get what he wanted.

On the long east side of the room were three windows, those at either end tall, narrow, single sash, from roof height to panelling about a yard from floor level. The big centre window is in the form of a bay with side lights, and here can be found an early example of double glazing. The panes themselves are divided up by leaded lighting into diamond shaped medallions. The serving table stood in front of the centre window. Right across the room and opposite the serving table is the only old carving in Tranby Croft. This is an ornate carved fireplace, roof height. No one can rightly say where it has come from though it seems to me likely that its previous home might have been Warter Priory, which had been purchased by Arthur's brother Charlie in 1875. This was a historic house — an Augustinian Priory was founded there in 1132 — but as soon as he got it Charlie determined to make alterations, and he ripped out the old panelling from the great hall and installed new, a portrait of himself being "artistically introduced"(15) into the new carved oak. Arthur's motto "Business is business" may well have meant that he was loath to witness the waste of what he might have called good timber; also, aware that there was some criticism locally that his new house lacked a feeling of the past, he could have used the old wood to make a double score. However, the fireplace poses many problems. It does not fit well and the top half does not match the lower. It looks older, is less intricately carved and has a duller finish. The carving in the lower half is ostentatious. There are four rectangular panels with oval centres, in each of which is a classical figure. Between the two innermost panels is an upright, narrow rectangle in which is carved a lady wearing an Elizabethan ruff with what appears to be a large goblet growing out of her head. Above this strange device is a lion's head — ubiquitous at Tranby. Seventeenth century Delft tiles

The Dining Room, looking north (from the Pressling/Woolrich bequest).

surround the fireplace itself. When the family were alone, the small round table seating eight persons was probably placed near to the fire, but more usually there were two of these tables, placed either side of the fireplace down the middle of the room. This was a pleasant room with an atmosphere of space and contentment. The walls were filled with paintings, and every flat surface with china ornaments.

Behind the fireplace wall, a corridor leading to the kitchens was very far from pleasant, there being no light of any kind which could penetrate to it. Later on, two latticed windows were driven through on either side of the fireplace, but the effect was limited, and the corridor remains dark to this day. The kitchens themselves were, however, very light and airy with plenty of room for the work to go on. Behind the main working rooms were a series of small pantries, blue tiled and with thick slate slabs providing a working surface, and an excellent place to keep the milk and the cream cool, since the outside walls faced north. They still remain, and are used daily. Opposite the kitchens, and across a red tiled corridor was the housekeeper's room and the servants' hall. By the end of the nineteenth century the family and servants in a country house might as well have lived in a different world, for there seems to have been an unwritten understanding that each group had a right to its own privacy. Corridors and back staircases led to all parts of the house, so that it was unnecessary for any servant about his or her work to disturb the family at all. None of the servants' rooms overlooked the formal gardens or the lawns, and the kitchen wing was far from the main part of the house. Not many of the servants were resident. The big house employed half the adult inhabitants of the nearby village of Anlaby, either on a full time or occasional basis. Those servants who were resident slept at the top of the house, males and females being strictly segregated. Mary Wilson prided herself that her young girl servants were well looked after, but I think she would probably have admitted that the task was not always an easy one. House guests as well as footmen sometimes had the roving eye.

Next to the servants' hall was the room where the housekeeper could be found. The huge cupboards are still there, and many a young kitchen maid must have watched, in fear and trembling, while one of the cupboard doors was unlocked and the commodity for which she had come was taken out, noted, and placed carefully in her hands. The housekeeper, (towards the latter end of the Wilsons' residence at Tranby she was a Miss Woolrich), was able to take breakfast and tea in her room where she would be served by the still room maid. She could also entertain the maids of those ladies who were house visitors, and she sometimes gave the butler sherry or wine there. Her room was well sited, almost at the corner of the drive, where the carriages turned south onto the gravel approach to the main door, or north, past the servants' hall to the stable block. She could see everyone who came and went at Tranby Croft.

The staff had a herculean task to perform. They were divided into day staff and night staff. The male servants under the authority of the butler were supposed to have little to do with the female servants under the authority of the housekeeper, cook or laundry mistress. The first job of the day staff was to get breakfast, a gargantuan affair, starting early at Tranby, because Arthur Wilson often wished to go in good time to Commercial Road, and lasting until the last house guest had partaken. It was served by the butler from a side table in front of the double glazed windows, and although it may have been more frugal when the family were alone, tea, coffee and possibly chocolate would be provided with plenty of eggs, porridge (with milk or cream), bread (brown, white, hot, cold, rolls or in slices), cooked meats, bacon and devilled kidneys. In the hey-day of Tranby Croft the butler was a Scotsman named Reid. The cook in a country house was, traditionally, a woman and usually addressed as "Mrs." whether she was married or not. By the end of the century many houses were employing male chefs. Arthur Wilson may have done this, but it is more likely that he did so in his London house than here in Yorkshire. Certainly, when the family were at Wolfreton, his cook was a widow, Mrs. Clara Harrison.

Punctually at ten o'clock Mary Wilson would appear in the kitchens to "pass the slate". This meant that she would give her approval of the day's menu, or would suggest alterations. As soon as this had been done, the kitchen maids were sent out to put on clean uniforms, in which they proceeded to prepare luncheon. Earlier in the century they might then have been able to get straight on with preparations for the evening meal, but by the time Arthur Wilson built Tranby Croft the tea party, to which a woman came hatted and gloved, had almost become an institution. Dinner, which meant a third clean uniform, was an elaborate affair which could last for three hours or more. The kitchen maids must have gone to bed dog tired.

(1) The Ellerman/Wilson Archives 4/4 Brynmor Jones Library, University of Hull.

(2) *Hull News* 27.1.1872 p.6 column b/c.

(3) *Hull News* 6.4.1872 p.4 column g.

(4) I am indebted to Iveson, Jarratt and Co. Hull for information supplied. Also to the Record Office, Beverley. 1873 LD 313 358; LD 313 359; 316; 360.

(5) See *K. J. Allison: Hull Gentleman seeks Country Residence 1750-1850* (East Yorkshire Local History Society 1981) p.26.

(6) *Hull Lady* 1900 p.29.

(7) Only a short time ago Andrew Bailey, one of the present gardeners, dug up a tree plaque on the south side

of the building. It recorded the planting of a Scotch Pine and appeared to be dated 1874, which would mean that the tree, now alas cut down, was one of the original plantings.

(8) *Journal of Horticulture and Cottage Gardener:* June 15th 1893 p.485.

(9) Verbal evidence from the late Mr. Henry Hall, who was a gardener at Tranby Croft and a great favourite with all the girls, who called him "Henry". He worked at the home farm when the Wilsons were still in residence, and he had a fund of stories about them.

(10) See Yorkshire's Progress in Commerce. Reprinted in *The Century's Progress* introduced by Arthur Raistrick (Brenton 1971) p.187.

(11) From information supplied by Mrs. Pat Labistour.

(12) *Hull News* (9.5.1874 p.6 column f).

(13) I am grateful to Mrs. M.P. Grady for this and other detailed identification - her eyesight in subdued lighting is very much better than mine.

(14) I would like to acknowledge help received from Mr. Christopher Ketchell and Ms. José Montgomery for all detailed information concerning Victorian tiles.

(15) *Daily Telegraph* 28.10.1907 Obit. notice.

CHAPTER FOUR

The Social Climb

The Holderness Hunt Years

The fact that Arthur Wilson could build a big mansion, buy a big estate, and farm what later amounted to 3,000 acres of land in the East Riding did not necessarily mean that this would endear him, or even make him acceptable to society in his area. That he did manage to integrate, and almost immediately, was mainly because he was both able and willing to perform a job which no other member of local society wished to do, namely to become the Master of the Holderness Hunt. When Arthur had been a small boy his father (himself no sportsman) had bought him a hunter. When he went to live in Wolfreton Hall, Arthur struck up a business friendship with a local breeder of horses, Henry Lambert, who sold him his next hunter, Slashing Harry, and many another after that.[1]

The Holderness was in the doldrums. The Master, Mr. James Hall of Scorborough had died, and the Hon. Alan Pennington, brother of the 5th Lord Muncaster (who sold Warter Priory to Charles Henry Wilson) had reluctantly taken over for a single season, refusing to do more as subsidies from the members were not forthcoming. By 1878 a fresh infusion of cash was necessary, and after some persuasion mainly by Christopher Sykes of Brantinghamthorpe, a friend of the Prince of Wales who needed all *his* money to entertain his royal friend, Arthur Wilson agreed to undertake the somewhat thankless task. He knew very little, since his hunting had been done in a rather aimless fashion, and the managerial side of the new job was a closed book to him. He was, as always, willing to learn, and his vast wealth ensured that the help he needed would be given unstintingly by those who wished to hunt, but had no wish to undertake any of the financial responsibility themselves.

Arthur Wilson said he was willing to hunt without any guarantee from the committee, (he was under no illusions as to why he had been selected for the job) but he would, of course, receive the subscriptions.[2] It cost him dear. Twice, in January 1886, and again in February 1895, he asked to resign because so little money was forthcoming. This the committee certainly did not want, and on the earlier occasion a special committee of five (with the aptly named Frederick Reynard as secretary) agreed to collect more, and did so. By the end of March Reynard was able to promise Arthur that £1,900 a year could be guaranteed from the subscriptions, and Arthur, mollified, carried on. Alas! the members soon slipped back to their former apathy, but were gingered up again in 1895, when they were made to realise what the alternative would be if they did not cooperate. Trouble, however, continued. In February 1897 *World* quoted Arthur Wilson as saying that the cost of running the Holderness was in the region of £4,000 a year, perhaps £150,000 in our money.

Although Arthur Wilson's appointment opened up a new era for the Holderness, (he stayed with them until 1904) he took care to respect tradition, and he kept the huntsman and whipper in who had served under Pennington. The huntsman was George Ash, who served from 1878 until 1881 and again from 1884 until 1900. During the three year gap, the huntsman was Charles Orvis, a son of the William Orvis who was drowned in a tragic accident in the locality at Newby Ferry in 1869. The story is worth the telling.

Orvis Senior was huntsman for the York and Ainsty, of which, later on, Arthur Wilson's son in law was master. On the 8th February 1869, on a glorious morning, the fox, after an hour's run, crossed the River Ure at Newby. The river was running high, for there had been flooding, and the fox was carried over the weir with the hounds close behind. They all got out safely, and the hounds immediately picked up the scent on the opposite bank. The flooding had made it impossible for the hunt to ford the river, therefore the ferry boat was brought across. Eleven horses and thirteen men at once pushed into it, dangerously overloading the craft. Speed being essential, the sides were now pulled up and chained — wrongly — so that as the ferry boat left the bank it began to fill with water and tilt. At this point the horse Swordfish, which belonged to Sir Charles Slingsby, the Master, jumped out, but in so doing caught one leg on the chain. This not only pulled the Master out with him, but further upset the equilibrium of the ferry boat, which turned right over. Six men were drowned, including William Orvis and Sir Charles Slingsby, although his horse, Swordfish, managed to struggle to safety.(3)

Charles Orvis, William's son, was with the Holderness at the time of one of the most important meets while Arthur Wilson was Master. The meet in January 1882 was a special occasion because the Prince of Wales, a personal friend of Christopher Sykes, was staying at the latter's house at Brantinghamthorpe. Most of the Yorkshire packs of hounds were represented, and it was estimated that 1,400 horsemen, 1,000 people in carriages and 4,000 footsloggers turned up.

"And when His Royal Highness came out on the terrace, the cheers that rent the air must have echoed in every valley of the district".(4)

The neighbourhood of Brantingham was difficult to ride over, being cut up by ravines and dales. This day's hunting started at eleven o'clock in the morning, when Orvis appeared with 18½ couple of the dog pack. The weather, as so often at this time of year, was far from ideal. One of our Humber fogs rose thick and fast and the first fox got away. The second one led them a pleasant gallop over Welton Dale and then promptly disappeared. The Prince, however, seemed to enjoy it all.

It was a good day. Tempers were relaxed. It was said that Orvis did not order a single hound to be kicked, and Arthur Wilson could reflect that night that so far as local society was concerned, he had now rather more than a foot in the door.

"Mr Arthur" as he was known, was an indulgent Master, perhaps because he had to learn the tricks of the trade when he was already in a position of authority, but Captain Reynard always remembered one occasion when he really did read the riot act. A certain Mr E. Harland had ridden throughout the day amongst the hounds. Full of indignation at such presumption, some members of the field complained to the Master, who therefore gave Harland "a thorough good rating". The complainants thanked him, and expressed approval of what he had done, whereupon Mr Arthur said "When I come to think of it, I did not give him half enough! and he rode up to him and let him have it all over again".(5)

The Wilson children were brought up to hunt, and Muriel and Clive, the two youngest, certainly rode as soon as they could walk. Later on the grandchildren carried on the tradition, and Tottie's three sons always rode with the Holderness whenever they stayed

Arthur Wilson. Photo by courtesy of the Guildhall, Kingston upon Hull.

with their grandparents. The Warter Priory Wilsons, particularly Millicent and Enid, made regular appearances, along with the Misses Constable of Watton and Misses Wade, whose father bought Brantinghamthorpe when Christopher Sykes died in 1899.

The hunt ball, during Arthur Wilson's time as Master, became even more splendid than it already was, and was accompanied by lavish house parties. In the late 1880s the Prince of Wales' elder son, Prince Albert Victor, was stationed at York, first with the 9th Lancers and then with the 11th Huzzars. During the hunting season of 1887-1888 he seems to have gone the rounds of all the local hunts, and was the guest of the Arthur Wilsons at Tranby Croft from Wednesday, 18th January until he moved on. The young Prince arrived at Paragon Station, Hull from York on a train which ought to have arrived at 12.15 p.m., but did not. He had asked that no fuss should be made, and the visit did start quietly enough when the reception committee, headed by the Sheriff, Mr Allison, and including Christopher Sykes and Arthur Wilson, took him off for lunch at the Station Hotel. He was then driven to the Artillery Barracks where he had promised to propose the inauguration of a branch of the Discharged Soldiers' Aid Society. This accomplished, he was driven off to Tranby Croft to give himself up to pleasure for the rest of his stay.

That night the annual ball of the Holderness Hunt took place in the Assembly Rooms in Beverley, which had been transformed by Mr Harry Hildyard of Cherry Burton House, Captain Rutter, who was Wilsons' Marine Superintendent, and Mr Leadbetter, the gardener at Tranby Croft. Flags galore floated from the ceiling, and included a Royal Standard, a Cross of St. George, and a Union Jack. The gasoliers were decked with evergreens and artificial flowers. In all the panels of the walls pines and spruce firs had been placed, and were lit with fairy lights and draped with flags, while underneath them were the trophies of the chase — foxes' heads, bits and spurs. The square hall had been made octagonal, since each corner had been cut off to make arcades which were furnished as lounges, and decorated like grottoes. Built of wood and covered with evergreens they were surmounted by Pampas plumes, arranged to simulate the Prince of Wales' feathers. The orchestra, Mr. Close's Quadrille Band, the most popular in the area, functioned from the middle of a decorated gallery at one end of the room, and below them a small drawing room had been created, which was decorated with greenery and small mirrors. Chinese lanterns and artificial roses hung from decorated arches above the galleries, so that the Victorian love of filling every nook and cranny was, at this event, thoroughly indulged.

The reception rooms had been furnished by the local firm of Elwell. Many paintings and water colours hung from the walls, and the organisers had even gone to the lengths of borrowing a huge candelabra which had been a wedding present to a former Master of Foxhounds, Mr. James Hall of Scorborough, whose death in a sense had made possible Arthur Wilson's entry into society. There was also some very good china, which the reporter from the *Hull News* believed was "supposed to have belonged to one of the French monarchs". It sounded very grand. There were two supper rooms, both heavily decorated, a small one for the Prince's party and a bigger one for everybody else. A couple of special trains were put on to bring house parties from Driffield and Nunburnholme, and between 400 and 500 persons attended. Dancing began round about 9.30 p.m. and continued until the early hours of Thursday morning. The Prince and the Arthur Wilsons arrived just before eleven o'clock, adding excitement, colour and delight to what was already an extravagant setting.

Next morning social Beverley was astir early. It was a glorious day and a huge turn out was expected for the meet, which was traditionally held the day after the ball, and at the

Grand Stand on the race course. Anyone who could borrow or beg a mount of any (or no) description appeared on it, and many carriages were driven up to watch. George Ash appeared with the hounds at exactly the time expected — but the Prince had not come, and it was half an hour before he did, during which time the crowd occupied itself by addressing comments, rude and otherwise, about both the hunters and their dogs. Finally, and no doubt to the great relief of Ash, the Tranby Croft party arrived, the hounds were inspected, and the hunt moved off, the Prince riding well to the fore all day — and it was a long day, for the hounds were not called off until the light faded.(6)

But Prince "Eddy's" day had not yet ended. At nine o'clock guests began to arrive for a ball at Tranby Croft itself. The extended ballroom had been treated to lavish decoration by Mr. Leadbetter, and in "Aladdin's cave" strings of coloured lights were suspended from the decorated ceiling as well as from the greenery around the walls. As this was a private party only 150 guests were expected, and the only special train ran from Nunburnholme to bring the house party of the Charlie Wilsons. Mr Close's Quadrille Band performed from the balcony, and a superb supper was prepared in the dining room. The bar was in the smoking room.

Amazingly the hunt turned out the following morning at White Cross and moved off when the Prince joined them at mid-day. The East Riding weather, never dependable at this time of year as the Prince's father had discovered not ten years ago, did its worst. Fog rolled up from the Humber, and before long the hounds were called off. The Prince was taken by Arthur Wilson to visit his agent, Mr Travers, in Beverley before returning to Tranby Croft.

The hunting seasons came and went. An interesting one was that of 1892-1893. At the

A Meet at Tranby Croft, 18th January 1907. Photo by courtesy of Mrs. D. White.

beginning the ladies were very much in evidence. The third week in October had been a particularly good one, and the last meet of the week was at Cottingham Castle. All the Wilson girls were there. A fox was found in the Cottingham cover and they ran it to Willerby, West Ella and Kirkella, a distance of seven or eight miles, then they lost it. The hunt moved in the direction of Hessle, to the south, and another fox was found in an osier bed there. They ran it towards Hull, but again lost it. They returned to Tranby where south of the pond was a horseshoe shaped stick heap and earth, where the foxes bred. A young lad was told to get in at the top with a stick, and draw a fox.(7) This he accomplished successfully (being rewarded with a shilling, which would be munificence indeed to him) and the fox led them to South Ella and back again to West Ella and Willerby but managed to save its brush.

A fortnight later there was an unusual occurrence when the hunt met at Tickton, near Beverley. Arthur Wilson had just given Ash the order to go, when a fox suddenly appeared and loped slowly *towards* the hounds. The company stared at it. It came on. When it was within 50 yards the hounds turned, it fled and the hunt was on. But the fox was lucky. A second fox crossed its line and the hounds were diverted. This fox led them a grand chase and was finally brought down near a greenhouse in the garden of the rector of Leven, a village several miles further east. The day was not yet over. A third fox was found near Riston. This one ran through Arnold, turned west, and crossed the river at Wawne. The terrain was difficult. There were many wide, open drains, and the fox was swift. There were many nasty falls, most of them among the ladies, but gradually the hunters tailed off and, again, a fox saved its brush.(8)

Those who have no use for fox-hunting would shake their heads grimly over the events of Thursday, 26th January 1893. This was the day after the Beverley Hunt Ball and, as was customary, the meet was at Beverley Grand Stand. There was a good turn out, not only from the locality but from the north of the county also. A fox was found very quickly half a mile away at Broadgate, but the hounds were onto it, it was bewildered by the spectators and was chopped at once. A second was found at Lamb Fold, and met with the same fate less than five minutes after it made its appearance. The hunt moved to the neighbouring Bishop Burton, and here, a fat fox was found in one of the plantations near the Hall, but again, the hounds were quick and the fox was chopped. The hunters were now considerably irritated. To them it was bad luck with a vengeance. However, a fourth fox appeared in Gallops Plantation, and this time the hounds ran hard through Brogdale and across the road into Deepdale. Eventually this fox turned for Beverley and they lost him in a garden, but, since the run had lasted an hour and twenty minutes, the hunters were more cheerful. They enjoyed what they called a "clinking run" which "pumped most of the horses out".

It was not, however, a trouble free run. David Dalby, the first whip, had put the hounds into a cover in Deepdale and was himself riding alongside the outer fence. Neither he nor his horse noticed that they were approaching a dyke until the horse shied, throwing Dalby. As bad luck would have it, there was a post in the fence at that very point, and Dalby fell heavily against it, striking his head an almighty blow which knocked him out. Fortunately a Doctor Walker was riding with the pack, and he was able to attend to the invalid on the spot. Dalby's head was bleeding profusely, but he was bandaged, and another member brought up a clergyman who happened to be present with his pony carriage, and he took the sick man home. It was months before Dalby could ride properly again.(9) He turned out several weeks later, but still felt giddy and sick and had to go back home.

He was not the only casualty that season. At the beginning of February Kenneth sought the advice of his doctor. He had hurt his back taking a gate some time before, but had thought little of it. Now the pain was excruciating. The doctor examined him and told him bluntly that if he wanted to make a full recovery, he would have to lie on his back for three months. Kenneth did as he was told.

Accidents were a perpetual hazard to the hunters. Arthur Wilson had put himself in bed for weeks in April 1888 when his horse slipped crossing a small drain. In leaping off he had fallen heavily against a gate and had broken a rib.(10) Both Clive and Muriel fell at a meet near Tickton in November 1897 when the fox was running fast, and Clive had a nasty accident in the 1903 season when he fell heavily and fractured his shoulder. Both were more fortunate than the wife of Dr. Smart of Leven, who badly injured her back when her horse fell back onto her; or Mr. Charlton, a fruiterer, who was passing through a gate when the wind caught it, and blew it back so that his horse shied, threw him, and then bolted — unfortunately before he fell clear. He was hurled against the gate post so violently that his arm was twisted backwards and the bone snapped. Jack, who happened to be riding alongside, immediately dismounted and, with the help of another member, bound up the injured limb quite expertly, and then sent for a carriage from Tranby Croft to take Charlton home.(11)

One of the most unusual occurrences took place on Saturday, 20th January 1894. The meet was at Tranby Croft. Arthur, Kenneth (now completely recovered), Clive, Muriel, and a young captain named Berkeley Levett (who had been at Tranby Croft at the time when an unfortunate game of baccarat was played) were out. A young lad was sent to the top of the stick pile, and as a result three foxes emerged. The first kill of the day came very soon, but a new fox was found near Eppleworth some three or four miles away, and this one made straight for the Hull and Barnsley railway line. Between Raywell and Little Weighton there was a very deep cutting. It presented no difficulty for the fox, but plenty for the hunt. The hounds followed close to the very edge of the embankment. Inevitably a few of them followed him down and, unable to negotiate the steep gradient, they fell and rolled onto the track, bruising and cutting themselves in the process. Once down, however, they siezed and killed the fox. While this was going on, a goods train came down the line on its way to Hull. The line itself was on a pronounced gradient, and the driver, Mr. Stroughair, had cut the steam off, and was allowing his train of 45 heavily loaded waggons to move at a fair speed. Suddenly he saw the hounds and realised that they were on the track. He applied the brakes at once, and made every effort to bring his heavy train to a standstill, which he could not do until he had reversed his engine. The noise was frightening. The terrified dogs tried to get back to the top of the cutting — an even more difficult manoeuvre than getting down it had been — and there were more injuries. Fortunately the train stopped in the nick of time, thus avoiding a wholesale slaughter.(12)

The Holderness Hunt had its part to play, if indirectly, after the Second Boer War broke out. On the 14th October 1899 Arthur Wilson at the Annual General Meeting reported that he had registered his horses with the government, and that ten of them had been taken for use in the Transvaal. It was not only ships, therefore, that the Wilsons had handed over for the duration. (Two of their biggest ships were offered as troop carriers and hospital ships throughout the campaign).

Finally, the time came when no amount of persuasion could keep Arthur Wilson at his post for longer. He was old and it was time for him to go. At a meeting at the Beverley Arms on St. Valentine's Day 1903, the committee met to decide how to honour him. The

A cricketing party at Tranby Croft, probably 1885. Muriel, Mary and Arthur are on the second row, to the right of centre. Raymond and Clive sit in front of them (from the Pressling/Woolrich bequest).

official honouring of Mr. Arthur took place on 12th January 1904 at Powolny's Hotel in Hull. The Lord Lieutenant, Lord Herries, who was chairman, presented him with an oil painting of himself as Master of the Holderness. It was a three quarter length portrait by A. S. Cope R.A. and was reputed to have cost them £600.(13) With this was an appreciation which read as follows:

> "Our Master is respected and loved by all as a thorough good sportsman, a most liberal man, a kind and steadfast friend and a most worthy follower of his predecessors in office."(14)

Lord Herries reflected on the great joy which would be felt by Arthur Wilson when, on looking round, he would see his wife, three sons, three daughters and two sons in law, all of whom were, or had been, keen fox hunters. Arthur responded heartily, although he had probably heard very little of what was said, being now very deaf (an affliction from which his mother had suffered acutely). It was right that he should be thus honoured. It was the end of an era not only in the history of the hunt, but in his own life too.

The new Master of the Holderness was Mr. Charles Brook of Kinmount. He remained with them only for three years.

Sheriff of Hull 1888-1889

Apart from his election as Master of the Holderness, the year in which the social progress of the Wilsons of Tranby Croft was most marked was the year during which Arthur was Sheriff of Hull. They had already made impressive progress, and were well

Tottie, aged seven (from the Ayre Collection).

Ethel, aged about five (from the Ayre Collection).

known outside the Riding and in London, where they now had a house on the outskirts of Belgravia. Photographs exist showing Mary Wilson and her two elder daughters at a distinguished house party at Wollaton Hall in early August 1884. It sets the scene admirably for their new life style. Eliza (Eisa) Mary, Lady Middleton, who was a sister of Sir William Gordon-Cumming (soon to be disastrously involved in a baccarat game at Tranby Croft) had organised a fancy dress bazaar in aid of the rebuilding of Wollaton Church. Queen Elizabeth I once visited Wollaton, so it was to that century that the guests were asked to turn in the creation of their costumes, each of which represented a Willoughby ancestor, and was almost certainly copied from a portrait.(15)

On 9th November 1888, and contrary to custom, the Sheriff was elected and installed on the same day as the Mayor, Dr Sherburn, who had already held the office of Sheriff himself. The voting for Arthur had been unanimous. His philanthropy and his deep pocket to match it, were by now very well known. At his installation Arthur made a speech in which he assured his supporters that he would do his best, and asked them to look in mercy upon his inexperience. Mary began her duties immediately. On the afternoon of the Wednesday which followed the election she and the Mayoress, Mrs Sherburn, held an At Home in the Town Hall. (Mr Leadbetter and his assistants had been sent from Tranby to work, in this case with the gardeners from the parks). Refreshments were served in the banqueting hall, and here, the local reporter joyfully proclaimed were found "all classes of citizens mingling amicably together, discussing the topics of the day".(16) The reception was held in the evening, which made it easier for some "working" people to attend, and indeed, many representatives of the "industrial classes" did come to pay their respects.

The following Sunday was Mayoral Sunday, when the civic dignitaries paraded to the

Grand Fancy Dress Bazaar, 1884 at Wollaton Hall. Mary Wilson sits at the far right on the front row. Ethel and Tottie stand second and third from the left at the back (from the Pressling/Woolrich bequest).

old parish church of Hull, Holy Trinity, for morning service. This satisfactorily concluded, they all adjourned to the Guildhall for what was euphemistically called "refreshments". The ex Mayor toasted Arthur Wilson, who once again reiterated his promise to do his best.(17)

Mary Wilson had always been eager to show forth her charitable instincts, and her new role gave her ample opportunity to do so. Before the end of November she had associated herself with a committee whose aim it was to provide breakfasts on Sunday mornings for poor children.(18) At the beginning of December, and with the full cooperation of Arthur and Charlie, she also promoted a Dramatic and Musical Recital in Hull for the benefit of young Mary Robertson whose London debut was to take place the following Friday.(19) Mary was ever willing to put her money where talent and dedication had already shown the road. The local churches and chapels did not appeal to her in vain. She was unable to open Albion Church bazaar at the end of November, but Arthur happened to have the time, and she sent him. The presence of a Wilson at such an event became synonymous with success.

Just before Christmas, Arthur was elected chairman of the council of the Yorkshire Agricultural Society; and he and his family saw the New Year in by entertaining the Mayoral party, the Grand Jury and members of the bar to luncheon in the banqueting room at the Guildhall. A fortnight later an event took place which was not only a milestone in the social life of the young Muriel, but also the beginning of a Hull tradition.

Muriel was young enough to have known no home before Tranby Croft. From the start she was trained to take her place in society as soon as she was old enough. She was still only thirteen years of age and had not been able to accompany her parents to many of their official functions. Because she was a lively girl, she found the restrictions irksome. However, her chance came in January 1889. Arthur and Mary, philanthropists both, had taken a great interest in hospital work in Hull, and particularly in the work that went on for the benefit of the Victoria Children's Hospital. This had been founded in 1872 and by 1874 Arthur and his wife were both vice presidents.[20] The hospital was in Story Street, and at the beginning of Arthur's term of office was bursting at the seams. There were many poor children in Central Hull, and the hospital, although doing a heroic job, needed to expand. A new site had just been acquired for it in Park Street, but the cost was such that no money was left to start the building. Mr Henry Allison, the Chairman of the Executive Committee, who had been instrumental in procuring the site, was so upset, that in January 1889 he resigned. The committee, however, sent for Arthur Wilson and confided their problems to his sympathetic ear. Arthur immediately handed them £1,000 which got the building job going.[21] A Grand Juvenile Fancy Dress Ball was now to be held in the local Artillery Barracks (whose drill hall was larger than any public room) and the committee then came up with the happy idea that the Sheriff's youngest daughter should be approached to receive the little guests. Muriel was delighted: for one night she would be the most important person in a big social occasion.

The ball exhibited all the Wilson characteristics of good and thorough organization. It must have been difficult to bring a completely festive atmosphere to a drill hall, but what Mr Leadbetter and Captain Rutter, the Marine Superintendent for Wilsons, could do was done. Flags were strung all over the ample ceiling, and moved like the waves of the sea. Beautiful flowers and foliage lined the walls. There was to be a band (Mr Close's), and the direction of events on the night was in the hands of Mrs Taylor, the matron of the Children's Hospital, and a team of nurses. The best known photographer in Hull, Barry's, promised to take pictures of any little guest (just like it was done at the big fancy dress balls in London), and the catering firm of Marshall made sure that there was plenty to eat. There was a kind of throne for Muriel at one end of the room. Mr Sherburn, the Mayor, lent it for the occasion, and Muriel was thrilled to hear that this was the gilded chair on which Queen Victoria had sat when she visited Hull in 1854. The children began to arrive at 7.15 p.m. and by 8 o'clock there were 400 of them in the hall. All were in fancy dress. Mary appeared in Elizabethan costume (perhaps the one she had worn earlier at Wollaton), young Jack was in hunting dress, Clive represented Prince Diablotine and Muriel, the star of the show, was his princess. During the evening the Master of Ceremonies called for quiet, and Muriel was invited to dance for the company. In the words of the reporter "Miss Wilson executed with admirable taste a tambourine dance which illicited hearty applause". It was an evening Muriel never forgot, and to the end of her long life she supported the Children's Hospital, which remained in Park Street for about the same length of time as was granted to Muriel on this earth.[22]

During the same week Arthur and Mary showed their support for the academic life of Hull by being present at the Annual Ball in aid of the Hull University Extension Society which was held in the Assembly Rooms. The aim was to endow a chair of either science or literature for which £2,000 was needed. Previous events of a similar nature had already resulted in a total of £800 having been collected, and it was hoped that this ball would outdo all the others. It did. One hundred couples attended. There was dancing to the band of the ubiquitous Mr Close until two in the morning. The Wilsons had done it again.

Their next challenge came only a day or two later when they led local society first at the Holderness Hunt Ball, and then at their own home. It was difficult to surpass the ball of the previous year, when Prince Albert Victor had been an honoured guest, but the hospitality was equally lavish. There were many house parties: but none was as big as that from Tranby Croft.(23)

That January the Arthur Wilsons displayed considerable interest in another project of vital importance for the cultural development of the town. A committee of influential citizens had met during the week of the Hunt Ball to discuss and, if at all possible, bring about the creation of an Art Gallery in Hull. The idea had first been aired in June, the previous year, when both Charles Henry and Arthur had guaranteed their support and Arthur had been made a vice president of the executive committee. Now, the chairman, Dr R.H.B. Nicholson, pointed out that a few weeks before, after they themselves had begun their campaign, an agitation had been started for a free library, as a result of which many of their supporters had moved over to the literary side. What he was now asking for was a guarantee fund of £200. He proposed an exhibition, a good one, and he thought that circulars should be sent round Hull and district inviting support. He told them that the Literary and Philosophical Society had agreed to let one half of the Royal Institution for a rental of £35, and they would throw open their own museum on the days when the art gallery was free, so that there would be plenty to see. He had, went on Dr Nicholson, the support of several influential families who had agreed to loan pictures, and among these were Mr Howard of Castle Howard, Charles Henry, Arthur, and John Graham Menzies, who was Tottie's husband. It was fitting that this project had the support of the Wilsons, and the Ferens Art Gallery, now an established and essential institution in Hull, contains a bequest of five pictures from Muriel, one of which might possibly have first been exhibited publicly at this early stage of the gallery's development. The committee had determined that it should be free if at all possible, but they considered that on either two or three days each week there should be a private viewing for students, when a charge of sixpence for each person would be made.(24)

At the very end of January, the Sheriff was invited to the annual dinner of the Hull branch of the United Kingdom Commercial Travellers' Association, and was asked to propose the toast "The Houses of Parliament". Arthur's political convictions had never been as well aired as those of his Liberal M.P. brother, Charlie who had sat for Hull since 1874, for Hull West since the reorganisation of 1885, and was still going strong. The Wilsons had traditionally tended towards liberalism, but Arthur, like so many other Englishmen, could neither understand nor condone the aged Gladstone's radical approach to Irish politics. Less than three years previously Gladstone, as a result of an ill timed revelation to the press (by his son, Herbert) of his real opinions about Ireland's future, and after a cliff hanger of a general election, had been forced to bring in Irish Home Rule at the very beginning of his 3rd Ministry in 1886. Members of his own party, appalled at this apparent switch of policy, split. The bill was thrown out, and Gladstone resigned. But he was not penitent. He never tried to regain the support of the rebels while there was still time, and he virtually reintroduced the same bill seven years later with the same result, although parliamentary circumstances were then very different. The rebels, first called Liberal Unionists, had joined the ranks of the conservatives by the turn of the century, and their leader, Joseph Chamberlain, had actually become a member of A.J. Balfour's cabinet. Arthur Wilson called himself a Liberal Unionist, and he made this quite clear in his speech to the commercial travellers.(25) So Charlie and Arthur, the best of friends in business, did not see eye to eye in politics, and there were some in Hull who regarded this as deliberate policy, since no matter which party was supported by the man in the street, he could look up to a Wilson brother who would share his views.

At the beginning of February the two brothers were sadly put out by the deplorable weather, and by an agitation and threatened strike among the seamen of Hull. They both believed the latter to be completely unnecessary. The shipping year had, in fact, opened gloomily for the firm. Their liner "Cameo" ran aground off Christiania, as she was leaving to return to Hull with 800 tons of merchandise. Within a month, the fine new ship "Hindoo" made its appearance before an admiring crowd in Alexandra Dock, Hull, but even this event had been attended by problems and danger. The ship had been built in Newcastle by Robert Stephenson and Co. Although not so long (by 17 feet) as the famous "Buffalo" which had been built four years earlier, she could carry nearly as much cargo, and would, in fact, be expected to take on 4,000 tons of coal and iron for Bombay. She left Albert Edward Dock, North Shields at about ten o'clock on the morning of Saturday, 26th January, under the command of Captain Douglas (a veteran of the Bombay run in the "Apollo"). It was a slow start. The vessel had to stand by because three small boats had collided in the Tyne, but as soon as the river was clear she did her measured mile (while the official party wined and dined and toasted each other below deck) and then headed south. There was a squall, which the ship rode out. Then the engines stopped, and it took five hours to get them going again.

"The stoppage resulted from the fusing of the packing of the high pressure piston and when the engines came to a standstill the estimated time for making all right again was one hour"

So said the *Hull News* but the estimate was over optimistic. Darkness fell,

"and there lay the fine new ship and her large cargo quite helpless on the water, the rain falling and the dark cloud masses for nearly half the time shutting out the lights on shore or rendering them very indistinct"

A major problem was to alert passing vessels in case the "Hindoo" was rammed. This fortunately was avoided. Another problem was drifting. The first cast of lead showed 38 fathoms and every subsequent cast showed that "Hindoo" was shoaling the water. Soon the cast showed 24 fathoms, but a short time afterwards, at about nine o'clock in the evening the engines were started up. They were kept slow for an hour after which the order "Full steam ahead" was given. The rest of the journey was uneventful.(26)

As if this was not enough, there was trouble at Constantinople where the "Mourino", which sailed between Hull and Odessa, caught fire though by some miracle the cargo was undamaged.(27)

Meanwhile the threat of a seamen's strike continued. In some quarters Wilsons had a fairly enviable reputation as kindly employers. For instance, in the difficult early spring of 1886 they had issued a daily distribution of food on board the "Juno", which was anchored in the Railway Dock. This received sympathetic coverage in the local press. Captain Pepper, who was responsible for the organization, had issued 850 meal tickets daily. The cook had spent every night in the galley, and had produced next morning a rich soup, which was to be eaten with a small loaf for each person. It is an indication of the quality of the food that on Tuesday, 30th March, 120 pounds of beef had gone into that stew, with quantities of turnips, carrots, peas, barley, oatmeal, onions and herbs. Each man was given a quart of soup and if, when all Wilsons' men had been served, there was any food left over, the other poor, starving creatures who crowded the gangway had been invited in and, as far as possible, fed.(28)

When, at the beginning of February 1889, a strike was threatened, the *Hull Times* commented that the stimulation for the strike was coming from outside Hull and was not in the best interests of the local men, pointing out that the firm not only gave steady employment to thousands(29) but also offered good conduct money of ten shillings each month paid onto the wages of those who had served satisfactorily for six months. The paper quoted verbatim the letter from the Secretary of the Hull branch of the Seamen's and Marine Firemen's Amalgamated Association to Wilsons' Marine Superintendent, and his letter in return. It appeared that the Wilsons had a good friend in the *Hull Times*.

"From Mr J. B. Butcher, Secretary
1 Railway Dock,
Hull
12th December 1888

To Captain Rutter, Sir,

At a special meeting held last evening on the wages question, it was resolved to accept Mr Wilson's offer of a shilling per week and five shillings per month, and that it should commence January 1st 1889, and I am desired to express the thanks of our members for the many acts of kindness and goodwill that you have evinced towards the society, and through you to Messrs Charles Henry and Arthur Wilson our gratitude for their generosity in listening to our appeal, and hope by our conduct in the future as in the past to merit a continuation of your help and goodwill."

The following day Captain Rutter wrote in reply:

Hull 13th December 1888
To Mr J. B. Butcher,

Dear Sir,
We are much obliged for your letter of the 12th inst. . . . and note your Society accept our terms . . . The matter has been brought before Mr Charles Wilson today, and he has requested me to inform your Society through you that the increase of wages so far as his firm is concerned may commence from the present time."(30)

The correspondence did not solve the problem. On Thursday, 7th February 1889 more than 200 members of the Seamen's and Marine Firemen's Amalgamated Association crowded at the quay of Albert Dock where the "Draco" was waiting to set sail and refused to let any of her crew go aboard. Several police officers turned up in answer to a call for help, and a crowd of more than 50 on the dock was dispersed. The ship then sailed, but not before three groans had been given for the police and Messrs Wilson. It was not the only incident. The very next day there was a similar occurrence when the "Humber", berthed in Railway Dock was about to leave for Dantzig. Again, about 50 men turned up on the quay and tried to dissuade the crew from going to sea. Three firemen were persuaded. The police appeared as before; and Deputy Chief Constable Jones, Inspector Matthews and half a dozen constables personally escorted the three turncoats on board to the accompaniment of loud groaning from the men on the quayside. The ship then cast off, and as it went through the lock pit a police guard stood by to prevent any member of the crew trying to jump off. The "Otto" was also in dock, but there was no bother here, as the men insisted on getting on with their work; but Captain Rutter was uneasy about the

"Buffalo" which was due to leave Alexandra Dock bound for New York. He decided to play safe and sent for Deputy Chief Constable Jones again, and he brought along Sergeant Pickering and several constables. As it happened, they were unnecessary. The ship sailed though with seven firemen short, but it was expected that they would pick up others down river.(31)

During the week ending 23rd February there were further agitations among the seamen. On Tuesday the 19th they held a protest demonstration in Drypool, and the following day, in the afternoon, a second committee meeting of the local branch of the National Amalgamated Sailors' and Firemen's Union to be held that week took place at the offices of the Union in Posterngate. This National Union had appointed the Chaplain to the Hull seamen, Rev. W. R. Welch, as mediator, and he now came to report to them how he had been received. Mr Welch assured the committee that the grievances of the seamen had been given a very good airing, and said that the Wilsons would be in contact shortly by letter. Sure enough they did write, but it was not at all what the Union had expected.

Hull February 20 1889

"Dear Sir,
... We beg to say that there is a misunderstanding as to Mr C.H. Wilson's action. Mr Wilson made no promise or even hinted at any intention to recognise the Union. We understand that the So-called National Union was formed about 7 months since at Sunderland and, as we have a Union of seamen and firemen in Hull, we do not consider that a branch of the Sunderland Union is needed".(32)

This letter greatly angered Mr Reid, the Union secretary, who thought that it would increase the bitterness of the seamen and firemen of Hull. He felt that Charles Henry was both unjust and cruel "using the great lever of his wealth to the disadvantage of the men." He was adamant that the Union was not a Sunderland union, and he wanted to know by what right "eighteen men of the local union dictated to the seamen of Hull and by what right — Divine or otherwise — Mr Wilson tried to impress their views upon them". He proclaimed those men to be fools who were prepared to do what they were told by Mr Wilson, and he was sorry that the Rev. Welch had not managed to do rather better.

Perhaps the only light relief in this doleful week was to be found in an incident reported at a meet of the Holderness Hunt at Bentley. A gentleman was making his way towards the starting point, and was passing the Borough Asylum when an inmate, standing at the gate, hailed him.

"Where are you going?" asked the inmate.
"To the meet, my man" replied the gentleman.
"What is that?"
"Gentlemen on horses, and hounds hunting the fox."
"How much are the horses and hounds worth?"
"Perhaps two thousand pounds."
"And how much is the fox worth?"
"Oh, nothing."

The inmate immediately opened his gate and gave the prospective hunter a hearty invitation to come in and join them.(33)

Industrial troubles there may have been, but the Wilsons steadily consolidated their shipping empire. Late in February their new liner "Iago" loaded for Bombay in the Alexandra Dock. As in the case of the "Hindoo" earlier in the year, she was built in the

North East by Raylton, Dixon and Co. of Middlesbrough, but she was a smaller ship. A week later the new steel screw steamer "Urbino" was launched by Robert Thompson and Sons, Southwick Yard, Sunderland.

The social round continued. The Victoria Children's Hospital held its annual sale of work in late February to collect money to supply instruments and surgical appliances to parents whose children had been in the hospital, but who could not afford the equipment their children needed. They also hoped to be able to send some children on holiday, either to the seaside or to the country. Young Muriel, who had earlier worked so hard to make the Fancy Dress Ball a success, was brought in again to declare the bazaar open. The text of her speech remains:

"Ladies and Gentlemen. I am very much obliged to you for asking me to open this bazaar. My mother tells me that the committee have made me a life member and I thank them very much for it. I shall always take a great interest in this hospital and the children of the poor people who are brought here to be cured. I hope you will make a lot of money today. I have great pleasure in declaring this bazaar open."(34)

There have been many worse speeches, and many more sophisticated speakers might have learned from the thirteen year old Muriel.

Early in the following month the Prince of Wales' elder son, the ill fated Prince Albert Victor, once again joined the Tranby Croft party and rode with the Holderness. It was unfortunate that the East Riding weather behaved in a less than gallant fashion. The meet was at Sigglesthorne near Hornsea, but it was bitterly cold, with snow and sleet at intervals throughout the day. There was, perhaps naturally under the circumstances, a good turn

House Party at Tranby Croft, 1889/91, including Prince Albert Victor who is seated second from the left on the front row. Jack stands behind him. Mary is seated in the middle of the front row. Arthur is third from the right at the back (from the Pressling/Woolrich bequest).

71

out, but before long the hounds were taken home, and the Prince and Arthur Wilson rode back to Beverley and visited Arthur's agent, Mr Travers at North Bar, who seems to have fulfilled a very useful and hospitable function when the elements forced the hunters to abandon the chase.

The following day the meet was at the kennels in Etton which, being fairly close to both Tranby and Beverley, meant that several ladies were able to venture out. The weather was wretched, and although there was a good run through Kilwick, which lasted an hour, continuous rain beat down and the fox got away. Once again the Prince and Arthur retired to Beverley, but the Prince soon left for York.(35) It was a pity about the weather, but the Wilsons had entertained a member of the Royal Family in their year of public office and service, and even if the sun had not been visible in actuality, metaphorically it had beamed upon them with its brightest rays.

Apart from his hunting activities at Tranby Croft, the Prince was also present at what might have some claim to be considered the most prestigious event in Arthur Wilson's year as Sheriff — the Sheriff's Ball. It was to take place on Monday, 4th March, in the Artillery Barracks, and was given in the Prince's honour. The local press shook their heads, "The large hall is not beautiful" they proclaimed, but the willing workers for the Wilsons well knew how to make it so. Once again, thousands of flags, banners and ensigns fluttered from the ceiling. Large mirrors were fixed along the walls at intervals, and the walls themselves were covered with climbing plants, evergreens and flowers, many of which were roses. These even appeared entwined amongst the greenery around the gasoliers, which were supplemented by the softer light of wax candles in brackets on the walls(36) a sight to make a modern fire officer feel faint with horror, disbelief and shock. There were chairs around the walls, and in each corner of the room stood an arrangement of palm trees which gave dignity and height to the immense hall, enabling the eye to travel easily upwards to the flag washed ceiling. For once a special platform had been erected for Mr Close's band, which would perform from a semi circular gallery built on top of a series of arches "which were radiant with plush and profusely decorated with flowers and trophies of the chase".(37) The flowers were springlike — narcissi, Stars of Bethlehem, jonquils and Roman hyacinths. The chase was represented by a hunting trophy, a fox's head and brush and hunting horns, arranged among yet more flowers. In the centre of the bandstand a standard had been erected, bearing the Royal Arms and the Prince of Wales' feathers. The space underneath the bandstand was equipped as a sitting out room. "Delightful", the newspaper called it, but it must have been rather noisy. The actual platform at the far end of the hall had been converted by Elwell into a drawing room. Here were tapestries and curtains, mirrors and "artistic furniture". Nearby was a billiard room, and this had been fitted out as a smoking room. There was also a small room set aside for playing cards — all the leisure activities of an English country house party seemed to be there for the asking.

The decorations were not only inside the hall, for an arcade had been created in front of the main entrance and was covered with bunting and lit by Chinese lanterns. Since it was expected that the guests would arrive by carriage, a circular approach had been made right round the huge Corporation Field, and this, too, was lit by double strings of coloured lights.

It was undoubtedly the biggest ball of the season. Crowds collected to watch the impressive display of wealth and authority, although it was a very cold night, frosty and the ground hard as iron. Between nine and ten o'clock that night 700 guests turned up and were received by Arthur, resplendent in court dress and carrying a sword, and his Mary, who wore pale blue velvet intermingled with pale blue satin and tulle and a panel brocaded with pearls. She had a diamond necklace, and a diamond tiara in her hair. Although dancing started at ten o'clock, the Prince was not expected for another half hour. Before he arrived everyone had to be there, and the party had to be in full swing. At his appearance the band stopped in mid stream, a drum roll was heard from outside, and then all stood to attention while the National Anthem was played. The Prince, wearing the uniform of a Captain of the Yorkshire Hussars, advanced between the double ranks of a guard of honour one hundred strong, and as soon as the ceremonial was over he led out Mary Wilson to head a set of the lancers, (in which set there were many representatives of the party from Tranby Croft). It is interesting to note that one member of the house party was Captain Holford of the 1st Life Guards. He was the Prince's equerry and, after the death of John Graham Menzies, became Tottie's second husband in 1912.

The Prince greatly enjoyed himself. Indeed it would have been surprising if he had not, for there was every comfort and every luxury. There were chairs and couches in abundance, screens to prevent draughts, little gas stoves near each group of seats, antique cabinets "that might have graced a mediaeval castle" and flowers "which seemed to invite the bees to come".(38) A very elegant dining room had been created out of the gymnasium. Its roof was draped with blue and yellow bunting. Its walls had been covered with turkey red cloth. Japanese umbrellas hung from the gasoliers and the walls were covered with paintings illustrating the works of poets, dramatists and humorists. Rabelais took his place with Dante, Shakespeare and Milton, who might have been surprised to see him there. There was also the head of a Madonna, a picture of brigands, and portraits of mediaeval moralists and divines. The Prince sat at a private table in the centre of the room, which, like the platform, was decorated with orchids and silver plate. The food was magnificent. It was a triumph of hard work, good organisation and a genuine flair for the spectacular. No one could doubt that the Wilsons had completely absorbed what the Riding had to teach them, and were now able to teach the Riding.

March saw one other interesting event. Charlie, who had already purchased one Scottish estate (the Kinord portion of the Marquis of Huntly's Aboyne property) now purchased another. This comprised 17,000 acres of the Cromar, also in Aberdeenshire and belonging to the Earl of Aberdeen. He paid £14,000 for it, a good price. Arthur and Mary appear to have had no hankerings after grouse moors. It was becoming increasingly obvious that their main interests lay further south.

During the last fortnight of March another ship joined the Wilson fleet. This was the "Clio" built by Grey and Co. in West Hartlepool. She was berthed in Alexandra Dock and immediately began loading a cargo consisting mainly of coal, which was to be shipped to Bombay. The "Clio" was an adaptable vessel but, because she had been designed for the Indian trade, the problem of good ventilation had to be taken very seriously. It was pointed out with pride that on the run down to Hull her stoke hole was nearly as cool as her upper deck.

A very sad event took place at Dover at about the same time. The "Buffalo" had sailed from Hull for New York, but it was discovered that there were nine stowaways in the hold of the ship. The poor, wretchedly clothed young men were put ashore, their dream of self improvement in God's Own Country shattered. It is tempting to speculate whether they would try to hitch a lift home, or whether they would try instead to reach London or Southampton and make another attempt.

At the end of March came Founders' Day at Spring Bank Orphanage. The Wilson family had given splendidly to this institution from the very beginning, so it was to be expected that, during his year as Sheriff, Arthur would try to make the day a memorable one for the children. First there was a service of thanksgiving at Kingston College, Beverley Road (which was Arthur's old school). Then the children formed a procession and, headed by their own band, and hoisting aloft their banners, marched home by a devious route, so that they might be seen by as many of the good citizens of Hull as was possible. That evening old students as well as present orphans were invited to a dinner in the main hall, provided by Arthur. This was followed by a prize distribution, but the Master of Ceremonies was — Charlie. He explained that Arthur had "a very bad cold in his eyes", which was only too true, and it was some time before he could rid himself of the infection.(39)

Everything that Arthur did as Sheriff must be looked at in conjunction with his interests as a business man. These could not be ignored, and recently the Wilson ships had quite literally been having a smashing time. The "Albano" was in collision with the "Glenavon" off Gravesend, as a result of which both ships sustained damage and had to return to port. In the North Sea, the crew of the little fishing smack "Crown" were picked up by the "Malmo" which had run them down. Their vessel had sunk immediately, but all lives were saved, and the crew were landed shortly afterwards in Hull. However, to offset this, a new steel screw steamer, "Douro", was launched from Richardson, Duck and Co.'s yard in Stockton at the end of May; and a serious fire in the forehold of the "Plato" (which was berthed on the east side of Princes Dock) was put out by the fire brigade, and the ship was saved.(40)

At the end of the hunting season it was customary for those gamekeepers living within range of the local hunt to be entertained on a grand scale. This year (as had happened often before) it was at the expense of Arthur Wilson, and it took place at the Beverley Arms. He himself was unable to be present, but Mr Travers, who spoke for him, said that he was particularly disappointed to miss the occasion, as relations between gamekeepers and the hunt had not always been friendly during the season, and he was anxious to establish harmony if he could.(41)

A more regrettable absence was on the occasion of the opening of what was described as Hull's "fine new art gallery" at the end of May, although Charlie, who was a member of the committee, was certainly there. For Dr R.H.B. Nicholson, the President of the Hull Literary and Philosophical Society it was the end of a long, arduous and sometimes distressing struggle, for he had met adamant opposition often coupled with incomprehension at what he was attempting to do. The opening took place at the Royal Institution, Albion Street, the premises having been lent for the occasion.(42) Where was Arthur? Was he, perhaps, in Gothenburg? His elder brother John West Wilson had died there, a naturalised Swede, on 24th May. He was 72 years old. Even a Wilson was not immortal. Soon after, he was in London. Since the birth of Muriel in 1875, the family had moved from their London house in Hyde Park Street, which was to the north of the park, to Belgravia, a more genteel area to the south of it, and they now occupied No. 13, Grosvenor Crescent, a tall, rather gloomy house, bigger than their last, and therefore more suitable for receptions. Thursday, 6th June 1889 saw one of the worst thunder storms London had suffered for a long time. The Wilsons were not entertaining that evening, but the curious Arthur, with his second son, Kenneth, his daughter Ethel's in-laws (Sir Edward Green the iron master of Wakefield, and members of his family) along with Frank Travers went to stand under the portico at the front of the house so that they could watch the storm. It was providential that after some minutes they decided to go indoors. Immediately the house was struck by lightning which dislodged a heavy coping stone forming the cornice, and half a ton of masonry fell upon the very spot where the group had just been standing. Some stones were hurled right across the road, and a footman, who had the bad luck to be passing at the time, was hit by falling debris as he ran for shelter. He reported later that the lightning dodged about all over the place and the crescent seemed to him to be a sheet of flame. Similar evidence came from the neighbouring Wellington Club, where the story went round that the lightning had set alight a box of matches in the smoking room.(43)

While Arthur was in London Charlie, having completed negotiations for his new estate in Scotland, was making his views about the seamen's strike widely known. As Sheriff, Arthur would not wish to have to mix awkward business problems with his less controversial social duties. Charlie knew he had to speak for both, and he did so forcefully and unequivocably at the Annual General Meeting in the Hull Seamen's and General Orphan Asylum in Spring Bank. Not only sailors and firemen were coming out, but efforts were being made to bring out the dockside labourers as well. This, said Charlie, would simply mean that owners would be forced to lay up ships, and that would mean no work for anybody. Did the men not realise what a lot was done for them by the charitable businessmen of Hull? It was time that the two sides should try to see each other's point of view. (His words have a contemporary ring.) "The other day" went on Charlie "I met a man in Posterngate who said he was destitute but unable to go to sea because of Unionist activities. And he *wanted* to go to sea. I believe there are many like him". Another man he had met had existed for the past two or three days on a few biscuits, and told Charlie that he had no hope of being able to pay his union subscription. "What a pity" Charlie said "that in this fine weather they are not earning money". He finished ominously by reminding his listeners that whereas in the North Eastern ports the regular trade was carried on almost exclusively by Scandinavian ships, in Hull at that moment it was carried on in British ships. The *Hull News* sympathised with Charlie, pointing out that, if left alone, Hull seamen tended to go on working and it would seem that the agitation was coming from men in other ports.(44)

The only "event" recorded by the newspaper during the strike was the appearance of George Reid, the secretary of the local branch of the National Seamen and Firemen's Union, before the Stipendiary Magistrate on a charge of disorderly conduct, and causing a crowd to assemble in Hull's Dagger Lane. At some point a policeman had come up and had sworn that he would "shift everybody".(45) In spite of the evidence of a witness that the policeman's words had actually caused the crowd to gather. Reid was fined £2.10.6d. The end of the strike came early in July. It had done nothing to disrupt the trade of the port, and the local society of sailors and firemen seemed fairly content with existing pay rates. Many men had returned to work because they had received no pay from the National Union, although within the last fortnight of the strike a whip round in other branches had produced a small sum for distribution. Reid became very unpopular. He then disappeared, no one knew when or where. His name was therefore blotted out on the sign-board of the Union offices in Prince Street.

While Reid was still in Hull there was a humdinger of a row between him and J.B. Butcher, the secretary of the Hull Seamen's and Firemen's Amalgamated Association at their half yearly meeting. Reid, who represented the National Union, came with supporters and at one point shouted that he would rather work with the Scandinavians than with

Mary Wilson, by L. Disanocs. Photo by courtesy of the Guildhall, Kingston upon Hull.

"those who call themselves Englishmen".(46) His supporters were nevertheless in a minority and lost heavily, which produced the following letter from James Rutter, Wilsons' Marine Superintendent, for Mr Butcher:

"June 20th 1889

"Dear Sir,
As the firemen and sailors' strike is now practically over, we think it only due to you to say that we have had offers of large numbers of firemen and sailors from abroad, and had it not been for your good management of the local societies, the greater portion, if not the whole of our fleet would now undoubtedly have been manned with crews from the continent, and although compelled to adopt this course, for the sake of the families of our townsmen, we should have very much regretted it."

The Wilsons had won, but the struggle between local and national unions was going on all over the country, and gaining momentum. It would not be so easy next time.

Meanwhile Mary Wilson was making Hull Hospital Saturday a great success. The Ladies' Committee master-minded a campaign to make sure that no Hull citizen could possibly remain unaware that funds were needed for the local medical charities. More than thirty stands were to be set up in central Hull on the second Saturday in June, and collectors arranged themselves in such a way that no corner of a single street was unmanned. The non-contributors who usually managed to steer an inebriated progress from street to street found themselves trapped. Even the passengers on board a tramcar were not safe — the ladies had been given permission to go on board and collect. The Artillery Band under Conductor Isitt was thumping ceremonially and thus adding to the impressive siege. When the proceeds were added up, a grand total of £455.15.11d was declared — the best on record. Mary had added £111.12.3d, and no other collector came anywhere near that figure. It was a far cry from the first year's collection in 1882 when only £17.10.0d was collected. The committee had enough this year to allow £200 to the Royal Infirmary, £100 each to the Dispensary and the Children's Hospital, £21 to the Homeopathic Institution, fifteen guineas to the Orthopaedic Hospital, and even five guineas to Lloyd's Hospital, Bridlington.(47)

The ship "Buffalo" was back in the news. This time Captain Malet was shifting horses not stowaways. The Wilsons were doing a thriving trade as live stock carriers, and towards the end of June the "Buffalo" left Alexandra Dock for Boston carrying 38 horses — young Cleveland stallions and mares, Clydesdales and a few Shetland ponies — the whole consignment having been bought by a single estate owner, Mr J. Harris of Fort Collino, Arizona, who had travelled in Yorkshire on several occasions, and on whose orders the animals had been sent down to Hull by train.(48)

A new screw steamer for the Norwegian passenger trade, the "Juno", was launched on Wednesday, 10th July from Earle's yard. This made a total of six new ships since the beginning of the year, but more was to come. In early August the "Polo" was launched from Earle's for the coastal trade. The first of these ships, the "Juno" was steel built with awning type deck — flush deck all fore and aft — and was framed on the cellular system with a double bottom for water ballast. The collision bulkhead, forward, was curved, a design thought out by Charlie because it gave additional strength where it was needed, and which was now to be generally adopted on all Wilson ships. First class accommodation was amidships. There was a big dining room, a smoking room, a ladies' room and the usual conveniences. The saloons were decorated in polished wood with some carved work, and some marble fittings. If a large number of passengers wished to travel, it was possible to extend the accommodation without trouble. The captain and officers were also berthed amidships. The crew quarters were forward. There were comfortable cabins aft for second class passengers, and emigrants travelled between decks. The "Polo" was a smaller ship with a raised quarter deck over engines and boiler. At the launch it was pointed out that Charles Henry had thought out a number of improvements, and that the launching was later than expected because of strikes. The speaker, Mr Seaton, said that strikes were giving Hull a bad name, and this was causing work to be taken elsewhere. A fortnight previously, Charles Henry had brought an order for a large passenger and cargo steamer, and he was also willing to place an order for two smaller vessels, but, because of the expected difficulties in getting through the work, one of the ships was being built by a firm further north, and this was a pity.(49)

However, the topic which filled the Sheriff's mind during that summer was not so much his ships — Charlie would be able to keep in touch during the parliamentary recess — but the Yorkshire Agricultural Society Show, which was to take place for the fourth time in its history at the Hull showground off Walton Street. This was a thirty acre site owned by Hull Corporation, who had purchased it from the North Eastern Railway Company. It included a fair ground area which was well cindered. The show had started in York in 1838, and in that year 68 head of cattle, 90 sheep, 38 pigs and 105 horses had been displayed, £549 having been paid out in prize money. Since then the number of entries had risen steadily.(50) It was important to Hull, as well as to Arthur Wilson, that the coming show should be the best ever.

Complicated and careful arrangements were being made. The cindered section would become a reception area for stallions and brood mares — the cinders could easily be rolled and turned if the weather proved to be wet. Six "elegant" new turnstiles were to be erected at the Anlaby Road end to admit the public. An area in the centre of the showground was to be reserved for members and ticket holders who would be free to come and go as they liked. Here, also, the secretaries would have their offices, separated into administration and finance, and there would be postal and telegraphic facilities. There was to be a huge implement yard and alongside it, and twice as big as the show had ever had before, a shed for exhibits with further covering to the left and right of it. The reception area needed to be extensive because of the expected heavy entry. In the main avenue of this area machinery would be seen in motion, and at the far end of the implement yard would be a working dairy. Not far from the dairy was the bandstand, that essential ingredient of the Englishman's day out. The Council of Administrators had thrown caution to the winds here, and had hired for the whole of the three days the full band of the Yorkshire Dragoons, (although they had taken the precaution of making a more humble arrangement with the Orphan Homes to "dep." where necessary). To the left of the dairy, a huge dining tent would be erected which would seat 600 members of the general public at one time. In Hull at this time there was a strong feeling against alcohol, therefore the Temperance Society was allowed to administer its own separate accommodation.

To the right of the machinery in motion, a shoeing forge was to be created. There was no grandstand here, but ample space for 400 spectators to watch the event at ground level. In the immediate neighbourhood was an exhibition of beekeeping, and near that, the cloakrooms, council rooms, and accommodation for the judges, stewards and their parties.

The foregoing only comprised one section of the show yard. In addition there would be the cattle stalls which would run the full length of the stockyard, for between two and three thousand entries were expected. In front of the horse boxes the grandstand was to be erected, its 1,500 seats to be covered in red cloth. There would be four large horse rings in front of it, where the judging would take place.

The Yorkshire Agricultural Society had to pay for all this temporary building programme, and although it received substantial help from its host, Hull Corporation, the seemingly bottomless pocket of Arthur Wilson and other private donors made matters a good deal easier. The total prize money, starting at £2,300, was more than it had ever been before. It was already known that the show of stock would beat all records, and that Queen Victoria, no less, would be a "large exhibitor".(51) (She would probably have found little amusement in reading this description). A tactful merging of the Hull Horse Procession Society's annual meeting with the grand parade of the Yorkshire Show also ensured that the last day would see a procession of at least 400 horses, again, the biggest and most impressive parade on record.

All that was wanted now was fine weather. This so occupied the minds of the committee that the announcement that the Children's Hospital could now claim to have bought and paid for the new site in Park Street (helped by Arthur's £1,000 and £250 from Charlie) and could also announce that £5,400 of the £7,235 needed to build had already been subscribed, was hardly noticed, great triumph though it was.(52) True that Arthur and Mary managed to tear themselves away for a flying visit to their London house, but it was because they had the honour to entertain the Duke of Cambridge (another royal friendship). The party included Lord Randolph Churchill whose meteoric rise in the Conservative party had so recently been followed by his equally rapid descent from grace,

Arthur and Mary Wilson at Swanland Manor. Mary stands third from the left in the middle row; Arthur stands fifth. His brother, Charles Henry, is on Mary's right (from the Pressling/Woolrich bequest).

and Christopher Sykes, Arthur's neighbour in the East Riding and a friend of the Prince of Wales for twenty years. By the beginning of August they were back at Tranby Croft to witness the final preparations for the show.

There was some grumbling now from members of the general public in Hull. To reach the show ground they would normally travel by tramcar, bus or waggonette and the cost would be one penny. For the three days of the show, however, the cost was to be "tuppence per person, per trip or per part of per trip" as Stanley Holloway might have said had he been there then. To the poorer people of Hull, and there were plenty, this seemed an unfair thing to do, and an example of sharp practice on the part of the organisers. The arrangements, nevertheless, had been made to some purpose. To prevent the snarling up of traffic needed a superior kind of organization which was expensive. Still, as the ordinary members of the public were aware, when they finally reached the show ground the entrance fee was no mean sum. On Tuesday, the first day, it would cost 2/6d until six o'clock in the evening. The price thereafter was 1/-, but this was a small fortune to a poor family. But the show was hoping to attract spectators and exhibitors from all over the country, the railway companies were obliging enough to run trips, and therefore the poor of Hull would have to put up with the situation.

All the stock was judged on the first day, and the entry, as had been hoped, was a record. There had been 516 horses on display when the show had been at York, but here there were over 600, including 130 stallions. Four thousand people passed the turnstiles that day and, with one unfortunate exception, the organization ran like clockwork. Just after the gates opened at nine in the morning the only serious accident of the week occurred. Joseph Cade, a 55 year old from York was erecting a building for the Water Gas Company of Horsforth when an explosion erupted in the purifier. A heavy lid shot into the air and, falling back, struck Cade on the head, felled him, and killed him. It ought never to have happened. A youth had been manipulating a gas engine unsupervised, and had thoughtlessly applied a light — a simple act with tragic consequences.

During the judging, much interest was concentrated on the section for the two or three year old hunting geldings and fillies for which the new prize of £35, donated by Arthur Wilson, was to be given. There was a good deal of local satisfaction when it was won by Mr Henry Barkworth of Tranby, Hessle, with a beautiful chestnut he had bred himself. By the third day the organisers were beginning to relax. It looked as if Hull's entry figures would beat those at Huddersfield the previous year. They stood at 66,249, but more and more visitors poured through the turnstiles as the hours went by, and on the last day the Hull total was 80% up on that of Huddersfield. The final assessment, that 76,575 people had attended the show, delighted the committee; but by that time, the Council of Administration had met a delegation from Harrogate, where the next year's event would take place, and were already starting afresh.(53)

Once the show was over, Arthur's attention switched back to the Holderness, since the new hunting season was about to begin. He presided at the puppy judging, which took place at the kennels at Etton, and followed it up by giving everybody a good dinner which was served in the paddock at the kennels. The ground was dry and very hard, but the season managed to get off to a good start.

Late in August Charlie and Arthur were toasted by the shore-gang of their firm after more than a hundred of these men and their wives had enjoyed an outing to Bridlington, during which they watched a certain Miss Beaumont ascend in a balloon and descend by parachute. After general thanksgivings they all trooped back to the station, caught the 9.45

p.m. train, and were in Hull an hour before midnight. This at least shows a different side of the coin — gratitude of the workmen to their employers for their jobs and for acceptable conditions of employment.(54)

A more critical attitude was noticeable when the Hull Seamen's and Marine Firemen's Amalgamated Association met in their rooms on Tuesday, 10th September, when their secretary, Mr J. B. Butcher pointed out how far Hull lagged behind other towns in the British Isles in what was available to the workmen. At the beginning of the month Mr Butcher had attended the Trade Congress, which took place over five days in Dundee. He told his listeners of towns where the only requirement to enter a hospital was ill health or disease, where free libraries were available, where shortly there would be elementary and technical education both free of charge, and where working men served on local committees; where, in short, the classes were beginning to fuse. Hull had nothing like this: nor had it a Humber bridge, whereas Edinburgh and Dundee could boast, in the Forth and Tay bridges, two of the most famous engineering feats of the age.(55) It is interesting how, in so short a time, Mr Butcher's attitude had changed. His attendance at the Congress seemed to have stiffened his determination to stand first, and only, for his members.

They thanked him for his report, and then the Association carried unanimously the following resolution, which left neither the Wilsons nor anybody else in any doubt where their sympathies lay in regard to the London Dock Strike, that milestone in Trade Union history, which had erupted in the West India Docks on 14th August 1889.

"That we, the members, express our hearty sympathy with the dock labourers now on strike in London, and view with admiration their self sacrifice and orderly conduct under very trying circumstances, and that we hereby show our sympathy by sending them £10."(56)

Meanwhile, the "Santiago", Captain Potter's ship, had turned in a remarkable performance of speed. She had left Hull for New York on 7th August. She discharged her cargo there, filled up again with general cargo (which included 498 head of cattle), and landed it at Hull only 29 days later, with the exception of the cattle, which had been put off in splendid condition at Gravesend. It was thought to have been the quickest two way journey between Hull and New York ever to have been made.(57)

Late September brought another important social occasion for the Sheriff. The Associated Chambers of Commerce held their Autumn Conference in Hull, and this started with a brilliant reception for them in the Town Hall, where they were guests of the Mayor. Eighteen hundred were invited: thirteen hundred came. The foreign consulate officials were resplendent in their colourful uniforms, and the uniformed services also stood out among the evening dress of the civilians. The guests were received at the foot of the carpeted and decorated staircase by the Mayor and Mayoress. The Mayors of Hull and Leeds both wore court dress, but many of the other mayors and delegates, who came from all parts of the country, preferred the plainer evening dress. Arthur Wilson was attired as a Master of Foxhounds.

One of the ways in which the Wilson brothers could always impress a visiting delegation, and at the same time show off the attractiveness of the East Riding, was to offer a mini-cruise down river, in one of their ships. On the Wednesday of the stay of the delegates from the Associated Chambers of Commerce, they were invited aboard the old "Orlando" which would take them past all the Hull docks. It was a beautiful September day, fine and mellow, the time of year when perhaps the Riding looks at its very best. So that the event was not orientated too obviously towards the Wilsons, the party assembled just after ten o'clock in the morning on the river steamer the "Manchester", which belonged to Manchester, Sheffield and Lincolnshire Railway Company. This little ship took the party from Victoria Pier and sailed them round Albert Dock. The Chairman of the Dock Company, Mr J. H. Ringrose, and other directors steamed in front of the expedition on the "Hercules", showed them the River Hull and the cattle wharf on the Citadel, and then took them back again to Victoria Pier to pick up their wives, who had either not been invited for that part of the tour, or who had not wished to come, pending the fairly lengthy trip down river later on. The "Manchester" also picked up a number of less important delegates before heading past Victoria Dock. If it had been intended to enter, a disappointment was in store, for an outgoing steamer had partly blocked the entrance, and Captain Hollingworth had to back out into the river and make for Alexandra Dock, the property of the Hull, Barnsley and West Riding Junction Railway and the Dock Company, and a source of great local pride. Here they saw the fine slipways and the shipbuilding works belonging to Earle's, where so many Wilson ships had been built. It was pointed out to them how the engineers (among whom had been Mary Wilson's brother Henry Smith) had made it possible to have a flow of water clear of the muddy sediment, which no visitor to the Humber could have failed to notice.(58)

The next stage of the journey was to board "Orlando", and the old ship was decorated with bunting from stem to stern, and had been made as clean as a new pin. The party was welcomed aboard by Captain Watson who had been with the "Orlando", a ship built for the Scandinavian mail and passenger service, for 14 years. He had actually been on duty twelve years previously when Charlie and Arthur had entertained 250 delegates of the Associated Chambers on another trip similar to this one. Four years before, his was the vessel chosen to open the new Alexandra Dock. The ship had prestige, and more than one delegate would regard her as an old friend. As the "Orlando" steamed slowly down river the guests, 350 in number, congregated below in the fore part of the ship where the banquet would be served. It had been cooked on board by the Chief Steward and his assistants. Spurn Point was reached, and soon they were off Grimsby, but here Captain Watson turned the ship and headed back to Hull. He knew the cross currents at the mouth of the Humber and the rough sailing they might be expected to get in the open sea. He also knew how well they were dining, and regarding this with humanity as well as humour, decided it would be a pity to spoil their day.

The very next week there was news from New York that the "Colorado" had arrived from Hull on 11th September after one of the fastest passages on record — 11 days, 20 hours. No daily distance (apart from the final day, which was incomplete) was less than 275 knots, and the best performance covered 302 knots. Just before Arthur Wilson's year of office ended, the new ship "Juno", launched the previous July and built for the Norwegian trade in passenger and mail service at Earle's, came up for her trial trips in the Humber. They were completely successful. "Juno" was brought out of Victoria Dock at eleven o'clock, by which time the steam tug "Zero" had ferried the official party to the waiting ship. The day was ideal. "Juno" sailed quickly down river on an ebb tide, passed Spurn Point and came up the Yorkshire coast as far as Withernsea. Although it was now November, the weather remained fine and clear, and the mid-day sun was warm. The second run was made against the ebb, after which two further runs were made, the mean speed of the four being 13 1/4 knots. A new act of parliament would come into force on 1st March, 1890 which would compel evey ship to carry sufficient boat accommodation for everyone on board. "Juno", in anticipation of this, already had her quota, and some of these boats had to be hung up, well above the heads of the passengers, for there was no room at all on the deck. Large permanent skids had been constructed, which were not beautiful to look at; and before long, when the ship would start to carry emigrants, she would have to carry additional collapsing boats, which would create another problem of stowage. Wilsons had been carrying emigrants successfully for years, and over the previous decade had averaged around 50,000 of them each year. During that period not one life had been lost — another indication of the meticulous attention to administration and high standards which, from the beginning, the firm had striven to adopt.(59)

In the second week of November Arthur Wilson held his last banquet as Sheriff in the banqueting room at the Town Hall. He invited all the officials of Hull Corporation, with Mr R. S. Pickering from the *Hull Daily News* and Mr W. W. Woodifield from the *Daily Mail*. These were the men among whom Arthur had worked for the last year, and after the usual reception, splendid meal, loyal toast and a few speeches, he got up, for the last time as Sheriff, and proposed the toast to "The Mayor and Corporation". He thanked them with genuine gratitude for their support, and wished the new Sheriff, Mr Robson, well, hoping that he would be able to do a better job than he himself had done. He then urged strongly that in the year to come great attention should be paid to working class housing in Hull. Much of it, he said, was sub-standard, and he felt that many houses could do with being pulled down as quickly as possible. He finished in a way that the local people were fast beginning to recognise. He told his audience how a Presbyterian minister in Hull, the Rev. Mr Duncan, whose church had been seriously in debt, had been offered £1,800 to clear it. The offer had come from the shipbuilder William Gray of West Hartlepool, and was conditional on the congregation putting up the rest of the money, which amounted to £450. Unfortunately this was a higher sum than they could afford, "but I have helped them" said Arthur, "Now, what about the Corporation?".(60)

It had been a full, exciting and successful year, and the Wilsons had established themselves more firmly than ever in the forefront of local society. Arthur may not have been a clever speaker — those who did not like him had more than once maintained that he was no speaker at all, and two years later, after the "Baccarat" furore the *Pall Mall Gazette* condescendingly asserted that "the leaders of the working men like to be spoken to in homely Saxon". This was probably not far off the mark, but he never wasted words, and his main purpose in speaking was usually made clear, even when he did not ram it home like a pile-driver. His great wealth had enabled him to make substantial contributions to charities and local enterprises. Not every wealthy man is prepared to do this, and Arthur Wilson continued to be generous for the rest of his life. By the end of the year the hardest part of the social climb was over. But no Wilson ever underestimated how much he owed to Hull; Arthur himself never forgot it, and seventy years later his daughter, Muriel, was to echo the same thankfulness, although by then she lived far away from the Riding.

(1) *Grimsby Daily Mail* 21.10.1909 Obit. notice, Arthur Wilson.
(2) *The Field* 23.10.1909.
(3) *William Scarth Dixon: A History of the York and Ainsty Hunt* (Leeds, Richard Jackson 1899) Chapter 4 pp.110-123.
(4) *Sketches of Beverley and the Neighbourhood* (John Kemp and Sons, Beverley 1882) p.81.
(5) *Captain Frank H. Reynard: Hunting Notes from Holderness (Truscott & Sons) c. 1914* pp.170-171.
(6) *Hull News* 21.1.1888 p.6.

(7) Ibid 22.10.1892 p.4 column g and verbal evidence from Mr Hazelhurst of Hessle.
(8) Ibid 12.11.1892 Supplement p.4. column b.
(9) Ibid 28.1.1893 p.4 column e.
(10) Ibid 7. 4.1888 p.4 column c.
(11) Ibid 1.4.1899 p.4 column b.
(12) Ibid 27.1.1894 p.7 column b.
(13) *Eastern Morning News* 22.10.1909.
(14) *J. Fairfax-Blakeborough: Yorkshire East Riding* (Robert Hale Ltd. 1951) p.268.
(15) From information supplied to Miss P. Raine by Jeremy Farrell, Keeper of Textiles, Museum of Costume and Textiles, Nottingham. Nottingham has a very similar group photograph of the event to ours at Tranby Croft.
(16) *Hull News* 17.11.1888 Supplement p.3 column g.
(17) Ibid p.4 column c.
(18) Ibid 24.11.1888 Supplement p.4 column d.
(19) Ibid 1.12.1888 p.8 column c.
(20) Ibid 3.1.1874 p.3 column e.
(21) *George Patrick: A Plague on You, Sir!* (George Patrick, Hull 1981) p.61.
(22) *Hull News* 19.1.1889 p.6 column f.
(23) Ibid 26.1.1889 p.5 column a.
(24) Ibid Supplement p.8 column c.
(25) Ibid 2.2.1889 p.4 column f.
(26) Ibid 2.2.1889 p.4 column d.
(27) Ibid 9.2.1889 p.4 column f.
(28) Ibid 3.4.1886 p.4 column g.
(29) It has been estimated that the Wilsons employed 10,000 men.
(30) *Hull Times* 2.2.1889 p.7 column b.
(31) *Hull News* 9.2.1889 p.8 column g.
(32) Ibid 23.2.1889 p.5 column c.
(33) Ibid Supplement p.3 column g.
(34) Ibid 2.3.1889 p.6 column d.
(35) Ibid 9.3.1889 p.4 column f.
(36) Ibid Supplement p.4 column b.
(37) Ibid Supplement 9.3.1889 p.4 column b.
(38) Ibid 9.3.1889 Supplement p.4 column b.
(39) Ibid 30.3.1889 p.5 column c.
(40) Ibid 6.4.1889 p.5 column c; 20.4.1889 p.4 column g; 25.5.1889 p.4 column g; 1.6.1889 p.5 column b.
(41) Ibid 27.4.1889 p.5 column b.
(42) Ibid 25.5.1889 Supplement p.4 column b.
(43) Ibid 8.6.1889 p.8 column d.
(44) Ibid 15.6.1889 p.6 column e.
(45) Ibid 22.6.1889 Supplement p.6 column g.
(46) Ibid 6.7.1889 p.5 column f.
(47) Ibid 29.6.1889 p.4 column e.
(48) Ibid 22.6.1889 p.3 column e.
(49) Ibid 3.8.1889 p.6 column g.
(50) *Hull Times* 3.8.1889 p.4 columns f/g.
(51) *Hull News* 13.7.1889 p.4 column g.
(52) Ibid Supplement p.3 column f.
(53) Ibid 10.8.1889 p.4 column d.
(54) Ibid 31.8.1889 Supplement p.3 column d.
(55) Ibid 14.9.1889 Supplement p.4 column c.
(56) Ibid 14.9.1889 Supplement p.4 column c.
(57) Ibid 14.9.1889 p.4 column g.
(58) Ibid p.6 column f.
(59) Ibid 2.11.1889 p.3 column d.
(60) Ibid
9.11.1889 p.6 column b.

CHAPTER FIVE

The Doncaster Race Week 1890 at Tranby Croft and its aftermath

The early part of September 1890 looked like being the greatest social triumph so far for the family at Tranby Croft. For some years the Prince had spent the Doncaster race week in the company of his friend Christopher Sykes, the Conservative M.P. for the division of Buckrose in the East Riding, at his house at Brantinghamthorpe, not far away. Christopher Sykes was the younger son of the colourful and eccentric Sir Tatton Sykes, 4th baronet of Sledmere. He was a diligent parliamentarian, but a lonely and solitary soul (he never married), and he hankered after high society. He had first met the Prince of Wales at Grimston in Yorkshire, since when he had made every effort to become an accepted member of the Prince's circle. He had achieved this ambition by the relatively simple expedient of producing endless and lavish dinner parties for the Prince, and these became famous, so that Disraeli introduced them into his novel *Lothair* in which he writes

"Mr Brancepeth was a grave young man. It was supposed that he was always meditating over the arrangements of his menus, or the skilful means by which he could assemble together the right persons to partake of them. Mr Brancepeth had attained the highest celebrity in his peculiar career — Royalty had consecrated his banquets, and a youth of note was scarcely a graduate of society who had not been his guest."[1]

Keeping the Prince amused could be difficult. In one sense Christopher Sykes was fortunate that when his dinners began to pall, he acquired another role. At one of these dinners, overcome for the moment with boredom, the Prince lifted a glass of good brandy and poured it over his host's head. The company gaped. The Prince was allowed to be rude, but not as rude as this. For the moment there was a complete silence, which the Prince noticed, and for which he had the grace to look regretful. Then Christopher spoke. Dripping from his own good brandy, which he did not even attempt to mop up, he said in his peculiarly squeaky voice "As your Royal Highness pleases." It was the perfect courtly answer, made completely incongruous by the extraordinary circumstances. The Prince realised this immediately, and burst into a hearty roar of laughter in which the relieved company promptly joined.[2]

Christopher was now a figure of fun, and the Prince's circle teased him unmercifully. Shortly after this incident he was deliberately locked out of a fancy dress ball, where he had arrived as a knight in full armour, so that he had to clank his way round and round the London house in an attempt to get inside. This drew the attention of a jeering crowd which fell into step behind him, as he continued his undignified progress. It was also said that he was kicked under his own billiard table and poked with the sharp ends of billiard cues, while on another occasion the Prince stubbed out his cigar on the back of Christopher's hand. Another member of the Prince of Wales' set, Mrs Hwfa Williams, maintained that Christopher knew that he was being teased, and willingly accepted the situation.

According to her the Prince would say "Come here Christopher and look at the smoke coming out of my eyes" and would then "playfully" pretend to burn his hand. The lady may have been right, but she called her autobiography *It Was Such Fun,* and she was sometimes able to see a joke in a situation which would call forth a very different reaction from her reader.(3)

By 1890 Christopher Sykes had entertained so much and so well, that he was on the verge of bankruptcy. He could no longer accommodate his royal friend. He explained his position to Lord Coventry, the head of the Prince's household, and it was decided to suggest to the Prince the name of Arthur Wilson as a likely host. The Prince had met him in the Riding in his capacity as Master of the Holderness Hunt, Prince Albert Victor had stayed at Tranby Croft only the year before, and Mary Wilson had the reputation of being a first rate hostess. The Prince accepted without hesitation, and the Wilsons received a list of names of those friends he would like to meet there, to all of whom the necessary invitation was dispatched.

The Prince had been taking the waters in Hamburg, but on Friday, 5th September he had returned to England, and on Monday, 8th September, travelled directly to the race course at Doncaster. After he had inspected the course, he and his party were driven back to the station where a special train was waiting to take them to Hessle, the nearest station to Tranby Croft itself, and this they were expected to reach at approximately ten minutes past five.

Tremendous preparations had been made to welcome the Prince, and the little station had undergone a complete transformation. On the south platform an elegant reception room had been created out of the waiting room, complete with luxurious carpets, and an oak dining suite upholstered in rich crimson velvet. All along the embankments on either side of the line were massed ferns and greenhouse plants. The station exit was banked by flowers and greenery too, and above all soared a triple arch, built up of foliage of yew and laurel and outlined with scarlet gladiola, white asters and yellow almandas. Between this arch and one of the signal posts a double line of flags waved.(4)

A huge crowd had gathered in the sunshine by the time the two handsome Great Northern saloon carriages, a composite and two brakes, drew into the station. The Prince stepped down onto the scarlet carpet, which ran the full length of the platform (just to be on the safe side), and was met here by Arthur Wilson, his host, who also greeted the equerry, the Hon. Tyrwhitt Wilson, and Christopher Sykes, who should have been the host, not the guest. The Prince of Wales was now led out of the station and up the somewhat steep slope, to where a sociable was waiting at the top. He was driven at once to Tranby Croft, followed by his equerry and Christopher Sykes in another carriage. Apart from the vast crowd at the station there were few spectators and few cheers along the route. Here, the East Riding Constabulary were in charge, and patrolled as far as the lodge gates where Mr Leadbetter, the gardener, and Mr Pickering, the joiner, had between them erected a magnificent triple arch, which included the word "Welcome" and the Prince of Wales' feathers in white everlasting flowers. Further up the drive two smaller arches underlined the sincerity of the welcome, as did the Union Jack which flew from the top of the tower — along with the flag of the Wilson Line.

The pattern of country house life meant that guests were free to settle in until dinner was called. At Tranby Croft the dressing bell sounded at seven o'clock, and the meal was served at about a quarter past eight. It was both lavish and impressive and would have consisted of at least 14 courses. The Prince sat at the centre table, which was a round one and could seat eight people. Mary Wilson was on his left, and Lady Brougham on his right. Arthur sat opposite. In the centre of the table was a massive silver bowl filled with orchids, coleus, crotons, tube roses and maiden-hair fern. Above this hung a silver lamp, shielded by a rose tinted lace shade, while the rest of the table was lit by a four branched silver candelabra. There were two other round tables placed at either end of the room, and the meal was served from the oblong table near the window and opposite the fireplace, where logs were blazing.

After the meal there was a short entertainment. Ethel Lycett Green was almost certainly the principal, if not the only performer. Since her marriage five years ago, she had gained a reputation in York for her singing and piano work, and she was a regular contributor of after-dinner ballads at the so called "Penny Readings", which were organised by the local gentry for the general public at the York Corn Exchange.[5] The Prince was always ready to listen to a song from a pretty woman, but he would be unlikely to settle for this kind of entertainment for a whole evening. Dancing for Prince Edward was out of the question. He was now 48 years of age, portly, and had recently eaten a very good dinner. After listening for a short time to Ethel's recital, he it was, no doubt, who suggested a game of baccarat. Arthur Wilson could not have been pleased. Baccarat, as the Wilson family very well knew, had been expressly forbidden at Tranby Croft since one night the previous autumn, when Arthur had returned home from Commercial Road late and tired, and had found an inebriated baccarat party in full swing in the billiard room where Jack and his young friends, soldiers and undergraduates were playing for high stakes. Arthur had stopped the game, confiscated the counters and had the table removed. Thus, when the Prince made his request, the Wilsons were put to some confusion. If Arthur allowed the game, his stern protest of the previous year counted for nothing. Yet his future sovereign was a guest in his house. His wishes could not be ignored. Mary Wilson, the perfect hostess, expressed a willingness to play, and sent a delighted Jack to prepare a room. It has been assumed that Arthur pleaded sickness or fatigue, and went to bed.

He may not have done this. For some days the Wilsons had had a strike on their hands. Between 50 and 60 shipwrights were out. For a long time they had received two prices for their labour, a minimum for "new work" and sixpence a day extra on "old work". The shipwrights maintained that work on board a vessel which had been to sea once, was "old work", and this was what the trouble was about. It is therefore possible that Arthur used the excuse of an industrial problem to wriggle out of an awkward moral dilemma, and he may have gone off to Commercial Road. Certainly he appears to have taken no further part in the activities during the rest of the evening.

Jack arranged the game of baccarat in the smoking room next door to the billiard room. The billiard room itself was full of young men who had gone there immediately after dinner, and were already playing. Since there was no suitable table, Jack had to improvise. He used two card tables with the smoking room table itself in between them. This was slightly higher than the others, but not noticeably so, but it was highly polished, and would therefore require a cloth. The only one which Jack could find was a tapestry one, and unsuitable, as the counters would not show up upon it. However, he set chairs round, and invited those who wished to play to come in. The Prince of Wales sat in the middle of one of the long sides, as he was taking the bank, which he would start, moderately enough, at £100. The rest of the players drifted in and took seats as they were available.

Baccarat is a simple game, requiring little, if any, skill. The long, narrow table should be covered with a baize cloth, on which a chalk line should be drawn all the way round, six inches from the edge. Stakes are placed beyond this line. The banker sits opposite to the croupier, if there is one. The punters sit round and all have counters of different colours, according to the amount they wish to stake. When called to "make their game" they put down the amount for which they intend to back the hand, and this is done before any card is dealt. A nine, or the nearest number to it, wins. A score of eight or nine is a "natural". An ace counts as one, a ten or the court cards are nil. The dealer now deals two cards to the right tableau, two to the left and takes two himself. If he has in his hand less than eight "pips" (for example, a four and an ace) he does not expose it. If he has eight or nine, in other words a "natural", he puts his cards down on the table. If neither side can beat his score, the banker has won. If the banker does not expose his cards, the punters look at theirs, and can, if they do not hold a total of more than four, ask for another. The banker also may take another card, but these cards are dealt face upwards. The banker now declares his points, and if both tableaux score higher than he does, he pays out to both. If one is higher and one lower, he pays out to one, and receives from the other. Each "coup" lasts about one minute. The banker continues to hold the bank until he has twice run through all the cards — or until he has been "smashed".

On Monday evening, 8th September, the left tableau was arranged in this fashion.

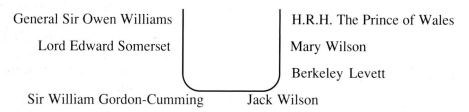

General Sir Owen Williams   H.R.H. The Prince of Wales

Lord Edward Somerset   Mary Wilson

Berkeley Levett

Sir William Gordon-Cumming   Jack Wilson

There was no problem about the counters. The Prince carried his own, made in very soft Russian leather, and with the Prince of Wales' feathers stamped on the back. When the game had been in progress for only a short time, young Jack Wilson became convinced that the man on his left was cheating. This was Lieutenant Colonel Sir William Gordon-Cumming of the 1st Battalion of the Scots Guards, a personal friend of the Prince over the last twenty years. Although Princess Alexandra had been known to describe him as a "vile snob", he had proved more than useful to the Prince in the past by putting his house, at 2 Harriet Street, at his disposal, so that he could meet his lady friends there. Bearing in mind the moral climate of Queen Victoria's court, it would hardly have been seemly for her eldest son to flaunt his amours under her very nose.

The *Sporting Times* called Gordon-Cumming "Possibly the handsomest man in London, and certainly the rudest". He was at this time 42 years of age, single, and a soldier of repute. He was a wealthy man, owning 40,000 acres at Altyre and Gordonstoun and a member of four important London clubs, the Turf, the Marlborough, the Guards and the Carlton. Florence Garner, who later married him, said he swaggered. His daughter, Elma, maintained that he played cards very badly, and also believed that relations between the Prince and Sir William had recently worsened, because the latter had "cut him out with a certain lady". Daisy Brooke, Countess of Warwick, ("Darling Daisy" as the Prince was known to call her) had been discovered in Gordon-Cumming's arms when the Prince arrived, unannounced, at Harriot Street on 6th September, the day after his return from the continent.(6) By then, it would have been far too late to change a guest list for the stay at Tranby Croft.

Whatever the truth of this matter, Gordon-Cumming's play on both this and the following night did give rise to the suspicion that he was cheating, although the accusations, like those of the witnesses before Pilate, did not always agree. He was said to be employing the dodge known as "la poussette", which meant pushing extra counters to join a bet already placed, when the cards fell fair; and by adding to his stake in a similar circumstance by dropping the soft leather counters from one closed hand over a single exposed counter, while his other hand concealed what he was doing. He was also accused of withdrawing money when his tableau was the loser, but this accusation, made by someone who had not actually seen the cheating, was later withdrawn in court.

At first young Jack had made no move, but he had continued to watch his neighbour's play with greater attention. When, for the second time, he felt sure that cheating was going on, he alerted the young subaltern sitting on his right. This man, a personal friend of Jack's and at the house party because he had been invited by the Wilsons, had the misfortune also to belong to the Scots Guards. In other words, he was now being asked to contemplate the ungentlemanly conduct of his own commanding officer. Contemplate it, however, he did, and later that evening assured Jack that cheating had taken place, and that he had witnessed it. Play was not halted until the Prince was ready to retire, which he did round about half past midnight. Jack then sought his mother, to tell her of what he was convinced he had seen. Mary was horrified, but her advice was definite and diplomatic. A scandal was to be avoided at all costs; Jack was to keep his mouth shut, and was to make sure that a proper table should be made available for play on the next evening. Jack also went to see Berkeley Levett, the young subaltern, but if he had expected cooperation from this quarter, he was disappointed. The young officer was already wishing he had never entered the smoking room that night, and he flatly refused to be involved any further.

Jack was an early riser. Next morning he was out in the grounds of the house, where he met his brother in law, Edward Lycett Green. He had already decided that this was the man whose advice would be most valuable, and he forthwith, and completely ignoring his mother's warning, told the whole story to Edward. Edward had been cubbing the day before, and had been too tired to play, although he had purchased a few counters for Ethel. However, he lost no time in making the information available to his wife, so that by now there were at least five people who knew.

During that morning, after the Prince was up and had breakfasted, he was able to inspect a valuable herd of Angus cattle. They belonged to a neighbour, Mr Arthur Egginton of South Ella. It was considered to be unseemly to expect the Prince to make the journey, so the animals trekked the mile and a half to Tranby, and were paraded across the lawn in front of the house. Shortly before noon the house party departed to catch the special train for Doncaster, which left Hessle station at five minutes past twelve. They spent the day at the races and then returned to the hospitality of the house, where the pattern of existence continued as usual until, after dinner and a short recital, the Prince once again suggested baccarat. This time the circumstances were very different. Since the previous night Jack had, possibly at the suggestion of the Prince, and his mother, ordered the butler to take a table from the pantry and cover it with green baize. There was even a chalk line six inches from the edge. This had been placed in the billiard room, beyond the table itself, and near the fire. It was the best thing the Wilsons could do to discourage cheating.

Later, it was to be a very important point at issue during the trial as to whether the five members of the house party who had by this time either seen, or had been told of the suspicion of cheating, did or did not make a pact to watch the movements of Gordon-

Cumming. They themselves maintained stoutly that there was no such plot. Yet why was Berkeley Levett playing? He had already stated, and would state again, that he wanted no part in the proceedings, and in spite of this he not only played, but played sitting opposite to his superior officer, where, presumably, he would be in an excellent position to observe events. Yet the Wilson evidence at the trial is clear that the seating on this second night was haphazard, and that probably the last two people to join the punters were Gordon-Cumming himself, and Edward Lycett Green, later the most significant witness. It is just possible that Berkeley Levett might have hoped that Gordon-Cumming would not appear, but this cannot be a strong argument, since the man himself was so far totally unaware of the hostility building up around him.

Whatever four of those in the know had determined to do, it seems certain that Lycett Green made a close study of the man under suspicion. The new table was a narrow one, no more than three feet wide, and from his lately acquired seat, Lycett Green had both a front and a side view. It is reasonable to assume that from this particular position Ethel's husband could easily see any cheating from Gordon-Cumming which occurred. It may well be true, as has been suggested, that Gordon-Cumming's habit of ridiculing the nouveaux riches had caused Lycett Green to feel resentful towards him. He himself did not know the man, but his wife, Ethel, was a regular visitor to Birdsall in the North Riding, where Eisa, Gordon-Cumming's elder sister, who had married Digby Willoughby, Lord Middleton, held extravagant parties.

The seating for baccarat on this second night of Tuesday, 9th September, 1890, so far as the participants could remember, was probably something like this.

Reuben Sassoon

Mary Wilson	Lord Coventry
H.R.H. The Prince of Wales	General Sir Owen Williams (croupier)
Lord Edward Somerset	Lady Coventry
Berkeley Levett	Lieutenant Colonel Sir William Gordon-Cumming
Edward Lycett Green	Ethel Lycett Green

Jack Wilson

Within a very short time Lycett Green became convinced that Gordon-Cumming was cheating at cards. Having been told the circumstances of the previous evening by Jack, Lycett Green could not ignore what he had just seen, and he went out to the smoking room next door, where he wrote a note to his mother in law, and sent a servant into the billiard room to deliver it to her. Mary refused to react. It seems certain that, at this stage, she did not, as some writers have suggested, wish to create a scandal. It seems equally certain also, that if she had not planned to watch Gordon-Cumming at the beginning of the evening, she could not now very well avoid doing so.

Play went on until the Prince was tired. Lycett Green had long since returned to his place and continued with the game. Strangely, there is no evidence to suggest that at this small table and in these cramped circumstances, any new witness came forward with a similar story of having noticed cheating. Perhaps Mary Wilson, Ethel and Edward Lycett Green half expected it to happen — and later said it did; but neither the Prince nor Lady Coventry appear to have noticed anything, although the Prince was nearer than Mary Wilson, and Lady Coventry was sitting at Gordon-Cumming's right hand. Nor, according to his evidence given later, did Berkeley Levett see anything untoward, yet he was sitting almost opposite the man under suspicion. At the end of this night's play Gordon-Cumming had won £225.00, which was £100.00 more than anyone else, and most of it had been won from the bank, or, in other words, the Prince of Wales. There is no argument that he did better because he was more familiar with the game than most of the other punters (which he was). There is no skill in baccarat. Either he had a run of luck, or he helped himself to get it. Strangely, also, there would not appear to have been any conversations behind closed bedroom doors on this night, unlike the previous one. If the Wilsons had had a pact to watch, presumably this evening's entertainment would have given them plenty to talk about.

During the night tragedy came to Tranby Croft. Mary's brother, Henry, had recently been far from well, and suddenly died at his bachelor residence at Crown Terrace on the Anlaby Road.(7) Mary was his nearest living relative. The news came before mid morning and, as was usual at country house parties, spread through the staff and guests like wildfire. So, in addition to a strike at the industrial headquarters, the unfortunate Wilsons now had to arrange a funeral and go into mourning. Gordon-Cumming returning from a stroll in the grounds, and still blissfully ignorant of the furore his conduct had created, met his hostess as she was descending the main staircase on her way out to the Anlaby Road. He later, at the trial, maintained that he had offered her sympathy, and had suggested that it might be easier for the family if the house party came to an end. Mary, knowing the importance of Wednesday's racing, insisted that this should not happen. If this is true, there is no suggestion here that Mary was out to make trouble. Indeed, a case could be argued that she had to be safely out of the house before there were any further developments, and when they came, they came from Lycett Green, her son in law, who had not been present on the Monday, and not from her own son, Jack, who, on that night, had seemed so anxious to bring the problem to a head. However, at the trial, Mary maintained that she could not remember this conversation on the stairs. It was a surprising story for Gordon-Cumming to have made up, and not really surprising that, under the difficult circumstances, Mary failed to recollect it.

That Wednesday morning became very gloomy. It was the most important day at the races but the Prince knew, none better, that death in a country house was incompatible with race-going. His irritability grew, and it was a great relief all round when a suggestion was made that the party should attend the races — wearing mourning. Out came Arthur Wilson's store of black ties and arm bands, and off to the races went the company, their respect for the dead plain for all to see. In one of the rail coaches that morning Edward Lycett Green found himself in the company of Lord Edward Somerset who, like Lord Coventry, had been a member of the Doncaster race week party at Tranby Croft the year before (and who, like the Prince Consort, was to die of typhoid some six years later). To him, Edward poured out the whole story, as he knew it. Lord Edward told his cousin, Lord Arthur Somerset, and later they suggested that Lycett Green should inform Lord Coventry, as head of the Prince's party. This was done and Lord Coventry, who had only played baccarat once before in his life, told General Sir Owen Williams, a senior army officer and a man of greater experience. Thus it was that, while dressing for dinner after the dressing bell had gone, Gordon-Cumming was visited in his room not by an accuser who had actually seen cheating, but by the two most senior members of the Prince's party who had not. Their demeanour was serious. Their words more so. They told the startled soldier that there had been a meeting in Lord Coventry's room. (It had consisted of Jack, his brother in law Lycett Green, Lord Edward and Captain Arthur Somerset as well as themselves; in other words, it included only two witnesses). They went on to say that as a result of the accusations, it had been decided that the Prince should be informed. In fact, although he did not say so, Lord Coventry had already done this. Gordon-Cumming was flabbergasted. He was also extremely angry when his accusers (only Jack and Lycett Green at this stage) were mentioned. "Do you believe the statements of a parcel of inexperienced boys?" he asked, and, because his relations with the Prince of Wales were long standing, he demanded to see his future sovereign. This he was allowed to do after dinner: because of the family bereavement it was not seemly to play baccarat again, although Berkeley Levett later remembered that "some round game" took place. With the Prince were Lord Coventry and General Sir Owen Williams, an incongrous group in the circumstances, since none of them had any direct evidence of what was supposed to have gone wrong. Gordon-Cumming maintained his innocence, and assured his friends (for such he had always believed them to be) that he was playing to the system known as the "coup de trois", which was easily explained, and which the simple souls at the baccarat table, most of whom seemed to be fairly ignorant of the game, did not understand. Gordon-Cumming had actually played on a piece of white paper on which he kept his score. He was betting in £5.00 counters, which were red and therefore easily seen. If he won in the first coup of a series, he would be paid £5.00 from the bank, would then add a further £5.00 of his own, and thus would stake £15.00 at the second coup. What he believed Jack Wilson had seen was not the altered stake for the first coup, but the new stake for the second. It sounded plausible. Gordon-Cumming was sent away and recalled some time later when the Prince of Wales had left the room.

During this second interview, which was with Lord Coventry and General Sir Owen Williams only, — the blind leading the blind? — Gordon-Cumming was asked to sign a statement which had been hurriedly prepared. It read as follows:

"In consideration of the promise, made by the gentlemen whose names are subscribed, to preserve silence with reference to an accusation which has been made in regard to my conduct at baccarat on the nights of Monday and Tuesday 8th and 9th September 1890, at Tranby Croft, I will on my part solemnly undertake never to play cards again as long as I live."(8)

Apart from this paragraph, the paper was blank. If Gordon-Cumming signed it, he would not know who would sign it after him, and therefore how many mouths were sealed. In any case the document, if signed, was the virtual equivalent of an admission of guilt, and Gordon-Cumming was continuing to claim his absolute innocence. No matter how hard he tried to explain his "system", or however forcefully he spoke, the two senior members of the Prince's party would have none of it. If he did not sign, he would immediately be exposed on all British race courses as a cheat and a liar.

The situation was more complicated because Gordon-Cumming regarded both of the Prince's men as upright and honest, and acting in his best interests. Later he maintained that both accepted that he was speaking the truth in continuing to affirm his innocence, but that the document was necessary to safeguard his Prince, his regiment and his hosts who were in such personal trouble. (Coventry and Williams denied this). Finally Gordon-Cumming signed, and some time after he had left the room, ten further signatures were added — Albert Edward, Prince of Wales, Coventry, Owen Williams, Arthur C.E. Somerset, Edward Somerset, Berkeley Levett, Arthur Wilson, Arthur Stanley (Jack) Wilson, Edward Lycett Green, and Reuben Sassoon, mentioned now for the first and only time. One can only wonder why it had been thought necessary to bring him in. Gordon-Cumming had already been advised to leave Tranby Croft as early as possible on the following morning, and this he did. He never asked who the signatories were.

And they were a most peculiar lot. Seven out of the ten could have no clear idea of what had actually happened, and of the three who said they had actually witnessed cheating, one had expected to see it, and another one had virtually been asked to watch for it in the middle of a game. Jack alone had, as it were, started from scratch. Or had he? The Gordon-Cumming family believed later that Sir William had been "framed".(9) Was it possible that several of the players were flipping the counters? Jack, at the trial later, gave a clear instance of Gordon-Cumming doing it, but was he the only one, and what exactly did it imply? Several of the punters were unfamiliar with the game, as was evidenced at the trial. And drink was flowing freely on both nights. How reliable could memories be? When Gordon-Cumming finally brought an action, he brought it against Jack, his mother, his sister Ethel and her husband, and Jack's friend, young Berkeley Levett, all of whom could claim to know what they were talking about. Yet neither of the two women were asked to sign the extraordinary document. If this was an endeavour to spare their feelings it was not a success — they were questioned thoroughly enough at the trial. As a cover up the document was slipshod anyway. It was revealed later that Lycett Green had consulted his father at the race course on the Wednesday, that is before Gordon-Cumming knew anything about it. Sir Edward Lycett Green may well have respected his son's confidence, and later it was generally thought that Lady Brooke had spread the tidings. She certainly earned for herself a new nickname "the Babbling Brooke", but who could have told her? And when? It can only be assumed that the clumsy and makeshift method to preserve secrecy was, apart from being unsatisfactory, entirely unnecessary. The story was already out, and if, as has been suggested, the purpose of the whole affair had been to remove Gordon-Cumming from society, success would seem to have been assured without it.

There was another important aspect too. When Lord Coventry informed General Sir Owen Williams and then the Prince, he was informing two high ranking soldiers, both of whom knew perfectly well that in a matter of dishonourable conduct of this kind, the proper procedure was to obey Queen's Regulations No.41 and subject the accused officer to a military court of enquiry. Gordon-Cumming himself knew this, and had even reminded his "friends" of this line of approach. Why did he not insist? He was, of course, outranked, and Gordon-Cumming would expect to stand by his friends against the nouveaux riches accusers, even if his friends were refusing to stand by him. Much was made of the danger that publicity would bring to the Prince. This is supposed to explain the desire for secrecy and the signing of the document, but Lord Coventry (with stiffening from Owen Williams), who explained to Gordon-Cumming how necessary secrecy was, was the very person who involved the Prince. Before he told the Prince he had unburdened himself to Owen Williams, who does not seem to have considered Queen's Regulation No. 41 at all. Was a military tribunal to be feared? Was the Prince's influence therefore desirable? Perhaps the Prince himself had dropped a hint that he was weary of Gordon-Cumming (after all, there was the incident with "darling Daisy" at Harriet Street the previous week). A hint would have been enough. Nothing has ever been said about the other guests. What did they know? How much did they guess? Was there ever a country house where the servants did not pass on interesting information?

Next morning the house party began to break up. The Prince had expected to stay until Friday, but Arthur Wilson conveyed him and his party to York, where he occupied his elder son's rooms for a night, and then joined his wife at Abergeldie. Arthur returned sadly to Tranby Croft to bury his brother in law, and deal with the strike, which was not settled until late in October, when a compromise was reached.

The baccarat scandal was not allowed to die. Gordon-Cumming realised this when he received a letter from Paris on the 27th December 1890 telling him "On a trop causé en Angleterre" and adding the information that not only was the story out in Paris, but in Monte Carlo as well. By mid January 1891 the London clubs had it. Before this, Gordon-Cumming had sought the advice of General Sir Owen Williams. Owen Williams was knowledgeable about baccarat, and even more about the British army in which both he and Gordon-Cumming served. The latter took his Paris letter to the General, and complained that the terms of the agreement at Tranby Croft had not been honoured. Owen Williams, playing for time, urged him against any precipitate action. A fortnight later, when Gordon-Cumming was told to his face by a lady that the affair was gossiped about all over London he sent a telegram to the Prince asking for an interview. It contained the sentence "It is clear, as I feared all the time, that the promise of secrecy made has been broken by those concerned."(10) The Prince acknowledged the letter, but would not see the unfortunate man, so Gordon-Cumming could now be in little doubt as to the value of the "friendship" offered by his social set. He could either let events take their own course (and this was the policy strongly recommended by the Prince to those to whom he was prepared to speak), or he could fight. Gordon-Cumming determined to do the latter.

It was an inevitable decision. Rumour was now so widespread that neither the Prince nor Gordon-Cumming would have been permitted to ride out the storm by inaction. First, Gordon-Cumming did what he should have done at the beginning, which was to seek an interview with his commanding officer, Colonel Stracey, and ask to be retired on half pay pending a military enquiry. This he did on Sunday 25th January 1891. Stracey did not admit to having heard the rumour, and at this stage had little advice to give. Later that same day Gordon-Cumming invited Berkeley Levett round to his house at No. 2 Harriet Street, and at half past five ushered the young officer into a small sitting room which led out of another room, the communicating door being locked during the interview. Berkeley Levett said later, at the trial, that the explanation given for this unusual action was that it would prevent the servants from overhearing the discussion. Gordon-Cumming, cross examined at the trial, denied that the door was locked. He had asked the young man to withdraw his allegation of cheating at cards. The young subaltern said that it would make no difference if he did, since Jack Wilson could never be persuaded to do the same. When this interview was recalled later in court, once again considerable discrepancies were revealed. According to Berkeley Levett, when he was asked to give evidence of the alleged cheating he had said "I must believe my own eyes — I saw you adding counters", but according to Gordon-Cumming he had simply said "I thought I saw something', I said 'What?' and he shuffled and said 'I don`t quite know'".(11) Nevertheless, at Gordon-Cumming's request, Berkeley Levett immediately got in touch with Mary Wilson (who was in London) and with Jack. Neither was prepared to recant.

Before Gordon-Cumming had the chance to make a further move he was sent for by Lord Coventry. It appeared that both Coventry and Owen Williams had made written statements shortly after the event. Coventry's was in a cheap diary (it had cost 18d), and had lain among the papers in his office for months. Anyone might have seen it.(12) Owen Williams had made a memorandum on the 11th September 1890, and this had been read and signed by the Prince, Coventry and himself. The Prince had then instructed Sir Francis Knollys to lock it up with the original document in safety at Marlborough House. The memorandum was explicit, and had been shown to Gordon-Cumming.

"We have no desire to be unnecessarily hard upon you, but you must clearly understand that in the face of overwhelming evidence against you it is useless to attempt to deny the accusation. So long as you comply with the conditions you have signed silence will be strictly maintained as far as we are concerned. In this we have dealt with you as old friends and in your interest, but we must plainly tell you we consider we have acted quite as leniently as we possibly could under the painful circumstances of the case . . ."(13)

As an example of an iron hand in a velvet glove this could hardly be bettered. It starts with an uncompromising belief that Gordon-Cumming was guilty. It then coldly informs him that if he keeps his part of the bargain they will keep theirs, but there is the ominous though unspoken threat that they cannot answer for anyone else's silence. The accused man was expected to stand by his friends who could easily find an excuse for forsaking him. Now the excuse was there; the story was out. Gordon-Cumming had been asked to see Lord Coventry because he had the memorandum at that point, but at the interview, as always when Lord Coventry was seen in action, Owen Williams was present. Gordon-Cumming received little comfort from it. He saw Stracey again. Stracey knew that the Prince was Commander in Chief of the Prince of Wales' Own Regiment and that his younger brother, the Duke of Connaught, was Colonel in Chief of the Scots Guards. He also knew that a general of the British Army had some connection with the scandal. He played safe and informed Sir Redvers Buller, the Adjutant General. He also said to Gordon-Cumming "Because you signed that document, you will never put on a sword again in the regiment. If you bring a successful action you will be allowed to retire; if you fail, you will be dismissed the service."(14)

A letter dated 28th January 1891 now came for Gordon-Cumming from Owen Williams, who was at his home in Great Marlow, Buckinghamshire. At a casual glance it would appear to be a concerned and kindly missive, but it is fascinating because of its underlying implications. It said:

"My dear Bill,
There was nothing left but to place yourself, as you have done unreservedly in Stracey's hands, and now all must depend, as you say, on the attitude of those who made the accusations to Coventry. You are quite at liberty to tell Stracey that you signed the document under *extreme pressure* and the *promise of secrecy,* but that you never acknowledged for a moment either to Coventry or myself the truth of the accusations brought against you. You signed by the strongest advice on the part of Coventry and myself, who were deputed to present you with the *ultimatum* and we were absolutely certain that unless you did so the accusations would immediately be made public, and that, therefore, your signature was the only possible hope of the avoidance of a horrible scandal . . . Coventry and I clearly explained to you that your signature was tantamount to an admission of guilt; but that while acknowledging this you signed as the only way out of the impasse, but in no way made any acknowledgment that you were guilty, but on the contrary strongly asseverated your innocence. . . Yours ever,
O.W."(15)

The letter is calculated and careful. In the first sentence it implies two things, that Owen Williams had a fair idea of the way Stracey would move, and that the "villains" of the piece were the five members of the house party who said they actually saw cheating. These were Arthur Stanley (Jack) Wilson, Berkeley Levett, Mary Wilson, and Ethel and Edward Lycett Green. In other words, Coventry and himself were only acting as the recipients of other people's confidences, and had done nothing to precipitate the furore. The underlinings in the letter are not without interest. Owen Williams admitted there was "extreme pressure", yet very shortly afterwards when he was visited by George Lewis (the solicitor recommended by the Prince, who would be acting for the five defendants) he was willing within half an hour to admit that no pressure had been put on Gordon-Cumming at all. The "promise of secrecy" too begs several questions. In whose interest was this? E.F. Benson(16) says Coventry and Owen Williams could not have been convinced of Gordon-Cumming's guilt or they would have had to apply Queen's Regulations No.41, and they did not. Both, as Gordon-Cumming said himself, were honourable men. Yet the Owen Williams memorandum, written as early as the Thursday of the Doncaster race week, gives a very different impression of Gordon-Cumming's alleged dishonourable conduct. Also, the senior members of the Prince's party maintained that silence had to be kept to safeguard the reputation of the Prince. Certainly the Prince had been banker in a game of baccarat where a punter was apparently seen several times to have cheated but, so he said, he suspected nothing. Was it therefore really necessary to bring him in at all? And who brought him in? Not the Wilsons who had seen, but the senior members of the Prince's party who had not. And who among them was likely to know the relevance of Queen's Regulation No.41? Surely only General Owen Williams. His evidence at the trial gives a distinct impression that he and Coventry were responsible for the secrecy. Bearing in mind his own military position, he must have either been frightened to set aside army regulations, or he must have felt it advisable to do so. But why? When? Finally, half way through his letter, Owen Williams speaks of the document which Gordon-Cumming had to sign, and says that he and Coventry were "deputed" to present him with an "ultimatum". In other words they, in consultation with someone else, had decided exactly how to act, and they had judged Gordon-Cumming and found against him. By that time they had interviewed the five accusers (whose knowledge of baccarat turned out to be sketchy) and they might have indicated to the Prince that there was a passable amount of evidence against the accused. Yet Gordon-Cumming had known the Prince for twenty years, and had been his personal friend for ten of them. Could not the Prince be expected to put up a fight for his friend?

Stracey now convened a court of five senior officers of the regiment who said that Gordon-Cumming must hand in his papers, not because of the scandal, but because he had broken Queen's Regulations, and his papers were therefore handed in to Redvers Buller to keep until the issue cleared. There were consultations in high places, and at one point Lord Coventry — and, inevitably, Owen Williams — appeared before Buller expressing indignation that Gordon-Cumming might be allowed to retire on half pay when he was a cheat. Where, said Buller, was their evidence! They were quite unable to substantiate their accusation, for neither of them had seen any cheating.(17) Gordon-Cumming had, by now, contacted his solicitors, Messrs Wontner, for a writ for slander to be issued against the five so called witnesses. Once this was done, the military enquiry had to be postponed until after the civil action. George Lewis had tried desperately to get the matter settled out of court (he had quite a reputation for managing such problems).

Already the affair was creating a wonderful opportunity for the free press, who had concentrated on a few definite issues from the beginning. On the whole Gordon-Cumming had their sympathy. They tended to be rather more cavalier in their treatment of the Prince, and on the whole stern in their condemnation of gambling. *The Star* said:

> "It is a pity that a soldier so useful to his country should retire from the army. Still, the Prince of Wales must be amused, and we must with good hearts freely relinquish our claims on great soldiers rather than have the baccarat parties of the heir to the Throne interfered with".

The magazine *Truth,* a kind of Victorian private eye, hit out at Prince Edward from a different angle:

> "The resignation if accepted, would be deemed to be the result of a belief on the part of the military authorities that Sir William Gordon-Cumming was guilty of cheating. And unquestionably, this view would be justified. Moreover, if Sir William is to be removed from the Army for not having notified his commanding officer that he had been accused of cheating, and that he had been induced practically to admit the truth of the accusation in order that the matter should be hushed up, surely some action ought to be taken by the military authorities against the officers who were present who urged him to take this course and who were quite ready that he should remain in the Army and in his clubs provided that the offence was kept secret".

After this statement appeared the information that Mr Labouchere intended to enquire in the Commons why Sir William Gordon-Cumming had had to send in his papers and retire from the Guards. This would open up the subject at the highest level.

Most papers gave an account of the events of 8th and 9th September 1890 as they understood them, and some added an account of how to play baccarat. *Central News* listed the names of the five defendants and the charge. The report continued that Gordon-Cumming now claimed, because of the loss of his credit and reputation and his suspension from military duties pending the trial, £5,000 damages against each of the defendants for their slanderous accusations. The matter of gambling in high places was thoroughly aired. The London correspondent of the *Manchester Guardian* reported in mid February that before answering questions in the House of Commons the day before, the Secretary for War, Mr Stanhope, had been to see the Prince of Wales, and both agreed that more strenuous efforts were necessary to discourage army officers from gambling. The correspondent of the *Yorkshire Post* said that the Prince intended to make it clear that in future he would not accept card playing as a means of entertainment at any country house he might visit.

Queen Victoria was furious about the whole situation. She approved neither of what her son had done, nor of his nouveaux riches friends, and no doubt she had already conveyed her displeasure to him in the strongest possible way. She had sent for Coventry and had asked him for a full account of what had happened. One can only wonder how Coventry would fare, with his inaccurate knowledge of the game, and his memory which, after four months, may well have been imprecise even with the help of the 18d. notebook. Coventry was somewhat deaf, and certainly bewildered. It seems unlikely that the Queen would get a clear picture of events from him.

It was now known that the trial would take place in the Lord Chief Justice's Court, Queen's Bench Division, at the beginning of June, but before that happened, the social life of the Wilson family continued to cause considerable interest. Half way through February they were visited once again by Prince "Eddy", the Duke of Clarence and Avondale, elder son of the Prince of Wales.

World described the event somewhat sarcastically:

"It is a moot question with me whether the Duke of Clarence and Avondale is an indifferent man, an impartial man, or a curious man. He has been visiting Lady Middleton, the sister of Sir William Gordon-Cumming at Birdsall House; he is now the guest of the Arthur Wilsons at Tranby Croft; he need only come on to Sandringham to have it admitted that he will have thoroughly boxed the compass of the baccarat affair."(18)

Arthur Wilson's progress in society continued; a month later, in late March, he was appointed High Sheriff of Yorkshire.

The same week his house caught fire. It happened round about half past eleven at night on Tuesday, 24th March. Muriel, his youngest daughter had been celebrating her sixteenth birthday. She and her maid, Mademoiselle La Court, had retired to their rooms at the top of the house, and on entering Muriel's bedroom one of them took a taper to light the gas and caught the window curtains which immediately flared up. They ran down to alert Arthur Wilson's agent, Mr Travers, who happened to be staying in the house. He alerted the staff who, until the Hull Police Fire Brigade turned up 35 minutes later, manned the hydrants. The ladies were escorted to a safe place clutching their most valuable jewellery and at one point, when it was feared that the whole house would be engulfed, the most valuable pieces of furniture were taken outside. Fortunately the damage was confined to a limited area. Muriel's room, which was difficult for the firemen to reach, was completely gutted; and Muriel complained that all her expensive perfume and toiletries had been burned. There was a huge hole in the ceiling and a considerable amount of reroofing was necessary. To do this, slates from the Honister pass were brought, since this was the area from which the original slates had come. There was some damage from the water which had to be pumped up by the Hull Police Fire Brigade. Arthur Wilson, informed by telephone, left his office in Commercial Road at once and arrived at the scene at the same time as the Hull Volunteer Fire Brigade and a brigade from Cottingham, but by that time the fire had been put out. Arthur estimated the damage at something between £500 and £1,000, but was thankful to say that it would be covered by insurance.(19)

At the end of April the local people were interested to learn that young Jack had been elected to the exclusive Marlborough Club on the personal recommendation of the Prince of Wales. If the Prince was angry with the Wilsons because of the scandal now exposed, this was a queer way of showing it. They had been advised to go to the Prince's recommended solicitor, Mr. George Lewis, for direction. Also they had lately taken a new town house, No. 17, Grosvenor Place, and the Prince of Wales was shortly to visit them there. Where he came, the rest of society would follow. The salon at No. 17 overlooked the gardens at Buckingham Palace. The Prince may have possessed an unscrupulous streak, but it still seems odd, unless he was absolutely convinced of the guilt of Gordon-Cumming, that his treatment of the two protagonists was so different.

(1) Benjamin Disraeli: *Lothair*, first published 1870, (Nelson) p.125.
(2) Christopher Simon Sykes: *The Visitor's Book* (Weidenfeld and Nicholson 1979) See Chapter 4.
(3) Mrs. Hwfa Williams: *It Was Such Fun* (Hutchinson 1935) p.126.
(4) *Hull News* 13.9.1890 p.4 column a.
(5) Ethel, Lady Thomson: *Clifton Lodge* (Hutchinson 1955) p.69.
(6) See *Sunday Times* colour supplement 2.3.1969. Article by James Fox p.29.
(7) Henry Wilson Ringrose Smith had become an engineer, had done his early training at Earle's and, in June 1874, had gone into partnership with Charles Amos. Their engineering and boiler making firm had its premises at Albert Dock. Arthur Wilson was a sleeping partner in the business, which did well, soon employing 300 workers. Over the next 20 years they built up to a work force of 800. When his father, Edward James Smith retired from the Leeds Post Office in 1879, Arthur and Mary Wilson installed him and his unmarried sister, Emma Anne, at Tranby Park, a prestigious mansion within a mile of Tranby Croft to the south west. Here, Henry joined them. When the old man died (21.11.1883), Henry and his aunt moved back into the vicinity of Hull, and on her death in 1884 Henry continued to live in the property on his own. (For short history of Earle's see *Arthur Credland: Earles of Hull*, City of Kingston upon Hull Museums and Art Galleries 1982 p.40).
(8) ed. W. Teignmouth Shore: *The Baccarat Case (William Hodge & Co. March 1932)* p.185. I have relied on this account for factual evidence throughout this and the next chapter.
(9) *Elma Napier: Youth is a Blunder* (Cape 1948) p.96.
(10) See: *Rt. Hon. Sir Michael Havers QC, Edward Grayson and Peter Shankland: The Royal Baccarat Scandal* (Wm. Kimber London 1977) p.42.
(11) *Havers, Grayson and Shankland: The Royal Baccarat Scandal* pp 43-44.
(12) ed. W. Teignmouth Shore: *The Baccarat Case (Wm. Hodge and Co. Ltd. 1932)*. p.218.
(13) Ibid p.52.
(14) *Havers, Grayson and Shankland: The Royal Baccarat Scandal* pp 49-50.
(15) ed. *Teignmouth Shore: The Baccarat Case* p.63.
(16) *E.F. Benson: As We Were* (Longmans, Green and Co. 1930) p.211.
(17) *Havers, Grayson and Shankland: The Royal Baccarat Scandal* p.57.
(18) Court and Social gossip column, quoted *Hull News* 28.2.1891 p.4 column c.
(19) Ibid 4.4.1891 p.6 column b.

CHAPTER SIX

The Trial and the Reaction of the Press

By the end of May details of the trial had been settled. The baccarat case would be tried by the Lord Chief Justice and a City of London special jury. Applications for seats were already pouring in, and more than ten times the number of seats available had already been asked for. The Prince had been informed by the solicitors on both sides that his presence would be requested. For Gordon-Cumming, Mr C.F. Gill an able and experienced junior, was led by the Solicitor General, Sir Edward Clarke Q.C., whose nickname "The Bayard of the Bar" spoke for itself.(1) Clarke was an essentially humble man, whose interests were simple. He neither liked nor understood high society. He was ingenuous and believed, wrongly, that others were equally so. Until his death Clarke believed in the innocence of his client, and because of this belief, at the time of the trial he spared no effort to prove that the accusers had been misinformed. He hoped to be able to convince the defendants that they had — possibly through ignorance — misinterpreted his client's movements during the games. Unfortunately for him, he discovered that each of the witnesses was adamant that cheating had taken place and that he or she had witnessed it.

The defendants were in the capable hands of Mr George Lewis of whom it has been written "His business was to save society from the consequences of its sins".(2) Lewis sent the brief to his senior, Sir Charles Russell Q.C. Thus there would be a battle between legal giants, and there could not have been a greater contrast between the two men. Whereas Clarke was humble, Russell was arrogant. Whereas Clarke had had to make his own way forward, Russell, a Roman Catholic from Northern Ireland, had introductions made on his behalf to the influential Irish Catholics in Liverpool. He took silk in 1872. Whereas Clarke's tastes were intellectual and often solitary, Russell enjoyed society, which he understood very well as his favourite pursuits were cards and racing. (He was later, as Lord Chief Justice, elected a member of the Jockey Club). Whereas, at the trial, Clarke tried to prove a misunderstanding of events, Russell was ruthless in his destruction of the opposition.

The judge, Lord Chief Justice the Right Honourable John Duke Bevan Coleridge, was well known to Russell and a personal friend. Clarke did not like him, although he admired his skill, and later wrote:

> "Coleridge was in the habit of repeating a witness's answer and quoting it in a subsequent question, and somehow the phrase as repeated or quoted was not actually the same as the witness had first used it . . . "(3)

Coleridge was deaf, and tended to nod off to sleep. At the trial his young wife sat at his right hand side, administering a judicious poke when necessary.

It was a very fashionable trial. Admission was by ticket only. Coleridge's daughter-in-law sketched the proceedings, and most of those present were personal friends of the judge. There were more women than men, and opera glasses and lorgnettes appeared all over the court. It took place between Monday 1st and Tuesday 9th June 1891. Clarke opened by establishing four important points. First, he said that Gordon-Cumming was at Tranby Croft not as a friend of the Wilsons, nor of the Lycett Greens (both of which families he knew slightly) but as a personal friend of the Prince of Wales. He made no secret of the fact that his client had stayed at Tranby Croft for a few days during the Doncaster Race Week in 1885, or that he had visited their London home several times, but he was an acquaintance not a friend. Clarke was aiming to make quite clear to the jury the social difference between his client and his accusers. He then described how to play baccarat and having given a clear exposition, described equally clearly Gordon-Cumming's system of play. Clarke believed that this system, properly explained, would cause the defendants to doubt their previous evidence. He was inviting them to consider the possibility that what they had witnessed was not an attempt to cheat, but an early stake in a new coup. He pointed out how, on his sheet of white paper (on which the red counters would be clearly visible), Gordon-Cumming alone had noted down the winners of each coup. He also seized this opportunity to scotch an earlier accusation made in their memoranda by Coventry and Williams, that Gordon-Cumming had been seen to withdraw part of his stake. This statement they now appeared to believe to be incorrect. Clarke wanted to know why, if one part of their evidence was suspect, how much reliability might be put on the rest of it. He was well aware that neither of these gentlemen had actually witnessed the cheating about which they had written.

When he brought Gordon-Cumming to the witness stand Clarke had to present him as an upright, honourable and brave soldier, to whom the very idea of cheating at cards was abhorrent. He asked his client how well he knew the defendants, and Gordon-Cumming admitted he was at Tranby Croft in 1885, had visited the London house of the Wilsons, and had also visited the Lycett Greens at Nunthorpe a couple of years previously. (Later on it transpired that it was he who had taught Ethel Lycett Green to play baccarat).

Clarke now took Gordon-Cumming through the events of 8th and 9th September, 1890, which he recounted readily enough, though it was obvious that the detail was by now far from clear in his mind. He remembered that, on the second night, when the new table had been provided, he had helped his neighbour, Lady Coventry, with her cards as she did not know the game. He recounted how he met Mary Wilson on the staircase on the morning of her brother's death, and noticed no suggestion of reserve in her manner, let alone coldness or hostility. The first hint of trouble, as he recalled, came at about eight o'clock that Wednesday evening, when he was waiting in his room for the dinner gong to be sounded, and was approached there by Coventry and Williams who made the accusation. He could not remember having asked the names of his accusers, or that any name was mentioned by the two senior members of the Prince's party. Clarke elicited from him that he was under the impression that already the Prince of Wales had been alerted. Gordon-Cumming had asked to see the Prince, who granted the interview at about eleven o'clock that evening, in the company of Coventry and Williams. The accused man had asked for advice, and had been told to leave so that his three friends (as they still were) could decide what to do. Recalled half an hour later, Gordon-Cumming was induced to sign the document, and was asked to leave while it was still exposed. He did not see all his accusers that night, and did not know whether all of them would be asked to sign the document. He was told by General Sir Owen Williams that Edward Lycett Green (regarded by Clarke as the most dangerous witness) wanted the record in case Gordon-Cumming afterwards denied the accusations and turned to attack his accusers.

Getting up to cross examine, Russell had two strong lines of attack. He knew perfectly well that, as an officer and a gentleman, Gordon-Cumming was subject to Queen's Regulation No. 41, and that he had ignored it. If a regulation existed whereby an officer would be enabled to prove his innocence, and that officer had chosen not to use it, the implication was obvious. Russell also knew that at no time between his accusation and his presence before the judge and jury had Gordon-Cumming sought to face his five accusers (although he had tried to get some of them to change their minds). This, an innocent man would surely have sought to do. Russell was perfectly safe in trying to probe. If the truth involved the Prince, Gordon-Cumming might well have felt the necessity to edit it, in order to protect His Royal Highness. The close cooperation between the Prince, Coventry and Williams was also useful to Russell. Both the Prince and Owen Williams were soldiers themselves, and therefore knew of Queen's Regulation No. 41. Neither had implemented it. Gordon-Cumming already seemed to have nowhere to turn.

Russell asked him whether, at his first interview, he was told the names of his accusers. He again replied that he had no recollection of this. He said that he had been bewildered by the horrid charges and had lost his head, although he admitted that he was sufficiently aware to ask for an interview with the Prince. He admitted that he had learned the names of his accusers at a second interview, but did not think he had referred to the male members of the group at any time by saying "What are they but a parcel of boys".(4)

Russell now demanded to know whether, at the first interview on the night of 10th September 1890, he had mentioned anything to Coventry and Williams about referring the matter to his commanding officer, the Duke of Cambridge. The last thing the Royal Family would want would be a further implication, and Gordon-Cumming dutifully replied that he had no recollection of using the Duke of Cambridge's name, or even that Owen Williams had advised him against this course. Such a reply would shift the onus of further misconduct away from a superior officer, and put Gordon-Cumming himself further in jeopardy. Russell had already asked him why he did not insist on a confrontation with his five accusers. His reply made him sound either trapped or evasive: "I cannot tell. It was an act of folly on my part, but I did not do so". When asked why he had signed the document, his answer was both unsatisfactory and pitiful. He said it was put to him "by those two friends of mine", (he said two, not three), "on whom I had placed implicit reliance" (he used the past tense) that there was no chance of proving his innocence against five witnesses and that unless he signed the document a horrid scandal would follow. It was not a convincing performance: it could not be so.

Russell continued by asking whether, after the document had been signed, Gordon-Cumming had not intimated that he would be at the races next day (possibly to avoid or forestall any attempt at gossiping). Owen Williams had rejoined "Certainly you cannot: you must leave the first thing in the morning". Gordon-Cumming agreed that this had been the suggestion, and that he had complied. Russell had thereby demonstrated to all hearers Owen Williams' lack of confidence in Gordon-Cumming's defence of his conduct. It also appears to demonstrate how much of the initiative lay with the General. On the second day of the trial, continuing the cross examination, Russell asked Gordon-Cumming outright "What interest had General Williams of his own to shield?", and at the third request Gordon-Cumming had made reply "I really cannot say", and repeated the same answer with reference to Lord Coventry. And Gordon-Cumming was himself a soldier!

The Prince was called to the witness stand on the second day. Clarke quickly established that he had not personally witnessed cheating, and that he knew nothing of it until informed by Coventry and Williams. The Prince said that Coventry told him before dinner on the Wednesday. Clarke knew that the Prince and Owen Williams were military men, therefore he could assume that if they had not chosen to apply Regulation No. 41 it was because they did not consider Gordon-Cumming to be guilty. Would the witnesses, however, seek to conceal "the foibles of a prince". Clarke must have been aware that, had the Prince not been a member of the party, the reactions of the rest of them might have been totally different, and far more rough and ready. He made the point that the Prince had not discussed the event with all five accusers, but only with Jack Wilson and Edward Lycett Green and an odd word to Berkeley Levett. He got the Prince to admit that he had read and approved of Owen Williams' memorandum.

It seemed that Clarke was still trying to make capital out of the difference in social status between the Wilsons and the rest of the Prince's party. It was said many times during the trial that the Prince, Coventry and Owen Williams were "honourable men". Jack Wilson was a wealthy shipowner's son and Lycett Green the son of a Wakefield iron master. Perhaps their view of events was less likely to carry veracity to the Prince than the fact that a high ranking officer had not considered it necessary to enforce the military code! Perhaps! As the Prince stepped down from the witness stand a juryman called a question. "What was your Royal Highness' opinion at the time as to the charges made against Sir William Gordon-Cumming?" The Prince answered readily enough, but in doing so he destroyed the impression Clarke had been endeavouring to plant in the minds of the jurymen. He said: "The charges appeared to be so unanimous that it was the proper course — no other course was open to me — than to believe them".(5) The Prince had declared for the defendants. So much for army regulations! And for social discrimination!

Owen Williams now took the stand. Gordon-Cumming (unlike Coventry) had been an intimate friend of his for twenty years, had travelled with him in Africa and India, had stayed in his house and sailed on his yacht. In his own evidence Gordon-Cumming had stated that he regarded the general as a just and true friend, and a man of the highest honour. Clarke established that he had been croupier the second night and had shared the bank with the Prince, but that he knew nothing of any misconduct during the game until about seven o'clock the following day, when he was asked by Lord Coventry to go to his room. Lord Coventry had heard of the allegations of cheating during that day from Lycett Green via Lord Edward Somerset. At this point Owen Williams appears as the innocent who became involved through no fault of his own. His memory of the composition of the party who now met in Coventry's room appears to have been hazy. He remembered that Lycett Green did the talking, as a result of which Owen Williams said he and Coventry felt it necessary to inform the Prince. No further reason for this involvement was either asked for or given, and the information seemed to have been passed on promptly, and before any positive decision had been made about tackling Gordon-Cumming. It also seems that the idea of secrecy originated at this time, as Owen Williams gave evidence:

"We had very little time for consultation, but I think it was proposed to make this suggestion, so that if possible the knowledge of this most lamentable occurrence should not pass outside the house".(6)

The document may have been under consideration before Gordon-Cumming was even interviewed. In the cross examination Owen Williams told how, later that night, the witnesses had been called together and he "in the absence of the Prince of Wales" had explained to them what would seem to be the best method of procedure under the difficult circumstances.(7)

This evidence points to the fact that, if indeed the document had already been mooted, some members of the house party at least, could not have been very interested in Gordon-Cumming's version of what had occurred. Minds had already been made up. When Coventry and Williams involved the Prince, there were two senior army officers present who were deliberating the issue. Did they really believe Gordon-Cumming was innocent? Were they, for some reason as yet unrevealed, seizing an opportunity to ostracize him socially? Lycett Green had been both vocal and adamant, but he had seen what he had expected to see, and at the time of this meeting it is not at all certain that Jack Wilson's evidence was given personally. Why were the senior members of the Prince's party so sure, that they dispensed with army regulations? And why did they create this new course of action?

The cross examination was skilfully handled by Mr H.H. Asquith Q.C. He put the spotlight on the information vouchsafed by Lycett Green, the iron master's son and Master of the York and Ainsty. Owen Williams agreed that when he introduced the subject of the advisability of a signed undertaking Lycett Green wanted none of it, his argument being that the matter ought to be settled straight away: "Everything is fresh in our memories now, and we can all swear what has occurred, and I think it would be far better that it should be made public."

Asquith asked whether Gordon-Cumming had been told of Lycett Green's desire to confront him. Owen Williams said he had — later in the evening. Asquith then went on to the delicate matter of how Lycett Green's support for the document could have been obtained:

"I told Mr Lycett Green" said Owen Williams "that that document would be tantamount to an admission of guilt on the part of Sir William Gordon-Cumming, and that once signed would render him harmless for the future. He was content with the explanation and promised to maintain silence".(8)

Owen Williams admitted his irritation when Gordon-Cumming mentioned the Duke of Cambridge (which Gordon-Cumming did not recollect having done). He had felt that his clique had already gone far enough out of their way to accommodate the accused soldier, and he had answered with asperity that the army authorities would be far less lenient than they themselves would with their document (the text of which had actually been written by Coventry). The cross examination had shown a sorely tried army officer, landed with an impossible situation and desperately trying to salvage some respect for the rest of them. But how could it be regarded as an attempt to keep the Prince of Wales out of it, when Coventry and Williams themselves had just brought him in?

Now it was Jack's turn. Nearly 23 years old and self confident, he stood before Asquith. He remembered the setting up of a makeshift table on 8th September and where people sat. He remembered watching Gordon-Cumming add two £5.00 counters to his stake when Lord Edward Somerset (at that point handling the cards) had a natural. Later he watched him flip a £2.00 counter onto his piece of paper with a pencil, and described the pencils used that night as flat carpenter's pencils with the words "Tranby Croft" stamped upon them. He remembered the fear shown by Berkeley Levett when, after the conclusion of the game, he visited him in his room and told him he would inform his brother in law, Lycett Green, the next morning and ask for advice. The young subaltern had made an adamant refusal to inform against a superior officer. He told of his mother's reaction. She had been very upset and had said "For goodness sake don't let us have any scandal here".(9) He told how he had arranged for a proper table to be placed in the billiard room for the second night's play.

On the Tuesday night Jack remembered again, quite clearly, the composition of his tableau, and how Gordon-Cumming had come up after Lady Coventry and Ethel were already seated and had asked if he might take the seat between them. Lady Coventry was inexperienced, and Gordon-Cumming had helped her throughout the evening. When, in one coup, the Prince of Wales declared himself "baccarat", Jack had seen Gordon-Cumming push a £10.00 counter just over the line, but some four inches away from his earlier stake. Nevertheless, he had asked to be paid for it, and it was at that moment that the Prince said he wished the stakes could be put in a more conspicuous place. On a later occasion when someone in Jack's tableau took a good card, Jack again saw Gordon-Cumming flick a £5.00 counter with his pencil. He said there had been more instances, but he was unable to recollect the details.

He remembered the journey to Doncaster on the Wednesday, when he had travelled with his brother in law and the two Somersets who, when told of the circumstances, recommended that Lord Coventry, as head of the Prince's household, should know. He remembered that on the journey back to Hessle that evening Berkeley Levett joined the group, but refused to be drawn into further action against a man who had been his captain for a year and a half. He agreed that Lycett Green was most anxious to confront Gordon-Cumming with the evidence, rather than sign the document.

When Clarke got up to cross examine he seemed at first to be out to make the young man look a fool. He asked about Jack's university career at Magdalen, and Jack admitted that he had not worked hard, and had not completed the course because his father took him away. He agreed, amid laughter, that he had gone into his father's business for a month, had then broken his collar bone, and since had taken little, if any, interest in commercial affairs. He may have appeared momentarily as a figure of fun (and indeed as a result of this day's work he earned the nickname, locally, of "Jack-in-the-box"), but as soon as Clarke tried to get him to agree to certain fundamentals in the memoranda of Coventry and Williams — statements which had been accepted by the Prince — he stood his ground and refused to be swayed. He would not agree that Mary Wilson, having informed her husband of the unfortunate affair, had agreed with the Lycett Greens and young Berkeley Levett that they should all watch Gordon-Cumming's play on the second night. So, in one sense, Clarke had failed. The young man may have appeared brash, conceited and callow, but on the major issue he knew what he knew, and Clarke could not shake him.

Now it was the twenty seven year old Berkeley Levett's turn in the witness box, and a most unhappy witness he was. He was first examined by Charles Matthews, one of Russell's juniors. He said he had known Gordon-Cumming for six years and they had been in the same battalion for a year and a half, had immediately got to know each other, and thereafter had become close friends. He remembered, on the Monday night, seeing Gordon-Cumming put two extra counters on top of a £5.00 one, but he did not, in fact, remember whether the man staked the whole lot in the next coup. He said his conversation with Jack in his bedroom later that night had lasted "about an hour".(10) He implied that there was an awareness among those in the know to watch Gordon-Cumming's play on the second night, (he said that both the Lycett Greens tried to speak to him about it, but that he had refused to listen). He said that he had implied this fact to Gordon-Cumming himself, when he was sent for to discuss the matter in Harriet Street the previous January. His evidence concerning the return journey from Doncaster on Wednesday, 10th September makes clear that the subject of cheating was discussed at length on this occasion, as well as on the journey out, and he had asked to be excused from participation because of his embarrassing position. Consequently he was not in the conference called in the early evening by Coventry and Williams. He was, however, called for after dinner that night to attend in the Prince of Wales' room. There, he met the whole gang — as well as the Prince there were Owen Williams, Coventry, both Somersets, Jack Wilson and Lycett Green. Once again he had explained his awkward predicament, but nevertheless, when asked directly whether he had seen cheating he implied that he could not deny it. He signed the document on Thursday morning, the 11th September, when Coventry brought it round to his room. He insisted that he had not broken his pledge of silence.

The cross examination got nowhere at all with Levett. His evidence was not vital. Lycett Green took the stand next, and Clarke knew that here was the man who might well hold the vital evidence, and who therefore was potentially the most dangerous. Lycett Green might have attempted, as Clarke later considered he did, to take upon his own shoulders the honour of his wife's family. He was quite open about the way in which he had learned of the cheating, and told Mr Asquith that on the Monday he did not play, as he had been cubbing all day and was tired. He did seem to remember taking in some counters for Ethel, his wife. On the second night he distinctly remembered watching Gordon-Cumming push a blue, £1.00 counter over the chalk line, and shortly afterwards, after looking round to see whether he was observed, watched him push a £10.00 counter over. Questioned about this, he said that he had no doubt whatsoever that the action was deliberate and against the rules of the game. When the stakes were paid Gordon-Cumming had said "There is £10 more to come here" and the Prince had then said to Owen Williams, the croupier "Owen, give him another tenner".(11) He was paid £15.00 in all, and Lycett Green had no doubt that it was dishonestly gained. It was at this point that he left the table and the room to write the note to his mother-in-law, which she ignored. The following day, Wednesday, he had confided his information, on the outward journey to Doncaster, to Lord Edward Somerset, who had asked to consult Captain Arthur Somerset. It was on the return journey, by which time Captain Arthur Somerset had been told, that it was decided to inform Lord Coventry. Lycett Green thought that the original report to the Head of the Prince's Household had been given by himself, although soon after he was joined by Jack and Captain Arthur Somerset. At some point Coventry asked to bring in Owen Williams, and did so. Again Lycett Green went over the evidence, insisting that all witnesses were convinced of cheating and would be prepared to face Gordon-Cumming if required to do so. In other words he was acting as spokesman, and by the Wednesday evening there had been communication between the actual witnesses. Lycett Green believed that the document had been brought in later that evening by Owen Williams. He himself had not liked it. Owen Williams had told him not to worry, as the signing of that document would in itself constitute an admission of Gordon-Cumming's guilt. The General now begins to look like the strongest member of the Prince's party. The strength of the defence still lay in the downright belief of each individual that he had witnessed cheating.

Ethel's turn came next and she gave the most important part of her evidence with clarity and conviction. Examined by Sir Charles Russell she admitted that she had only played baccarat a few times. She had noticed nothing unusual during the first night's play, but had heard her husband's story the following morning, and had accepted it as being the truth. Baccarat started on the second night at about eleven o'clock or it could have been half past that hour. She had not been told about the new table, but naturally noticed it. She would not agree that she had been on the look out for cheating, and pointed out that Gordon-Cumming came late to the table, and her husband almost last of all. She was able to describe how Gordon-Cumming held his hands, with the left one covering the right, and she remembered his pushing up a £10.00 counter just on the line and asking the Prince to pay out £15.00. The Prince said something like "I wish you would put your stakes in a more conspicuous place — I never saw that".(12) The money was, however, paid out; the counters were returned to the heap, but later she observed Gordon-Cumming push a £5.00 counter over the line with his pencil, and shortly afterwards collect £10.00 from the bank.

Again, the cross-examination revealed little. Ethel agreed that her husband had brought in £5.00 worth of counters for her on Monday night. She never staked more than 10/-, and had not won once. She was asked whether her husband had suggested telling her father about the circumstances of the play, but she kept her head and said that her mother was well aware of what had happened, and if she had thought it necessary she would certainly have informed him.

The fifth day of the trial saw Mary Wilson called to the witness stand. John Welcome has called her "the weak link".(13) She started off by saying that she had some knowledge of baccarat. She affirmed that she had no knowledge that cheating had taken place during Monday night's play, but she had noticed that her son, Jack, "had a rather surprised air. I could not make it out. I thought he was puzzled about something".(14) He appeared to be trying to attract her attention and then looked down at the table, but, until later, when she saw him in her dressing room, she had no idea why. She and Jack discussed the new table, which would be properly marked out to prevent cheating. She did not mention the matter to her husband that night, because he came in very late. Like her fellow witnesses, she maintained that there had been no conspiracy to watch Gordon-Cumming's play on the second night, and that it was purely accidental where most people sat. She herself had been requested by the Prince of Wales to sit on his left (which meant that she would play in the left tableau, not the one in which Gordon-Cumming and the other members of her family were playing). She did say, however, that while they were still in the drawing room listening to Ethel's songs, Jack came up to her and whispered that the new table had a chalk line right round it near the edge. He had said "It is virtually impossible (to cheat)".(15) This must have put the matter to the forefront of Mary's mind if, indeed, it was not already there. When her son-in-law, Lycett Green, came back into the billiard room after sending her the note which reported the cheating, she had shaken her head at him, but that was all, as play was still going on. She could remember no details with clarity, but she had noticed Gordon-Cumming cheat twice. The first time he put a £10.00 counter on top of a £5.00 one which he had already staked. It was done quite openly, and she could not understand why other people did not react. He was helping Lady Coventry who "had a run", and the second time she noticed the cheating was when Lady Coventry had a natural (or nine points). The cards were thrown down and she saw him push a £10.00 counter over the line with his pencil. "I am perfectly sure" she said "that before the natural was declared his stake was only £5".(16) Next morning she had to leave Tranby Croft because of the death of her brother, Henry. She did not recollect meeting Gordon-Cumming on the stairs, or any conversation with him as she was leaving the house. Most of the guests had departed on the morning of Thursday, 11th September, but she recollected that Lord and Lady Coventry, General and Mrs Owen Williams, Lord Edward and Captain Arthur Somerset "and others" stayed on for a further day. This information was given during the cross-examination by Sir Edward Clarke, and it is interesting that Mary should have identified by name the very people who seemed to have had more to do with directing operations than anybody else.

Concerning Tuesday night's play, Mary admitted that Gordon-Cumming had usually played a £5.00 stake. Clarke then asked her if anyone had staked as much as £15.00. Mary's amazing answer was "I don't think any one till my husband played". Clarke said "Did he play the first night?". Mary replied "I think so".(17) There was no other evidence given at this trial to the effect that Arthur Wilson senior was even in the building on either of the occasions when baccarat was played. Mary herself had previously stated that she did not inform him of the trouble on the first night because he came in very late and was tired. It is possible that several witnesses knew far more than they were prepared to say. Mary may have been one, and Clarke's persistence may have flustered her. She was no longer young, and youth can sometimes be more rigid than experience. Mary was 48 years old. Although she was normally clear headed, her house party that September had gone sadly off the rails. Her husband was unhappy and preoccupied, her brother had died, a house guest had been accused of cheating at cards, and the Prince of Wales had been a guest in her house for an extended stay for the first time. The Prince had to be protected. But why bring in Arthur? He was so patently innocent. Was Mary not flustered at all? Did she know something which she was not prepared to divulge, and did she therefore deliberately drag in a red herring? Clarke certainly did not probe further. He did not see her as a vital witness. He checked as to when Mary spoke with the Prince about the cheating she had witnessed. This had been on the morning of Thursday, 11th September, before the Prince left Tranby Croft for York.

With her evidence Clarke had challenged the last of the actual witnesses, and he had gained little. He may have made it quite clear to the jury that none of the defendants were skilled players, but he had not been able to shake a single one of them with regard to their main conviction. Now Lord Coventry was to be called. Could Clarke shake his story to bits? Would it be of any use if he did?

Coventry was examined by Russell who probably knew that he would give a repeat performance of General Owen Williams' earlier evidence. Welcome(18) described Coventry as charming, well liked, and a member of the Jockey Club who, thirty years earlier, had won the Grand National in two successive seasons. He was also Master of the Buckhounds, a political appointment which the Prince of Wales axed as soon as possible when he came to the throne. He was quite deaf, not in the least clever, and was unused to gambling. His appearance on the stand would hardly seem likely to present Clarke with a challenge. He had not witnessed cheating, he was not a solider who might be expected to know all about Regulation 41, and when the problem had been brought to his notice, his immediate reaction had been to call in Owen Williams.

Coventry had no hesitation in telling Russell that he and Williams had involved the Prince of Wales because there had been a long standing friendship between the Prince and Gordon-Cumming, and because of this, the two gentlemen felt that they could not allow that friendship to continue if the Prince remained in ignorance as to what had occurred. He said that Lycett Green had explained the circumstances in the early part of the evening of Wednesday, 10th September in the presence of Owen Williams, Jack Wilson and Captain Arthur Somerset. He and Williams had then confronted Gordon-Cumming before dinner. (Coventry remembered the interview as taking place in the smoking room).

108

They told him that his accusers were Jack Wilson and Lycett Green. They did not mention Subaltern Berkeley Levett. Gordon-Cumming had responded by exclaiming that they were surely not prepared to take the word of "a parcel of inexperienced boys".(19) He had then asked to see the Prince.

The Prince had seen him after dinner, but the two senior members of his party were there too. Gordon-Cumming protested his innocence, but the Prince reminded him that there were five witnesses against him. Gordon-Cumming now suggested that the Duke of Cambridge, the Commander in Chief of the British Army, should be informed, but Williams disuaded him, saying that although he was perfectly free to do as he liked, the Duke would not be prepared to take such a lenient view of the case as they would themselves. Once again the initiative seems to have been thrown back on General Owen Williams. However, later in the evidence, Coventry's memorandum written, according to him on Thursday, 11th September, was read out in court. It contained the text of the agreement and the signatories, and it would appear that this, at least was his own work. Coventry agreed, in response to further questioning, that the Prince had spoken with Jack Wilson, Edward Lycett Green and Berkeley Levett, and that Lycett Green had reiterated that he wished to confront the accused. Coventry thought that Gordon-Cumming had been told of this, but if he had, he had never taken it up. (Russell was slamming home an important point here, with an easy witness). He said that the idea of a signed document had started with himself and Williams, and Russell then asked him how Gordon-Cumming had reacted when faced with it. Coventry said he had called it tantamount to an admission of guilt, and added that the actual witnesses thought so too. He maintained, however, that there was no pressure to make Gordon-Cumming sign, and in his opinion the accused man did not lose his head when he did so. He was still thinking in terms of approaching the Commander in Chief, but when he had asked Williams and himself for advice, they had told him to sign. Russell asked whether, when Coventry gave this advice, he believed Gordon-Cumming to be guilty. Coventry said bluntly, and unequivocally, that he did. Russell had gained a further point.

When Clarke rose to cross-examine he knew he had his back to the wall. This witness actually knew very little, and his personal opinion, which might have counted for something, had gone against the prosecution. Clarke did what he could, and thoroughly bewildered Coventry in the process. It was fairly easy for him to find inaccuracies in Coventry's memorandum, but when he did so Coventry returned that his statement was only written to give a general impression of the case. Clarke did, however, get his witness to assert that he genuinely believed that there was collusion among the witnesses to watch for cheating, and that he and Owen Williams had introduced the document because they were anxious to prevent a scandal in which the Prince of Wales might become involved. Finally, Clarke asked him whether, since he had stayed on for an extra day at Tranby Croft, cards were played on the evening of Thursday, 11th September, but Coventry had no idea.

Russell, summing up, tidied a few loose ends, but his was, in no way, such a vital performance as that of the Solicitor General, Clarke, which followed. Clarke pointed out the unfairness of removing Gordon-Cumming from the army whilst allowing other superior officers involved to stay on. He pointed out that not one of the actual witnesses wrote a memoir, yet throughout the hearing reference was made to the memoirs of Coventry and Owen Williams, although both manuscripts had been proved to have been inaccurate on several points. (Owen Williams' precis, for instance, had spoken of a systematic withdrawal of stakes by the plaintiff, and an agreement to watch between the five members of the house party who later became accusers. Both of these statements had been categorically denied). Inaccurate as the written statements had proved to be, Clarke thought they might well be more reliable than memories trying to recall the events of nine months ago. He mentioned that Tuesday and Wednesday were both exciting days at the racecourse. On the first day the Prince's horse had won; on the second day the St. Leger was run. Entertainment both at Doncaster and at Tranby Croft was lavish. Clarke wondered whether the guests' powers of observation would have been keen enough after such hospitality. He made it clear that he considered the Prince of Wales, Coventry and Owen Williams to be completely dependable. The two latter gentlemen were explicit in thinking that there was a conspiracy to watch Gordon-Cumming on Tuesday night, and Coventry had even written this down. Apart from Jack, he thought that all the witnesses saw what they expected to see. He thought that Berkeley Levett had simply seen a "coup de trois", and under cross-examination, when asked if he had witnessed dishonest play, he had had to say "I had been told that he was cheating".(20) Clarke felt that this was very significant and pointed out that Gordon-Cumming's red counters were placed on a piece of white paper so that everyone could see at a glance what he was doing.

The Solicitor General was convinced that the "hot headed boys" had told their story to people who had no business to know, while young Jack had neglected to tell his experienced father who had every right to know. "Instead" said Clarke,

"they seek an experienced counsellor, a man of the ripe age of, I think, thirty-one . . . Mr Lycett Green — whose capacity is that of a Master of Hounds who hunts four days a week, and Lycett Green promptly takes it up; he feels that the whole reputation of the family has been committed to him; and instead of going to Mr Wilson, who was entitled to know, he goes and tells his father, was was not entitled to know at all, and then for the most foolish of all reasons he tells his wife".(21)

He spoke of the audacity of Mary Wilson who had asserted that she had forgotten about the new table for Tuesday until her son reminded her. Nor could he believe her evidence when she said she saw Gordon-Cumming cheat at a point when no-one else did. She was farthest away of any of the five observers, being the only one not in the right hand tableau, where Gordon-Cumming himself was. Also, everyone at that time was concentrating on Lady Coventry who, helped by her neighbour on the left — Gordon-Cumming — was winning for them.

Clarke then attacked the peripheral evidence of the accusers. Jack slipped up on detail; he was unsure, for instance, as to who drew the chalk line around the new table. Coventry could not even remember whether cards were played on his last evening. Lycett Green had been unable to remember whether Gordon-Cumming had in front of him a piece of paper, a tumbler, a pencil, or whether he was smoking. Clarke found it odd that certain things could be observed with such precision, while others were completely unnoticed.

He felt that the Prince had not been told the whole story, and had been ill advised by Coventry and Williams. Clarke categorically admitted that he was unable to see how they persuaded themselves that the composition and the signing of the document was an honourable course of action. He made it quite clear also, that Gordon-Cumming himself wished to protect the Prince and implied that his signature on the document showed his willingness to be sacrificed. Gordon-Cumming was far too well known on the race course not to be missed, and when he did not turn up, Clarke could well imagine the veiled hints which knowledgeable members of the house party would give to enquirers as to his whereabouts on the day on which he left Tranby Croft.

He pointed out again how Gordon-Cumming had wished to consult his Commander in Chief right from the start, and was dissuaded from doing so by the Prince's party, Owen Williams saying at one time "I was nettled at the suggestion".(22) Clarke thought that if Gordon-Cumming had sent in his papers straightaway, said as little as possible, and asked to be retired on half pay he might well have got away with it, but he did not do this. He told Stracey the whole story, which precipitated the investigation. Therefore, Clarke said, Gordon-Cumming had not, as had been suggested, tried to slip out of the army. Finally Clarke pointed out that Gordon-Cumming asked for help from Coventry and Williams not only at the beginning of the affair, but also when the gossip began to build up. He obviously respected their integrity.

Clarke still differentiated clearly between the "gentlemen", like the Prince, Coventry and Owen Williams for whom he made excuses, and the nouveaux riches Wilsons and Lycett Greens. He tried to show Jack, the originator of the whole affair, as the spoiled darling of a very wealthy family, without a single vestige of real initiative in him. Lycett Green was mercilessly lampooned as a "Master of Hounds". Even the apparently entirely innocent Arthur did not escape. His absences, and the way in which his wife had presided over the evenings' entertainment led Clarke to make the statement that Coventry and Williams "did not know - could not possibly know - the sort of ornamental position that Mr Wilson appears to hold in his own house."(23) And these people, Clarke would appear to be saying, were preparing to crucify Gordon-Cumming. Clarke had done well, and as he sat down voices were raised and there was applause. "Silence" thundered the Lord Chief Justice, "this is not a theatre".

Clarke, as a prosecutor, may have been less than fair to the Wilsons, but the judge's summing up made it crystal clear whose side he was on. John Welcome has described it as "a literary exposition, polished, skilful and fiendishly unfair".(24) Coleridge began by stating the main issue — did Gordon-Cumming cheat? He reminded the jury of Clarke's point that most of the witnesses saw what they expected to see, then added that all the evidence was of the same kind — adding to a stake when circumstances were favourable and it was safe to do so. Jack, he said, had certainly not seen what he had expected to see. On that first night he had ignored what he thought might possibly have been cheating until he saw it again, plainly. Berkeley Levett obviously saw something about which he was unhappy, because he did not wish to look again. Lycett Green, when he left the game on Tuesday night was in a very difficult predicament. The Prince of Wales and seven ladies (no less) were present in the room. How could Lycett Green stand up and denounce a cheat in such a situation? It is interesting how little Coleridge had to say about the evidence of Lord Coventry. He had even less to say about that of Owen Williams. He wished that Clarke, in the heat of his fervour had not called Coventry "a false friend",(25) and was interrupted by Clarke who said he regretted this. So, the judge had made his feelings clear, but what about the repeated request of Lycett Green that the accusers should be allowed to confront the accused man? This seemed not to trouble Coleridge. Each of the defendants had done what seemed to him or her to be best. Lycett Green was no exception; he believed what he had said, and what he had seen. So, in their different ways, had the other defendants.

Coleridge tackled the ridicule which the young defendants had suffered at Clarke's hand. Lycett Green's unaristocratic beginnings had been held up to view. Jack had been made to look a brash young fool, when his shortcomings at university and later in the family business were brought up. Coleridge asked whether this was fair. He rehabilitated Arthur Wilson, speaking of "the honourable pursuit of merchandise"(26) and the fact that his "great position" was the result of hard work. He implied that Mary would certainly not be the only lady who would be delighted to have the Prince of Wales as a guest in her house. Then he went on to make a remarkable statement and, by backing it up with reference to the evidence of men whose social background was unimpeachable, seemed to turn one of Clarke's conjectures inside out. He said:

> "Some people I would not believe guilty of a thing if I saw it. Perhaps that is too strong; but nothing would persuade me of the guilt of a man whose heart and head I had known, unless I saw the act beyond all possible doubt. I would then say, well, human nature is human nature, and I suppose he did it."(27)

Coleridge now reminded the jury that Gordon-Cumming had never asked to be confronted by his accusers. It was a telling point and the judge was on safe ground. Gordon-Cumming himself had admitted it under oath. Coleridge went on to say that if Coventry and Williams had broken a military rule it was with the best of intentions. He also pointed out that the breaking of a military rule was not the main issue. (The military enquiry would come later, but this was surely a neat bit of side stepping). He pronounced himself satisfied with the Owen Williams precis and said he thought it was very well drawn up, but since the witnesses had not seen it, it was not surprising that they differed from it on certain details. He underlined Gordon-Cumming's now almost pathetic reliance on the good offices of Coventry and Williams, and leaned towards the supposition that he could not expect any further backing from them if, in fact, he were guilty. He said the Prince, like everyone else, had the right to relax. As a final thrust he asked the jury what innocent man could possibly have signed that document.

The jury retired on this seventh day of the trial, Tuesday, 9th June 1891 at 3.25 in the afternoon. They took 13 minutes to reach their verdict and found for the defendants. Mary Wilson was waiting with an addressed telegraph form in her hand — she seemed to know what to expect. The jury stayed behind to ask for more money, which was not popular. No more popular was the Wilson party, who had to be steered through an empty court to an exit at the side, as a well-dressed crowd were waiting to boo at the front, but they had survived to go on to even greater things. For Gordon-Cumming it was socially the end.

The Reaction of the Press

As a result of this trial the newspapers had a field day. There was some sympathy for Gordon-Cumming, and *Truth* said "No dog would be hanged on the evidence that convinced a jury that Sir William Gordon-Cumming had cheated at cards".(28) *The Times* which said it wished that the Prince as well as Gordon-Cumming had agreed never to play cards again, said of the convicted man: He "must leave the army, must leave his clubs and must no longer consider himself a member of that society in which he has moved so long. Condemned by the jury to social extinction, his brilliant career is wiped out. Such is the inexorable social rule. A man who defrauds his friends whom he meets at the card table has forfeited his honour. Society can know him no more".(29)
The Daily Chronicle was rude about the Wilsons, but far ruder about the Prince.

> "It is enough to say that the readiness of the Prince of Wales to dispose of himself as 'a prize guest' . . . in rich but vulgar families, where his taste for the lowest type of

gambling can be gratified, even at the cost of dishonouring the proudest names in the country, has profoundly shocked, we may even say disgusted, the people who may one day be asked to submit to his rule".(30)

The *Hull News,* however, concentrated on the Wilsons and printed the whole of an article from the *Pall Mall Gazette* entitled. "The Wilsons of Hull by One who has studied them". It mentioned how: "In a recent year, the brothers were said (probably with exaggeration) to have divided a million between them. . . . Every third ship which is registered as due in Hull every week is a Wilson liner." It maintained that the Wilson brothers were a real team, spoke with one voice and, in public at any rate, never opposed one another, even though Arthur was a Unionist and Charlie the Liberal M.P. for West Hull. Neither could be said to be a gifted speaker. "Mr Arthur Wilson makes no more pretence of coherent oratory than a country gentleman presiding at a farmers' dinner", and Mr Charles, although able and shrewd in business, was "not a tactful speaker". Their charity, however, was real and abundant, though their great wealth and influence tended to produce sychophantic behaviour. "A recent Mayor, in recounting all that the Wilsons had done in Hull, actually wept to think that the term of Mr Arthur Wilson's shrievalty had expired".

On the whole, the Wilson image was not tarnished beyond redemption. The Prince of Wales had a more difficult time, because he was far more vulnerable. The press seemed to concentrate upon his vices and largely ignore any virtues he might possess. He was attacked politically, socially and religiously. The Venerable Dr Douglas of Montreal wrote:

"The awful spectacle is presented of the heir to the throne publicly acknowledging complicity in gambling transactions".

The famous social and religious writer, W.T. Stead, spoke of a device called "The Prayer Guage". He worked out how often the prayer for the Prince of Wales had been offered up in churches, the only result being a card scandal. In his *Review of Reviews* in July 1891 which collected up literature and cartoons concerning the baccarat scandal, with particular reference to the Prince, he started off by elaborating on this point.

The cartoons were endless. The American issue of *Judge* on 17th June showed various Lords and Ladies kneeling before a statue on the plinth of which was inscribed 'His Royal Highness, the Prince of Wales'. On top of the plinth was the figure of the Prince himself. His feet were labelled "card box" and "poker". His shins were formed from dice. Above his knees, "stock gambling" was written, above that "race betting" and above that "Rules of Baccarat". His crown was made up of playing cards.(31)

Puck on 17th June produced a throne room with shocked guards standing to attention. In the foreground, the huge figure of an irate Victoria, wearing a cross between a crown and a widow's cap, and carrying an outsize feather duster which she grasped as if it were the proverbial rolling pin, was berating the tiny figure of her son, who was dressed in a small boy's smock with the label "Ich deal" across his stomach. In her other hand she held a scroll, which was labelled "Record of His Royal Highness the Prince of Wales: Keeping Low Company: Inveterate Gambling Propensities: Advertising Actresses: Hard Drinking: In Debt to Everybody: Loose Morals: Generally Fast: Too, Too Fond of Baccarat".(32) The most famous German cartoon showed the great door of Windsor with the Prince of Wales' feathers above it and, again, the motto "Ich deal". Among the English papers *Ariel,* on the 20th, showed the deck of a Wilson liner. Sir William was falling off the rigging onto the head of the Prince, from whose mouth the cigar had fallen, and from whose pocket cards and counters had spilled onto the deck. A handsome young woman was holding out her arms as if to save him. The caption read "Cumming down".

Criticism came from as far away as Australia. *The Sydney Bulletin,* before the trial on 16th May 1891, showed a wolf peeping in at the door of the palace, claws bared, and round its neck a label saying "Debts". Victoria was pushing on the door to keep it closed. Her son was hiding behind her and was attempting to cover his face with her skirt. The *Australian Boomerang* of the same date repeated the theme. Victoria was holding out to her son a money bag containing £300,000, and the caption read:

"Says Her Gracious to her graceless Son and Heir, 'This is flat!
Just this once I'll help to make your banker square; Mind you that!
If you promise me as follers -
To provide for 'Cuffs and Collars'(33)
And to plank none of the dollars   On baccarat'"(34)

The most famous of all the cartoons appeared in *Truth* in the supplement to the Christmas number, 25th December 1891. It took the form of a double page spread in colour, and showed a number of ladies and gentlemen sitting at a green baize table with a well defined chalk line round its edge playing "A Quiet Round Game". Anyone who knows the old billiard room at Tranby Croft will have no difficulty at all in recognising it, and those who do not, will immediately recognise the Prince of Wales who, cigar in mouth, was shown seated on the far side of the table to the right of the picture, handling a card with the Prince of Wales' feathers upon it. Every person seated round that table can

"A quiet round game". The cartoon published in the "Truth" Supplement, Christmas 1891. From the copy presented by Major & Mrs. Iveson to the Hull High School for Girls.

easily be identified.(35) Gordon-Cumming, his sheet of white paper plainly visible, was looking straight ahead. He, too, was smoking. Berkeley Levett, seated opposite, was obviously communing with the ceiling. At the far left of the picture Jack, Lycett Green and Ethel were looking with alarmed concentration at something in front of Gordon-Cumming which the viewer cannot see. Behind them, peeping through a curtain, and wearing his dressing gown, was Arthur Wilson. An alcove actually exists where he was shown to be standing, but it would have been impossible to hide there without first crossing the room. In front of the group, a corner of the billiard table could be seen. On it were cigars (the box was labelled "Princeps"), and wine (the bottle was labelled "Mumm"). One or two empty bottles were shown rolling round the floor, which was wine stained. At the back of the picture was a choice selection of what might loosely be termed 'Art'. From the left there was a large portrait of Arthur Wilson as Master of the Holderness, then came an equally large one of an "ancestral" Wilson — an old salt, sitting on a bollard and holding a little wooden boat with a Wilson Line flag on it. Next came the fireplace, easily identifiable with the real one, on the mantelpiece of which reposed no fewer than eight portraits of the Prince of Wales in differing dress, including court dress, military uniform, wearing a homburg hat, and resplendent in a kilt. Hanging out over the right hand side of the table was what appears to be a Wilson Line pennant (a red circle on white), but on close inspection the circle contains the Prince of Wales' feathers.

The main part of the Christmas number took the form of a lengthy poem which purported to be an admonition from the Prince's nephew, Kaiser Wilhelm II, to a member of a European Royal House who had let the side down badly. The Kaiser spared no rod:

"We royalties stand on a plane of our own
And I have persistently studied
To select my acquaintance from people alone
Who are quite 'comme il faut' and blue blooded,
But you, it would seem, have your friendship bestowed
Not on well born or recognised entities,
But have hastened to choose as your friends, parvenus
And wealthy but vulgar nonentities".(36)

Some papers made the charge that the Prince's lot was unenviable because he was given so little to do, which encouraged him to get into trouble. *Figaro* said:

"'If' the English "want princes to be prepared to act as Kings, they must not keep them entirely out of the domain of politics. If they want the princes solely as ornaments, they ought to make them a suitable allowance. If they don't want princes at all, let them say so. Meantime, they have no right to flagellate Queen Victoria's son with the maxim . . . that a prince has higher duties to fulfil than an ordinary individual. Prince! he is so little of a prince, the Prince of Wales".(37)

A year or two later, in France, the question of espionage was raised, and the fate of the innocent Jewish army officer, Alfred Dreyfus, became submerged in the wider issue of the continued existence of the Third French Republic. A study of the reaction to the baccarat scandal, which originally involved another soldier, looked at one time as if it could have built up into a full scale attack on the British monarchy, but Britons are slow to rouse. Victoria, so recently out of favour with the general public, had now become a venerable figure, and had made no secret of the fact that she disapproved of her son's behaviour. Edward, too, rode out the storm with dignity. His position forced him to fight with one hand behind his back, but he was at least able, through a personal contact, to make a peace offering to the Established Church.

He sent a message one morning to summon the Archbishop of Canterbury, Edward White Benson, to Marlborough House. He told his spiritual advisor that he believed the whole church to be condemning him as "a gambler and worse".(38) He was sufficiently upset to imply that the Archbishop himself was leading the crusade. The Archbishop bluntly told him that this was not so, that he himself had been particularly careful not to take sides, but if the Prince wished to have his private judgement on the subject, he could certainly have it. In the end, an amicable discussion took place.

The Archbishop and the Prince then exchanged letters, and the Prince wrote from the Royal Yacht "Osborne" at Cowes on 13th August 1891:

"My dear Archbishop,
. . . I have a horror of gambling and should always do my utmost to discourage others who have an inclination for it, as I consider that gambling, like intemperance, is one of the greatest curses which a country can be inflicted with.
Horse-racing may produce gambling or it may not, but I have always looked upon it as a manly sport which is popular with Englishmen of all classes, and there is no reason why it should be looked upon as a gambling transaction".(39)

So to the Prince, it was a matter of degree; and to some members of his public this must have seemed a very accommodating theory. The Tranby Croft incident had highlighted an undesirable trait in late Victorian England, but when all the shouting was over, it seemed that the majority of Englishmen had come to expect a high standard of conduct from their Royal Family. Prince Edward learned his lesson from that.

Like the Prince, the Wilsons also rode out the storm. Their social image did not appear to suffer. Royalty continued to visit them, but the Prince of Wales was not a member of their Doncaster race week house party ever again. His favour continued. Jack, recently admitted to the exclusive Marlborough Club on his nomination, was soon able to add political honours to his social ones, though the latter was due to family rather than royal influence. However the first wedding present sent out by King Edward VII soon after his accession, was to a member of the Wilson clan.

The consequences for Gordon-Cumming were socially disastrous. On 12th June 1891, a notice in the *London Gazette* told of his exit from the army "the Queen having no further occasion for his services".(40) Four days later, General Owen Williams wrote from the Turf Club to Lycett Green: "It was as clear as anything could possibly be that Cumming had cheated in a barefaced and systematic manner . . . and we were as lenient as possible under the circumstances".(41)

On the same day, Gordon-Cumming resigned from the Carlton Club. He had, however, married. The ceremony took place the very day after the conclusion of the trial, at Holy Trinity Church, Sloane Street, and was by special license. His bride, Florence Garner, was one of three daughters of an ex-Commodore of the New York Yacht Club. She had been born into a wealthy home on Staten Island, but at the age of four she was left an orphan when her parents were drowned in a boating accident.(42) Gordon-Cumming's sister, Eisa, wife of Digby Willoughby, Lord Middleton and the friend of Mary Wilson, had not been present at the trial, but she defied the Prince of Wales by attending this wedding, and she was one of very few who chose to do so. Of this event the Prince wrote to his son, George,

"Thank God! the Army and Society are now well rid of such a damned blackguard. The crowning point of his infamy is that he, this morning, married an American young lady, Miss Garner (sister of Mme. de Breteuil) with money".(43) This was true. Florence brought with her a personal fortune of £20,000 a year, which enabled her husband to live in comfort on his Scottish estates at Altyre and Gordonstoun, but society cut him dead. He once told a daughter "Among a host of acquaintances I thought I had perhaps twenty friends. Not one of them ever spoke to me again".(44)

Gordon-Cumming's daughter, Elma, tells how, as young children, she and her brothers and sister were staying at their uncle's home in the Avenue des Bois de Boulogne in Paris. Florence's elder sister, Lita, had married Henri de Breteuil, who "was small but very grand".(45) He was also very pro-British, and was a friend of the Prince of Wales. In March 1881, for instance, at a time when the Prince was being deliberately discouraged from taking any diplomatic interest in his country's well being, "Uncle Henri" had arranged a private consultation between the Prince and the fire-brand French politician Gambetta.(46) It went very well, especially since Gambetta was no more charitable about Bismarck than the Prince would have been himself. After the Baccarat Scandal Lita, for some years, had to break all contact with her sister, but when children came along to both families, the rules were relaxed a little. On this particular occasion all the children were together when the Prince called. He was curious and asked to see the Gordon-Cumming brood. To his credit, Uncle Henri pronounced that "he could not, while pursuing the parents with hatred, inspect the children like specimens in an aquarium."(47)

Gordon-Cumming's marriage was not a happy one and eventually, her fortune drained, Florence left her husband who died in May 1930 at the age of 81. Florence had already died in 1922. The family house on Staten Island became an orphanage. During the Great War, however, Queen Victoria's grandson, King George V, was glad to accept the services of Sir William's eldest son, Alexander, who was a major in the Queen's Own Cameron Highlanders and won the Military Cross. After Gordon-Cumming's death, the house at Gordonstoun was sold to a German educationalist, Kurt Hahn, who turned it into a school which became well known. Prince Philip Duke of Edinburgh went there, and since 1960 his three sons have also received their education at Gordon-Cumming's old home. Perhaps, in a roundabout way, he has been rehabilitated.

(1) *John Welcome: Cheating at Cards* (Faber and Faber 1963) p.71 et seq.
(2) *Havers, Grayson and Shankland: The Royal Baccarat Scandal* p.52.
(3) Quoted *Welcome* p.76.
(4) ed. *W. Teignmouth Shore: The Baccarat Case* p.47. I have relied consistently on the Teignmouth Shore transcript of the trial in the remainder of this chapter.
(5) *Teignmouth Shore* p.79.
(6) Ibid p.82.
(7) Ibid p.90.
(8) Ibid p.90.
(9) Ibid p.116.
(10) Ibid p.142.
(11) Ibid p.152.
(12) Ibid p.166.
(13) *John Welcome: Cheating at Cards* (Faber and Faber 1963) Op.cit.
(14) Teignmouth Shore p.172.
(15) Ibid.
(16) Ibid p.173.
(17) Ibid p.178.

(18) *John Welcome: Cheating at Cards* op.cit. p.143.
(19) Teignmouth Shore p.181.
(20) Ibid p.240.
(21) Ibid p.243.
(22) Ibid p.256.
(23) Ibid p.221.
(24) *John Welcome: Cheating at cards* Op.cit. p.157.
(25) Teignmouth Shore p.270.
(26) Ibid p.272.
(27) Ibid p.274.
(28) 18th June 1891.
(29) Quoted *Sunday Times Colour Supplement 2nd March 1969,* article by J. Fox.
(30) *Quoted Hull News Supplement.* 6th June 1891 p.3 col.c.
(31) *Review of Reviews* p.16.
(32) Ibid p.17.
(33) 'Cuffs and Collars' was a name often applied to the Prince's elder son, the Duke of Clarence and Avondale.
(34) *Review of Reviews* p.19.
(35) Lycett Green, Berkeley Levett, Lord Edward Somerset, The Prince, Mary, Reuben Sassoon, Ethel, Gordon-Cumming, Lady Coventry, Owen Williams, Lord Coventry.
(36) *Truth: Christmas Number 25th December 1891* p.20.
(37) *Review of Reviews* p.31.
(38) *E.F. Benson: As We Were* (Longmans, Green and Co. 1930) p.214.
(39) Ibid pp. 218-219.
(40) Quoted by *Sir Charles Petrie: The Victorians* (Eyre and Spottiswoode 1960) p.64.
(41) *Sunday Times Colour Supplement* op.cit. p.30.
(42) *Elma Napier: Youth is a Blunder* (Cape 1948) p.25.
(43) *H. Montgomery Hyde: Their Good Names* (Hamish Hamilton: 1970) p.162.
(44) *Elma Napier: Youth is a Blunder* op.cit. p.21.
(45) Ibid p.46.
(46) *Gordon Brook-Shepherd: Uncle of Europe, The Social and Diplomatic Life of Edward VII* (Book Club Associates 1975) pp. 69-70.
(47) *Napier* op.cit. p.48.

CHAPTER SEVEN

Charity and Local Society

In April 1891 Arthur Wilson had become High Sheriff of Yorkshire, and by doing so could be said, socially, to have climbed to the top of the local tree. His chaplain was his old friend Rev J. Foord of Kirkella, and his Under-Sheriff Mr Edwin Gray of York.[1] The Grays were an old York family and Edwin was a senior partner in a firm of solicitors. His wife, Almyra, an Anglo-American, was far more go-ahead and lively than most of her contemporaries. Like Mary Wilson, she was ambitious for her husband, who was himself perfectly content to remain in that sphere of life to which he had been called; but Almyra Gray overreached herself, and as a result had to endure being snubbed by her former so called friends. She was, however, a woman of determination, picked herself up, performed wondrous feats of social improvements and finished by joining the suffragettes.[2] Mary Wilson managed to avoid this fate, but she drove herself equally hard and, in Arthur, had a more willing partner than did Almyra.

The Spring Bank Orphanage

One charity, which continued to work to good effect in Hull for over a hundred years, was the Hull Seamen's and General Orphan Asylum, the foundation stone of which was laid on 29th March 1865. Thomas Wilson and his eldest son, David, had contributed largely to the foundation. Trinity House had donated an acre of land in Spring Bank, but Thomas soon realised that far more money would be required, and he offered a further £1,000 provided that double that sum could be guaranteed from other sources. His appeal was successful, and from that time not only Thomas, but his sons David, Charles and Arthur became benefactors, and remained so.

Soon the building had again to be extended, and a new Wilson Wing was built, like the rest of the building in a somewhat ecclesiastical style, by R. Sergeant from plans drawn up by Smith and Brodrick. Charlie and Arthur officially opened the new premises in February 1876, at a ceremony which took place in the basement where the refectory was.

When it was Charlie's turn to speak he said that he and Arthur regarded the new wing as a memorial to their father, Thomas, who had always taken such pride and interest in the orphanage, and whose portrait would now hang on the wall in the new building, which made provision for a further 80 children. During a meal which followed, several new subscriptions were announced, including one from David of £100.[3] The new wing came into use immediately and was filled with girls — overfilled, in fact. The premises were still not big enough. David, Charles and Arthur came to the rescue again; a further extension was built to the south at the cost of £2,000, and was opened by the Archbishop of York in April 1882.[4] This was particularly laudable, because the brothers were now also supporting the Hull District Railway Servants' Orphanage. They organised a Grand

Ballad Concert to collect money for it on Wednesday, 28th November 1883, staged at the Artillery Barracks.

Even this event paled before the Grand Bazaar held in aid of the Spring Bank Orphanage in November 1884.(5) For months previously work had been going on, a lot of it being in the hands of ladies like Mary Wilson and their sewing groups. One zealous supporter had been Emma Smith, Mary's aunt. She it was who had given up all ideas of romance in Cottingham when she undertook, with Victorian humility, to look after her widowed father, Lord Henry Smith; and two years later moved with him to her brother Edward's motherless establishment in Brixton, where she reared his children, of whom Mary was the eldest. She had continued to manage Edward's household, moving with him to Leeds; and on his retirement in 1879 from the Postal Service, came with him to Tranby Park, a country house less than a mile and a half from her niece's residence. When Edward died in 1883, Emma Anne had gone to live with her bachelor nephew Henry Wilson Ringrose Smith, now a successful partner in the engineering firm of Amos and Smith, at his house at 3 Crown Terrace, Anlaby Road. Even Henry became involved in the project for the orphanage, and had been made Bazaar Secretary.

So much material was collected that only the biggest hall in Hull — the Artillery Barracks — could house it all. It had the additional advantage of a room at the back which could be made into a concert hall for 600 people, and a room at the side which was big enough to serve refreshments — then, as now, an excellent money spinner. A good band was hired, and at various times throughout the four days of the bazaar, concerts, plays and piano recitals would take place, and Mary Wilson, who was alive to the latent talent in Hull exploited it here for the benefit of the performer as well as for the orphans, and also made sure that her own family led the way by exercising their musical and dramatic gifts in support of the cause. Even the North Eastern Railway was approached, and as a result trains to York, Beverley, Withernsea and Hornsea were rescheduled to run at a time a little later than usual on the last evening.

As might be expected the cost of admission was not cheap. Season tickets, which included the opening ceremony, could be had for 7/6d each, and this was reasonable since it would cost 5/0d to attend the opening ceremony alone. Two events clouded the opening ceremony. The Duke of Albany, who with his wife had agreed to perform this function, died; so the Duke of Edinburgh and his wife, the Grand Duchess Marie of Russia, came instead. A second death was that of Emma Anne Smith. She had suffered from a bowel blockage, and died on Thursday, the second day of the bazaar. Speaking from the platform on that day Charles Henry expressed his sympathy for her nephew, who was continuing to take an active part in the organisation, and paid tribute to the tireless little lady who worked until she could work no more.(6)

The Duke and Duchess of Edinburgh had been staying at Brantinghamthorpe with Christopher Sykes, whose path would again cross that of the Wilsons, with ill starred effect. The Royal couple went first to the Infirmary, where the Duke opened a new wing which had been built at the expense of David, Charles and Arthur, and contained a "Tottie and Ethel" cot. After this they came on to Spring Bank, and were shown all round the orphanage by Charlie, so that they now had a good idea of what the organisers of the bazaar had already done, and what they were aiming for. When they drove down Park Street, they were met outside the Artillery Barracks by Arthur, who escorted them into the bazaar. Charlie's daughter, Enid, presented the bouquet, the band played the National Anthem, Charlie made a speech of welcome to the Duke and Duchess, the Duke made his speech, and the bazaar was well and truly opened. Mary and her daughter, Muriel, both had stalls. Mary's was one of three in the centre of the room. A striking object she had for sale was a huge plush fan "of considerable dimensions."(7) Its central portion was of plaited white satin, beautifully painted with flowers by Tottie, who, like her mother, had also painted several screens, which were an absolute necessity in the draughty Victorian houses. There was a good deal on the stall which had been given by the Wilson Line captains, who had been asked, long ago, to keep a look out for unusual objects. This, they appear to have done, since one of them donated an upright stuffed Russian bear. The donor, Captain Rutter, who became a tower of strength to the Wilsons on any occasion of this sort, had asked, perhaps wisely, that the bear should be raffled.

Muriel had two stalls near the platform. Being only nine years old, she had opted to sell dolls. Young as she was, she was also involved, with her cousin Enid, three years her junior, in the theatrical productions, and took part in several of the one act plays. There was never really any doubt about the success of the enterprise. The *Hull News* dutifully reported each night that hundreds of Hull citizens patiently waited to gain admission, and from time to time the organisers were forced to suspend entry until the interior had cleared.

As a result of these great efforts the organisers netted over £5,000, and even after the deduction of the considerable expenses there was left in hand a useful sum for further building, and this was added to in 1893, when the orphanage benefited to the extent of a further £1,500 from David's will.

Each summer the Wilsons organised an outing for the orphans of Spring Bank. Usually Bridlington, was the destination; but on Tuesday, 21st August 1894, for the first of many times, the orphanage outing was to Tranby Croft. It was carried out with all the Wilson flair for careful and accurate preparation; and it needed to be, because the day was dull, and there was even rain at one point. At half past twelve, 200 children had left the orphanage in wagonettes, and on their arrival Mary Wilson, having had seven children of her own, led them straight into a marquee to be fed. The Wilsons never underestimated the therapeutic and psychological value of good food. Then there were games to be played in the garden, and in a big field near the house, a steam roundabout "with all the latest improvements" had been installed, much to the delight of all the children. At five o'clock they were called back again to the marquee. Nor was this a modest repast, as the local paper reported "the provisions being of a really sumptuous character",(8) and after this the younger Wilsons organised competitions and races, while Arthur and Mary entertained the adults of the party to a quieter dinner in the marquee. It was all over by eight o'clock, and when the children left, there was hardly a child present who had not won some useful or pretty prize. By 1897 Mary Wilson had established a tradition that the orphanage children should always have a midsummer treat out at Tranby Croft.

Waifs and Strays

During the summer of 1888 Mr Anderson, one of the Guardians of the Sculcoates Workhouse in Hull had written humbly to Arthur Wilson to ask whether his "poor waifs and strays" could come out one fine summer's day and play in only a little field somewhere on the Tranby estate. He was not asking for much, but a day in the country in the fresh air would do his poor little souls a power of good. The kind hearted Arthur well knew that he could expect a request like this from every charity in Hull, but he was delighted to help, and had promptly arranged a Fete for them — the first of its kind.

The Church of England, to which the Wilson family had always paid far more than lip service, had its own Waifs and Strays Society. In December 1893 a large and fashionable crowd assembled at the York Diocesan Home for Waifs and Strays (which was in Clarendon Street, Hull), to give their support to a bazaar there. Mary Wilson was President. The patrons were told that 30 girls, many of them taken from the streets of Hull, were being cared for, but that the future was uncertain because local subscribers were few.(9) Nevertheless the home continued to function if not to flourish, and in August 1898 Mary Wilson had a Grand Fete at Tranby Croft to help. This was not a "production" specifically aimed at children, and was therefore more spectacular then ever. The family worked with their usual dedication. The Union Jack flew from the tower. On the west front, to the back of the house and near the billiard room, a maypole had been set up. Seventeen year old Clive had taken a job which appealed to him greatly. Wearing a broad brimmed flat panama hat, a waistcoat with revers, a bow tie, and with his sleeves rolled up, he ran the American Bar, a cigarette permanently between his lips. He sold every kind of drink imaginable, including the Tranby Tickler (for the faint hearted), Gin Slings, and Corpse Revivers (for those with a jaded palate). A fortune teller from London, Mme Teresina, had been engaged, and she operated from a delightful little summer house on the west lawn, which survived until the vandalism of the mid 1970s forced its removal.

Mary Wilson had opened up her home so that guests who had not seen it could tour the reception rooms and the hall for the price of one shilling. She probably supervised this herself, but although the price was high Mary believed in giving value for money. The open air swimming pool was also available, at a charge, and teas were provided for those who still had any money left. As a variation on what was by now a well established theme, the fete did well.(10)

Sailors' Charities

The Wilson brothers were careful for the well being of sailors coming into the port of Hull. A Sailors' Rest already existed in Posterngate, in the Old Town of Hull, but the premises were far too small and, by 1897, desperately in need of repair. Once again Wilson money was poured out, and in mid June Charles Henry officiated at the reopening ceremony. However, further additions were still needed to make the place into a good recreation centre for visiting sailors, and with this in mind a Grand Bazaar was arranged to take place at the Artillery Barracks — where else! — over a period of three days in February 1898. The target was the massive sum of £2,000. Both the Charles Henrys and the Arthurs worked with tremendous energy. On the opening day a glittering assembly brought out a great crowd of sightseers, so that the reporter from the *Hull News* said, with real feeling, that the crush was "truly awful".(11) Throughout the three days Muriel and Clive ran theatrical performances, which included "Kitty Clive", for which Muriel became famous, and "Little Toddlekins". Clive, a very popular entertainer, sang in the café chantant in the coster style — a favourite of his. The bazaar was another resounding Wilson triumph, the total amount taken amounting to £3,012.8.3d. Mrs Charles Henry was top scorer with £465, beating Mrs Arthur, but only just, as she took £446.2.6d.

Hull Hospitals

Another charitable institution which enjoyed the continuous patronage of the Arthur Wilsons was the Victoria Children's Hospital, which had been founded in 1873 to accommodate the poor, sick children of Hull.(12) A house was bought in Story Street, equipped, and opened to patients at the end of February 1874, the cost being around £2,700. Queen Victoria was graciously pleased to sanction its name four years later. At first, there were only eight beds, but all too soon the little hospital was bursting at its seams, and it became necessary to purchase a new site, a suitable one being available in Park Street. This took every halfpenny the committee possessed, and to complete the picture of gloom the Chairman, Mr Henry Allison, no doubt suffering somewhat from nervous exhaustion, resigned in January 1889, although he had been Chairman since the beginning of the enterprise.

At this time Arthur Wilson was sheriff. He was already financially involved with the problems of the hospital and now he, perhaps more than anybody else, was able to instill heart and new life into the despondent committee. He became their chairman, gave them £1,000 to start their building fund, and, as has already been told, lent his daughter, Muriel, to be hostess at the Children's Fancy Dress Ball held later the same month. As this event was a financial success, building was able to start almost immediately, and Mary Wilson laid the foundation stone of the new hospital on 22nd February 1890. The following year, on 22nd July, the official opening was performed by Arthur and Mary. It was a dignified, colourful and popular event, and the whole length of Park Street was crowded with spectators. From London had come Sheriff Farmery with his footman, both gorgeously apparelled, and, in their state coach, the Lord Mayor of London and his Lady. Local worthies included Charles Henry M.P., for once taking second place to Arthur, and the procession was rounded off by the Mayor of Hull, Mr Frank Pease, also in full regalia, who was escorting the Marchioness of Salisbury who formally opened the door of the hospital with a gold and jewelled key.

Hospitals, however, absorb money like their furnaces absorb coke. At the Annual General Meeting held in the board room of the hospital, late in May 1894, the President, Arthur Wilson, underlined a desperate need for it. They had started the year, he said, with a balance of £98, but already they had a debt of £600. As things stood there was no chance of paying it off, because subscriptions only amounted to £578. In a town the size of Hull, said Arthur, this was disgraceful. He also believed that the Victoria was losing out on legacies. Money was often left to the Hull Infirmary, but unless the department to which it had to go was specified, the money went elsewhere, and the children's hospital was nearly always overlooked. Arthur thought that a special endowment fund should be set up. He also pointed out that contributions lately had been fewer because Hull was still recovering from its part in "that absurd and utterly uncalled for dockers' strike" — Arthur did not always choose his words diplomatically or fairly — and to add insult to injury this had been followed up, through no fault of Hull, by the coal strike.(13)

1897 was the year of Queen Victoria's Diamond Jubilee. A Celebration sub-committee was held early in April to decide what to do with the considerable amount of money they were prepared to spend. Several men wished it, or much of it, to be used for the new Art Gallery. Sir James Reckitt and Arthur Wilson, however, did not, and Arthur said bluntly that it should be used to provide Hull with more nurses. At this, Mr Martin Samuelson promised that during the year a Nurses' Home would be provided at a cost of £2,000, and also volunteered the information that Arthur would give £500 and his firm 25 guineas. The home, at 21, Charlotte Street, very close to the house where Arthur took his young bride nearly forty years previously, was opened to receive nurses in February 1899.(14)

In January 1899 the now well established Children's Fancy Dress Ball seems to have started a new tradition. Just before supper, the children were asked to get into a long line and, while the band played, made a slow, serpentine Ornamental March to the supper room. This enabled them to show off their elaborate costumes in a way which had not been possible previously. One little boy dressed as a gnome even travelled the whole distance balanced on a large ball, from which, surprisingly, he did not tumble.(15) In 1902 the ball was held on New Year's Day, and cabs began to arrive very early, because mothers were determined to have their children's beautiful fancy dresses showing to the best possible advantage. A gale blowing outside meant that the poor little girls would need longer ministrations to their ornate hair styles. Muriel arrived punctually at half past seven. It took her half an hour to greet all the children who then danced for a further two hours, while their parents sat out in the small hall. Ethel's smallest boy Peter, (his real name was Francis) was quite the star of the show. He was dressed as a Jack Tar and danced an English hornpipe, which was so much enjoyed that he followed it up by dancing a Scottish one. At ten o'clock the children made their circuitous procession to supper after which they went home and their parents danced.(16)

The hospital continued to grow. In 1901 electricity was put in, and during the next twelve months three houses in Park Street were bought and adapted. The outpatients' department was also enlarged. There was a new dressing room for the children and a new mortuary, consulting rooms, and a post-mortem room. At the official opening on Saturday, 21st November 1903, it was stressed how essential this extra accommodation had become. Previously the department had been able to take a hundred outpatients, but on the Friday before the opening of the new rooms 170 patients had turned up. These alterations had cost £1,100. Arthur had given £200 outright, and the committee had so far collected a further £500. Mary, who had opened the new block officially, put in another fiver on the spot, and a gentleman of the committee, Mr Spring, had the satisfaction of outdoing a Wilson by putting in £20.(17)

In 1948 the hospital was absorbed into the National Health Service, but continued to do its valuable and heroic work. Arthur and Mary were now long dead, but their grandson Arthur Wilson-Filmer was still acting as Chairman of the House Committee. Muriel, who had worked so hard on its behalf almost from the beginning, died in 1964 knowing that the hospital, like her, was moving to a new sphere. Lacking facilities and equipment, it was officially closed in 1967, the children having been moved to the new multi-storey Hull Royal Infirmary, from the top floors of which, looking north east, the old building can still be seen.

The Hull Royal Infirmary itself was also the recipient of Wilson generosity. Between 1884 and 1885 a new wing was built, and David, Charles and Arthur handed over £6,000 in their father's memory. The foundation stone had been laid on 1st October 1884 by the Duke and Duchess of Edinburgh, at which point the Infirmary, previously known as the "General" became the "Royal". Just over a year later, on Guy Fawkes night, the new ward, eye department and outpatients' department were officially opened by Lord Herries, and continued to give service until a different kind of firework display — a direct hit from one of Hitler's bombs — razed it to the ground.(18) In January 1890 Charles and Arthur headed the list of donors to the hospital with a handsome £250 each. Charlie, in particular, had practised what he had preached, for in the previous November he had made an impassioned speech to the effect that the wealthy men of Hull could be far more charitable to the hospital, and were being shamed by the working class.

Both brothers supported a Grand Charity Ball at the Public Rooms, Jarratt Street, Hull in June 1890, which did something to persuade the Hull élite to part with their money for a worthy object. When David Wilson died in 1893, he bequeathed £1,000 to the Infirmary, a sure indication of his anxiety for its welfare, and when Colonel Harrison Broadley, the hospital's President, died in 1895, Arthur Wilson was elected in his place. The Wilsons supported, though they did not mastermind, the annual ball for the Orthopaedic Hospital. In 1897 this took place early in November in the Public Rooms. Mary was present although wisely she did not, as many women did that night, wear the colour of the new season — yellow. Loyal to her Queen, she wore black, in this case trimmed with white lace, and set off by her magnificent diamonds. Clive, who escorted her, wore hunting pink. In the early winter of 1901 Mary took her great friend Mrs Travers to see Mr A.E. Hiscock's *The Playwright* at the Theatre Royal. She was pleased to see that the place was packed, for the proceeds were to go to the Orthopaedic Hospital.[19]

New ways of obtaining cash for all the hospitals were constantly being tried. On August Bank Holiday Monday 1898 the new Wilson liner "Idaho" moored in Alexandra Dock, was opened for inspection by the public. Contributions were asked for, on behalf of the Hull and Sculcoates Dispensary. £4.0.10d was collected.[20] Similarly, in Railway Dock, the Royal Mail steamship "Montebello" could be examined between eleven o'clock and five, contributions in this case going to the Victoria, and it was promised that during the afternoon the ship would be lit by electricity, still something to be marvelled at by many working people. This project did rather better, £12.3.9½d was contributed at the gangway, and a further £1.4.1d in the captain's room.

Victoria Mansions

One of the most remarkable and charitable acts of Charlie and Arthur Wilson was the creation, in 1903, of a huge block of accommodation called the Victoria Mansions. It stood in Great Passage Street, Hull, quite close to the Wilson Line offices in Commercial Road. Charlie was the chairman of the company which ran the project, Arthur was a director. In this block there was provision for 400 single working men on a short or longer stay basis. Most of the men would undoubtedly be dock workers or seamen, but there was no restriction as to who could apply.

The building was huge. It had a large basement with four floors above it. The main hall was octagonal, and from it doors led off in all directions to the public rooms. The floor of the hall was of concrete; teak garden seats were spread around, and the place was decorated with potted plants. The smoking room also had teak seats and tables for 120 men, so that it could be used, if necessary, as an overflow dining room. There were easy chairs and fireplaces at either end of the room. At one end of the main dining room, and separated from it, was a shop supplying cooked and uncooked food. A service lift brought this up from the catering department in the basement. There was a service room with a gas stove, where the lodgers could borrow crockery, pans and other necessary equipment. Normally, dirty crockery and utensils would be left on the dining room tables to be collected by staff and sent down on the lift, but there was a lodgers' scullery with hot and cold water, where they could wash up after making tea or after a meal at an unusual hour. There was also a reading room, a barber's shop and a tailor's.

On every landing there was a housemaid's sink and a supply of drinking water. Each bed was in a separate cubicle, and all cubicles had windows out to the open air. The bedsteads were of iron, with wire woven mattresses, a horsehair mattress on top and a bolster. Blankets, sheets and a quilt with an embroidered design of the head of the late Queen upon it were provided along with a chair and a shelf. The project was called "The Working Man's Hotel" by some, "cheap labour for the Wilsons" by others. It was run as a business venture, but under no circumstances would the directors and shareholders take more than 4% on their investments. The hostel fulfilled a need for the best part of a century.(21)

Education

It would have been odd if the Wilsons, so generous to the poor and sick, had not showed an interest in local education. Less than a month after the expiration of his office as sheriff Arthur Wilson became involved in the negotiations to set up a Church of England High School for Girls in Hull. Since the death of the Rev. John Hymers of Brandesburton in 1887 it had been decided that a large part of his fortune, some £50,000, would be spent on the creation of Hymers College, a public school for boys in Hull, a project in which Arthur Wilson had already shown interest. The feminist, Miss Christina Bremner who, with her sister, Janet, kept a girls' day school at No. 1, Clyde Terrace, Anlaby Road, had tried unsuccessfully to obtain part of the Hymers bequest for the education of Hull girls and was still preaching her gospel. Now it seemed, she had a powerful ally in the Church of England. A circular was issued stating that the object of such a school would be "to provide at reasonable cost — from £9 to £15.15.0d per annum, according to age — a thoroughly good and practical day school education in all branches of learning with definite religious church teaching."(22) The parent body would be the Church Schools Company Limited; founded in 1884, the Company already had 24 schools. A school in Hull could now be built providing that the locality could raise "not less than 250 shares of £5 each with £4 paid". A list of promised share purchasers and the identity of the buyers was given. At the head of this list was Arthur Wilson who took 50 shares, his nearest rival being Mr F. R. Pease, who took 20, and then the Mayor of Hull, who took 10. Thus began the association between the school and the family which remains to this day and will, please God, continue to remain.

The beginning of November 1893 saw the official opening of Hymers College. It was an all male ceremony as befitted an all male school. The Lord Chancellor, Lord Herschell, who performed the task, was staying at Warter Priory with Charlie, and both Charlie and Arthur were present. At the end of this part of the proceedings the members of the official party joined their wives for the official reception at the college, after which they all made their own way to a banquet in the Town Hall. Hymers College was thus well launched.

Academically it was an immediate success. Financially it was something of a headache. Pupils, they did not lack, and the inevitable result was that further building became necessary very soon, the first priority being a large and well equipped gymnasium. Hull society approached the problem in a way which was entirely typical of the era — they would have a ball, and in the college hall at that.

The arrangements were so lavish that it is a wonder there was any profit at all, but no doubt the Wilsons and others put their hands deeply into their pockets. The permanent floor being hopeless for dancing, a London firm was called in to lay down a special dancing floor a few inches above it. This floor covered the main part of the hall, but did not extend under the balconies, which were on three sides of the area. Between the pillars which supported the balconies and the walls, luxurious carpeting had been laid down, which made an ideal kind of promenade. The boys who saw it must have come away thoroughly bemused at what appeared to be happening to their school. The staircase to the balcony was also carpeted. Once more Mr Leadbetter brought plants and ferns from Tranby Croft, and created, amongst other things, a sitting out area under the north balcony. Out came the Wilson Line flags as well, and these were hung, as usual, all over the ceiling. Mr Close was back again with his band, and Mary Wilson was also back in her black satin, this dress embroidered with gold sequins, with a red rose in her corsage. Muriel was magnificent in white, with an apron with passementerie of silver lace. The dress had a pouched bodice, with pink malmaison carnations, and in her hair, at the front, she wore a single pink rose. Dancing went on until two o'clock in the morning.(23)

Hymers College and the Hull High School for Girls soon became important educational establishments in the life of what was now the city of Hull. Wilson money continued to be given to good effect here. Less obvious was the work done by Arthur and Mary to help music and drama in Hull, outside as well as inside the established schools, and also by attending concerts and participating themselves in aid of a deserving charity.

Music and Drama

The well established Hull Musical Union was staunchly supported by both Arthur and Mary. Its members often held concerts in the Assembly Rooms, and these were convivial and noisy, and Arthur thoroughly enjoyed them. On 22nd February 1893 the room had been arranged in continental style, small tables and chairs in little groups dotted all over the place, even in the galleries, which the *Hull News* reporter gloomily described as very draughty. "The draughts in the north balcony are most dreadful" he said, and added that those who came would be lucky not to catch a cold. Arthur and Mary and other members of the family who did come, were luckier than the unfortunate reporter, and were given a table plumb in the middle of the hall, so that they would be well buttressed from the four winds that blew by the convenient placing of the other tables. There was coffee and other refreshments, and a whole army of waiters to bring it and — surprising to our more fastidious sensibilities — smoking was permitted. The atmosphere thickened steadily as the concert proceeded, but the choir appeared to thrive on it.

Their first offering, a well known glee called "Strike the Lyre" was not good, the singers were uneasy, and the entries and the pitch were ragged and inaccurate. However, after Mr Russell's performance of "Come into the garden, Maud" and Mr Newton's rendering of "The Holy City" things went far better, and there was a fine execution of a vocal trio, which brought forth hearty applause from the Wilson family. Arthur's vote of thanks (Mary was the musical one) was genuine — he liked a hearty noise because, for one thing, he could hear it.(24)

When the choir held its next concert, on Wednesday, 21st February 1894, it had obviously decided that conviviality took precedence even over musical expertise, and had simply billed the concert as the "Smoker". The guests, including Arthur and Mary, numbered no fewer than 1,200, which filled the Assembly Rooms in Jarratt Street, and such a good time was had by all, that at eleven o'clock no-one had even begun to think about the votes of thanks. So, sensibly under the circumstances, all the thanks were taken as read, and "the strains of 'God Save the Queen' were probably never warbled amid such a volume of smoke before".(25)

1893 was the year in which the Thomas Wilson, Sons and Company Brass Band made its first public appearance on August Bank Holiday. Formed nine months previously among the permanent outdoor staff of coopers, carpenters, smiths and allied crafts, the band numbered some thirty players. It was a remarkable achievement to have got them to play at all, for most of them had been unable to read music, and had no instruments. Charlie and Arthur made an initial big donation, others joined in, and good instruments were bought from Booseys in London. The conductor, Mr Hills, an experienced musician from the Hull Artillery Band, was willing to teach as well as conduct. Mr Linnell, the treasurer, was equally enthusiastic. During the year the band had practised regularly, often four nights in the week, and now they made their debut at Mr Linnell's home in Sutton. "Florid music is, as yet, scarcely attempted"[26] the local reporter wrote, somewhat condescendingly and, as it turned out unnecessarily, for the second concert, which was held on Wednesday, 28th November 1894, showed just how much progress had been made.

Several soloists emerged, including one cornet player, Herbert Green, who was very popular. By 1899 the band was sufficiently skilled to take part in, and win, several small competitions. In that year a euphonium player from the Hull Artillery Band joined their ranks and took the solos. His name was Wilf Brocklesby, and from that moment his future, and that of the band were closely linked. Seven years later they entered, and won, the Peoples Challenge Shield against 24 competitors at the Crystal Palace Festival.[27] The firm was amazed — and delighted, and promptly handed over more cash. Clive, by now a Director of the firm, had become the band's President, and they could not have wished for a better. He took a real interest in their progress, and used his considerable influence to find venues for them to play, so that they were able to have experience of performing at civic occasions, at Tranby Croft and other big houses in the area, at the seaside and at private receptions.

In 1908 through Clive's influence, 17 members of the band became attached to the East Riding Yeomanry (Wenlock's Horse), the regiment to which Clive, a major since his service in the Boer War, belonged. The band survived until 1942, still under Brocklesby, and still winning prizes, although since the 1920s, because of the addition of woodwind, it became a "military" and not a "brass" band. Between 1924 and 1925 it was one of the early broadcasters for the BBC, which required some stamina, since these broadcasts were apt to last most of the evening (from 7.30 pm until 11 pm).

On Saturday, 19th October 1929, Mr Brocklesby steered his musicians, now called the Ellerman's Wilson Band, to victory at the 9th Annual Military Band contest held in the Zoological Gardens at Belle Vue, Manchester. There were 17 competitors so it was no mean triumph, and was shared by most Hull people who had an interest in the firm and who also had a radio. It was shared too by Captain Bean of the "Borodino" on his way back from New York. He, like everyone else, was puzzled when, in the middle of 'Finlandia', the playing suddenly stopped. No explanation was given by the BBC, but it transpired later that the lights in the Great Hall where the broadcast was being recorded had suddenly failed, and until they went on again the band had little choice but to keep silent.

Since the band survived for 50 years, it might be said that the Wilsons were thus literally instrumental in helping to give half a century of good music to the Hull area. Equally important, the existence of the band gave to many of the workmen a lifelong interest, skill and pleasure they might otherwise never have enjoyed. But services to music were also delivered on a far more personal basis. If Mary Wilson had any reason to believe that a talented local youngster needed financial support or professional guidance, she was willing to provide both. Consequently a promising young violinist, Ethel Weightman, was invited to play at Tranby Croft, and Mary cajoled, bullied and pestered a distinguished gathering to lend her their ears.(28) Mary discovered this latent talent in Hull children by interesting herself in the local music schools, of which there were two. One was run by Miss A.J. Martin A.R.A.M., who became very famous under her married name of Mrs Russell Starr. Mrs Starr had been born and educated in London. She had spent no fewer than six years at the Royal Academy of Music studying the usual programme of harmony, counterpoint, analysis and history as well as taking piano lessons with Walter Macfarren, a pupil of Cipriani Potter, who had received instruction from Beethoven.(29) When she left the Academy, she moved at once to Hull taking her mother with her. Her mother, who had struggled hard so that her daughter might qualify, was stone deaf, and never heard a single one of her performances. Miss Martin, as she still was, quickly became the local representative of the Associated Board. She also became a Fellow of the Royal Academy of Music, a comparatively rare distinction for one in her circumstances, in 1899. Several of her pupils gained the L.R.A.M.

Each month after the school had had time to establish itself (it was founded in 1888) Mrs Russell Starr organised a musical evening in her drawing room, which was, fortunately, big enough for performers, instruments and audience, who were parents and friends. No pupil was ever left out, no matter how limited her ability.(30) To this school came a very young and talented piano pupil, Ethel Liggins. Her father, Thomas, had a building yard and sawmill in Great Union Street, Hull, in partnership with a Mr Hockney. In June 1894, at the age of eight, Ethel was already sufficiently developed technically and interpretively to perform at a pupils' concert. She had already come to the notice of the Wilsons who installed her at Tranby Croft at certain times during the years, probably when there was to be a concert at the house, since Ethel certainly played for Mary's guests.(31) Tradition has it that she played for the Prince of Wales also. Almost certainly Mary Wilson was responsible for arranging Ethel's London debut in 1896 at the Queen's Hall before a distinguished audience. The child played a staggering programme of 17 pieces ranging from Bach to Sterndale Bennett and Moszkowski. She displayed a sound technique, interpretive skill and a steady nerve.(32) Her prowess was acknowledged not only in the local press, but in *World* and *Vanity Fair,* when Ethel repeated her programme a month later at one of Mary's exclusive dinner parties in Grosvenor Place.

Unfortunately a less rosy picture was painted when she performed in Hull the following January. Something had upset her immediately before the concert, and she had played the first half of the programme before she really settled down. Our local critic, although impressed by the undoubted skill and talent of the young performer, said he would have appreciated a singer to relieve the monotony of the instrument, but he agreed that, with the exception of Raff's Polka, there was no sign that the child was being forced beyond her powers, and he gave credit to the "careful and judicious way in which she is being trained."(33)

A year later Ethel was a pupil of Herr Kwast at the Hoch Conservatoire in Frankfort, and already, in May of that same year she had been chosen to perform Haydn's Concerto in Db with the orchestra, a feat she accomplished from memory and with resounding success. Soon after this she went to Vienna to study with Theodor Leschetizky, changed her name to Leginska, which was suggested to her by Muriel's great friend, the singer Lady Maud Warrender, and went on to become a famous soloist, teacher and composer based in America. She once dedicated a suite she composed to the Wilson family, and when she died in February 1970 she was probably one of the very last to remember the famous days of Tranby Croft.

Mary did not confine her help to musicians. She also took a young actress, Gwendoline Brogden, under her wing. After a number of recitals locally, including at least one performance at Tranby Croft, Mary launched Gwendoline at a matinee in London. The girl went on to enjoy a distinguished career in musical comedy, and was one of those actresses (like Annie Croft, who also had Hull connections) playing at the Gaiety in the Strand at the end of the career of the famous George Edwardes.(34)

Gwendoline worked throughout the First World War in London. In Alfred Butt's *Passing Show* of 1915 she sang what Denis Castle described as "a blatently recruiting number", "I'll Make a Man of Every One of You".(35) The first production after the armistice of 1918 was *The Kiss Call* by Fred Thompson, and here Gwendoline played alongside Evelyn Laye, Stanley Lupino, Binnie Hale, and the now unreliable G.P. Huntley. It ran for 176 performances.

In 1910 she had married an actor, Basil Samuel Foster, a member of a famous Worcestershire cricketing family. Tall, athletic and good looking, (he played the young lover to Phyllis Dare in *The Sunshine Girl*), he became lead actor and singer at the Gaiety. The couple were happy for some years but in 1921 Basil Foster left Gwendoline and their only child Mary. Five years later she divorced him. In 1927, when she heard of the death of Mary Wilson, her old benefactor, Gwendoline Brogden travelled back to Anlaby to attend the funeral service, and thus paid tribute to one who had helped her when she had most need.

Gwendoline Gertrude Brogden had been a pupil at the school of Madame Alice Sharrah, A.T.C.L., who had founded the Hull School of Music in Story Street in 1887, when there were only six pupils. She was immediately successful, and managed to hold her first concert in the Royal Institution only two years later. The year after that, the young principal took her courage in both hands and booked the Assembly Rooms. Seventy pounds was taken at the door, a thing unheard of, said the local paper, for an amateur concert at that time.(36) It is possible that Mary Wilson encouraged Madame Sharrah to make this move. On at least one occasion Mary hired the hall herself for a huge matinee for the school, and Gwendoline on this occasion was a member of a dance group.(37) Madame Sharrah married Mr William Henry Simpson in 1894, when all her bridesmaids were pupils. Mary Wilson respected her dedication, and when Alice formed a band of mandoline players, Mary at once arranged that they should perform at the very next entertainment she had to organise. By 1914, 1060 pupils had passed through Alice's hands, and she, by then, had large and commodious premises which included a music room with seats for 200 listeners, and her staff had risen to eleven — eight governesses and three masters.(38) It is a touching fact that when Madame Sharrah retired from the school in 1938, after fifty years' service, a mandoline and piano duet was performed during the concert which was given in her honour in the Guildhall, Hull.(39)

In spite of the great support given by the Wilsons to music, there is no doubt that their main interest was in drama. In Gilbert and Sullivan, however, the two combined. A programme exists of a performance of *Patience* in the great hall at Tranby Croft from 30th January until 3rd February 1882, surely a very early performance of this work in the north.(40) It was master-minded by Mary Wilson, Tottie played the Lady Angela, and Ethel took the part of Patience, the dairymaid. There was a pretty programme with the location, Tranby Croft, at the top right hand corner; a heraldic beast with the motto "semper vigilans" (identical with the one appearing in the woodwork of the fireplace in the billiard room); a swallow in flight above the title, and below it, a spray of lilies of the valley. Almost certainly the production would be in aid of some charity, but the programme itself gives no indication as to what it was.

Clive was the most rumbustuous of Arthur and Mary's seven children. He never aspired to sing or play classical music, although he appreciated it. After he joined the territorials he was much in demand at smoking concerts where he would sing in the coster style. Nor did the more erudite playwrights particularly attract him, but he joined the East Yorkshire Dramatic Society and this provided, through contemporary comedy, an outlet for his histrionic talent. In a single week in February 1896 he was involved in two local productions. On the Monday night the society put on F.C. Bernand's play *Betsy*. Seats at the front were three shillings, at the back, one shilling. Clive took the part of Adolphus Burkett, who was sued by Betsy for breach of promise, but got away with it. The play was a rollicking comedy, and was played for all it was worth by Clive and several other gentlemen; but one of them, Captain McManus, who was supposed to have an Irish accent, kept on forgetting it, and several of the young ladies were plainly scared of the footlights, and their performances were very inhibited. Although the play made a late start — perhaps the stage hands were inhibited as well — and the intervals were "very, very long"(41) the play was, surprisingly, a success.

A more disciplined and more tongue-in-the-cheek production was put on at Tranby Croft the following Thursday by the redoubtable Mary Wilson, who was seeking to aid the Anlaby schools and other local charities. Not a seat remained empty, and every available space for standing room was also filled. "Diamonds" remarked the reporter from the *Hull News*(42) "were as common as blackberries in autumn". The play was G.W. Godfrey's *The Parvenu*, which concerned a disagreement between Sir Fulke Pettigrew "a cad of highest order of merit", whose ancestors had fought with Harold at Hastings in 1066, but whose purse was now empty, and Mr Ledger, a self made man and radical M.P., whose "Hs" had been omitted from his "Heddication", who had no known ancestors, but whose heart was in the right place. One presumes that Mary gained a cheerful satisfaction in making her wealthy and influential friends pay for hearing this.

As a curtain raiser Muriel and Sir Harry Bellairs danced a piece called "Highwaymen". They did well, which was a good thing because the twenty year old Muriel had to follow it up by playing the part of Sir Fulke Pettigrew's wife — a matron of fifty, if she was a day. Clive pranced all over the stage as the Hon. Charles Tracey, and was very popular. The Countess Cairns, playing the Pettigrew daughter Gwendoline, had but a small part, which was another good thing as she suffered from a bad attack of stage fright which made it very difficult for Captain Jeffcock who was attempting to act as her lover. In spite of Mary's organisational qualities all did not go smoothly, and Mrs W. James, whose part demanded that at one point she should eat an apple, put herself in danger of a stomach ache since the curtain got stuck at that precise moment, and she was forced to go on eating.

Another interest very dear to Mary's heart was the Yorkshire Needlework Guild, with which she had been associated almost from the beginning. Compared to some of the more flamboyant Wilson ventures it lacked glamour, but it gave practical help to many poor and struggling families. During the year 1898 for instance, 9,443 separate articles of clothing had been made or collected, plus 1,303 blankets.(43) A grant was made from the Guild in 1898, and thereafter continued to be made, to the unhappily named Guild of Brave Poor Things — the crippled and otherwise handicapped local sufferers. Long after this time the

"*Masks and Faces*"

A 3-Act Comedy, written by Tom Taylor and Charles Reade.

Dramatis Personae.

Sir Charles Pomander	MR. EILLE NORWOOD
Ernest Vane	MR. T. HOLDEN
Colley Cibber	MR. J. C. LLOYD
Quin	MR. H. GUINNESS
Triplet	MR. PAUL A. RUBENS
Lysimachus	MASTER ROY HOLDEN
Call Boy	MASTER KEITH MENZIES
Snarl	MR. BARNES
Soaper	MR. H. POTTER NEWTON
Burdock	MAJOR BARRINGTON STEPHENS
Colander	MR. HEBDEN
Hunsdon	HON. EVELYN FITZ-GERALD
Pompey	MASTER GUY HOLDEN
Peg Woffington	MISS MURIEL WILSON
Mrs. Vane	MRS. BEERBOHM TREE
Kitty Clive	MRS. RUPERT BECKETT
Mrs. Triplet	MRS. RINGROSE-VOASE
Roxalana	MISS GWENDOLINE BROGDEN
Guests	{ MRS. J. G. MENZIES { MRS. E. LYCETT GREEN

Programme for one of Mary Wilson's matinees in the Palace Theatre, Hull, from 18th to 20th April 1901, during the Second Boer War. Photo by courtesy of Mrs. Hazel Jeffs.

132

name was mercifully changed to The Hull Braves, and the Victorian overtones of charity were thus obliterated. Another grant went to the Sheltering Home for Girls, founded half a century ago by philanthropic citizens including Thomas Wilson, though its headquarters had now moved to No. 37 Peel Street.

The Church

The enviable social status now enjoyed by the Tranby Croft family was associated not only with their generous help to charitable organisations, but also, outwardly at any rate, with their devotion to the established church. Arthur Wilson and his brothers and sisters had been carefully nurtured in the essentials of their faith and creed by their devout parents, and the training would appear to have borne good fruit. It was perhaps fortunate that there was, in the immediate vicinity of Tranby Croft, an excellent opportunity to make a contribution towards the work of God through Mammon. At the time of Arthur and Mary's marriage, the local parish churches in the Anlaby area were All Saints', Hessle and St. Andrew's, Kirkella. In 1865, just before they came into the Riding, a small red brick church had been built at Anlaby by donors who included Mary's relative Frances ("Fanny") Ringrose-Voase. It was administered by the two neighbouring vicars. By 1883, by which time Arthur had established his family both in his great house and in local society, the church was in danger of falling down, its thin walls being completely unable to support the weight of its roof. Here was an opportunity which neither Arthur nor Mary would want to miss. They ascertained that £1,500 was needed to rebuild, and promptly organised a bazaar in the grounds of Tranby Croft which, to their entire satisfaction, produced just over half the sum required in one fell swoop. The rest of the money was soon provided through private donations, and when the work had been done, the Tranby Croft family worshipped there as regularly as the previous generation of Wilsons had done at St. Mary's Lowgate. Both Arthur and Mary became churchwardens, a proof of the value of their services; this was a time when there were few female churchwardens around.

They added considerably to the furnishings and decorations of the church. Before the official opening of the reconstructed St. Peter's in 1885, Mary's father, Edward James Smith, had died. He had completed a distinguished record of service in the Leeds Post Office at his retirement in 1879. He had then come to live with his unmarried son, Mary's brother Henry Wilson Ringrose Smith, now a partner in Abel and Smith's Engineering Company of Hull, at Tranby Park, little more than a stonesthrow from his daughter's residence, but he survived for only two short years. In his memory Mary now bequeathed a carved oak reredos. It was divided into the usual three sections, each one "filled with handsome needlework flowers on a dark ground",(44) (was this Mary's own work?), and on each side of the reredos was the small figure of an angel, carved in oak. These still survive, until recently perched rather uncomfortably on top of the main entrance door, one at each side, but the reredos itself has gone, no doubt a victim of the anti-Victorian attitude in the earlier part of this century.

The chancel floor was retiled, and this was paid for by John Peter George Smith, Mary's uncle, and that same John who had picked up the knuckle bones of skeletons on the Greenwich river front more than half a century ago. He had since moved to Liverpool, had married, and had a son, Francis Rawdon Smith, who settled in Ironbridge into which neighbourhood eventually John himself came, and died there. Mary and her Uncle John also paid for the oak choir stalls in the chancel.

Mr. Leadbetter, the most famous of the Tranby gardeners, holding a spade which Edward, Prince of Wales, used on three occasions. Photo by courtesy of Miss Newton of Hessle.

Raymond (from the Ayre Collection).

Even the children played their part. Raymond, Arthur and Mary's third son, did not survive long enough to go to Eton. Shortly after his thirteenth birthday, and just before Christmas 1885, he succumbed to what was then known as perityphlitis. He was in London, which implies that he was at his preparatory school, and his father came south and installed him in a suite at the Langham Hotel. What could be done, was done. Nurses were in attendance day and night, but the child suffered for thirteen days, fighting the intense pain until all his strength was gone, and death took him. Muriel and Clive now purchased and dedicated to his memory a two light stained glass window. This was placed in the north aisle of Anlaby Church. The left light shows a little lad in a nightgown being called to approach Jesus. Underneath are the words "Jesus called a little child to him". The other light shows the same lad, now at the point of death, being lifted by his mother into the arms of a compassionate angel. The words "God has heard the voice of the lad" confidently assert that the child's sufferings are now over, and indeed, in the tiny window at the apex, there is a picture of Jesus with the child, now smiling and happy. It must have been a comfort to his young sister and brother to know that Raymond was in safe hands. As Victorian children they were allowed to comprehend the ruthlessness of death.

Even in later Victorian times and after Charles Lyall and Charles Darwin had said their say, the village church still dominated local society. Mary Wilson always tried to attend the weekly Mothers' Meetings, which were often spent in making clothes. Mary, and her daughter Muriel, were both excellent cutters, and Muriel regarded this as a duty, and rarely made excuses. If neither of them could attend, Mary would send her maid to preside at the head of the table and do the job.(45)

As good Anglicans the Wilsons endeavoured to support the Church of England on a wider basis than simply within their own parish. Charles and Arthur were both patrons of a Grand Concert given on 12th December 1883 in aid of the Choir Fund of St. John's Church, Newland. Ten years later they were still offering help. The premises at the church had to be enlarged, and a debt of £600 had been incurred. Arthur and Mary gave great support to a bazaar in the Public Rooms to offset this debt. The bazaar lasted three days to give everybody plenty of time to buy. The main attraction, as so often when an event was under Wilson management, was the tableaux vivants. It was perhaps this enthusiasm for what might be termed living art that helped to give the Victorians such a reputation for enjoying their dressing up. No movement was allowed in the tableaux vivants (which, by the beginning of the Second World War, had degenerated into what were inaccurately called "waxworks"). The group simply held a pose for perhaps as long as two minutes, and the artistry was in the grouping and the complete stillness of the participants. Muriel shone in work of this kind. Her Cleopatra (for which she wore a breathtakingly beautiful gown) was described as "stunning". There was also "The Martyrdom of Faith" a scene representing the time of the Spanish Inquisition, a "reproduction" of the popular picture "The Doctor" by Luke Fildes, and two funny scenes "Walls Have Ears" and "The Barber". Only in the final scene was there any movement, and here Muriel was given the opportunity to dance. This was certain to rouse the audience. Special souvenir programmes containing details of all events had been specially printed in red, blue and gold and these, too, helped to earn extra money.(46) The £600 mark was passed before the end of the second day.

It was a great blow to Cottingham church when David Wilson died in February 1893. He had been a churchwarden and consistent helper for years, and his quiet devotion was a further example of the efficacy of the teaching of Thomas and Susannah to their large and ebullient brood. It was perhaps a dreadful warning of things to come that, shortly after his death, the stained glass window which he had had installed in memory of his father, Thomas (which had cost him fully £800) was damaged by hooligans. Fortunately Wilson money enabled the church to send for a glazier from Belgium who was able to match his new glass to the original remaining in the window.(47)

In July 1897 one of the famous Tranby Croft Open Days was given in aid of the great parish church of Holy Trinity in the Old Town of Hull, but sometimes Mary would help a church about which she knew very little. St. Mark's in East Hull served a poor parish and there was desperate need of £1,500 for new vestries, and a further £1,000 for cleaning, a new organ, and outside repair work. The vicar had been at his wits end before he contacted Mary Wilson, and when he dared to approach her, he told her frankly that he did so because he knew that she would give a generous donation. Since she brought Muriel and Clive with her, he probably got three.(48)

Sometimes the charitable events in aid of church funds led to some quite extraordinary happenings. One of these took place at a Fancy Dress Ball in Beverley on the 9th January 1902. The purpose was to obtain funds for new building at St. Mary's Church (which became Clive's church after he married, and was where his two children were christened). It was a children's ball, for these were usually very successful, and it took place in a beautifully decorated Assembly Rooms which had been made to look as much like fairyland as possible. The children were received by Jack's wife Florence, or Queenie, as the family called her. She was presented by the Mayor, Mr Elwell, before proceeding with her duties.

"Then a tootle-tootle was heard, and a little girl in a white muslin frock, big sash and a white baby hat came running in, blowing a tin trumpet. When she was about to shake hands with Mrs Stanley Wilson it was seen that the 'little' girl was considerably taller than the lady, and everyone shrieked with laughter. The perpetrator of the joke was too well known to be able to hide *his*, yes, *his* identity long, and that daring little girl vanished very early in the evening."(49)

Mary Wilson must sometimes have thought that her only value to some local Christian communities was as an opener of bazaars and similar events. Indeed she said as much when, on Wednesday, 12th August 1903, she opened the two day bazaar and garden fete in aid of the little church at Rowley, near Beverley, a hamlet where her grandson, Arthur, Jack and Queenie's elder boy, would one day live. The object of this event was threefold, to pay off the debt on the recently installed heating apparatus, to do the same for the new organ and, if possible, to raise enough funds to build a parish room in Little Weighton, nearby. It was a daunting challenge, but Mary made it clear to her listeners that the last aim had her entire approval. How nice, she said, would a parish room be for a working man. He could sit and read the paper there after his hard day's toil, play backgammon, or divert himself in some other way. She then declared the fete open; and soon afterwards an entertainment was given on the rectory lawn, in which the star performer was Muriel who once again "enhanced her reputation as a gifted elocutionist".(50)

Weddings

With such a large circle of friends and acquaintances who belonged to society, the Wilson family regularly attended engagement parties, weddings and christenings. Muriel, being both wealthy and attractive, could hardly escape, and in the late summer of 1894, when she was nineteen years old, her engagement was announced with Lord Willoughby de Eresby, M.P. for the Horncastle division. If this marriage had come about, it would have linked the Wilson name with one which was centuries old.

Muriel's marriage was arranged for the end of November, and the couple were said to be looking for a small town house. Financially, this should have presented no difficulty. Lord Willoughby de Eresby was very well off, and it was rumoured that Arthur was considering that he would settle an allowance of no less than £4,000 a year on his daughter.(51) However, before September was out, an official announcement gave the news that the marriage would not take place, and no reason was given.(52) Unhappily, it was not the only time when Muriel's matrimonial prospects came to naught.

Her friend Mary Constable of Wassand was more fortunate. Her wedding with George Bulteel of Pamflete in South Devon did take place. This was on a glorious day in early April 1897 at the little parish church of St. Lawrence, Sigglesthorne, a mile away from the family home, and deep in the East Riding countryside. Several members of the Wilson clan had received invitations and Arthur and Mary, Jack and Queenie, Kenneth and Molly duly put in an appearance though they probably did not, as most of the guests did, travel by a special train which ran from Hull Paragon at midday. Muriel, however, was one of a group of three ladies and four gentlemen who should have caught this train, but managed to miss it. This was most unfortunate because the next one, a normal service train, was not due to leave until five minutes past two, ten minutes before the start of the wedding some twenty miles away. Few events could put Muriel off her stride. She went to interview the Passenger Superintendent, Mr E.L. Davies, and as a result of her blandishments he agreed to run another special train and, what is more, arranged for it to be cleaned and brought round to the platform at once. He told them that it would be best for the train to run straight through to Hornsea, the end of the line and a mile away from Sigglesthorne Church. This would prevent it from being held up by the earlier special, and no doubt he assumed that Muriel, with her natural imperiousness, would have no difficulty at all in procuring further transport at this point.

It was not the Superintendent's fault that the party missed the wedding. The second special train had reached Hornsea just after two o'clock, and a mad dash in a carriage would have got them there. But Muriel's group arrived on the platform at Hornsea to find that every single vehicle and already been appropriated. There remained, however, the railway rullymen's horse which was cropping quietly near the line. Muriel sent a porter to fetch it, and they all went round to the premises of a certain Mr Beal, who owned a small trap, (this being more suitable for the conveyance of ladies than the rully itself). It was only possible for the ladies to get into the little carriage, and the gentlemen were told unceremoniously that they would have to walk. Thus they all set off, but, passing a hawker's rully, the gentlemen were also enabled to hitch a lift. By now it was half past two, and as there was still some distance to go, the party decided to make for Wassand itself, which was nearer, and therefore make sure of attending the reception. The butler and housekeeper must have got quite a shock when they saw them arrive.

The choice of wedding presents for those who already had everything is interesting. Mary Wilson gave the young bride a diamond monogram pin cushion. Muriel gave her a jewelled fan, Ethel and Edward a writing table, and Kenneth and Molly another one.(53)

Late in May 1898 Charles Henry and Florence gave a ball to celebrate the engagement of their young daughter, Joan, with the Duke of Manchester. (Their eldest daughter, Millicent, had married Sir Charles Hartopp three years previously). Arthur, Mary and Muriel attended, and watched the presents flood in, but almost immediately the wedding was postponed until September. The occasion gave the reporter from the *Hull News* the opportunity to voice his opinion that the three daughters at Warter Priory, although very beautiful, were not to be compared with their cousin Muriel who, he said "has won and holds a position in smart society seldom attained by smart, titled married women".(54) The Wilsons, he went on, had entered London society a few years ago "and are now not only in it, but of it". Mary Wilson was recognised as one of society's best hostesses. "Her parties are of the highest and smartest, and the Tranby Croft episode", the Baccarat Scandal, "is not openly alluded to". It was not a flattering comment to the Warter Wilsons. After all it was their daughter who was getting married.

Shades of Muriel! At the beginning of July a further postponement of Joan's wedding was announced, this time for a year. The bridegroom was, in fact, away. He had set off on a round-the-world-tour, and was said to be heading for Australia. He was so very young, commented the *Hull News*, but when he returned, he would get married.(55) Alas! Joan changed her mind; but this time she stood the course. Her engagement to Guy Fairfax of Bilbrough Hall, near York, was announced early in May 1899 and, the marriage itself was celebated, as Millicent's had been, at St. Mark's Church, North Audley Street early in July. It was a very fine wedding. Daisy, Princess of Pless was a guest, and the little daughter of the Hon. George and Mrs Keppel was a train bearer.

Within the Tranby Croft family, those weddings which did take place clearly indicated the success of their social climb. Between 1885 and 1907 all the children except Raymond, who died, and Muriel, whose choice was so great that she appeared to be unable

137

to make up her mind, did marry, and marry well. The two elder girls were the first to go, although the younger, Ethel, beat her sister by a short head, her wedding taking place locally on Thursday, 23rd April 1885. Ethel's husband, Edward Lycett Green, was the son of an influential Wakefield iron master. His father, Edward Green, had leased the Elizabethan Old Hall at Heath, where the family had now lived for some years, but in 1879 and 1880 he had had built a delightful Victorian mansion at Ken Hill in Norfolk, his architect being John J. Stevenson who built it in the then advanced Queen Anne style.(56) It was hardly finished when the Prince of Wales heard that excellent shooting was to be had there, and so he came down to pay them a visit. The rise of the Greens ran parallel to that of the Wilsons, for both made much money and practised philanthropy and, like Charlie Wilson, Edward Green served his birthplace in parliament, though Charlie's service was three times as long as his.(57) Edward had invented a preheating system known as Green's Economiser, which he successfully marketed. His wife, formerly Mary Lycett of Bowden, gave her matronymic to all her children who became known by both surnames. Young Edward had been told by his father to "ride the family into society" which the young man proceeded to do quite literally when he became the Master of the York and Ainsty in 1886 — another parallel with the Wilsons. At the same time his father was enobled, and took as his motto "Waste not" which was certainly logical.(58) By the time of this marriage Arthur and Mary had their London house at 13 Grosvenor Crescent, but the marriage, as befitted two individuals born in Yorkshire, took place at the Parish Church in Hessle, the rebuilding of the Anlaby Church not yet being complete. It was one of the events of the year.

The Wilsons' family friend Rev. J. Foord, the vicar of Kirkella, and Rev. A. Kaye, the vicar of Hessle, conducted the service jointly, and the organ was played by Captain Hullett who had been involved in the amateur theatricals at Tranby Croft earlier in the decade. When the wedding party had returned to the house the local photographer, Mr Drinkwater, had made everything ready for the official photographs which were taken straight away before the wedding breakfast. The breakfast was a very grand affair, served in a large marquee brilliantly illuminated by electricity, which had been erected on the west side of the house. That evening a dinner at the Station Hotel in Hull suitably finished off the day of rejoicing. All the regular staff at Wilson's were invited to this, heads of departments, captains, engineers of steam ships and senior clerks being fed in the quadrangle of the hotel. Firemen and outdoor staff had their celebration at the Cross Keys Hotel, and junior clerks were entertained at the Wilson Line offices.

One important guest who was unable to attend the wedding was Charlie. He was wheezing and sickly when he left Warter with his wife. They got as far as brother David's house in Cottingham, but by that time all that Charlie wanted was to go to bed. The bronchial attack was a severe one, and the doctor insisted that he should stay where he was. His wife and David went on without him. Apart from jewellery, the young couple received handsome presents from the family. Edward himself gave Ethel an old marqueterre tray and a silver coffee pot. His parents gave them a brougham, a Broadwood grand piano (which Ethel would adore to have), a Louis Quinze clock, a Brussels lace veil, a chest of plate and a set of furs. Arthur and Mary added a silver mounted dressing bag and a double Chippendale settee. The official gift of Ethel's brothers and sisters consisted of silver backed brushes, bottles, boxes, and a looking glass in a case. Raymond, however bought a personal gift, a fitted handbag, and no doubt Ethel treasured it after his untimely death later that year. Young Clive felt that what Raymond could do, he could do; and he

Menu du Déjeuner.

Printaniere à la Royale.

Cotelettes d' Agneau aux Petites Pois.

Cailles bardées aux feuilles de Vin.

Saumon à l' Norvegienne.

Pâte de Pigeons de Bordeaux.

Galantine à lá Parisienne.

Jambon. Bœuf à l' Aspic.

Quatiers d' Agneau.

Salades d' Homard.

Oeufs de Pluviers en Aspic.

Cailles à la Bohemienne.

Filets de Fruites à la Montpelier.

Cotelettes de Mouton en Belle Vue.

Chand froid de Poulets.

Langue découpées à l' Aspic.

Petites Pains de Volaille.

Poulets rotis découpées.

Crèmes à l' Italienne.

Gelées Variées.

Pâtisserie Assortie.

Luncheon menu for the wedding of Ethel with Edward Lycett Green (from the Ayre Collection).

139

presented his sister with an olivewood almanac. Uncle David gave a £50 cheque. Uncle Henry Smith gave them an antique silver tea service. Three of the housemaids at Tranby gave an oak biscuit box, and the vicar and choir of St Peter's Anlaby, for whose church the Wilson family had recently done so much, presented them with a large and handsomely bound copy of *Hymns Ancient and Modern*. The Tranby Croft weddings were off to a good start.(59)

Tottie's marriage to John Graham Menzies took place less than two years later, on Tuesday, 8th February 1887, in the now completely rebuilt Anlaby Church. The bridegroom always known as Freddie, a member of a family of distillers of Scotch whisky, hailed from Linlithgow. Once again Tranby Croft was decorated, a triumphal arch near the house proclaiming "God bless the bridal pair" and "Long life and happiness". Flags waved on top of it, there were hunting trophies there too, and the crest Arthur Wilson had adopted - a griffin's head turned left, and the motto "Semper vigilans". As before, monograms of the two young people appeared on the arches which decorated the drive. Flags waved at the top of the tower, and from a second arch which stood at the entrance to the park, a message wished "Health, Prosperity and Happiness" to Tottie and Freddie, and also romantically pronounced "Hearts and Hands Uniting".

The bridal procession left Tranby Croft at 2.15 pm and all the way to the church the bridal party was cheered by crowds which packed the pavement every inch of the way. Tottie, who had a sweet face and gentle expression, wore the traditional white dress in satin with a long train. Her six bridesmaids (Ethel had ten), wearing cream brocade skirts with grey overskirts and coats of cream satin merveilleieux, included Muriel and the three Warter cousins Enid, Joan and Gladys. They carried bouquets of pink roses, and were each given diamond brooches with "8th February 1887" inscribed upon them.

This was a very important wedding for St Peter's which had, in the words of the local reporter, been "transmogrified". Ten times the number of people who could be accommodated had turned up, and most of them were now waiting near the entrance gate, from which an awning of crimson cloth covered the carpet along which Tottie would walk. At the church porch climbing plants flanked an inscription which read "Live in Love".

Rev. J. Foord commenced the marriage service in which he was assisted by the bride's cousin, Rachel's son, the Rev. Edgar Lambert. The large and fashionable congregation took part heartily, knowing that bells would be ringing in Hull in honour of the occasion, and that all the Wilson ships in dock would be decorated overall, and would be sounding off their sirens to add to the joy of the wedding day. When Freddie and Tottie had departed, the guests straggled back to their rooms to prepare themselves for the ball, which was held that night at Tranby Croft. It was another very successful Wilson wedding.(60)

The appearance in court of "Jack in the box" at the time of the Baccarat Scandal seemed to have done the son and heir of Tranby Croft no harm. In fact, Jack's wedding came soon after the furore had died down, when on Wednesday, 24th February 1892 he married Alice Cecil Agnes, daughter of the late Sir Edmund Filmer, 9th Bart. and Lady Filmer (who gave her away), a girl whose family traced their descent from Edward II in the fourteenth century.

They were married at St Peter's Church, Eaton Square, not much more than a stone's throw from his parents' new London residence in Grosvenor Place. February is not the most attractive month for a wedding, but with Lent coming on Jack and his bride, Queenie, either had to get a move on, or wait. The guest list included the Archbishop of York and his family, the Duke and Duchess of Wellington, the Earl of Coventry (shades of baccarat) and the Earl of Chesterfield (soon to become the husband of Enid Wilson of Warter Priory). But there was a hefty contingent from the Riding and York, which included Sir Joseph Terry of chocolate fame, the Russell Starrs (so devoted to the well being of music and drama in Hull), old Mrs Voase from Anlaby House, and David Wilson making one of his last appearances with his widowed sister Elizabeth Sanderson.

At precisely 2.15 in the afternoon the choir (perhaps not so precisely) singing "When Morning gilds the skies" led in the bride and her mother to join Jack and his best man, Sir Cecil Pery Van Notten Pole, at the chancel steps. The ceremony was actually conducted by Rev. J. Foord, the Vicar of Kirkella, but he was assisted by the Vicar of St. Peter's, Rev. J. Storrs.

Queenie wore a dress of rich, white, duchess satin, plain, with a long court train, and draped with old Point lace. She was followed by six bridesmaids, two of whom were her sisters. They, too, wore white. The reception had been arranged by Lady Filmer to be held at the residence of Baron and Baroness Henry de Worms in Grosvenor Place. A charming feature was the bestowing of favours by the bridesmaids. Each of them had small ornamental hampers in white wickerwork trimmed with green to match their own dresses, and they handed out sprigs of orange blossom, sprays of white heather, and bunches of forget me not, each in its own little basket.

This was certainly the smartest of the three weddings so far. The presents were magnificent. Jack gave his wife a diamond ring, a diamond pendant, a watch with the date 1892 engraved upon it in diamonds, a diamond bandeau for her hair and a diamond tiara.[61] After the honeymoon he brought her back to Yorkshire where they settled in a small country house at Raywell, some three miles to the north east of Tranby Croft. Here they raised a family of two sons, and Jack turned his attention to politics. He had always been a Conservative by commitment, unlike his father, who was drawn into it after his disappointment over Gladstone's acceptance of the principle of Home Rule for Ireland in 1886. The two of them together became a formidable team.

Would Kenneth be able to follow Jack's lead in the matrimonial stakes? He was very different from his mercurial brother. Slower of speech, indeed he had a slight speech defect, conscientious and hard working, he might well have shown little social ambition for himself. However, the 1890s saw gay parties at 19 Grosvenor Place; the friendship of the Prince of Wales and the Wilsons was known and accepted by society, and when Kenneth did marry, on Thursday 27th June 1895, it was the same all over again. This wedding also took place at St. Peter's, Eaton Square, but Rev. J. Foord of Kirkella did not come to take the service. Instead it was the bride's uncle, the Hon. Rev. Augustus Byron M.A., Rector of Kirby Mallory in Leicestershire who did the job, assisted by Rev. J. Wallis of Hindlip and Rev. John Storrs, whose church it was.

Kenneth was marrying Molly Hacket, daughter of Mr George A.B. Disney Hacket J.P. of Moor Hall, Sutton Coldfield. For her wedding Molly wore a gown of ivory duchess satin with a very long, plain, beautifully shaped skirt and bodice. She was one up on Queenie, for she had seven bridesmaids, Muriel being the principal one. The two young women were, in fact, great friends. They were both very fond of Winston Churchill, almost their exact contemporary, who used to take them out to dinner. Indeed, the second bridesmaid was Maud Spencer-Churchill. The youngest was Phyllis, the second of Edward and Ethel's two girls. The best man was Charles Henry's eldest son, also called Charles but known to the family as Tommy. The reception was held at the home of Lord and Lady Hindlip at 33 Hill Street, Berkeley Square. Lady Randolph Churchill was there, and so was Lord Edward Somerset, who had played baccarat at Tranby. Much of the honeymoon was spent at Bayham Abbey, Lamberhurst, Kent, as Kenneth preferred this to going abroad as his brother had done. As at Jack's wedding the Wilson ships were dressed overall and sounded their sirens, and once again the bellringers at Holy Trinity Church were paid to peal all the day.(62)

Kenneth brought his wife to live at Roehampton Court. In 1903 their only child, Hilary, was born, and from that moment Kenneth was her devoted slave. Hilary inherited her father's retiring disposition, though as a little child she prattled readily enough. When the family moved out to Wimbledon at the end of the First World War, by which time the Wilson family business had been sold, Kenneth was able to live the life of a country gentleman, and develop and extend his estate at Cannizaro.

Clive's marriage did not quite run according to plan, although it was the most romantic of the lot. He had fallen in and out of love several times, but in the latter months of 1906 he had determined to marry his sister's Italian tutor, Elvira Maria Ercilia, daughter of Carlo Magherini of Florence. Elvira had been at Tranby Croft for some time, for she had attended the opening ceremony of the Victoria Buildings for the workingmen of Hull with Muriel in 1903. When Clive announced his intention, his parents, with a fair amount of experience to guide them, thought that he might soon change his mind. He did not, and would not, and on Thursday, 24th January 1907 he and Elvira were married at 2.30 in the afternoon at St. George's Church, Hanover Square, "the ultra fashionable church for such gatherings" as the local paper said.(63) Few people knew Elvira. She was slight, dark, graceful and very beautiful, and she was a Roman Catholic; but Clive, who was a handsome lad, cheerful and adaptable and always good company, swept her completely off her feet, and she was as much in love as he was himself. Clive was also a hero. He had served with distinction in the Second Boer War and held a D.S.O.

Many guests came from the Riding and a detachment of yeomanry "of whom the bridegroom is a popular and distinguished officer" lined the aisle in their scarlet and blue uniforms which went well, the *Hull News* reporter said later, with the red carpet. The best man was Clive's good friend, the solicitor Jack Travers. Elvira's family did not attend, and she was given away by Mr Lockett Agnew, the art connoisseur, at whose home in Portman Square the reception was held. Unlike the previous brides Elvira did not wear white. Her lovely gown was of the palest grey chiffon over silk of the same shade, and was made in half Empire style, which suited her slim figure. She wore a large hat of pale grey tulle with a grey feather and a band of silver tissue gleaming among the tulle. Her shower bouquet contained pink roses, and her one bridesmaid was little Hilary, Kenneth's daughter, now nearly four years old, and as charming as she looked in a long picture frock of pale pink velvet, a silver Juliet cap on her head with a sprig of mistletoe in it. She performed her duties admirably.

The fully choral service was taken by the resident rector. Just before the benediction an unusual and elaborate setting of "O Perfect Love" was sung, the second verse of which was taken as a solo by a very good choirboy. Clive and Elvira both looked radiant and happy.

Mrs Lockett Agnew received the guests at the reception. She, too, was wearing a half Empire style gown in Wedgwood blue silk. Mary Wilson was in mole grey voile with touches of turqouise blue velvet. She wore a big grey hat with feathers. Tottie wore a striking outfit of emerald green cloth topped by a gauzy pale blue hat. Ethel might not have been pleased with the *Hull News* reporter who described her, somewhat ambiguously, as

Family snapshot c.1896 in the Billiard Room at Tranby Croft. Back row, left to right: Edward Lycett Green, Arthur Wilson, Muriel, Molly, Kenneth and Freddie. Middle row: Ethel (with Francis on her knee and David standing beside her), Clive (with Phyllis Green on his knee), Mary Wilson, Nancy Green, Queenie (with young Arthur on her knee) and Tottie. Front row: Stewart Menzies, Eddie Green and Keith Menzies. Photo by courtesy of Mr. Raymond C. Wilson.

"looking wonderfully young". She was wearing black velvet with a little French "bowler" hat of green velvet with feathers, which were mauve. Queenie, Jack's wife, wore mulberry velvet with a big, feathered purple hat; Molly, Kenneth's wife was in black velvet, elaborately braided, and her hat had two cerise feathers on it. Muriel was in pale blue with an ermine stole, and a big hat covered with pale blue feathers. Nancy Green, now a young lady of almost nineteen, was in pink, with pink feathers in her hat. Jack's fair haired eleven year old boy, Arthur, came. Perhaps he felt a little out of things, for he was rather too old for Hilary. She was having a lovely time, and seemed to bear no traces of the reserve which came later. Clive had given her a lovely little diamond pendant with two large pearl drops, and she danced round the assembled company showing it to anybody who would look.

Once again the ships hooted and the bells rang in Hull. The stable workers at Tranby Croft and Beverley were given a dinner in honour of the occasion, and a similar treat was arranged for the members of A Squadron of the Imperial Yeomanry at the Walton Street Riding School which was where Clive had done his training. The honeymoon, as might be expected, was spent in Florence so that the bride's family could meet her husband. Fred Wilson, old Thomas' artistic son and therefore Clive's uncle, was still alive and living there. He was now married and it is interesting to speculate whether Clive chose to renew the relationship.(64) After the honeymoon the young couple settled at St. Mary's House, Beverley, to the east side of the church. There, their two children were born. When, some years later the house burned down, they moved to a house on the edge of the Beverley Race Course, which was always known as Little Tranby. There the children grew up, Thetis, called after her Aunt Muriel and her great grandmother Smith, and Raymond, whose name commemorated his father's brother who did not survive to manhood because so little was known by the medical profession about how to treat appendicitis.

Funerals

With a family as big as that of the Wilsons, it was perhaps surprising that some of them ever came out of mourning at all, and in the late Victorian era quite a number of elderly people did not. One of the saddest funerals of that time was that of Arthur Wilson's friend Christopher Sykes. By proposing Arthur as Master of the Holderness way back in 1878, Christopher had helped to make possible the family's social success, and he must have mused sadly sometimes how much more fortunate they had been than he had himself. It will be remembered that he was seriously embarrassed financially at the time of the Baccarat Scandal in 1890, and shortly afterwards he knew that he would have to sell his estate at Brantinghamthorpe. He had served his Prince not wisely, but too well. Before the decade ended he was a very sick man, but he still answered the Prince's call for service, although physically he was totally unfit to do so. In 1898, while Christopher was taking a cure in Hamburg, the Prince fell on board the royal yacht and broke his ankle. This put him in bed which he could not abide, and he sent for Christopher to come and cheer him up. Christopher was, in truth, entering on his last days on earth and was feeling so ill that he begged to be excused. The Prince would have none of this, and summoned him again. The whole of the latter part of Christopher's life had been spent in serving His Royal Highness, and in spite of his extreme exhaustion he was incapable of ignoring this second call to duty. Somehow he struggled to the yacht and presented himself. The Prince, who was by no means heartless, took one look at him and realised immediately that he should not have come. When, shortly afterwards, Christopher asked to be allowed to go home, permission was immediately given. He died ten days before Christmas. He was not an old man, only 67 years of age, but his life style had worn him down, as it had worn down his financial assets. The net value of his personal estate was declared to be nil. His father, Sir Tatton, had once won a gold racing cup at Lincoln. This Christopher had originally intended to give to Lord Rosebery (who won the Derby as Prime Minister twice running); instead, it was now given to the Prince of Wales, a true example of devotion in life and death.(65)

Entertaining for pleasure and profit

The late Victorian era highlighted rejoicing and grief, which was regarded as natural, and on the whole there was no studied plan to try and avoid it. This seems to have applied particularly to the wealthy and socially acceptable. While life remained, they were determined to live it to the full. January was usually an excellent month for parties, also the weather during that month normally left much to be desired from the point of view of outside activities. January 1899 gives a good example of how society entertained itself in the Riding.

The first event was the "White Rose" ball held in the Assembly Rooms, York on the 12th. It was organised especially for one hundred unmarried ladies of the county, among whom were Charles Henry's Enid and Joan, and Arthur's Muriel. That same week most of the party were at the Sheriff's Ball in Hull, and it was said to have been the best since Arthur Wilson was sheriff ten years previously. This year the hosts were Mr Harold and Miss Elsie Reckitt (whose family marketed that famous washing day standby Reckitt's Blue, and later on, Dettol). They lived at Swanland Manor, less than a mile from Tranby

Croft, and the Wilsons had visited Mr Harold's father, then Mr James Reckitt but since enobled in 1894, from their very early days in the Riding.

"The cream of Hull Society" wrote the reporter from the *Hull News* "were there, and direct countenance was given to the reception by the presence of Mr and Mrs Arthur Wilson and party from Tranby Croft, and many other county families."(66)

After such a glowing testimonial, it is not surprising to find that Mary Wilson chose to wear a dress which she knew would be one of the most striking in the room. It was in black and white with sleeves of ecru lace which also draped the bodice and was caught up "with many magnificent diamond brooches". The collar was in the Elizabethan style, and she wore a wig to match it, wide across the front. Muriel played up to this without overdoing it. Her dress was of black net, sequinned, and she wore a bunch of lily of the valley on her shoulder. Her wig was a high one with hanging curls, and on top of it waved a black ostrich plume.

Next it was Charles Henry's turn. His ball, during the same week at Warter Priory "may very properly be designated the East Riding gentry's ball", so wrote the reviewer.(67) Since the house was some 2 1/2 miles from the nearest station, Charlie had organised no fewer than 50 broughams to pick the guests up there, and he had ordered one special train to leave Hull at 9.30 in the evening, and a second to leave York at a similar time. Preparations at the Priory had been going on for days, and had called for major reorganisation. Armies of servants had moved in. Between two and three hundred gilt chairs had arrived, and Herr Wurm's White Viennese Band (which had made a big impression at York earlier in the week) had been told to come to Warter. Charlie's chef was working miracles with sugar confectionery. He created, among other items, a huge steamship, a lighthouse, a four-in-hand and a hansom, and all were lit from inside by electric bulbs. On the night of the ball one individual was hired to do nothing else but open oysters, and several women, whose skill with a knife was guaranteed, were there simply to cut bread — and cut it very thinly.

There were to be 300 guests, including not only Princess Daisy of Pless who, born a Cornwallis West, was often around the social scene, but also her tall, fair husband, Prince Henry, who wore a white uniform. There was also Mr Cecil Brownlow who later in the year travelled with a Wilson party to America, and George Cornwallis West who became, a year later, the young husband of Jennie, the widow of Randolph Churchill. At the ball, the guests took part in one of the favourite pastimes of late Victorian society — the cotillion. It was hardly a dance, but more like a procession which wound its way to the dining room in serpentine fashion, thus allowing every dress and every uniform to be displayed to the fullest advantage. The little children at the Fancy Dress Balls to aid the Park Street hospital were fond of doing it. The cotillion at Warter had a centrepiece. A Miss Katie Ward was dressed as the Queen of Flowers, and she sat in a decorated Russian sleigh which was pulled by a donkey, fortunately a docile one.

It was arranged that the ball would end at 3 o'clock, when the 50 broughams which had been waiting patiently all night lined up to transport the guests back to Nunburnholme station, in time for the trains to Hull and York, which were due to leave at four. Thomas Lockey, a cab driver from Hessle Road, Hull had deposited his load at the station and had begun his solitary clip clop back home in the bitter cold of the January morning. By 5 o'clock he was well past Market Weighton, and was heading for the hill top route over to Beverley. Suddenly he saw in front of him one of the new fangled motor cars. It was in the middle of the road, and did not move as Lockey approached. As he came alongside the cabman reined in, and jumped down to investigate, which was easy to do as the car was an open tourer. Lockey had thought that the vehicle was unattended, but it was not. Huddled on the driving seat, chilled to the bone, and so near collapse that for some moments he was incapable of speech, was one of the guests from the Priory. The poor man had left the party at one o'clock and, with a friend, had attempted to drive to the house of Mr George Duncombe (a stalwart supporter of the local Conservative party) where he was staying. This was in Beverley, and the car had broken down some seven miles short of its goal. No doubt it found the steep hill to the east of Market Weighton too much of a challenge. The friend at this juncture had rather ungallantly opted to walk the rest of the way. This much Lockey was able to educe from the frozen gentleman, though with difficulty. He realised from his own experience that the situation was a dangerous one. To leave the gentleman where he was might well be fatal. He persuaded him to get into his brougham, covered him with all the rugs that were there, and delivered him safely to Mr Duncombe, who identified him as Mr Edward Clifton from London.(68) Mr Clifton recovered and was none the worse for his experience, but he must have taken back to the south country the impression of a vast and frozen Yorkshire, as many another had done before him.

A week later it was the turn of the Tranby Croft Wilsons to made their contribution to the month's festivities. They, too, had 300 guests, many from the ranks of the aristocracy, and they also had the same Viennese band. They had, however, gone to tremendous trouble over the floral decorations — always a feature at Tranby Croft. The house blazed with light. The reception rooms blazed with colour. The main door was closed so that the ante hall could be used as a sitting out room, and very pretty it was with its dainty furnishings and masses of flowers. The modest side door was given unwonted stature on this night, since this was where the guests would enter. From the drive to the door was a covered way, and the corridor which led from the door to the central hall had had a temporary dado of red and blue tacked onto its wall. The hall floor shone with polish and the balcony above was festooned with greenery and smilax. A special supper room had been provided in a tent on the croquet lawn, and this was entered from Mary Wilson's morning room. It was decorated in cream and gold, and against this were massed arrangements of scarlet poinsettias, there was no other colour. Two tall palms stood at either end of the ridge pole.

For this night, the normal dining room was given over to serving refreshments, with seats in the corners for those sitting out the dances. All the tables had cloths of fine drawn linen, and that on the long buffet table was decorated with a swallow in flight. A cover on one of the side tables was even more remarkable. It showed huge strawberries worked in a heavy padded pattern. In this room large bunches of grapes grown in the Tranby vineries were suspended from silver bars. The drawing rooms were all thrown open and were heavy with the scent of roses, lilies (there were lilies of the valley as well as amaryllis), malmaisons, carnations and azaleas. Dignified palms stood in every one of them. The electrically lit conservatory beyond the drawing room (which was part of Arthur Wilson's rebuilding of the 1880s) was fitted out with comfortable sofas, and here Mary had placed Moraco's portrait of the latest scion of the family, Jack's young son, Arthur, as well as several signed photographs of members of the Royal Family.

Mary dressed for this occasion in her usual black, but Muriel, with her dark beauty, was breathtaking in pink mousseline de soie, with many frills around the skirt. On her shoulder a big rosette of black chiffon caught the ends of a sash powdered with chiffon.

Banksia roses formed the shoulder straps.(69) The beauty of the setting and the dresses and uniforms was almost excessive, even before they got down to the business of the evening. Local society needed stamina to get through January.

The Wilsons were a very patriotic family, and by 1899 Britain was again at war with the Boers. Their contribution to the war effort was both generous and valuable. By 1902 the soldiers were coming home, and in November of that year there also came to Hull, General French who, unlike some other generals who were considered to have bungled badly during the war, had "his hero worshippers in Hull and did well after the relief of Kimberley".(70) Arthur and Mary, whose son Clive had been out to the veldt, offered the hospitality of Tranby Croft and on Friday, 3rd November, just before six o'clock in the evening they drove their guests to the Guildhall in Hull where they all had dinner with the mayor and mayoress, Mr and Mrs Alfred Gelder. After this they drove out to the barracks, where the mayor made a speech. He was glad to tell his listeners that a subscription list to pay for a monument to those who had fallen in the war had already reached over £1,000. General French also made a speech, and this took many people by surprise. They had thought of him as a man of action, but he proved to have a slow and stammering delivery. Nevertheless, he was well received, and after he sat down the members of the Hull Musical Union got up and, with their soloist, Miss Kennedy, proceeded to sing suitably. The *Hull News* wrote up the event, perhaps less than tactfully, under the heading "Big Guns and Little guns".

The following year the Prince and Princess of Wales visited Hull on 12th May 1903. By now Arthur and Mary were beginning to leave the limelight to their children, and were no longer so much in the news as they had been, but when the royal train steamed into Paragon Station they were there on the reserved platform, waiting to meet the royal couple. A crowded programme had been prepared, which included the unveiling of a statue of the late Queen Victoria and the opening of the square where the statue stood, which would henceforth be known as Victoria Square. The statue stands to this day, our late beloved Queen enthroned above — of all things — some public lavatories, the expression on her face bearing mute testimony to the fact that she is not amused.

At night, after the departure of the royal guests, the Wilson males congregated in the Imperial Hotel, Hull where the officers and men of the East Riding of Yorkshire Imperial Yeomanry (A Squadron) dined, if not wisely, extremely well. Captain Arthur Stanley Wilson M.P. the Commander of the Hull Squadron, presided. Captain Clive Wilson D.S.O. proposed the toast to the Mayor, Sheriff and Corporation. Arthur Wilson responded to the toast "Our Guests", and Oswald Sanderson proposed the toast to the Regiment.(71)

In mid October 1906 the Boer War was in the news again. A three day event had been organised in the Assembly Rooms in aid of the Imperial Yeomanry and the Walton Street Riding School. This took the usual form of a fashionable bazaar, being opened on the first day by no less a person than "Bobs", Lord Roberts of Second Boer War fame. He was staying at Escrick Park, the guest of Lord Wenlock, and would be his guest of honour at the Hull barracks, for Lord Wenlock commanded the East Yorkshire Imperial Yeomanry (of which Clive Wilson was an active member). "Bobs" would arrive at Paragon Station in mufti, but would be immediately shown into the Station Hotel where he would change into his Field Marshall's uniform. A guard of honour, consisting of twelve men from the A Squadron would then escort him to the Riding School where Clive would receive him. After his inspection of the unit, "Bobs" would go on to the Assembly Rooms, and after his reception there by the Lord Mayor, Sheriff, and officers of the East Riding Imperial Yeomanry, would proceed to open the bazaar.(72)

This had been carefully and lovingly constructed to represent a camp at Scarborough Castle. All the usual stalls were there, and members of the Wilson clan much in evidence. There was a gypsy fortune teller, and also a concert in the Lecture Hall. Muriel was to recite "Hal the Highwayman" and Clive would sing his coster songs. Upstairs Molly directed a café chantant, which had secured the services of a Ladies' Banjo Band. When they were tired, Mr Tom Holden and the Beverley Coons would entertain. Karl Kapps' Blue Hungarian Band played all the time. It would not be the organisers' fault if "Bobs" were not entertained. However, he listened to none of it, for he had another appointment to see Hymers College. So he missed the rifle range, and the American Bar which Clive came to run as soon as he had finished singing, but "Bobs" had got the bazaar off to a good start and the outcome was all that the organisers could have wished. It could hardly be called a charity, but defence of the realm was an issue which would have great significance in the very near future.

(1) *Hull News* Supplement 18.4.1891.
(2) *Ethel Lady Thomson: Clifton Lodge* (Hutchinson 1955) pp. 82-83.
(3) *Hull News* 5.2.1873 pp. 3 and 4.
(4) See *J.D. Hicks: Our Orphans* (Lockington Publishing Co. 1983) pp. 22-25.
(5) For an account of the Bazaar see *Hull News* 4.10.1884 4.10.1884 p. 3 cols. a/g, and *J.D. Hicks* op.cit. pp.22-25.
(6) *Hull News* 11.11.1884 Supplement p.4.
(7) Ibid 4.10.1884 p.3 cols. a/g.
(8) Ibid 25.8.1894 p.5 col. d.
(9) Ibid 9.12.1893 p.3 col.g.
(10) Ibid 13.8.1898 p.2 col.e.
(11) Ibid 12.2.1898 p.6 col.d.
(12) See also *George Patrick: A Plague on you Sir* (Archibald and Johnsons Ltd. 1981) pp.57-59.
(13) *Hull News* 26.5.1894 p.8 col.d.
(14) Ibid 10.4.1897 p.2 col.g.
(15) Ibid 7.1.1899 p.10 cols. d/e.
(16) Ibid 4.1.1902 p.4 col.c.
(17) Ibid 28.11.1903 p.10 col.d.
(18) Rhoda Lamb: "The Life and Times of Charles Henry Wilson, 1st Baron Nunburnholme 1833-1907". (Unpublished thesis submitted for the Department of Social Studies, Hull University 1974. p.25).
(19) *Hull Lady* December 1901 p.7.
(20) *Hull News* 6.8.1898 p.8 col.c.
(21) Ibid 15.8.1903 p.9. See also Rhoda Lamb op.cit. p.26.
(22) Ibid 16.11.1889 Supplement p.4 col.a.
(23) Ibid 4.9.1893 p.5.
(24) Ibid 25.2.1893 p.5 col.c.
(25) Ibid 24.2.1894 p.6 col.g.
(26) Ibid 12.8.1893 p.6 col.c.
(27) *Ellerman's On Shore and Afloat* 31.3.1970 p.20.
(28) *Hull Lady* No. 7 1902 p.4.
(29) Almost certainly George (later Sir George) Alexander Macfarren 1813-1887.
(30) *Madame Fashion in Hull* April 1901 p.2.
(31) *Hull Daily Mail* Tuesday, 31.5.1983 p.6 col.a/d. Information for this article was supplied by Dr. and Mrs T. Broadbent, biographers of Ethel Leginska, to whom I am personally indebted for information.
(32) *Hull News* 13.6.1896 p.8 col.f.
(33) Ibid 16.1.1897 p.3 col.f.
(34) *W. Macqueen Pope: Gaiety, Theatre of Enchantment* (W.H. Allen 1949) See references to Brogden.

(35) *D. Castle: "Sensation" Smith of Drury Lane* (Charles Skilton Ltd. 1984) p.191.

(36) *Hull Daily Mail* 9.4.1938 p.5 col.d.

(37) Ibid 23.11.1927 p.5 col.a. Event recalled in obit. notice of Mary Wilson's death.

(38) *O'Hara: Men of the City 1914* (Hull City and County Printing Co. Ltd.).

(39) *Hull Daily Mail* 9.4.1938 p.5 col.d.

(40) I am indebted to Dr Philip Muller and his patient for information concerning this programme.

(41) *Hull News* 15.2.1896 p.6 col. c.

(42) Ibid.

(43) Ibid 10.12.1898 p.3 col.d.

(44) *Bulmer's History and Directory of East Yorkshire* 1892 p.668.

(45) *The Hull Lady* No. 7 1902 p.23.

(46) *Hull News* 16.12.1893 p.6 cols.b/c.

(47) Ibid 7.10.1893 p.5 col. b.

(48) Ibid 23.4.1898 p.2 col. c.

(49) *The Hull Lady* February 1902 p.34 col.b.

(50) *Hull News* 15.8.1903 p.3 col.f.

(51) Ibid 1.9.1894 and 15.9.1894 p.3 col.f.

(52) Ibid 22.9.1894 p.3 col.a.

(53) Ibid 10.4.1897 p.2 col.f/g and *Hull Times* 10.4.1897 p.10 col.b/d.

(54) Ibid 21.5.1898 p.6 col.f.

(55) Ibid 9.7.1898 p.3 col.d quoted from "Belle" in *World*.

(56) *Burke and Saville: Guide to Country Houses Vol. 3 East Anglia* (London Burke's Peerage Ltd. 1981).

(57) Edward Green served from 1885 to 1892, Charles Wilson from 1874 to 1905.

(58) see *M. Girouard: The Victorian Country House* (Yale University Press 1979) chapter 29 p.366 and article by James Fox in *Sunday Times Colour Supplement* 2.3.1969.

(59) *Hull News* 25.4.1885 p.8 col. a.

(60) Ibid 12.2.1887 Supplement p.4 cols.a/b

(61) Ibid 27.2.1892 Supplement p.4 col.d.

(62) Ibid 29.6.1895 p.3 col.e.

(63) Ibid 26.1.1907 p.7 cols.a/b.

(64) Ibid

(65) Ibid 19.1.1899 p.9 col.c. Also *Christopher Simon Sykes: The Visitors' Book* op.cit. pp.101 & 104.

(66) Ibid 14.1.1899 p.8 cols. a/b.

(67) Ibid p.12. col.b.

(68) Ibid 21.1.1899 p.8.

(69) Ibid 28.1.1899 p.10 col.b.

(70) Ibid 4.10.1902 p.3 cols.b/c.

(71) Ibid 16.5.1903 pp.9-10.

(72) From Scrap Book 1, compiled by Joseph H. Vickers, of events locally 1905-7, p.96. The extract is from the *Eastern Morning News*. I am indebted to Mr J.D. and Mrs M.D. Hicks for the use of this material.

CHAPTER EIGHT

The Wilson Line ships in the late Victorian and Edwardian era, and the story of the only indentured apprentice

While Arthur and Mary were building up their impressive social prestige the family firm was being transformed by Charlie and Arthur. When they took over in the mid sixties David had already decided to leave them to it, and virtually ceased to influence their policy. By the early '70s Wilson ships had a regular service to Norway, Sweden, St. Petersburg and the Riga, Stettin and Dantzig. Large steamers also served Odessa and Constantinople as well as Trieste. A service was opened to Bombay, Columbo, Madras and Calcutta, and another one to New York and Boston. More and heavier ships of over 3,000 tons were built for the company. By the time of the Baccarat Scandal there were over 10,000 workmen in the employ of the Wilson brothers; who were said to be netting a personal income of £100,000 each in a good year.(1)

Such success did not come easily. When the brothers had decided to go for New York it was a tricky business since they were putting themselves in direct competition with Liverpool, but they persevered. In 1892 the Wilson and Furness lines started a joint service between Newcastle and New York which functioned every ten days. Four years later the London/New York and London/Boston services were coordinated. The brothers were helped here by the local knowledge of the Sanderson family, kinsmen of the late Edward Rheam Sanderson, who had married their sister Elizabeth. (Edward had had an idiosyncratic temper which could terrify his wife; and he periodically threw his breakfast, if it did not satisfy him, into the local river which ran close to the house where they were living in Epworth. When this happened his family would shake their heads and announce that he had "Trented his breakfast").(2) Thanks to the help of the Sandersons as well as to their own business acumen, the American Line became one of the most successful.

Wilsons were by now wealthy enough to buy up other shipping lines. In 1878 they acquired the seven steam ships of Brownlow, Marsden and Co., one of Hull's earliest steam ship companies. Early in 1894 the coasting trade between Hull and Newcastle was bought, and nine years later 23 ships belonging to the Bailey and Leetham fleet joined Wilsons.(3) In 1904, a year after the firm of Earle's Shipyard and Engineering Works had gone into liquidation, Wilsons bought it. Earle's, the firm which had employed and trained the young Henry Smith, Mary Wilson's brother, before he became a partner with Charles Amos, had set up a yard in Wincolmlee in the early '50s, and for a long time had taken the lion's share of ship building for the Wilson Line. In 1907 Wilsons were said to own 99 ships, and the story went around that if the total reached 100 they would have to buy a war ship to protect their large fleet. Therefore, as one ship came out of service another took its place. They now had more than a third of the foreign inward tonnage of shipping at Hull, and owned 56% of the total tonnage of the port.(4) The Hull dock area which, when Thomas had been a young man had covered about five acres, was now spread over 150 acres, and in this development the family had played a signficant part.

In 1891 the firm had become a private, limited company. The nominal capital was £2,000,000 in 20,000 shares of £100 each but not a single one reached the open market. Relations between the Wilsons and their employees had usually been good. But the times they were a-changing, and during the last quarter of the nineteenth century trade unions quickly became a serious challenge to the autocratic rule of the masters. When the Wilsons took over Earle's, they did so because they had no wish to see the firm closed having done business with it for so long. The yard had suffered much neglect and there was no other buyer. Charlie and Arthur were not engineers or ship builders and a hefty sum — some £200,000 a year — had to be poured out to improve yard facilities. They had saved many jobs, but if the brothers expected steady and friendly relations with the work force, they were too sanguin. The continual demands of well led men and the threat of strike action made the new acquisition a permanent source of anxiety.

The local union, the Seamen's and Marine Firemen's Association, founded in 1887, had as its secretary Mr J.B. Butcher, who negotiated a closed shop with the Wilson Line. However, this union soon came under pressure from the National Union, and in January 1889 Mr George Reid was sent down from Glasgow to address a meeting in the Friendly Societies Hall in Albion Street. Here, he made a personal attack on the Wilsons, affirming that though the local members thought that the brothers had done much for Hull shipping, Hull had paid them back with interest. He was interrupted by a voice at the back which told him that the said Wilsons had made thousands of widows and orphans happy.[5] Strikes there were during this year, but the Wilsons were still far stronger than their opposition. The shipwrights were out again at the time of the baccarat party, but a compromise was reached without undue strain. The same was not true of the strike of 1893.

A branch of the Dockers' Union had been founded in Hull in December 1889, and was no doubt fired by the enthusiasm of the dedicated Ben Tillett, who came on several occasions to Hull to address the workmen. It was soon well organised and very strong. These years were hard: unemployment was increasing as in most areas of Britain, and Hull suffered particularly in winter, when ships were frozen up in the Baltic as well being laid up in the Hull docks. Until now Charlie and Arthur had kept out of the Shipping Federation, which had been founded in 1890 by the ship owners, who had their own register of seamen, and only accepted those who agreed to work with non union men. However, in February 1893 when there was a greater shortage of work than anyone could remember before, the Wilsons came in. The Federation had decided to support a National Free Labour Association, whose secretary, William Collinson an ex driver of omnibuses, would supply free or "blackleg" labour to replace, in this case, members of the Dockers' Union who were refusing to work. On 6th April the dockers had come out. They would work with free labour providing that it was not given precedence, and were willing that foremen and clerks should be organised in a separate union. Charlie, however, had refused to agree. Why, is not entirely clear. It is very clear that he was not now shrinking from confrontation; perhaps he regarded the rivalry of the union as something which ought to be thrashed out once and for ever.

The Free Labour Association was obviously threatening to the union, and although the Shipping Federation had maintained that it would not discriminate between unionists and non-unionists, it nevertheless brought in 400 free labourers, some from as far off as London, on the day before the strike became official. From now on and for the next six

151

weeks, which was the length of time the strike lasted, there was an overwhelming display of force. By the end of the first week there were 1,000 free labourers in Hull, some of them from Cardiff. Police were drafted in from Leeds, Nottingham and London. The fact that they were not local meant that they had no personal knowledge of, or sympathy with the strikers, and that tougher action might be expected from them. They were supported additionally by military force to protect the free labour moving in. Ben Tillett arrived early in the strike to debate with Charlie, who refused to consider a compromise. He was now out to win, and win he did. The strike ended in the complete capitulation of the strikers, and the local union secretary's attempted suicide.

It may have signalled the end of militant trade unionism in Hull for a decade, but it did not all go the shipowners' way. Stronger words had been spoken than ever before. In Parliament Keir Hardie had persistently harrassed Mr Asquith (a Wilson supporter at the time of the Gordon-Cumming trial), and had got from him the revealing fact that 4 of the 38 magistrates in Hull were ship owners and a further 19 had financial interest in the shipping companies.(6) Next time, the struggle would be far more even.

Very early in the next year Arthur Wilson responded to the toast "the Town and Trade of Hull" at the Railway Guards Friendly Society's annual dinner. The speech is interesting because the blunt Arthur told his audience what, in his opinion, was needed to make Hull great. He began by recalling the strike, and said that the merchants and traders of Hull had won the right to be masters of their own businesses, and should not be controlled by irresponsible union leaders. He then went on to another controversial issue of the previous year — the acquiring by the North Eastern Railway of the old Hull docks. The time for change had come, he said. He promised, with his friend Mr Pease, he would see to it that Hull's interests were well looked after. He obviously appreciated the competition which would be offered by the proposed Manchester Ship Canal, but he called it "a big and exaggerated Holderness drain" and maintained that it would not give so much opportunity as their own "great Humber". He was adamant that the managers of the railway should keep the trade in the ports of Hull and Liverpool.(7) Five years later he was a supporter of the Joint Dock Bill, and when it passed he said, in a speech at the Annual General Meeting of the Subscribers and Friends of the Humber Industrial Training Ship "Southampton", that he hoped in future that the town, corporation and mercantile community would work with the railways (the North Eastern and Hull and Barnsley lines) instead of against them.(8) Arthur's business instincts and his local pride seem to have been marshalled in that order.

How dangerous was the life of a sailor of the Wilson Line in late Victorian England? The great parliamentary reformer, Samuel Plimsoll, who in 1875 was able to get the principle (at least) of the Plimsoll Line established in parliament by throwing such a wicked temper that his enemies sat stupified, was very anxious to prevent unnecessary shipping losses. He held up the Wilson Line as a good example of "what blessed life-saving results the adoption of good precautions is attended" which, if of doubtful grammatical excellence, at least implies that the Wilsons cared. He also quoted a statement from the Insurance Department in Hull, dated 4th February, 1889 which said:

"Our steamers are mostly cargo steamers, sailing to all parts. For the past eight years 1881-1888, our losses have reached £2.3.1d% on the value of our fleet. We have now 74 steamers afloat, and of these we run the entire risk of 59; the remaining 15 are of high class and value, and of these 15 we run at least half the value, in some instances considerably more than half the value: the balance we insure in London."

To this statement Charlie had added the comment "We had last year 72 steamers and no loss", to which Plimsoll adjoined "74 steamers and eight years are conclusive. There is no luck in it: it is simply the proof of what we can do."(9)

Of course there were collisions. One occurred on a Saturday night late in January 1893 in the Humber, between the "Galileo" and a Bailey and Leetham ship, the "Esperanza". The Captain of the "Galileo", George Henry Jones, said he had left New York on the 7th of the month with a cargo of 3,500 tons of general merchandise. He had arrived off Spurn at 6.30 in the evening of the 21st, and had taken a Humber pilot on board. The ship had moved at full speed up the Humber to Paull, at which point the engines were reduced to slow. It was now half past eight, they were in mid channel, the weather was clear and the water smooth. They passed several outward bound vessels on the port side and altered their course, by the Paull Clough lights, a little to the north to allow those vessels more room. Then they spotted a steamship's green and mast-head lights on their port bow about a mile and a half away. The pilot asked Jones for one blast of the steam whistle to show that the "Galileo" would not incline to starboard. This was answered at once by two blasts from the oncoming vessel. The pilot requested one further blast, but this one was not answered. The vessel was now two points on their port bow, and apparently moving full steam ahead, while the "Galileo" was still maintaining her speed of four knots. The pilot realised the likelihood of a collision, and therefore had the engines stopped. He put the "Galileo" into full speed astern and helm to port, and ordered three blasts of the whistle. And still the outward bound ship came on. The "Galileo" had been moving full speed astern for about three minutes (it was by now about half past nine) when the second ship crossed their bows. Her starboard side hit their stern with much damage to it and the bow plates. Immediately the engines were stopped and then put onto slow ahead, so that the ships should be kept together. The "Galileo's" starboard cutter and the company's tug "Jumbo" were both sent to help to get the passengers from the "Esperanza" on board the Wilson Line ship. Captain Jones felt that the collision ought never to have happened. The captain of the other ship had starboarded her helm. If it had been put to port when the first blast from the "Galileo" was given, the "Esperanza" would have got by.

The captain of the "Esperanza" was Edward Mason. He had just left the Humber dock for Hamburg and was carrying 12 passengers and 600 tons of general goods. He described the weather as hazy, with a light wind blowing from the north, and a smooth sea. He had sailed down the Humber at 10 knots and was on the bridge with the chief officer. An A.B. was on the look out on the forecastle. He maintained that the mast-head and side lights were burning brightly. It was about nine o'clock, when his ship was close to No. 10 buoy, that the A.B. reported the "Galileo's" mast-head and green lights between half a point and one point to starboard, at a distance of three quarters of a mile. He put the helm to starboard to give the "Galileo" more room in the south channel and gave two blasts to tell the other pilot that he was on the starboard helm. He then steadied the helm and gave two further blasts without reducing speed. He blew three times, but by then the ships were very close and the "Galileo" came stern on to their starboard side midships, and cut them below the water line, doing serious damage. He said that from the time he steadied the helm until the collision the ships were in a perfectly straight channel. He thought that the collision was caused because the "Galileo" ported her helm and tried to cross his bow.(10) It is not recorded in the local paper what the Official Receiver of Wrecks made of this controver-

The "Galileo", built 1881. Photo by courtesy of Hull City Museums, Town Docks Museum.

sial evidence.

That winter of early 1893 was a severe one. The "Rollo" had been icebound in Gothenburg but her captain was determined to get away as soon as possible. There are ten miles of river between Gothenburg and the sea, and this had been frozen for weeks. Packed ice had made it impossible to get through the Kattegat. On 4th February there was bright sunshine although 15 degrees centigrade of frost were registered. The "Rollo" lay close to the quay, in a good position for moving down river, but there was no open water to be seen anywhere. Further down the river, the London Mail steamer was equally anxious to get away. After two hours struggle, and helped by the icebreaker, she did so, at 1.30 in the afternoon. She headed off down river, closely followed by two smaller vessels. The ice closed in immediately they had passed. It was now "Rollo's" turn. The icebreaker connected up the "Rollo's" strong wire and began to pull. The wire snapped as if it had been made of string. The icebreaker returned and fixed its own rope, taking greater care this time, and the "Rollo" moved slowly away from the quay.

The 400 or so emigrants on board cheered. Most of them had already been out to Canada, and were now returning there having been "Home" for the winter. At this time the return fare from New York via Liverpool and Hull to any Swedish port was £4.10.0d (£4.50), and this included food and railway expenses. So, instead of staying in Canada during the slack season, these emigrants had preferred to live cheaply back at home with their families or friends. It made financial sense for them to do so.

The "Rollo" proceeded down river, making very slow progress to begin with because of the broken ice. Friends seeing off the passengers were able to walk alongside the ship, keeping pace with it. Skaters whizzed past, although the "Rollo" was on full steam. Then

154

it was discovered that two men were still on board who were seeing off friends, and who had not realised that the ship was moving out. The engines therefore had to be stopped, and the two then climbed down a ladder and walked off, back across the ice. The channel was so narrow that this could have been done almost anywhere. Shortly after this, a steamship in front of "Rollo" smashed her bows on the ice. This meant that the icebreaker had to go ahead and cut a new channel round her, otherwise the rest of the queue would never be able to move. This was done. Further down the channel, where the river was two miles wide, men were fishing from holes in the ice, each one having rigged up a small screen to act as a wind break. Ponies dragging light sledges were also moving across the river.

It was sunset by the time "Rollo" had reached the Kattegat. Looking south, nothing could be seen but a vast frozen sea of packed ice, extending limitlessly. "Rollo" steered a northerly course and kept clear, although the look outs were on duty throughout the night, making sure that no icebergs loomed up out of the darkness. It was so cold that throughout the 20 mile crossing from Sweden to Denmark the ship was pushing against ice. It was only about half an inch thick, and therefore no real problem, but it was smooth as glass, and every star in the heavens was reflected on its surface. Apart from the movement of the ship, everything was still in this immensity. Skagen lighthouse was reached after seven hours and Hull after 48. It was a memorable trip.

A fortnight later Captain Soulsby of the "Milo" returned to Hull with a tale to tell. He had left Stettin eleven weeks previously on 5th January 1893, but had been unable to make headway because of the ice. So he had put back to Swinemunde (now Swinoujscie) which was little more than a village, and there he had to wait for two months. The inhabitants of Swinemunde were pleased to see the sailors, and were quick to take advantage of the unexpected emergency. They charged double for everything the men required, though they did put on dances three times a week to cheer everybody up. Captain Soulsby said that the ice here was twelve inches thick, and the tin of water which was always placed by the cabin stove on the "Milo" was invariably frozen solid by morning, even though the fire was never allowed to go out. Milk, which had to be bought on shore, was frozen into a solid block when it was purchased.

Finally the ship got away in hazy weather and, like the "Rollo", was in continual danger from icebergs, so that a sharp look-out was essential. As the temperature gradually increased the fresh water tank, which like everything else had been frozen solid, burst, but this was the only bad luck the "Milo" suffered before reaching Hull.

Strange and inexplicable events occurred no matter what time of year. At the end of April 1893 the "Cameo" was returning across the North Sea when the second officer, Mr Norton, informed Captain Potter that a lifeboat had been spotted, and that it appeared to contain bodies. Mr Norton was asked to investigate, and he discovered that the lifeboat belonged to the S.S. "Noranside" of Newcastle, which presumably had been lost. There were five men in the boat, all dead, so Mr Norton, having written down all their particulars, as well as the particulars of the circumstances in which they were found, buried them at sea. The crew of the "Cameo" were puzzled because there was no indication as to what might have happened. The first body lay over the stern sheets. It was that of an officer, perhaps 40 years of age. He wore new wellington boots and had on a long brown overcoat. He was going bald and had short clipped whiskers. The crew thought he might have been first mate. The second body, they thought, was that of a fireman. He was young, slight and fair, and was wearing dun trousers and a shirt, under a short, brown jacket. The third body also seemed to be that of a fireman. This man was older, probably between 30 and 35 years of age: he had a dark complexion, marked from smallpox, and a dark moustache. He was short and stout. The fourth body, again, seemed to be that of a fireman about 30 years old and sturdily built. This man's hair was non-existent above the ear on one side of the head, the result, the crew thought, of a previous incident, but they also thought it would make identification easier to know this. The last body was found underneath the seats of the boat. This was a young man in his late 20s who was wearing no life jacket. However, he was wearing the typical hand knitted jersey, and so the crew concluded that he probably was a sailor. He, too, was fair, with a fair moustache, and on the little finger of his right hand he wore a plain, gold ring. The boat itself was fully equipped, although nothing had been done to place the gear, and the rudder had not been shipped. It seemed to the crew of the "Cameo" that a collision had taken place and that the men had had little time to get into the boat. Their clothing was very thin, and would have afforded no protection. The second officer thought that they had been dead about two days, but he pointed out that there were no signs of personal suffering.(11)

In the following July Captain Gordon and the "Rollo" were involved in another spectacular, but this time less hair-raising, event. Gordon was carrying 160 passengers on what was known as a "Polytechnic" trip to the North Cape. On the way they passed Dr Nansen on the "Fram". He was just starting out on his attempt on the North Pole, and the "Rollo" saluted him by blasting on her foghorn, while the 160 passengers cheered him as loudly as they were able. Dr Nansen was obviously pleased, because he came up on deck to wave and acknowledge the support from Hull.(12)

Captain Standish of the "Livorno" had a less than auspicious meeting with members of the Russian royal family. He was turning his ship, fully laden with cargo, in the basin in the sea canal above Cronstadt. This was the place where such a manoeuvre would be expected to take place. At the same time, however, Grand Duke Alexis, brother of Tsar Alexander III and Admiral of the Fleet, was bringing his yacht down to Cronstadt, and approached as Captain Standish was making his turn. The Grand Duke's captain stopped the yacht and prepared to wait, only to be ordered by his master to proceed. Captain Standish backed the "Livorno" so that the royal yacht would have more room to pass. The Russian vessel, however, attempted to cross his stern and a collision was inevitable. The yacht, of course, came off worse. Her deck bridge was down, and the total damage to her was later estimated at 75,000 roubles. Fortunately the Grand Duke was unhurt, though his captain had a leg injury. Nor did the "Livorno" sustain any appreciable damage, but Captain Standish was "requested" to present himself on board the royal yacht. This he did in fear and trembling — the horrors of Siberia were not unknown in Hull, which already had a small Jewish community exiled from Russia because of the cruelties of Pobedon-ostzev, minister of Alexander III, who had said that one third of the Russian Jews must die, one third must emigrate, and the rest must assimilate. These people had already told their tales. The Grand Duke, however, proved himself willing to accept responsibility for the accident, and a relieved Hull captain returned to his ship.(13)

A very strange occurrence was the loss of the "Apollo". She was a good ship and had been launched in 1889 for the Bombay run, carrying out coals and general cargo, with machinery on the upper deck, and returning with general cargo and grain in bags. She coped well with heavy weather. In January 1890 she was put on the New York run and carried general cargo, sometimes including cattle in the 'tween and upper decks. (She once carried 400 head of cattle without a single loss). From February 1891 she had been on the Antwerp to New York run, and had last been checked for sea-worthiness in

Antwerp late in May 1893. In February 1894 the "Apollo" was in New York, ready to sail, with a 3,442 ton cargo for Antwerp, 500 tons of it in coal, 2,416 tons in corn (which was stowed in bulk in the lower holds) and the rest, lighter in weight, was stowed 'tween decks. Mr W.A. Ellis, the Surveyor to the Board Underwriters at New York, signed a certificate to show that he had witnessed the loading, and that it had been carefully done. The captain of the "Apollo" had also sent a letter to Wilsons' Marine Superintendent, Captain Rutter, to confirm this.

At 10.30 in the morning of 11th February 1894 the New York pilot, William Hall, took the "Apollo" out of the dock at Holboken, New Jersey, and he later said that she was handling and steering well. It was one o'clock when he disembarked outside the bar of Sandy Hook, at which time the weather was fine and clear. He was the last person to have any knowledge of the "Apollo", which simply disappeared. The commissioner to the Board of Trade heard the evidence. It included the ship's history from the beginning, but it was a mystery which was never solved.[14]

The conveyance of chemicals was always a hazard. The bulk of this trade came down from Newcastle in the coasting steamers and was then transferred onto the big ships crossing the Atlantic to New York, but some of it was carried in Wilson Line ships directly from the Tyne. The "Rialto" left the Tyne in February 1897 carrying chemicals, and on 5th March this cargo exploded, setting fire to all the rest and killing the third engineer, Mr Howe. After fighting in vain to control the flames, Captain Rippett declared that this was a policy no longer feasible, and he gave orders for the ship to be abandoned.[15] It was by no means the only example of a ship being destroyed by her cargo. Some years previously the "Santiago", homeward bound, was lost when her cargo of cotton ignited.

There were occasions when casualties resulted through no fault of the elements. In March 1899 the "Chicago" was lying at Charlestown when two of the firemen, Thomas French and Robert Scott, came back after a night out in which they had got very drunk. Neither had been aboard the ship for long. For French, a widower of 42 left with five children to bring up, it was his second voyage; for the 24 year old Scott, it was his first. The argument must have started in a pub. The two men came out of it and began to fight. Other members of the crew separated them for the time being and got them back into the dockyard. Here, the quarrel flared up again, and the two men fought their way up to and onto the "Chicago", where a stout-hearted crewman, Thomas Riley, rushed in to separate them. He managed to do this, but the drunken French staggered in front of an open hatchway and, before Riley could haul him back, fell 35 feet into the hold, which killed him. It was a tragic end to over-indulgence, and more tragic on account of his young, growing and now completely helpless large family. His ship, the "Chicago" was a new one, and the biggest of the Wilson fleet. When she had to be named, in Autumn 1898, there was already a vessel of that name, which had been built in 1884 for the New York trade. This ship was now given the new name "Salerno" in order that the bigger vessel could take the name the Wilsons wanted it to have.

In October, 1899 Britain once again found herself at war with the Boers of the Transvaal and the Orange Free State, and our troops went off to Cape Town singing "We're soldiers of the Queen, my lads". The Wilsons spared nothing in their personal war effort. Charlie's two sons, Tommy and Guy, and Arthur's Clive all went out to the veldt. The Wilson women organised one charitable event after another, and at a single cafe chantant, organised by Mary, £400 was raised for the Mayor's Transvaal War Fund. Charlie and Arthur handed over a ship, and they did this at a most significant time. On 10th

City of London Imperial Volunteers embarking on the S.S. "Ariosto" during the Second Boer War. Photo by courtesy of Hull City Museums, Town Docks Museum.

December Gatacre had been defeated at Stormberg, one day later Methuen suffered the same fate at Magersfontein, and only four days after that, Buller lost at Tugela River. The newspapers called it "the Black Week". On the 20th December, the Lord Mayor of London, presiding at a meeting of the City of London Common Council, announced to the assembled throng how heartened he was by the generosity and loyalty of two Yorkshire brothers, who had made the largest individual gift to the country so far during the war. The Wilsons undertook to provide and equip the "Ariosto" (built in 1890 and 2,376 gross tons) to carry out to Cape Town, initially, 500 men and 50 officers of the Special Volunteer Corps which was to be raised in the City to serve out on the veldt. (They were soon known as the City Imperial Volunteers). One of the officers sent out in this way was Tommy. The Lord Mayor said that the Wilsons' gift was the equivalent of a subscription of £15,000. Charlie had not been in favour of war, and had spoken out in the Commons on more than one occasion during the past year against war mongering; but now that the die was cast, he was not one to hold back his efforts towards a successful outcome.(16)

Some of the most luxurious liners that ever sailed did so in the Wilson Line in the Edwardian era. They were the last word in scientific efficiency too. In May 1909 the "Aaro" made her maiden voyage, and was described as "a floating hotel".(17) She was the first Hull steamer to be fitted with the Marconi wireless telegraph, and her Captain Cowlrick wirelessed the following message to Tommy, by now 2nd Lord Nunburnholme, and his family "230 miles N.E. from Spurn, everything most satisfactory". It was a little bit of history of which Tommy was very proud. "Aaro" steamed at 15 knots. She had a spacious first class dining saloon panelled in fumed oak, which would take more than 100 passengers at a sitting. The oak parquet floor was covered with rich and thick Turkey carpets.

The ship's lounge was equally magnificent. The panelling here was of mahogany, and the windows were of bevelled glass. The smoking room, which was panelled in walnut, was divided into bays; the floor covering was of india rubber patterned in white squares with black dots. The first class staterooms were all midships, and there were no upper berths. Each cabin had a cabinet folding lavatory, a fresh water supply, mirrors, racks and candle lamps, and the ventilation was said to be excellent. There was also a big promenade deck, and the deck shelter was closed in overhead and on three sides.

This magnificent ship could carry 120 first class passengers and 60 second class ones (who were housed quite lavishly above the engine room). Third class acommodation was also available for 100 passengers in cabins each of which contained four or six berths, and this was at the stern of the ship. The "Aaro" was expected to reach Christiansand in 33 hours and Christiania in 47. The fare for the voyage was £4.15.0d.(£4.75) single, and £7.10.0d (£7.50) return first class, and £3.5.0d (£3.25) single, and £5 return second class.

This wonderful steamer was soon outclassed — in the very next year — by the "Eskimo", built by Earle's, and the new darling of the Wilson line. Sailing the same route, the "Eskimo" liberated the "Aaro" and the "Oslo" from the Christiania trade, so that they could go on to Stavanger, Bergen and even as far north as Trondheim, and thus the whole of the Norwegian trade could be carried on in the new, fast ships. Lord and Lady Nunburnholme, Charles Henry's son and daughter-in-law, travelled as first class passengers on the maiden voyage, and Tommy had plenty to tell the press about the new twin screw, which he said was a novelty, and apart from being a safety device would help

The "Aaro", built 1909, a casualty of the 1914-1918 War. Photo by courtesy of Hull City Museums, Town Docks Museum.

159

considerably to prevent rolling.

The bridge of this steamer was fitted with every modern device — docking telegraphs, telephone communication throughout the ship, electric patent log, signal lights and a telemotor steering gear coupled with a reply dial for every motion of the quadrant for three gears; it was 40 feet above the loaded water line. The promenade deck had thick plate glass at the fore end, which meant that passengers could sit there in rain and a head wind and observe what was happening from a sheltered position. Lounge chairs, garden seats and a wireless telegraph office could be found in this part of the ship.

On the deck below was the lounge, fitted with the usual thick, rich carpeting and with furniture à la Chippendale, and specially made by the aptly named Hull firm of Craft and Sons of Beverley Road. There was also a grand piano and well filled book case "the firm having joined the *Times* book club". The grand promenade deck stretched uninterrupted for over 100 yards and was designed to give the passengers the best possible view of the fjords.(18) In early July came the news that the "Eskimo" had been chartered by the Admiralty for their guests at the Coronation Review for King George V and Queen Mary at Spithead.

Before leaving the subject of shipping it would be worth while to tell the story of Robert Henry Stutt whose fortunes — if such they were — were, in his early days, bound up with the Wilson firm. His father had been an engineer trained, in five years' apprenticeship, at the Hull firm of Rose Downs, after which he had gained experience at sea. He then came home periodically for six monthly intervals, during which time he worked for and obtained his ticket for 4th, 3rd, 2nd, chief, and even extra chief engineer, the last of which he got in 1882. By this time he had become a family man with several children, and this

The "Eskimo", built by Earle's Shipyard, Hull, in 1910. Photo by courtesy of Hull City Museums, Town Docks Museum.

had meant that, during his study periods, it had been necessary for him to get temporary work in Hull, and Robert remembered that he was once employed in helping to repair dock gates for Blundell Spence. Some time later when the child was four years old his father was at sea in a Wilson ship when she ran into a severe storm during which, because of the pitching of the vessel, Stutt senior was thrown onto the engines. His neighbours dragged him clear, but he was seriously injured. He never worked again, and died two years later as a result of his injuries. His wife, with several small children to care for, was forced to accept charity where she could get it. The Board of Guardians in Fern Street allowed her a five shilling (25p) grocery order each week, and this was handed over with the name of the shop where Mrs Stutt had indicated she would like to trade inscribed upon it. Robert remembered that from time to time some member of the family would be required to offset the debt by chopping wood at the workhouse. Eventually Mrs Stutt secured rooms in the neighbourhood of Kingston College, which were reserved for captains, chief engineers and their widows.

As a schoolboy Robert visited Tranby Croft regularly. His uncle, Mr Pickering, was head joiner there, and later became estate manager (his daughter, Mollie, was Muriel Wilson's god child). When he wished to go to visit his uncle at Tranby Croft Robert had the choice of two "bus" services from Carr Lane in Hull. The first, a wagonette with two horses, left the White Horse pub and ended its journey at Granby's in Hessle Square, the cost being 3d.(1p). Diagonally across the way from the White Horse Mr Binnington, the originator of the East Yorkshire Motor Services, set off from the Black Horse, and went as far as the Red Lion in Anlaby village. Robert was often the only customer on this "bus". At conker time he used to take along a large black bag, and with his cousin Bob Pickering, would pick up the conkers which lay strewn all over the ground in the wood just beyond the gate house, well out of sight of the mansion itself. This was fairly safe, but occasionally the boys dared to turn their attentions to the crab apple tree in front of the house — a far more dangerous escapade. Eventually Robert would return home with his all but impossibly heavy bag. It had cost him 6d. to travel to the conker site, therefore at school during the next week he sold his haul — eight conkers for one halfpenny — and usually made a modest profit.

When he was fourteen years old it seemed natural to Robert's mother that her son should enter the firm for which his father had worked, and for which he had even given his life, and on 16th October 1908, standing in front of Arthur Wilson — the only time in his life when Robert remembered seeing him — the lad became a fully indentured apprentice to learn the job of a shipping clerk. Normally apprentices were not indentured, and went to and remained in one department only. The sad circumstances in which Robert's family had been cast was probably the reason why he was treated differently, and was to receive training in every department. The indenture was to serve from 19th February 1908 for five years, and contained the following instructions:

"During all and which said term, the said apprentice his said master well and faithfully should serve; his secrets keep; his lawful commands should do; fornication or adultery he shall not commit; hurt or damage to his said master he shall not do nor consent to be done, but so far as he may be able shall prevent it, and therefore give notice to his said master; taverns or alehouses he shall not use or frequent unless he be about his master's business; at dice, cards, tables, bowls, or any other unlawful games he shall not play; the goods of his said master he shall not waste, or lend, or give to any person without his master's license; matrimony within the said term he shall not contract; nor from his master's service at any time without leave absent himself; but as a true and faithful apprentice shall order and behave himself towards his said master and family, as well in words as deeds, during the said term; and true and just accounts of all his master's goods, chattels, and money committed to his charge, or which shall come into his hands, faithfully he shall give at all times when thereunto required by his said master, his executors, administrators or assigns."

In return for what Robert Stutt later called the "signing away of his body and soul", Wilsons undertook to:

"teach, learn and instruct him, the said apprentice, or cause him to be taught, learnt and instructed, in the Trade, Art or Mystery of a Shipping Clerk which he the said Master now uses, in the best and most effectual manner."(19)

Robert was to be paid £10 during his first year, £20 during his second, £25 during his third, £30 during his fourth and £35 during his final year. His mother, Mary Jane, was to provide him "with all suitable clothing and other necessaries" and to help with this she was given £13.13.0d (£13.65) by the Municipal Charity Trustees under the Thomas Ferries Charity, which had been set up in 1630 to assist fatherless boys to be bound apprentice to a good trade.(20) Mrs Stutt was given £3.3.0d (£3.15) immediately, with a further £3.3.0d to come after a year, £2.2.0d twelve months later and a further £2.0.0d. a year after that. Finally, at the end of the apprenticeship there was to be a further donation of one pound, but not one of these sums would be paid if Robert did not produce a certificate, signed by his master to say that he had minded his studies well, and also his duties. This help must have been a Godsend to the poor widow. A suit of clothes could be purchased for less than a pound, and the boy could start his new life without shame as to his appearance. The important document had to be signed by both mother and son, in the presence of W. A. Ouzman, Clerk to John Watson. The common seal of the company was affixed in the presence of George Hickman, manager, and H. J. Tarn, the company's secretary. On 19th February 1913 the document recorded that Robert Henry Stutt had completed his apprenticeship satisfactorily, and this was again signed by H. J. Tarn.

The apprenticeship began in winter and Robert was placed, to begin with, in the post department, which received and sent its own telegrams by morse, radio having not yet arrived at Commercial Road. Two gentlemen from the post office looked after the boys in the department. One of Robert's job was to copy letters, and for this purpose there was a ledger book which consisted of 500 sheets of very thin paper. Near to his desk was a large pot of water with a paste brush balanced on it. Robert would wet the top sheet of the ledger with this brush, after which the ledger would be subjected to pressure and the water squeezed through to the sheets underneath. The boy soon learned to control the amount of moisture according to how many letters needed to be copied at once. He then placed each typed letter (the Wilson correspondence was always typed) underneath a damp sheet with the writing uppermost. He next placed a backing sheet behind each letter, and once again subjected the ledger to pressure. This brought the copy through from the typescript to the back of the thin wet paper, which was sufficiently transparent for it to be read. Robert was a good worker; he was moved to the railway department and became eighth boy.

Even during his first year there were three nights of overtime each week, and in these days there was no extra pay. On Tuesdays, Thursdays and Fridays his work ceased at five

162

o'clock in the afternoon, but on Mondays, Wednesdays and Saturdays it went on until three o'clock in the morning. The boy walked to work each morning from his home, now in Brunswick Avenue. He had to leave at seven to be in time for the eight o'clock start. He had no bicycle; they were still a novelty and scarce, and he could not have afforded it anyway. Between noon and half past one he trekked back for a good lunch — sandwiches would not have kept him going on an overtime day, and a carefully contrived stew (perhaps a sheep's head with vegetables) would be as cheap. His mother was hard put to it, for Robert's wages, which amounted to 3/10 1/4d (19p) a week, were only paid to him at the end of every quarter year. He would be back at his desk at half past one and worked straight through after the bookkeepers had gone home at five o'clock. If he wanted a drink, he had to go through to the lavatories at the back and cup his hands under a tap. At last, at eight o'clock, came what he described as "a jolly good tea", but this had to last for the rest of the night.

Robert's department handled five ships a week, and there were 500 bills for each ship. He remembered dealing with the Antwerp service on Monday, Wednesday and Saturday and, also on Saturday, the service to Ghent. Each bill had to be copied. When Robert became head boy he was sometimes left at night with a big black leather topped box which contained manifests and bills of lading and these had to be put on board the outgoing ships. It was often a struggle to find the time to do it. Ships would not willingly miss a tide, and there were times when an outgoing vessel was on the move through the Humber dock lock pit when Robert and the box arrived. He would then get a boatman with a long hook to swing his box aboard and, if this failed, he would have to get a tug and sail down the Humber after the ship. Consequently, there were overtime nights when he did not reach home until five o'clock in the morning. He would walk down Kingston Street, where waggons were being shunted across by means of ropes, in the flickering light of oil lamps. Their light enabled the lad to see the scurrying of the rat population on the dock side — there were a great many of them. On such nights it was hardly worth while going to bed.

On those nights when Robert got home "early", he had to spend a couple of hours at the Technical College, for each year it was necessary for him to gain a First Class Certificate in French, shorthand, commercial English and commercial geography if he wished to obtain the increased salary. Fortunately he was a bright boy, giving up his one free day on Sunday each week to preparing the next lot of homework, and so he kept his head above water, and was once awarded a Pitman's Shorthand Dictionary as a prize.

After his apprenticeship was complete Robert, unlike the non-indentured clerks who remained in the one department, had a working knowledge of them all, and his salary was £50 a year, whereas theirs was only £40. He now went into the Russian department where conditions were very hard and it was necessary from time to time to work right through the night. (Soda water and milk were provided after the eight o'clock tea). Accuracy was all. A balance had to be obtained between what was loaded onto the ship and what was stated on the bills and manifests. The clerks were told that not a single package must be lost, or Wilsons would be fined thousands of roubles. This work was so onerous that eventually Robert took his salary book to his chief, a man he knew as Bill Elliott (although that was not his real name) who was a superintendent at the Wesleyan Chapel in Argyle Street. He asked this gentleman for a rise and presented his book. "Leave it there" said Bill noncommittally, and when, after a few weeks Robert went to fetch it back he discovered, although no one had troubled to tell him, that he was now earning £60 a year. He now heard from a fellow clerk that anyone who was working in the Russian department, in the St.

Petersburg division, was worth £10 more than anybody else, so he again presented his book, and was awarded a further rise, bringing up his salary to £70 a year. Here it remained until 1914 when Robert joined his local regiment, the Hull Commercials, and very shortly found himself over in France.(21)

He never returned to Wilsons, but it was the end of an era, not only for him but for them too. Charlie and Arthur were now dead, and the firm, which had been their very life, was soon to pass virtually out of Wilson hands altogether. The heyday was over.

(1) *Hull Times* 6.6.1891 p.3 col.c.
(2) From the personal jottings of Alice Minna Wathen, grand-daughter of Edward Rheam Sanderson. The original script is in the possession of Adrian Sanderson of British Colmbia, great great nephew of Charles Henry. I am indebted to Ben Charles, IVth Baron Nunburnholme for permission to use the material.
(3) *Hull News* 25.7.1903 p.10 col.b.
(4) *Hull News* 25.7.1899 Quoted J. Bellamy: 'Some Aspects of the Economy of Hull in the Nineteenth Century with special reference to Business History' (Hull University Thesis 1965) p.169.
(5) *Hull News* 19.1.1889 Supplement p.8.
(6) For general background to the strike see *H. Pelling: History of British Trade Unionism* (Pelican 1963) pp. 93-123. See also *Rhoda Lamb: The Life & Times of 1st Baron Nunburnholme* op.cit. pp. 39-41; *Eastern Morning News and Hull News; Victoria County History,* East Riding p.260.
(7) *Hull News* 20.1.1894 p.6 cols.c/f.
(8) Ibid 5.8.1899 p.3 col.g.
(9) Ibid 9.3.1892 p.4 col.e.
(10) Ibid 28.1.1893 p.8 col.c.
(11) Ibid 6.5.1893 p.4 col.g.
(12) Ibid 22.7.1893 p.5 col.c.
(13) Ibid 5.8.1893 p.3 col.e.
(14) Ibid 21.8.1894 p.3 col.e.
(15) Ibid 20.3.1897 p.3 col.a.
(16) Ibid 23.12.1899 p.6 col.e.
(17) *Eastern Morning News* Monday, 31.5.1909 From the Hicks Collection.
(18) Ibid 4.6.1910 From the Hicks Collection.
(19) All information concerning the career at Thomas Wilson, Sons and Co. Ltd. of Robert Stutt is from the late Robert Stutt himself, who generously gave me a detailed account before his death in December 1986.
(20) *Handbook to Hull and the East Riding of Yorkshire* ed. T. Sheppard (Brown 1922) p.136.
(21) See *A History of the 10th (Service) Battalion the East Yorkshire Regiment* (Hull Commercials) (A. Brown and Sons Ltd. London and Hull 1937). Mr Stutt was intensely proud of his regiment's contribution to the fighting on the Western Front.

CHAPTER NINE

Edwardian England and the Wilsons

London Society

Splendid as the social life of the Wilsons had become in East Yorkshire, it was only one area of social activity. After their association with the Prince of Wales had become more firmly established, they were able to be accepted into the London scene. They had had a house there for a long time — longer in fact than they had inhabited Tranby Croft. Muriel had been born in 1875 at No. 28 Hyde Park Street, and ten years later they had moved to the more exclusive south side of the park, to No. 13 Grosvenor Crescent, a terrace built on the site of the famous Tattershall's, and on the edge of Belgravia. Brother Charlie was nearby at No. 41 Grosvenor Square. By the end of the decade they were casting their eyes round the corner to an even more prestigious site. The building of No. 17 Grosvenor Place had, for some reason, lagged behind the rest of the block, which had been built in the sixties by Thomas Cubitt. By 1890 it was available for occupation.(1) It occupied a desirable corner site and was a magnificent, solid, substantial French styled building, its steeply sloping roof giving it an additional fifth storey, unlike the other houses. It overlooked the gardens of Buckingham Palace. Here, the Wilsons came in 1890. Unlike their socially unconscious father, Arthur and Charles Henry became members of prestigious London clubs. They were both members of the Bachelors', but Charles Henry, a liberal in politics, favoured the Reform Club rather than the conservative Carlton, where Arthur went.

Mary Wilson's balls at 17 Grosvenor Place were magnificent. Her flower arrangements were famous, even for this extravagant style of hospitality. As one local reporter put it, if anyone wished to sit upon a sofa which had cost £1,000 and look at flowers which had cost half as much again, he could not do better than visit the Arthur Wilsons in their London home.(2) As the visitor entered the hall, he would very likely see in front of him a tall palm plant, banked up with crimson rambler roses, white hydrangeas, lilies, marguerites and many different kinds of fern. Nor would this be the only display. The side tables would carry baskets of pink roses and ferns too. At the foot of the stairs would be a stand on which pink roses, smilax and ferns would be arranged in tiers. The buffet, which would be in the morning room, would abound in ferns, palms and flowers, whilst, in the dining room, there might well be a pyramid of orchids on one table, and a group of large pink malmaisons standing high on a second one. Bright red lilies would be placed in vases, and there would also be massive bowls of pink roses and malmaisons in various parts of the room, wherever there happened to be a space. Even the ballroom had its share. At its far end would be a wonderful display of red tile carnations. As a general rule, all flowers for display were sent down from Tranby Croft by Mr Leadbetter, though misfortune, bad weather, or the necessity for haste could sometimes mean that all, or part might have to be purchased in London.

There were times when some of Mary Wilson's guests did not arrive until after midnight. Society was such a whirligig that the attendance of the same people might have been requested at two or even three houses on the same night. At the party on Monday, 3rd July 1899 many of the principal guests came straight on from a concert at the Rothschilds: Lady Rothschild herself did this. The same thing had happened in reverse when, on 18th July, 1898 Mary had arranged an elaborate and very large dinner party. Before the guests had finished their meal, Arthur, Mary and Muriel had gone off to the Court concert, which preceded Mrs George Bentinck's cotillion — which was where the family ended its social activities for that night.(3)

Earlier that year members of the Wilson family had attended the first drawing room of the season at Buckingham Palace. Mary looked splendid: her court gown had a petticoat of black sequin and lisse embroidery over white gaufre. The corsage and tunic were of black satin embroidered with sequins, and her train was of black satin Oriental, lined with pale blue and veiled with black lace. Muriel's pale blue crepe-de-chine gown was embroidered with diamonds and white lace applique. Her train was of blue Orient satin entirely covered with flounces of soft white tulle. A spray of La France roses was arranged on her left shoulder. Kenneth's wife, Molly, wore a black net gown, and Ethel pale blue satin (a colour of which she seems to have been very fond).(4)

Charing Cross Hospital held a bazaar at the Albert Hall in the late June of 1899. Mary sold buttonholes, and was obviously very good at the job, as she got ten guineas for one of them.(5) It was an exceedingly hot day, and Mary must have sweltered, for she was wearing a black dress with cream embroidery and covered with sequins, surmounted by

The Wilsons' London home, No. 17 Grosvenor Place, taken from Chapel Street. From the Author's own collection.

166

a corn coloured net toque with sprays of gold and feathers. Muriel, and others were in charge of "Flowerland" and they all wore white silk and crepe gowns with bands of coarse cream lace. These were open necked and the sleeves of lace and crepe were almost transparent. Muriel's hat was a large, black ship hat of tulle, fastening at the chin (which must have made it even hotter).(6)

Perhaps the most splendid party of the late Victorian era was the big Costume Ball at Devonshire House in the year of the Diamond Jubilee, 1897. The extravagance of the fancy dress was greater than ever, as we have good reason to know, for a photographer captured every one of them. The Duchess of Devonshire was dressed as Zenobia, Queen of Palmyra and the Duke as Charles IV of Austria. Alexandra, Princess of Wales, not only attired herself gorgeously as Queen Marguerite de Valois, but was attended by an equally splendid little page. Leonie Leslie, sister of Winston Churchill's mother, Jennie, was Brünhild, complete with spear, shield and plumed helmet. The Prince of Wales' confidant, Soveral, the Portuguese Ambassador, was dressed as his illustrious country- man the Count D'Almeda. There was also a strange partnership of two sisters who, remembered Lady Maud Warrender, went to the ball as the Furies "and wore hair nets to keep their hair tidy".(7)

Muriel, always spectacular, had appeared as Vashti, but to the watching Mrs Hwfa Williams, all paled before the exquisite simplicity of Tottie Menzies as Titania. She wore a flowing white gown with a long train bordered with stars. She held a bunch of lilies as tall as herself, and her lovely golden hair fell loosely to her waist.(8)

Two years after this event the Second Boer War broke out, and before it was brought to a final, satisfactory conclusion Queen Victoria had died, and at last, in his old age, Edward, Prince of Wales would be King of England and her Empire Overseas. When he was crowned, on 9th August 1902 (which just happened to be Mary Wilson's birthday) the expected streams of laudatory epistles came flooding in. The Mayor of Hull Mr William Alfred Gelder (who would be knighted the following year), had already given permission for a special Coronation Ode, and this was written by Duse Mohammed, who had been born in Alexandria and educated in England. Duse Mohammed thrived in this country. He became passionately interested in theatricals and made a name for himself as an elocutionist, but his professional work was as a reporter for the London dailies.(9) Now he produced Hull's own Coronation Ode which contained the following lines:-

"And e'en as the 'First Merchant Prince' did feat
The Third King Edward at his loyal board,
So the Seventh Edward — thy present King —
Following where Plantagenet had led,
With Princely grace — born of urbanity —
Became leal Arthur's guest at Tranby Croft,
And Charles, the elder of the Wilson race,
Like the great Michael, entered Parliament,
To legislate for Britain — and thy good."(10)

Duse Mohammed was not the only person to compare the Wilson family with the mediaeval De La Poles. Commercially they were probably ahead, but they never had the political influence of the older family, and their rise and comparative decline took place over a far shorter period. Socially, however, in this new reign, they lacked nothing, and it is interesting for instance, that when King Edward paid his state visit to Vienna in

September, 1903, Arthur and Mary found it necessary to visit Carslbad.(11)

Muriel, still unmarried, revelled in the social round. Her mother was recognised as an excellent hostess, but Muriel was known as an interesting, lively and attractive member of any house party, and it was well understood that the King appreciated her company when he was visiting the great houses of the land. So, invitations were seldom lacking. Muriel was nearly always a guest of the Duke and Duchess of Devonshire at Chatsworth at the time of the New Year Festivities. She was almost certainly on her way there on 4th January, 1901, when an incident occurred which showed that, like Lady Maud Warrender, she was of impressive stature and strength. She was travelling by train, which was beginning to lose speed before pulling into Doncaster station, when a fellow passenger rose to leave the compartment, reached out, unfastened the door — and slipped. Muriel moved like lightning, managed to grab the unfortunate man under the armpits, and bracing herself against the sides of the open door, succeeded in holding him up until the train reached the station and stopped. She probably saved his life.(12)

In the autumn of 1902 she was at Rufford, the home of Lord Savile, where Dame Nellie Melba had been persuaded to sing. "It was such fun" as Mrs Hwfa Williams continually said, but there were times also when the greatest tact was necessary, as in 1903, when Muriel's friend, Lady Maud Warrender, organised a concert at the Albert Hall for the Union Jack Club. Here, the Leeds Choral Union were to give the first performance of Elgar's Coronation Ode, the words of this one written by A.C. Benson (son of the Archbishop of Canterbury at the time of the baccarat scandal). During this performance the King had the misfortune to fall asleep. This, Lady Maud could easily see, as the box in which she and Lady Elgar sat, was right next to that of the King. She immediately asked her companion to move to a "better position", but one from which she would be unable to observe her sovereign. Fortunately the King soon woke up.

It was perhaps at Chatsworth that the performing skills of Lady Maud and Muriel were most appreciated. The Festivities were big and impressive, and there could be a danger of fragmentation — always a hostess' nightmare. The guest lists were very grand. They always included the Marquess de Soveral, the Portuguese ambassador, who was one of the few men who appeared to enjoy the complete trust of King Edward. His presence was inevitable. He was often treated with nervous good will, which could be akin to jealousy. He was a swarthy man, and because of it was dubbed "the Blue Monkey". He had a reputation for breaking hearts, but not all women liked him, although Muriel on occasions acted the part of the adoring female. Princess Daisy of Pless considered his close friendship with the King to be dangerous, as she was sure he made his dislike of the German Emperor, Wilhelm II (Kaiser Bill) very obvious to his royal friend.(13) Princess Daisy was married to a German, but she need not have worried. King Edward had long ago made his mind up about his nephew, and, privately and discreetly, would probably have been hardly more charitable than the Portuguese Minister.

During the Chatsworth Festivities of 1904 the King very often played bridge with Mrs Keppel in a separate room, and everybody else kept together. Queen Alexandra sometimes grew bored with this, so Muriel and Maudie and others got up impromptu concerts and dances in the corridor where the band was, and thus passed the time away. On one night, just after the Queen had danced with Soveral, some house guest wondered aloud what difference to a person's height his shoes would make. This thought appealed to the Queen. She promptly kicked her own shoes off — whereupon everybody else did likewise. Then she proceeded to try on all the other shoes in the room, thoroughly enjoying herself, and walking around for some time in Willie Grenfell, Lord Desborough's old pumps.(14) Dancing at these house parties often went on until three or four o'clock in the morning, after which, those who had taken part would often sleep on until mid-day. When the King was a guest, however, his movements dictated those of everybody else.

In some ways society had what we might call an unsophisticated idea of fun. They were, for instance, very fond of the Families Game. Mr and Mrs Pus had two daughters Lu and Poly; the O'Graphs had a rascally son, that sinner Mat O'Graph; Mr and Mrs Ow'n Lawns had a son whose name was Moses.(15) They roared with laughter when an unfortunate printer misheard a telephone direction concerning a funeral leaflet, the last item of which was listed as "A Few Remarks by Chopin". Above all, they loved to dress up and act, and the main purpose of the Festivities was the production of theatrical work, at which both Muriel and Lady Maud were impressive. It was probably at the house party of 1904 where they both took part in a play written by Mrs Dora Knatchbull. They were dressed as Eastern characters, and Lady Maud remembered wearing a green and gold costume designed by Percy Anderson, with a helmet on her head and a fine steel spear. When the play was over, the King suddenly seized the spear from Lady Maud, announced that he would now do some pig sticking with it, and promptly pursued a terrified guest the whole length of the long gallery, at the double.(16) Occasionally they did venture into the outside world. Later in that visit the whole party wrapped themselves in their furs, and motored over to Hardwicke Hall to look at the tapestries, children lining the road and waving flags as the royal car drew near.(17) In 1907, one evening after dinner, Queen Alexandra announced that she wished to play baccarat. The party had to comply, but when she retired early, they split up. Lady Maud, Princess Daisy and others played poker, but Muriel, Lord Elcho and Lord Desborough (he of the old pumps) played a more innocent battle of dominoes with Lady de Grey, (yet another Viking, standing slightly taller than Lady Maud at 6' 1 1/2").(18)

A further incident shows Muriel as not only resourceful and sympathetic but also as a quick thinker, and involved — unfortunately for her — Princess Daisy of Pless. The party was at Alloa House, the piece which was being acted was called "A Pantomime Rehearsal". Princess Daisy tells us:

> "Just as I was going on stage I half tripped over what I thought was some of the cord of the electric lights. I did not take any notice. But when I came off again, Muriel Wilson, who had been just behind me, said with a sympathetic face, 'My dear, *how awful* for you' and gave me a little bundle of silk and lace. It was *not* my petticoat. She had seen something hanging down, and as it was too late to stop me from going on the stage, she gave it a little tug and down 'they' came."(19)

Some of the parties organised by Muriel's friends were almost unbelievable in their magnificence. Florence Hwfa Williams had married a man of remarkable business ability, who played a considerable part in the amalgamation of the Savoy group of hotels — the Savoy, Simpsons, Claridges and the Berkeley. Her husband advocated the opening of smart new restaurants in the hotels, and to get the idea off the ground, his wife organised dinner parties there, followed by a dance. They only invited their friends, but at the first party which they gave at the Savoy (which occurred on the night Gladstone died) no fewer than 375 persons sat down to dinner, and the party went on until four o'clock in the morning. At another of her dinners at the Savoy, Chaliapine was present, and at a small party at Claridges she secured Caruso.(20)

169

The Wilsons had done it. Hard work and shrewdness had put them into the world of society where Mary, at any rate, wished to be, and where her children seemed totally secure. When they were not in London for the season they were at their beautiful villa on the Riviera, or hunting in the Riding. But they had reckoned without the Grim Reaper — as they would certainly have described him. Within two short years he struck again, and again, and again, and left both Charlie and Arthur's families bereft. The best years were over, suddenly stopped, and for seventeen years Mary realised and remembered that of the two great blows, the death of her husband and the end of her life in society, it was the first which was the real tragedy.

The Villa Maryland

During the nineteenth century the English had virtually taken over the Riviera. Even Queen Victoria had succumbed. Prince Leopold had been recommended to visit Mentone because of his haemophilia, and his mother had been to see him there in 1882. She was attracted by the area and its climate, and followed up the visit by going to Grasse in 1891 and Cimiez (Nice) after that, travelling south early in March, when the winds of Britain were still cold and biting.(21) Her son, the future King Edward VII, was equally fascinated, but preferred Cannes to Cimiez. He would ensure that his yacht "Britannia" would be there when he arrived, so that he could entertain privately on board. The rest of the Royal Family also visited the area and Prince Arthur, Duke of Connaught, in particular loved it and during the 1920s spent a season there every year, first at Beaulieu, then at Cap Ferrat, which was where, at the turn of the century, Arthur Wilson's Mediterranean villa was built. Cap Ferrat had already attracted several well known and talented individuals, and would attract many more.

The architect chosen by Arthur Wilson to develop the site he had managed to buy, was Harold A. Peto. Peto came from a family of individualists. His father, Samuel Morton Peto (1809-1889) was born in Woking (where, at one time, some of the Smith family lived), but at an early age he had been apprenticed to an uncle, Henry Peto, who was a builder at 31, Little Britain, near St. Paul's. In 1830 this uncle had retired, and Samuel and another nephew, Thomas Grissell, inherited and developed the business. One of their commissions was Nelson's Column, which was erected in 1843. Another was Somerleyton, Suffolk which was remodelled by Peto, regardless of expense, and contained a huge winter garden 100 feet square. (A passion for gardens was to be a characteristic of Harold's work, later on). After 1840 Samuel had begun to take an interest in railway building and, during the Crimean War, had suggested and constructed 39 miles of track from Balaklava to the army entrenchments before Sebastapol.

Harold had been born in 1854, and there was never much doubt that he would become an architect. He joined Ernest George, a well known and sought after Victorian architect, when George's partner, Thomas Vaughan, died in 1875, and he stayed with him for 22 years. George enjoyed popularity and a reputation perhaps greater than he deserved. He was influenced by Norman Shaw's Old English style, but broke away, and by the time Harold Peto joined him, his eye was very definitely on the nouveau riche country house market. Nevertheless, with Peto, George built in 1882 an immense house at Buchan Hill, Sussex, for an ostrich-feather merchant named Saillard. Mark Girouard calls it "exotic" and makes the comment "One could have done with more Buchan Hills".(22) Much to Girouard's disappointment "as George's practice grew more aristocratic his buildings

The central avenue in the lower garden, Maryland (from the Pressling/Woolrich bequest).

The cypress walk, Maryland (from the Pressling/Woolrich bequest).

became better behaved", but the romance of his early training remained with Peto. George became famous for his line sketches washed in sepia, which showed his clients (many of whom pined for a personal history) what a beautiful "old" house they would eventually get. He was a good draughtsman, but the sketches gave little indication of architectural detail or texture of materials. Goodhart-Rendel mentions how rival architects would point out the difficulties of constructing an interior to fit in with the fanciful exterior whilst still being convenient.(23)

Peto learned a lot from George — not least how to charm his clients. Most of the country houses on which he worked were in the south of England, but one, Monk Fryston, was in Yorkshire. He had plenty of experience of building houses in London, and was with George when he designed a villa at Antibes.

By the time Peto left George he was thinking not simply in terms of building a house, but also of harmonising house and estate, and formal planning with informality of plant growth. Arthur Wilson's commission at Cap Ferrat gave him the opportunity to develop these ideas, and also gave him an outsize headache. By now the English had introduced the formal garden to the inhabitants of the Riviera, who would never have done it themselves — it was far too pricey; even the provision of water necessary to keep the plants and flowers alive would involve considerable expenditure, and poor and thrifty as they were, any flowers they grew would have to have economic value for them. However, pioneers like John Taylor, a Suffolk gardener who later became a land agent, and Dr James Henry Bennet, who created his own garden with the help of "an intelligent peasant"(24) had already shown what could be done, and thyme, juniper, rosemary, cacti and geraniums as well as chrysanthemums, all flourished, and for the first time green lawns could be seen.

When Arthur Wilson decided to have a permanent residence in the Riviera he found land at a premium and very difficult to obtain, especially where he wanted it, and the best he could do was to buy up four acres on Cap Ferrat. The site was enough to put the fear of inadequacy into any architect.(25) The cape itself is a thin finger of land which pushes itself out into the Mediterranean. On all sides the land slopes upwards to a rocky summit, and it was up there that Arthur Wilson's purchase was to be found. Peto had not only to resolve the problem of land falling away on every side, but worse still, a peasant road ran right through the middle of the property. This gave access to several very small holdings, mere plots of ground, not all of which Arthur had acquired. The road, therefore, could not be obliterated, but at least it was a cul-de-sac. How on earth could Peto turn such unpromising material into a thing of beauty?

Fortunately he knew the area well, and had just finished a house in the neighbourhood, now known as the Villa Silvia. Equally fortunately, he knew Arthur Wilson, having done business with him on a previous occasion. He had been a lover of fine furniture and objects d'art throughout his life, and since he was steeped in the history, art, and literature of the Mediterranean, particularly Italy (his poor health had forced him to live there for some time) and the Riviera itself, he was less likely than some to be guilty of tastelessness.

He decided to incorporate the obnoxious little road into his scheme. The house itself would be built just to the north of it, on the highest point of the land. This would give it a south facing aspect, near the road but above it and, bearing in mind the structure of the cape, there would be spectacular views from every direction. Peto saw that the eastern aspect was the least impressive, so the house was sited to that side, with its offices close to the eastern boundary of the property. The road was twelve feet below the top of the plateau, which was to be the floor level of the house, and, as the ground fell precipitously on the southern side, the architect realised that it could be hidden from both house and terrace. First he arranged that a retaining wall should be built on either side of the road to the height of what would become the main building. There would be a bridge to span it with steps going down to left and right to the level of the southern part of the garden, which was on the opposite side of the road to the house.

The house itself would be set 40 feet back from the miserable road, but Peto boldly decided that it should be entered from the road itself. Between the house and the road he erected a two storeyed arcaded and vaulted cloister with an angled staircase leading up to the main hall. At the entrance to the cloister the road had been considerably widened on its north side, and a round arched doorway with wrought iron gates led inside. The cloister was cool and pleasant. In the centre was an old and beautiful marble bowl, or tazza in the middle of which a winged boy stood poised on one foot holding in his hand a small cup, from which a stream of water flowed. The water filled the bowl, which had been placed on a decorated pedestal, and overflowed into a larger pool set into the floor of the cloister. The walls were arcaded, the lower enclosed storey built in rough stone from the Pont du Gard quarries. The shafts of the upper tier, which was open to the Mediterranean wind and weather, were of a shell pink marble, half polished. Climbing plants decorated the walls at both levels.

Turning west from the upper storey of the cloister instead of north into the main hall, the formal gardens were to be found. Peto had had the retaining walls and balustrade on both sides of the road covered with a profusion of flowers, ivy leafed geranium, rosemary and lotus peliorhynchus reaching right down to the road. Just where the road turned north to accommodate the entrance to the villa he had built a little bastion, jutting out in a semi-circle over the road. From here, one of the best viewpoints in the estate, the whole of the lower garden and the rocky coastline to east and west could be seen. Moving westwards alongside this northern wall the residents would have on their right the green lawns of the sunken gardens. Descending a few steps they would come first to the bridge which linked the two halves of the estate, and then to what they learned to call the Fisherman's Cottage. This was one of the few original buildings retained by Peto, but it came just at the point where there was a slight bend in the road, and the architect realised that he could use the structure to hide the imperfect line. He gutted the cottage and opened out its walls so that it became a shelter. Paths from the bridge and the far side of the Fisherman's Cottage led due north across the lawns, and were intersected at right angles by other paths from the villa, and these led to the western end of the estate. However, if one moved straight through the Cottage and continued along the side of the northern boundary wall, the Cypress Walk was reached. Arches decorated with climbing plants spanned the Walk, and similar arches were placed on top of the boundary wall, their shadows making loops on the pathway as the Mediterranean sun shone down upon them. To the north of the Walk Peto laid out a square of formal gardens, intersected at right angles by paths, in the same manner as the lawns, but there were far more intersections here. In the very centre a low circular platform had been laid down in concrete, and on it stood a huge Roman corn jar. Standing here, and looking directly across the gardens to the east, the door of the main hall could be seen. Turning west and looking towards the far end of the property one could see an almost semi-circular pool with free flowering arum lilies in it, and a garden temple, arched and pillared, behind it. Peto had also introduced antique columns into the parterre. They formed pedestals for classical figures. The beds were filled with dwarf mimosas, orange trees, azaleas and the westringia and among the flowers were peonies, dicentras

In the wild garden, Maryland (from the Pressling/Woolrich bequest).

Maryland, viewed from the cloister (from the Pressling/Woolrich bequest).

and lilies. Paths from the north west and south west corners of the parterre ran round the back of the pool to the temple and formed a semi-circle. They were contained by a pergola, solid at the back, but forming an open colonnade on the garden side. Peto left the old olive trees which had been there during the peasant occupation alone, and many of their knarled and ancient boughs stretched over and into the pergola, giving a sense of timelessness to the beauty Peto had created.

Peto wanted to link the formal with the informal. At the northern end of the little estate, beyond the high lawns and the house, there was a wild garden. Here was shade, and nature running riot. Little stone stepping points appeared at intervals, and grass paths meandered through the area, unevenly on an uneven surface. Among the old olives Peto set clumps of iris, narcissi and anemone and these bloomed and spread, sprawling in joyful profusion in every direction. Indeed, one section of this garden became known as the iris field, and Muriel Wilson would come here often to sit quietly and gaze, without ever taking her fill, on the beauty of the land and the tranquility and fragility of this natural garden. Crossing the bridge that spanned the peasant road (which had a high arch to keep well clear of laden carts) one came into the lower garden. The immediate problem with which Peto had to deal was its steepness. He built a small, semi-circular bastion, or view point on the south side of the bridge, rather like the one near the cloisters, and from here, steps descended to left and right gently curving round into the garden before reaching ground level. To the south and immediately in front of the bastion Peto created a stepped central avenue, with paths off to left and right at different levels, and leading down to a levelled area with a circular pool containing a two tiered marble fountain (brought from Venice) and, behind it and at the extreme edge of the southern boundary of the property, a small temple. Shortly after

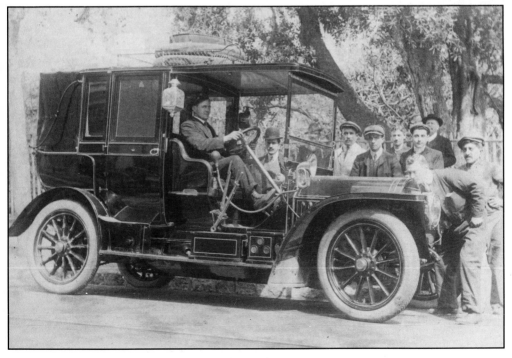

Mary Wilson's De Launey Bellville, Cap Ferrat 1906. Photo by courtesy of Dr. T. Debney.

the Second World War the Maryland stepped avenue received unexpected publicity when a sequence from the ballet — film *The Red Shoes,* which starred Moyra Shearer, was filmed there.

Peto had an eye for colour. He planted lavender bushes and echium at the feet of the tall cypresses which bordered the central avenue so that a blue-grey colour predominated, and this was repeated throughout the garden. To the east of the steps down from the bridge a pergola was built. Its back, below the level of the dividing road, was of rough cast brick completely obscured by greenery. The garden side had a brick colonnade, topped by plain, square capitals at intervals, on which rested the supports for the cross rafters. Looking east, the sea and the surrounding coast could be seen through the gap in the cypress border, but such was Peto's skill in planting that the immediate neighbourhood was hidden, thus gaining privacy for the Wilsons and their guests. The pergola was filled with rose blossom, and was the most colourful part of the lower garden. This was a more informal garden than the one above, but was therefore more restful. At the north west corner of this part of the estate Peto put the gardener's house and, next door to it, the garage, both of them having access to the little road.

Peto's first problem with the villa itself was that it should not look too big for its surroundings. The site was only small. His second problem was that he had to build a Mediterranean house for an Englishman, and many Englishmen were horrified at the idea of a house which had few enclosed rooms. But Peto was bold. He built a villa which gave the Wilsons the opportunity of enjoying fresh air whenever they wished, but at the same time included a sufficient number of well heated rooms for their comfort if a cold spell should occur.

Alongside the hall, which lay immediately to the north of the cloisters and above which were the guest rooms, was an open terrace, and beyond that and immediately under the main bedrooms, was a loggia. The path to the loggia was bordered thickly with violas and aubretias. Peto's love of Italian architecture could be seen in all aspects of the building. The villa was full of angles, corners and roofs of different height, and because it was necessary for the eye to shift continuously to take in the main lines of the architecture with its often exquisite detail, the actual size of the house hardly registered against the tall trees along the terrace walk on the north side of the dividing wall.

Peto had already shown his love of ancient Italian objects. Coming upstairs from the cloister court with its ancient tazza, one would see, on reaching the parapet in front of the hall door, that an old heraldic panel had been built into the outside of it, and there were rare terra-cotta roundels on the spandrels of the cloister arcading both inside and out. The ones on the outside were, in fact, fine copies — it would not have been sensible, even had it been possible to acquire originals, to expose such treasures to the weather at all seasons of the year.

The enclosed rooms of the house formed a long rectangle from which the south west corner had been removed to form the loggia terrace and part of the sunken gardens. The hall, which would normally be approached from the cloisters but could also be entered from the terrace, was a dignified but not very large room, some twenty by twenty six feet. Opposite the cloister entrance was a huge open hearth with a hood supported by stone pillars. To the east, a double door led to the library, and to the right of the fireplace as one faced it, was a round headed and curtained archway which led to the staircase hall, the very centre of the house, from which all other rooms could be reached. The ceiling of the hall was of the beam and rafter type, the spaces between the rafters having painted corbels showing coats of arms and the like. The furniture in the room included Louis XIII chairs in walnut covered in petit point. To the west of the fireplace was the door to the loggia, which could be seen from the Roman corn jar area of the parterre if one looked back towards the house; and from the same wall a huge window opened onto the terrace giving a fine view of the whole length of the upper gardens as far as the pool and temple at the western end. Two windows on the south side looked into the cloister court.

On the far side of the staircase hall Peto built the dining room which projected further north than the line of the house wall. This enabled him to have not only three large windows which spread over the entire breadth of the room, but also narrow windows at the east and west to complete the bay. This room was only a short distance from the boundary but, because the land fell away rapidly, Peto saw that little could be imposed between the immediate foreground and the more distant shore line. However, he built up a platform surrounded by trees and plants, and placed in the middle of it a tall column on which was a winged goddess, bow in hand, her long cloak flying behind her and one foot poised on a globe. Across the bay the distant villas and houses of Bieulieu sweltered in the sun, and rising behind them heaved the Maritime Alps.

The dining room itself, some 30 feet by 20 feet in area, was conceived by Peto as a typical refectory of the South. Its walls were absolutely plain, and the roof had perfectly plain plaster vaulting, supported by carved corbels which projected only slightly into the room. Walls and ceiling were both whitewashed to give a cool and restful atmosphere, and Peto had installed an antique fireplace. The furniture chosen was Swiss of the late 16th or early 17th century. There was a particularly fine dining table, which could be extended by drawing out, the top was inlaid, and it had carved, ornate trestle legs. The squarely built,

Some of the staff at Maryland. Miss Frances Woolrich, the last housekeeper, is standing on the left (from the Pressling/Woolrich bequest).

straight backed chairs had carved backs in sympathy with the carving on the trestles.

A few feet to the west of the dining room door and the door into the loggia, the corridor came to an end before the most magnificent door in the Villa Maryland. This was the double door into the salon. It had been carved in the Spain of the 16th century, and each door was symetrically divided into square and oblong panels, there being no fewer than 48 in all. The room beyond was, and indeed needed to be, the largest room in Maryland. It ran north-south for 40 feet, and the big door was sited in the middle of the long eastern wall. It was set into a shallow recess, and immediately opposite it, a huge bay jutted out into the trellised rose garden, at the north western corner of the house. A door window enabled the family to gaze down one of the paths to the high lawns, the parterre, and, slightly to the south, the temple at the west end of the property. It is only when the full length of the garden can be seen that it can be realised how restricted the site really is — a further tribute to the genius of Peto's planning.

On the north wall of the huge salon was an equally huge fireplace of 15th century Italian work. On top of it stood, at either end, two large ornamental elephants each carrying a vase. It is not easy, looking at these tall ornaments, to realise that the height of the room is a full 16 feet. The richness of the decoration on the fireplace is carried through elsewhere. The walls were hung with red damask, a careful copy of an old Italian pattern. The caisson ceiling was deep and massive, divided into plaster squares within each of which was an elaborately fluted roundel. The chairs, all chosen with great care, were upholstered in damask and petit point tapestry. Cheerful, oriental rugs on the floor underlined the warm and welcoming atmosphere of the house.

Probably Arthur and Mary never appreciated this house as much as Muriel did. No house anywhere ever displaced Tranby Croft in Arthur's personal affections. The name Maryland implies that the Mediterranean villa was built as a present to his wife; it was certainly a status symbol for her, and Mary appreciated such. After the house was completed, Arthur was spared very few more years, and after his death Mary was a changed woman. Muriel, however, loved it, and it was probably her favourite of all the Wilson houses. She continued to visit it regularly until, in the early 1960s, she became too old and frail to travel there. Before her death the house passed to a member of the Warde family, into which she had married.

Mr Reid, the butler at Tranby Croft, who lived at one time in the stable block and later went to farm at Bentley near Beverley where the Wilsons owned land, regularly brought back from Maryland orange branches bearing fruit, to be shown to the people of Anlaby who marvelled at the sight. These were the lotus days, but like Muriel they have now gone for ever, though the distant flashes from the lighthouse as the sun goes down over the sea remain, as she used to see and love them.

The Grim Reaper and the End of an Era

The Edwardian social whirl was an Indian Summer, and like an Indian Summer short lived. For the Wilsons it was even shorter than for the rest of their friends and acquaintances. On 27th October 1907, Charlie died very suddenly. He had not been well, and had actually seen his doctor earlier in the day, but had eaten a good Sunday lunch and was sitting on a sofa, chatting to his relative Mrs Cecil Wellesley when he suddenly lifted up his hands, and all was over. Arthur suffered bitterly. He was devoted to his brother, his alter ego. Their personal differences, and there had been many, had not mattered. At work, and work had been a focal point of their lives, they had always been as one.

Charlie, a parliamentarian by inclination, had sat for the Hull constituency from 1874 to 1885 when, after Gladstone's second great Reform Act, the constituency boundaries were redrawn. After the change, he represented Hull West without a break, until the experienced old Scot, Campbell-Bannerman, needing new blood in the House of Commons, made it possible for him to become a peer. He took the title 1st Lord Nunburnholme, from the little village near his residence at Warter Priory. His eldest son, Tommy, took his place as representative of West Hull, and was as staunch a Liberal as his father. Charlie had never been a prolific speaker and, more often than not, had confined his attentions to the subject of shipping about which, it must be presumed, he could speak with authority. Unlike Arthur, he had never cared for race meetings, and he had never entertained a party during the Doncaster race week. He was sometimes referred to as "the Napoleon of the North" but, great ship owner though he was, he was not deficient in humanity. In his young days he had believed in the rightness of the recognition of trade union members, and he had always maintained that cooperation between employer and employee could bring nothing but good. Even during the strike of 1893, by which time Charlie had learned to fear more from the unions, he subscribed handsomely to the fund for strikers' wives and children, saying he "could not bear to see little children suffer".(26) But he was blunt, sometimes to the point of rudeness, and in its obituary the *Hull Daily Mail* wrote:

"To Charles Wilson was due the praise of saying what he meant. It might not be pleasant, it might be inexpedient, it might even be unjust, but if it was uppermost in his mind at the time, he said it, and people could simply please themselves whether they liked it or not."(27)

The same attitude was noticeable when he was dealing with his constituents. Charlie never nursed them — he never had to do so, and many of them regarded him as immoveable as an institution. He *expected* their vote, and the prospect of a parliamentary defeat probably never entered his head. He was a more astringent man than Arthur, and probably not as popular, but he had been generous to a fault to local charities.

The next blow fell some five months after the death of Charlie, but it was less severe. Frederick Wilson had, in some ways, been a thorn in the flesh of his commercially minded brothers, and had lived the life of an artist in Florence. Since the death of old Thomas he had repeatedly asked for money, and had certainly been under the impression that he had not had his fair share. He had married an Italian girl, Maria Luisa Musetti, to whom all his goods and chattels were now left.

Arthur had barely had time to recover from this second shock when there came the tragic news of the death of his 23 year old nephew, Gerald, Charlie and Florence's youngest boy. He had hoped to be able to pursue a career in the diplomatic service and with this aim in view had gone, in June 1908, to study in Berlin. In late September he had started for home, but, understandably for a young man, had broken his journey in Paris. The day before his death he had taken a motor drive from which he had returned late. He had then eaten dinner, had a hot bath, and had gone to bed. His servant had discovered him unconscious the next morning, and had fetched a doctor. It was too late. Gerald died at five o'clock that afternoon. Once again Arthur made the bitter pilgrimage to Warter, where the boy was laid to rest, like his father, in the Italian gardens which had been designed by Florence. They lay in front of the house, and the headstones, since removed to a private area of the graveyard behind the church at Nunburnholme, could be seen from the windows.

But death had not yet finished with the Wilsons. Christmas 1908 was carried through at Tranby Croft with all the usual festive cheer and good will. On Boxing Day, Arthur took to his bed with stomach cramps, which he thought at first was caused by indigestion. The local doctor was called in. Dr Murray examined Arthur and was worried enough to call in a Hull colleague, Dr Frank Nicholson, who was no more easy in his mind than his friend. Together they sought the help of a London specialist, Mr Pearce Gould, who told them, what they had suspected, that Arthur was suffering from cancer. As was the custom then, a room in the mansion was turned into an operating theatre, and Arthur was given surgery, which was pronounced a success. Mary spoke optimistically to her husband, but she knew that the writing was on the wall. Arthur recovered sufficiently to make the journey to his lovely villa at Cap Ferrat at the end of January. Thus he was spared the harshness of an East Riding winter. He returned to London at the end of June, but not, alas, to enjoy an English summer, but to undergo a further operation. This was performed on 4th July, and bought him a little time, so that at the end of that month he was able to travel back to his beloved Tranby Croft to end his days there. He tried to visit his headquarters in Commercial Road, but the effort was too great, and those who saw him said that he looked thin and drawn. He was often pushed out into his garden in a bath chair, and lived long enough to witness the flowering of the dahlias, his favourites. The end came peacefully on 21st October and the hey-day of the Wilson Line was at an end.

Arthur had lived longer than any other son of Thomas Wilson. When he died, there were only two of his sisters left out of the original fifteen children. These were Emily, wife of Arthur Harrison, a corn merchant of Cottingham, and Rachel, third wife of Joseph Lambert, also a merchant of Cottingham. Before Emily, the last survivor, died in 1921 the Wilson firm had passed into other hands. It had survived for only two generations. Arthur had been a loving husband and father; he had also been a shrewd and dedicated business man. Born and educated in Hull, he, like Charlie, had been willing to devote his life to the development of family business interests. Before he died, he must have been aware of the difference of approach to life of his Eton educated, socially orientated sons. Jack was already a Conservative Member of Parliament, and unlike his father had supported that party from the beginning. Arthur had turned away from Gladstone at the time of his party-breaking Home Rule for Ireland measure; but once turned, he had turned for good. When Joseph Chamberlain looked like splitting the Conservatives over Tariff Reform, Arthur did not budge. Less than four months before his death he had written:

"This country is faced with a most serious and dangerous problem in the Budget . . . I say we have now to decide between the Socialism of the present Government, and a policy of Fiscal or Tariff Reform, and I, without hesitation accept Fiscal Reform."[28]

Arthur had been full of pride when Jack had won Holderness for the Conservative party in 1900, but Jack would be a politician, not a ship owner. The gentler and conscientious Kenneth could be expected to do his best, but he lacked his father's ruthlessness in business, and his relationship with his cousin Tommy Nunburnholme was certainly not as close as that between his father and his uncle. Clive, the youngest brother, intended to enjoy his life to the full. He was a soldier, a polo player and an amateur actor and singer: he did not enjoy the prospect of being chained to an office desk for twenty minutes, let alone twenty years. It is just possible, though hardly probable, that his sons managed to hide from their ambitious parent the fact that they saw no necessity to continue the business.

Neither had the sons the same affection for their father's house. Jack did not wish to live there. Kenneth's wife, Molly, hankered after the society of London, where indeed they settled, and Clive, on his marriage, had gone to Beverley. Perhaps Arthur, at 72 and very deaf, died early enough not to have realised all this, but Mary knew. It was her lot to live under the new régime for a further eighteen years, but in one sense she had died with her husband.

Hull mourned him too. The day he died, the large bell at Holy Trinity Church tolled for an hour and a half. He was buried, however, in a new vault in Kirkella cemetery and eventually a tall celtic cross was erected above it. The local people said it was on a bee line between the tower of Tranby Croft and the church tower at Kirkella, where Arthur and Mary and the children used to worship when they first came out to the Riding. It is a likely story, and this kind of symbolism would have appealed to the dead man, who loved his home and his church with passion. At his funeral, the vault was lined with single white dahlias, his favourite flower, and at either end was an anchor and a heart, also in flowers. It was fitting that this should be so. Charlie and Arthur had loved the family business so much that, to their sons, they had been the family business. If the fates were not going to allow it to continue, at least this token served as a mute illustration of the third great love in the life of Arthur Wilson of Tranby Croft.

Mary was supported by every member of the family with the exception of Jack's wife, Queenie, who was abroad. The floral tributes were so numerous that the swimming bath was emptied and the wreaths placed there. King Edward VII, the Duke and Duchess of Connaught, Prince Francis of Teck (Muriel's friend), the Grand Duke Michael of Russia and his wife, Countess Sophie Torby, all sent messages of sympathy. On the day of the funeral Arthur's body was brought down to the library (that Aladdin's cave with its gold bedecked ceiling), and the Union Jack, flying from the tower was dipped. A succession of farm rulleys were draped with purple velvet, the first being for the coffin and the others for the family wreaths, and at a quarter past two in the afternoon the coffin was brought outside, its lid completely hidden by Mary's wreath - a cross of scarlet salvias with here and there a carnation. It bore a card with the words "My darling, God bless and keep us both, your loving and devoted wife". It was a message of faith. Even in her devastation Mary still recognised that somewhere, somehow, a part of her still belonged to Arthur and a part of him was still hers. This proud, apparently dominant woman, had now been bequeathed the impossible task of reconciling the outlook and standards of her dead husband with the very different attitudes of their progeny. She never really tried: she knew it was beyond her.

The procession formed and moved off, the rulleys being driven by the oldest farm servants. Mary travelled by car, immediately behind the coffin. There was a service in Anlaby Church and, at precisely the same time, one in Holy Trinity Church, Hull. To the latter came the children from Spring Bank Orphanage and the Newland Homes. There were also many Wilson employees, and a contingent of the Imperial Yeomanry of which both Jack and Clive were officers.

The procession reached Anlaby Church, where the vicar, Mr Stromberg, was waiting to take the ceremony. The gentlemen had walked behind the rulleys, and had been followed by the servants. The ladies came in cars. Arthur's coffin, draped with the Wilson Line flag, was carried in, and the service began. It included one of his favourite hymns,

"Lead, kindly light". By three o'clock the mourners had reached the graveside. Here, the service was conducted by Arthur's old friend Rev. Foord from Kirkella, and another favourite hymn, "Abide with me", was sung. The cemetery gates had been closed to the public until after the mourners had left, but before the end of that service the gates fell open, because of the great pressure from the crowd, and the people moved in. There was no unruliness, they were quiet and respectful, but they had wanted to pay their respects to a man who had so often given help where it was needed, and by the time the family turned from the vault side, the little cemetery was full of those who sympathised and wanted them to know it.(29)

As was the custom, a poem in Arthur's memory duly appeared in the local newspaper. Sycophantic we may call it, but it was better than the token appreciation which so often suffices today.

"O, stay thy hand, Grim Death! Thy sickle keen,
Full many a day hath busy been, . . .
Thine aim is sure, for thou hadst dealt a blow
And laid another Prince of Commerce low. . . .
Here lived a man who scorned the miser's yoke.
His purse an 'open seseme' to poor and needy folk;
He loved the simple life, nor cared for pomp or show,
And used his wealth to lessen human woe, . . .
But oh! thy maw is greedy for these, the good and true,
The worst thou leavest, the best (alas, too few)
Thou takest one by one, and sure we are
The world is all the poorer since they have crossed the bar, . . .
Sleep on! Sleep on, beloved! We lay thee gently down
To rest in Mother Nature's arms till God shall claim His own. . . .
And on the Resurrection morn triumphant faith will sing
'O, Grave, where is thy victory, O Death where is thy sting?'"(30)

Perhaps a gentler offering, printed earlier by the same newspaper, is more to our taste (at least its genealogy is impeccable):

"His life was gentle and the elements
So mixed in him, that Nature might stand up
And say to all the world — This was a man".(31)

After the funeral Mary and Muriel went to winter in the Riviera. The boys, by the terms of the will, were to sell the town house, but allow Mary to move such furniture and effects as she would like. A smaller house was found for her at No. 21 Charles Street, and she and Muriel, the only unmarried daughter, went to live there. It was Mary's last home, and a long twilight after a glittering noonday. The social climb, brilliantly successful as it was, had cut the umbilical cord which had bound the Wilsons to the East Riding, and instead of a pervasive presence, they became only a memory.

(1) The building lease was granted to Robert John Waller, builder of Lyall Street in 1875, retrospective to the building commencement in 1867. (I am grateful to Mr W.W. Ellis of the Grosvenor Office, 53 Davies Street for this information).
(2) *Hull News* 8.7.1899 p.9 columns c/d.

(3) Ibid 2.7.1898 p.2 column c.
(4) Ibid 14.5.1898 p.3 column a.
(5) Ibid 24.6.1899 p.3 column f.
(6) Ibid 24.6.1899 p.10 column f.
(7) *Lady Maud Warrender: My First Sixty Years* (Cassell 1933) p.70 Lady Maud, or Maudie, as Muriel and her friends called her, was a woman of Viking proportions - she stood 6' 1". She was a granddaughter of Lord Shaftesbury, the factory reformer and philanthropist, and she was a philanthropist herself. She acted with Muriel, sometimes before the Prince of Wales, but more often she sang. She had a rich contralto voice, and it was no doubt Muriel who persuaded her to sing once in Beverley Minster.
(8) Mrs Hwfa Williams: *It was Such Fun:* op.cit. pp.75-77.
(9) *The Hull Lady* June 1902 p.41.
(10) Ibid Canto 111 p.4.
(11) *Hull News* 5.9.1903 p.10 column e.
(12) Ibid 28.12.1901 Epitome of the year.
(13) *The Private Diaries of Princess Daisy of Pless 1873-1914* ed. D. Chapman-Huston (John Murray 1950) p.79.
(14) Ibid p.102-103.
(15) *Lady Maud Warrender: My First Sixty Years* p.83.
(16) Ibid p.79.
(17) *Princess Daisy of Pless* pp.102-3.
(18) Ibid p.160.
(19) Ibid p.100.
(20) *Mrs Hwfa Williams: It Was Such Fun* p.318.
(21) *Patrick Howard: When the Riviera was Ours* (Routledge and Kegan Paul 1977) chapter 4.
(22) *Mark Girouard: The Victorian Country House* (Yale University Press New Haven and London 1979) p.82.
(23) *ed. Peter Ferriday: Victorian Architecture* (Jonathan Cape Ltd. 1963) p.69.
(24) Quoted Howarth op.cit. p.59.
(25) Much of my information about Maryland comes from two articles on the house and grounds, which appeared in Country Life 3.12.1910 and 10.12.1910.
(26) *The Star* 28.10.1907.
(27) *Hull Daily Mail* 28.10.1907.
(28) *Standard* 22.10.1909 Obituary notice.
(29) A scrap book once in the possession of Ellerman's Wilson contains cuttings from newspapers from all over the British Isles. Unfortunately these are not all adequately identified. The book is now in the possession of the University of Hull but I am grateful to Mr M.M. Webster, late of Ellerman's Wilson who allowed me to see it.
(30) *Eastern Morning News* 26.10.1909.
(31) Ibid 22.10.1909.

CHAPTER TEN

The Sons

It is after looking at the careers of the children of Tranby Croft that this story will end, although the family itself flourishes, multiplies, and is scattered throughout all parts of the world. The elder daughters, Tottie and Ethel, had joined other families, and were busily engaged in bringing up their children miles away from Hull. We hear of them incidentally, but the careers of the boys and of Muriel, who married too late to produce a family, have a good deal of relevance if we are to have a fair record of the results of their training at the hands of Arthur and Mary. Unlike their parents, the sons had started out from a position of strength, both financially and socially, and there was not a single "son of Hull" among them.

Jack (Arthur Stanley)

At the trial of the baccarat case in 1891 Jack had received an unenviable press, and had acquired his nickname "Jack in the box", but this had neither subdued his natural exuberance nor held him back socially. Less than a year later he had married Alice Cecil Agnes Filmer who bore him two sons, Arthur and Robert. Queenie's own father had died without male heirs, and the title and property, at Sutton Place, Staplehurst, Kent had passed to her brother, Sir Robert Marcus Filmer, but he also had no issue. Consequently on the death of Sir Robert in 1916 young Arthur, providing that he added the surname Filmer to his own, was to inherit the property. So he eventually became Arthur Thomas Filmer Wilson-Filmer, which somewhat confused the local people.

This, however, belonged to the future. In the 1890s Jack continued to live a witty, jocular, hectic and "modern" lifestyle at his comfortable home at Raywell House, some three or four miles from his old family home. At this time there were many people who dismissed him as nothing more than a dilettante, and stories such as the following were legion. Jack complained that he was haunted by one of the latest hit-tunes "The honeysuckle and the bee", and lamented that he seemed unable to stop singing it. "I'm not surprised it haunts you" exclaimed his blunt friend "Considering how you murder it". A trivial story, but most of the stories about Jack were trivial. He was, nevertheless, made of a finer temper than many imagined; and he now determined to enter Parliament, the first member of his immediate family to consider it at all.

Unlike the Warter Priory Wilsons who had, by now, plenty of parliamentary experience of the liberal persuasion, Jack, like Arthur, was a conservative and Arthur, who had never had any political aspirations himself, now gave his support whole-heartedly to his son. The chance came in the year 1900 when Britain, under a conservative government headed by Lord Salisbury, was struggling to conclude the Second Boer War in South

Africa. Charles Henry had had serious doubts on the issue, but once the die was cast, he threw himself enthusiastically into the patriotic struggle. Being a liberal, he stood in opposition to the government on other issues, and this was acceptable to his electorate. Commander Bethell, the member for the Holderness division, was not a liberal. Yet he, a conservative, dared to raise his voice in criticism of his government. There was plenty to criticise. The concentration camps in which the captured Boers had been placed were horrific, but the Commander's attitude caused offence to his local supporters, and encouraged the small executive committee to choose another candidate for the forthcoming election, which was expected late in the year.

Here was Jack's chance. The Arthur Wilsons had been somewhat overshadowed by the Charlie Wilsons so far this year in the matter of war work, and their image needed a boost. Charlie's eldest boy, Tommy, was, at the beginning of the year, Sheriff of Hull. He had, however, been granted leave of absence to go and fight. In mid January he had been sent out to the veldt and a contingent of colleagues, family and friends went south to see him go. Lord Chesterfield, who would very soon become a member of the family by marrying Tommy's sister Enid in the next month, was not present, but wrote that he expected the young man to do well, adding significantly "He is a Wilson. What more need I say? To you in Hull, this speaks volumes".(1)

To be fair, the balance between the two sides of the family had been somewhat redressed the following month. At the time Enid Wilson married Lord Chesterfield, a patriotic presentation of tableaux vivants in aid of the wives and families of the members of the Brigade of Guards took place at Her Majesty's Theatre. The American Mrs Arthur Paget was primarily responsible for this masque of War and Peace, which was described as the best dress-up since the Devonshire House Ball of 1897. Muriel Wilson was outstanding in two guises. As the Spirit of War she wore a long, blood red cloak of crepe de chine, a breastplate of oxydised silver with a helmet to match, and she carried a flaming torch of battle in her hand. A very quick change was necessary as she had to appear again immediately as the Spirit of Peace, but she simply stripped off the red cloak to reveal a simple white garment. A wreath of red and white roses was then placed on her head, and the flaming torch was exchanged for an olive branch. More than one national paper described her performance as breathtaking and spectacular.(2)

Mary Wilson had followed up this effort within the week with a Cafe Chantant at the Hull Assembly Rooms. She had assembled forty "waitresses", who wore red skirts with white muslin aprons on top, bodices which at the back looked like Eton jackets, and had white fichus in front, with sleeves of white chiffon tied with little red and blue ribbons. These "waitresses" sold programmes at "more or less abnormal prices"(3) and "unblushingly" asked for tips. But Mary had to accept defeat in a certain quarter. Molly, Kenneth's wife, asserted her individuality by wearing a scarlet muslin cap instead of the white mob caps of muslin which the rest had been asked to wear. She had also attached red and blue streamers to her bodice. There was an entertainment in which Muriel, Ethel, her daughter Nancy, and the little girl Gwendoline Brogden all took part. Gwendoline starred in "The Jewel of Asia" while Muriel recited "Roberts of Kandahar" and "The Absent Minded Beggar" written by Kipling to have a direct appeal to charitable instincts.

Clive had felt unable to watch Tommy go to the front and do nothing himself. He and his relatives Oswald Lambert and Harold Sanderson had also volunteered for service in Mr Paget's Corps of Imperial Yeomanry, and they had sailed from Southampton as part of the 8th Division in mid March.(4) After this, however, there was a long silence, and during it, public attention switched back to Tommy who returned to England in early October, but before that, had diligently informed the local people of his adventures. He had told them of the scarcity of food, how the soldiers lacked a change of clothing, what "piquet" duties entailed, and how he was nearly captured by the Boers in February, but escaped by a night march to the Modder River Camp. He had written in April to tell that he had met Mrs Grober, the wife of a Boer general, who told him that she loathed Kruger, Chamberlain and the Cecil Rhodes capitalists who were responsible, the Free State Boers believed, for bringing on the war so that they could "seize the gold" in the Witwatersrand mines near Johannesburg.(5) All of this Tommy dutifully transcribed, and his proud parents handed it on to the newspaper, and thus kept his memory green.

Arthur and Mary, in view of Clive's silence, had nothing to tell which could compete with their nephew's stories, though they did their best. In April they organised the Annual Fancy Dress Ball for the Victoria Children's Hospital, although they knew there would be little profit. This was all very well, but it did not really match the contribution from Warter, and Mary knew it. The possibility of Jack's candidature for the Holderness constituency was an answer to a prayer.

Jack was determined to stand. It appealed to his pride as well as his patriotism and fighting spirit, and when the executive committee met in Beverley in mid June, Arthur Wilson made sure that it was well aware of his son's political ambitions, and he might also have reminded them how much a wealthy man could do for their funds. Consequently, the following Saturday 16th June 1900, the *Hull News* reported that at a meeting of the Holderness Conservative Association, it had been unanimously decided to recommend Mr Arthur Stanley Wilson to the association for adoption as conservative candidate. A fortnight later he was officially adopted to fight against the Liberal candidate, Mr Lawrie.

Not every local conservative was delighted with the turn that events had taken. On Wednesday, 18th July the Beverley Conservative Club met to elect a new president to replace Lord Londesborough, who had recently died. They elected, unanimously, Mr G. A. Duncombe, their chairman, and in his proposal Mr J. R. Lane said very forcefully that they all wanted him, and it would be a good thing to give a rap to the Holderness executive by letting them know that in Beverley they would all have backed Mr Duncombe as their future member. Mr J. Edgar, who seconded the motion, was even more forthright. He reminded his listeners how, at the Annual General Meeting, he had stressed the suitability of Mr Duncombe as a proper person to succeed Captain Bethell, although it now behoved them to give all their support to Jack. The retired secretary of the club, Mr C. Stephenson, joined in at this point, and the meeting became something of a free for all against poor Jack. "Mr Arthur Stanley Wilson has been pushed down our throats" Mr Stephenson said, and added that the club's protest at the way in which it had been done should be written up in the minutes.(6)

Mr Duncombe, the unanimously elected president, now spoke in a manner far more gracious than any utterance heard so far. He allowed himself one crack at Jack, saying that he had done precious little for the party in Holderness, and had rarely been seen at any of their meetings. He hoped that the young man would begin to make a thorough study of politics, get the feel of the constituency, talk to the electors and note their requests, and that he would also join their club, so that they could be sure that he would match up to the glowing report issued to them by the executive committee.

They need not have worried. Wilsons never did things by halves. From that moment Jack stalked the constituency, and his baptism in public speaking was performed the following Saturday at the Annual General Meeting of the Holderness Conservative Association in Beverley itself.

On Wednesday, 8th August 1900 the Holderness Hunt puppy judging took place. This was held at the kennels in Etton, and after the judging Arthur Wilson invited a large company to lunch in a marquee. Jack was on to an easy wicket here. Surrounded by members of his family and before a large audience, well wined and dined and therefore captive, he also had the advantage of listening to his father's build up before he himself rose to propose "The Health of the Judges". Arthur was able to tell his audience with pride that one of his sons was serving the government on the battle field, and now another was doing his best to serve it at home. The family had at last heard from Clive, who was now acting as galloper to General Bruce Hamilton. Arthur said his youngest son was well, and was at Bethlehem, where 4,000 Boers had recently surrendered to General Hunter. It was a good introduction, calculated to rouse the patriotism of every eater and drinker.

Jack now rose, and in proposing the judges' health reminded his hearers that they too would soon be placed in a position to judge, and would have to choose between a party disunited, leaderless (a reference to Gladstone's controversial Irish measures) and with no coherent policy, and one with a strong and trusted leader and a policy both right and just. The atmosphere became even more euphoric.

It might well have been Muriel's influence that brought the young Winston Churchill to Beverley at the end of the month. At this time Winston was neither so well known, nor had he the reputation for political brilliance formerly enjoyed by his unpredictable father, Randolph. Nevertheless, he was a good catch. The meeting was at the Assembly Rooms and every available seat had been filled long before it was due to start. Two of the three galleries had been made available to the public, and these also had been filled. The third gallery contained a brass band which would play during the interval, and also whenever there was a need for a patriotic gesture. Jack made his, by now, customary speech before moving a vote of confidence in the government. This time, however, he analysed in detail the legislation of the last Liberal government of 1892-1894 and compared it unfavourably with a single session (the first, though he did not say so, when election pledges had to be seen to be honoured) of the present Unionist ministry.

The red-headed Winston sat through all of this in amazement and some consternation, which grew no less when the M.P. for East Dorset, the Hon. H. N. Sturt, made a further contribution, none too short, which ended by congratulating the Holderness conservatives in securing Jack as their candidate. Winston was now allowed to get up, and the band, previously alerted, rendered loudly and with more exuberance than finesse "Soldiers of the Queen". The audience, somewhat taken aback, forgot to sing, but they cheered heartily enough at the end. Winston began by saying, no doubt with some feeling, that all the major issues had already been covered, and that he, too, was sure that Jack was a first class candidate. He then spoke for a full three quarters of an hour. At this stage of his career his speech was fast and that, plus the slight impediment of a sibilant 's' which so far he had failed to correct, meant that much of what he said would not be entirely intelligible to many of his hearers; but there was no doubt about either his dedication or his charisma, and he finished in a style which anticipated his famous utterances two generations further on:

"The great cause for which you have fought will not be allowed to weaken and wither away in the hands of those people who care nothing about it. The fruit of your victory will be preserved to those who come after us and they, in their turn, will be proud and grateful to you."(7)

Arthur Wilson drummed the same lesson home in his vote of thanks.

It had hardly been a straight-forward week for Winston. He was staying at Tranby Croft which had caught fire the previous Wednesday, 29th August. It turned out that the second housemaid had lit the gas in bedroom No. 6 (one of the two best rooms in the house) at seven o'clock, but she had failed to notice that the window was still wide open and that the curtains were blowing. These caught fire, and considerable damage had already been done to the room before the fire was noticed in the house by a servant coming along the balcony and seeing smoke billowing out from under the door. The City Police Fire Brigade was sent for immediately but, before it arrived, Mr A. Atkinson, Mr Cutting, the coachman and other servants had put the fire out. What damage there was, was paid for from insurance, but some guest, and it may well have been Winston, must have been seriously inconvenienced.(8)

Early September was a time of hard campaigning. Jack spoke at Etton, Leven and Hedon, after which support from his family tailed off for the time being while they entertained a party of glamorous and illustrious guests for the Doncaster race week. But Arthur was in full fighting trim by the time Jack was due to speak at the Assembly Rooms, Withernsea. In offering up a second vote of thanks he apologised for not giving a political speech — he knew a lot more about commerce, he said. He hoped they would support Jack. If it rested with the ladies he was sure, without a shadow of doubt that they would return his son by an overwhelming majority.(9) Everybody laughed, but Arthur was a shrewd man. He had lived for 37 years with a woman who knew her own mind, and very often got what she wanted. Feminism was in the air. Arthur was no feminist, but it might help his son.

Jack now intensified his campaign, and was addressing audiences, one after the other, on every night of the week, preaching the gospel according to Lord Salisbury, even in the smaller villages so that nobody could complain that they had not had a chance to size him up. Occasionally he cast apprehensive glances at what the newspapers were saying about his rival, the liberal candidate, Mr A. J. Lawrie, but Jack was a habitual optimist, and his confidence hardly ever wavered. Arthur was working for him, and Arthur's influence, locally at any rate, was greater than most. Polling day fell on Wednesday, 10th October, and the election issue was never really in much doubt. In the previous election Commander Bethell had won the seat with a majority of 1,029 over his liberal opponent. Jack increased the majority to 1,787. Arthur was overcome with emotion when Jack expressed his thanks to his supporters outside the Sessions Court in Beverley. With tears running down his cheeks he declared "This is the proudest moment of my life", while Jack, hardly the modest violet (but then, politicians have never been renowned for modesty) declared in barely grammatical English: "Ladies and Gentlemen, we have won a great victory. I have been returned by the greatest majority that a Unionist member for Holderness has ever been returned by" (The Unionist party was, of course, of very recent origin, a fact which, perhaps in the heat of the moment, Jack had forgotten). He then paid tribute to the fair fight put up by Mr Lawrie, and thanked the presiding officer, Mr Todd. He was carried shoulder high to his carriage, from which the four horses had been unyoked, and was now drawn by his supporters to the Beverley Arms. There was a balcony at the level of the upper storey, and here Jack again received the congratulations of his supporters, after which he opened telegrams of congratulation from Lord Salisbury himself, his nephew and heir apparent, Mr A. J. Balfour, and from Captain Middleton, the chief agent of the conservative party in England. Arthur and Mary went down to London with their son, so that they might be present at the opening of Parliament.

The year 1903 posed problems for the government. The mercurial Joseph Chamberlain left office and went to the country to plead for a new fiscal policy which would do away with free trade on which, during the Victorian era, many believed Britain's prosperity had been built. Balfour, now the conservative Prime Minister, had tried to meet him halfway, and had only succeeded in aggravating both wings of the party. The conservative electorate did not know where it stood. During the summer and early autumn Jack did not find it easy to reassure them. It was almost second nature to him to make fun of his rival, the prospective Liberal candidate for Holderness, who rejoiced in the not unknown name of Wilberforce. (The emancipator of slaves had come from Hull). "I told him" Jack said, at a conservative conference for 300 delegates at his home at Raywell, "I told him I thought Holderness did not want emancipating".(10) But this was not good enough, and at the end of October it was Jack's business to make his position crystal clear to the Council of the Holderness Conservative Association at Beverley. He did his best. He said he supported Balfour, but was not sure how far he intended to go. He did not see any reason for not supporting Chamberlain. He rightly said that the principle of Free Trade really had gone for good, since England still had a free import system whereas every other country had a tariff wall. He ended:

"I tell you that it is my intention to loyally support Mr Balfour in his present programme and I trust that Mr Chamberlain's policy may eventually become the policy of the government. I have no intention of in any way opposing the government: that is the last thing I shall do."(11)

It was not an entirely convincing performance, although Jack was attempting to take the professional politician's line of being all things to all men, and it drew forth his Uncle Charles Henry's fire. Charlie was speaking the same week at St. George's Hall in Hull, and was, apparently, musing on the development of the Wilson fleet — which, of course, included food ships. He told his audience that when he entered his father's office some 50 years before, the total steam tonnage of the United Kingdom was 168,000 tons, exactly the tonnage of his own firm, which had been checked a few days previously. He implied that Free Trade had been responsible for this, and said that if his nephew, Jack, was going to follow Chamberlain and bring in import duties, he would have to go round Holderness, converting his constituents to a policy of dear food.(12)

Jack finaly pledged himself as a "whole hogger" on the question of Joseph Chamberlain's Tariff Reform policy, which split the Tory party and let in the Liberals with their Labour allies, so that Balfour had to concede victory to the wily Scot, Campbell Bannerman. The policy of the new government was therefore, of necessity, Liberal but with a Labour flavour. Jack had only just managed to hold on to his seat. The *Hull News* of Saturday, 27th January 1906 had published a very explicit cartoon headed "Just — and only Just", which showed a winded horse labelled "Tory Party" pulled up short at a fox hole, with Jack on hands and knees in front of it, dragging the unfortunate fox, labelled "Holderness" and still trying to get away, out of its hole.(13) Jack had polled 4,441 votes and Mr Wilberforce 4,411, so the majority had only been 30.

Jack's speeches seem to have been vitriolic and critical but, in no apparent way,

191

constructive. When he repeated his Aunt Sallies in Aldbrough, one heckler, and there were many, asked him the very relevant question whether the House of Lords ever threw out a Tory bill. Jack was no Winston Churchill, whose parliamentary knowledge and fighting spirit could already be harnessed to defend and maintain his dignity. Poor Jack blustered and answered that he could not say, but thought they probably had; which assessment would hardly take the heat out of the heckling, and might well have precipitated a moment or two of bitter mirth.(14) Jack never really learned to whip up popular emotion and fervour, and even at Westminster his reputation rested on his practice of exasperating the opposition by wicked little interruptions, which were really only a form of heckling.(15)

In 1909 Jack was present in the Commons while the Land Tax issue, feared and hated by many of the country gentry, was being debated. On two occasions that evening he saw Mr Lloyd George, whose measure it was, in close consultation with Mr Emmott, the chairman. The second time he noticed this he called out "Are you arranging it?" which caused the chairman to rise to his feet and rebuke him saying "That is a most improper observation to make". Liberal M.P.s also howled in displeasure.(16) It was no doubt because of such incidents that the obituary, that year, of Arthur Wilson in the *Belfast Irish News* contained the sentence "The late Mr Arthur Wilson was the father of Mr Stanley Wilson, M.P. for Holderness, whose perkiness and occasional impertinence have been responsible for more than one 'scene' in the House of Commons".

Jack was, however, from his roots, a son of Hull, and he could be passionate indeed when he felt the safety of the area to be threatened. In March 1903 he had asked the President of the Board of Trade whether, in view of the evidence recently given before the Royal Commission on Coast Erosion, he was aware that immediate steps needed to be taken to protect further the sea banks in the area between Kilnsea and Easington. Otherwise there would be a danger of the sea breaking through into the Humber and changing the navigable channel. Jack pleaded, though to stony indifference, that the Conservative government should make special provision for the defence of the Humber bank. The problem is still with us today.

After Arthur's death, which Jack felt keenly, (indeed he suffered a nasty attack of quinsies, something to which his father had also been prone, possibly because he had taken a chill at the funeral) he had to decide what to do with Tranby Croft. Nobody wanted to live in it. The place continued to function, but any personality of its own that it might once have had had gone for ever. In May 1913, after 28 years' service, Mr Leadbetter, the head gardener, finally retired, and that was a further blow to continuity.

Since his father's death the press had been somewhat kinder to Jack, and he was applauded when, at the beginning of the First World War he offered to serve his country in any way he could. He became an army captain and a King's Messenger, and in December 1915 was travelling aboard a Greek steamer, the "Spetzai", which was plying between Patras and Messina, and had the company of Colonel Napier, formerly Military Attaché at Sofia, and a Dr. Finlay. This ship was sighted by an Austrian submarine on the 4th December, at which time she was about 80 miles from the island of Zanti. The submarine fired a short burst across the bows of the Greek vessel, which hove to. The submarine now approached with her guns trained on the "Spetzai" and ordered the captain to come aboard, bringing the passenger list with him. This would give away the presence of the English group, who would certainly be sent for. Jack had in his possession a bag containing government correspondence, so he quickly stuffed this through a porthole and watched it drop into the sea before he obliged the Austrians with his presence. His quick thinking was, however, of no avail. The bag refused to sink, and the Austrians were able to row round and pick it up. Jack and Colonel Napier were now taken prisoner, but Dr. Finlay, in his capacity as a Red Cross officer, was allowed to rejoin his ship and proceed on his journey. Much later, when Jack returned to London, a military court of enquiry was held to determine whether he had done all in his power to safeguard the precious documents. He was exonerated from any charge of misconduct, and the matter was then referred to the Foreign Office, where it was decided that in future all such bags should be perforated, so that in the event of their being cast upon the waters they should not be seen again for many days.

The Austrian submarine now headed for its home base, but on the way was attacked by one of our own patrol boats. Jack and his fellow passengers understandably found it difficult to decide at this point whose side they were on. Fortunately for them the Austrian vessel managed to throw off her pursuer, and came in close to land, where she was joined by an escort of torpedo boats. These, however, were attacked almost at once by an enemy submarine, which launched a torpedo that came very close indeed to where the imprisoned Jack lay. He felt himself doomed, but after some general firing the submarine withdrew.(17)

Colonel Napier and Jack were first taken to Vienna, and then interned for the duration of the war at Salzerbad. Here were 260 Russian officers, 15 Frenchmen from the Air Service and the Mercantile Marine, and 21 other Britons who had been captured, like themselves, from merchant ships, many of which had been torpedoed. Salzerbad was a health resort, but the prisoners, although fairly well treated, were woefully short of exercise. They played badminton, and that was all. Accommodation was in villas, and was comfortable. The Russians ran their own kitchen, but the British were fed by the Austrians, and came to rely very heavily on food parcels from home. Jack believed they received the same rations as the civilian population, and on his release maintained that there was an acute shortage of food in the area. The prisoners were allowed to send and receive as many letters as they liked and were able to get, but as the war went on, the problems of transporting mail became more acute, and it would take between five and six weeks for a letter to arrive from England. Jack received books from the Prisoner of War Committee, and was therefore able to organise a small lending library. Newspapers were allowed, but they were Austrian or German. Nevertheless, they always gave the British communiqué, so Jack and his fellow prisoners were not entirely bereft of information.

Time passed very slowly, but when he had been a prisoner of war for almost 20 months Jack received a letter from home which told him that his sister, Muriel, was to marry a young army officer, Captain Richard Warde, in Anlaby Church on 1st September 1917. He realised that he would not be able to be there. All through his imprisonment he had hoped for an exchange, but invariably had been disappointed. Suddenly, out of the blue, he was told that his case had been discussed in the House of Commons but the Austrians were asking for two officers in his place. Jack knew that this would be unacceptable, but the fact that his case had been discussed gave him hope, and he wrote at length to Baron Slatin whose business it was to look after the interests of the prisoners of war.

Baron Rudolf Slatin, or Slatin Pasha as he was sometimes known, was of Austrian birth, but by the time of the outbreak of war in 1914 he had lived for nearly 30 years in Egypt and had become Inspector General of the Egyptian forces. This meant that he was faced with two impossible alternatives. He could not bring himself to fight against his native Austria, but neither would he pursue a policy which might harm his adopted country. He had therefore resigned his commissions, and had returned, a private citizen, to Vienna, finding an outlet for his energies and his philanthropy in working for the Red Cross movement.(18)

The Baron did not reply to Jack's letter, but ten days later, on 28th July, two officers arrived at the camp to see him, and told him that they had made many proposals for his exchange, but now a letter from the Austrian War Office had been obtained, which placed him at liberty. Jack regarded it as an added bonus that he was allowed to leave the camp two days later, on 30th July, which was his birthday. He always maintained that his release was an act of courtesy on the part of the Austrian government. He paid no money; there were no conditions; he could even have returned to serve at the front had he pleased. Back on British soil he said he hoped that the British Government would reciprocate such an act of generosity.

While he had been in Salzerbad Jack had written regularly to friends in the East Riding, for he knew that as an M.P. he could not afford to be forgotten. He now sent to his constituents the message "No reception by request". He might as well not have bothered. The Beverlonians had decided to ignore his request and prepared themselves to do him honour. On 1st September he led his sister, Muriel, down the aisle at Anlaby Church, but that was the only interruption in his tour of the constituency. The following Tuesday he was given a loyal reception from the Beverley Working Men's Club who were having a whist drive. They stopped their dealing for long enough for Jack to make a speech, in which he told them of the hair raising stories printed in the German newspapers about Hull. In Salzerbad he had believed that Zeppelins had raided the area, that Monument Bridge, the Dock Offices and King Edward Street, all in the centre of the city, were demolished. He had been given to understand that Hull had almost ceased to exist, and Beverley had also been laid waste. The men listened with interest as Jack relived the past. Then he left them and went to the Market Place Picture House where he could see how he had performed his role at Muriel's wedding, as the eight minute film was being shown there.(19)

By the time these events occurred, the Wilson Line was a thing of the past. Jack had never pretended to have much professional interest in it, and the mantle had therefore descended on Kenneth. After the deaths of Charles Henry and Arthur, Kenneth had become Chairman of the new Board of Directors. Tommy, now 2nd Lord Nunburnholme, was Deputy Chairman, Oswald Sanderson(20) was the Managing Director, and Clive and Guy (Tommy's only surviving brother) completed the Board.(21) The coming of the First World War convinced this younger generation that the time had come to get out. They lost 49 ships during the course of it. In the autumn of 1916 the Board was anxious to sell, and the ascendant star of John Ellerman was willing to buy.

Sir John Reeves Ellerman was the son of Johann Herman Ellerman of Hamburg. His was a Lutheran family which, for generations, had been merchants and corn millers. Johann had come to Hull where he had continued as a corn merchant and ships' broker, and then became the Hanoverian consul. He had married the daughter of a local solicitor, Anne Elizabeth Reeves, and in 1862 young John had been born. The child was left fatherless at the age of seven, but he was of an independent spirit, and by the time he was fourteen he had entered a chartered accountant's office in Birmingham. Two years later his wealthy grandfather died, and John was able to buy himself into the business. Soon he moved to London, and began his life long interest and association with shipping firms.

He never looked back.

There was some squabbling about the take-over. Jack was out of the way in Austria, but Tommy caused strain in the negotiations by holding out for a different settlement. He was overruled, although Kenneth had told Oswald Sanderson that he did not "want Ellerman to think them too keen".(22) The company now became Ellerman's Wilson Line Ltd. Sir John Ellerman was Chairman, but continuity was preserved in that Oswald Sanderson remained as Managing Director, and Kenneth would sit on the Board. The people of Hull found the new situation difficult to comprehend. "Charlie would never have sold out" a docker told the Sunday Chronicle, "And neither would Arthur" added his workmate; but their sons had done it, and the close link between the Wilsons and Hull was fraying badly.

In its editorial, The Eastern Morning News, one of the local newspapers, wrote an "obituary" and in doing so tried to find the reasons behind what had happened, and at the same time tried to allay the fears of the local people about possible job losses. The editor pointed out how greatly English shipping had suffered recently. Neutral countries had been able to make far heavier profits than England, and had not been subject to the heavy taxation demanded by our own near-exhausted government. When the war was over, such countries would be able to bring serious competition to the English shipowners, whose fleets had been depleted because of submarine attacks. However, the name 'Wilson' would survive, and the red and white house flag would continue to fly over the ships. When Wilsons sold out, their fleet had dropped in number to 70, with a gross tonnage of 184,084 (112,924 net). Three vessels, the "Oswego", "Chicago" and "Domino" were being built, which would bring the total tonnage to 197,480 gross (121,294 net), and with the seven vessels held in conjunction with the North Eastern Railway Company, the final tonnage of the 80 vessels would stand at 204,191 gross (124,038 net). In contrast to this, Ellerman Lines Ltd. of Liverpool had a fleet of 97 vessels (gross tonnage 462,000) and ranked eighth in the world, whereas Wilsons ranked 28th.(23)

How Charlie and Arthur would have grieved to hear it!

After he had returned home Jack's life altered considerably. His wife's brother, Sir Robert Filmer the 10th and last baronet, had died of war wounds the year before, and Jack and Queenie's son Arthur had adopted his mother's family name and had consequently inherited Sutton Place, Staplehurst. Jack's health was no longer so robust, and he not only ceased to ride to hounds, but in 1921 declined to serve Holderness any longer as its M.P., although he continued to be a staunch Conservative, and was re-elected President of the Holderness Conservative Association only a week before his death in 1938.

The sudden and untimely death of his younger brother, Clive, may well have influenced him, and even frightened him into taking this course. The Holderness Conservatives rallied round to show their appreciation, and at a Garden Fete held in the grounds of Tranby Croft on 4th August 1921 (the anniversary of the declaration of war in 1914, as it so happened) a presentation was made to Jack on the front steps of the house. It took the form of a framed and illuminated statement of appreciation of his 21 years' service. So the political infant of 1900 had just managed to come of age.(24)

Jack's new interest became the Turf. Again, this was almost certainly due to Clive's death, and Jack took over his brother's racing colours, the white jacket with the green sleeves and the red cap. He became well known and was described as a genial and popular paddock personality. His horses were trained by Captain J. C. Storie, though a few were handled by Captain P. Whitaker. "Knight Error", trained by the latter, was the winner of

Jack Wilson (from the Pressling/Woolrich bequest).

the Lincolnshire Handicap in 1931. Jack had got him for £500, not a large sum; and a mare, "Anna", which had been thrown in for luck at the time of the purchase, won a good race at Gatwick. "John James" won two handicaps in 1935, but Jack's favourite horse was one of his early winners, "Count Ross", who took the Liverpool Hurdle in 1922 and was both a hurdler and a racer on the flat. He sired the winners of 61 races. Jack became a steward of several race meetings and a director of Thirsk race course.

In 1927 Mary had died. Arthur had allowed her the use and occupation of Tranby Croft during her life time. By February 1929 Jack had become the sole owner, but he seems to have had little affection for his old home and continued to live at Raywell and, when in London, at 26a Davis Street, Berkeley Square. He decided to sell the effects of Tranby Croft. In three days in mid-October 1929 the house, the pride of Arthur and Mary Wilson, was stripped of its antique and modern furniture, its silver and its ornaments. Buyers attended from all parts of the country. A beautiful mahogany kneehole roll top writing desk was knocked down for £23 (although the local paper considered it to be a good price for the time). A Louis XV upholstered settee with old needlework panels went for £28, an old English wall clock in a black and gold laquered case fetched £21, a 16 by 25 foot old border Persian carpet brought in £250 and a smaller one sold for £104. A buyer paid £72 for a pair of fine old Chippendale chairs, while an antique grandfather wing chair, Queen Anne period and upholstered in silk brocade went for £35, and a second one for £27. Rather surprisingly a great deal of interest was shown in a Louis XV parquetaire writing table 4' 7" by 2' 6", and the bidding closed at £360. After this a set of five mahogany Chippendale chairs went for £180, a Chippendale dressing table for £30, and a pair of Chippendale mahogany chairs with carved legs and bull claw feet for £80. An antique mahogany Chippendale leather backed armchair was sold for £134, and two others for £29 and £56. A small Louis XV writing table (6 feet by 3) was sold for £65, and a chiming bracket clock in a hand carved case for £22. At the end of the first day the delighted auctioneer, Mr Edward Ellwell, verified that over £2,000 had been realised.(25) It must have been a sad day for those who had loved the house, but not all the pieces left the district. Only a few years ago I was able to identify a work box bearing the initials M.E.W. and the date 1863. It turned up in a house less than two miles away from Tranby Croft, and no doubt its present owner was pleased to learn that it was almost certainly a wedding gift to Mary Wilson whose industry in embroidery was proverbial. A sewing table, beautifully inlaid, also has a home less than ten miles away in North Cave.

From this time onwards Tranby Croft was opened up only for hunt balls, garden parties and the like. The period of comparative neglect, from which the advent of Hull High School for Girls saved it, was beginning to be felt if not seen. Jack's health continued to deteriorate. Gone was the slender young man, and he became portly, flabby, sporting a huge moustache. A colostomy was necessary, and henceforth he became a semi invalid. He lived to see the family break up. Clive had gone in 1921; Muriel's husband was killed in a horrific accident in 1932, and two years after that, Ethel died at Ken Hill. Like his father, Jack soon had to seek further surgery, and at the age of 69 he entered a London nursing home where, on 12th April 1938 he died.

Jack's generation never held the affection or enjoyed the deep interest of the local people as his father's had done, but there was more now to interest the working man. Horizons had broadened since the First World War. Nevertheless, in his own way Jack was committed to them as surely as his father and mother had been, and he was sadly missed by the little children of the Seamen's Orphanage, which had now moved out to

Hessle. The opening of the new premises at Hesslewood had been done by Mary Wilson back in September 1921. Jack and Oswald Sanderson, nervous of her ability to stand the strain of the ceremony, made no secret of the fact that she had been the driving force behind the move. When he died, Jack had been president of the orphanage for many years, as well as being president of the Old Boys' Association, and his generosity and charm, which all Arthur and Mary's children possessed, had made him popular with the orphans. He had sent regular gifts of rabbits and hares to them, and had paid for their Christmas dinners for years and on these occasions there were always sweets and toys for each child. He had always asked the children the same two questions, which became a ritual: "Have you had a happy Christmas?" and "Did you have a good Christmas dinner?" When house guests were in residence at Tranby Croft, Jack would often take them with him to see, and sometimes to entertain the orphans.(26) The previous January one such guest had been the Countess of Dudley, better known to ordinary mortals as the comedy actress Gertie Miller, and she was with Jack again when he paid one of his last visits in Hull, to the children's fancy dress ball in aid of the Victoria Children's Hospital. Arthur would have been proud to know that in this respect, as well as others, Jack was a chip off the old block.

Edward Kenneth and his daughter Hilary, Countess of Munster

Kenneth, the quiet son, had married Molly Hacket, a friend of his sister Muriel, in the summer of 1895. Since then they had lived at Roehampton Court, where they remained throughout the period during which their only child, Hilary, was growing up. Hilary first saw the light of day in her grandparents' house at 17, Grosvenor Place on 9th March 1903. Fair of face (she was born on a Monday) she was, and remained, a gifted but solitary child.

Shortly before the beginning of the First World War Kenneth had begun to show an interest in the purchase of Cannizaro Park, Wimbledon, but negotiations were only completed in 1920, when he was able to purchase it. It cost him £30,750 and was the first time that the house had been sold.(27) The house was of some interest historically, and its first known owner had been Thomas Walker, who was living there in 1727.(28) Walker's portrait was introduced into a picture by Hogarth entitled 'Monamy showing a picture to Mr Walker'. Monamy was a marine painter, and Thomas Walker had been his patron. Walker stands on the left beside Monamy, who is showing to him a seascape on an easel. That picture is by Monamy and is signed. The rest of the painting is by Hogarth.

A later occupant of the property was Henry Dundas, politician, Privy Councillor and Cabinet Minister, who later became 1st Viscount Melville. He probably came to Wimbledon about the year 1786, and the house soon became a meeting place for his political friends and colleagues, and even George III. More often came that great and lonely figure the Younger Pitt, and for him a room was permanently set aside. Dundas married, as his second wife, Lady Jane Hope and on his estate he planted a wood, which is still known as Lady Jane's Wood and lies on the south west corner. The next tenant was George, IVth Earl of Aberdeen, destined to become Prime Minister in 1852 and to lead, with the greatest possible reluctance, the English nation into the Crimean War. This same Lord Aberdeen would later be shown letters from Mary Wilson's father, which would complain about the lack of organisation for the soldiers' mail.

Perhaps the most colourful of all the occupants of the hosue was the man who gave it the name by which it is known today. Francis Platemone, Count St Antonio, was said to have been a poor Sicilian nobleman. He married a wealthy daughter of Commodore

George Johnstone, the Governor of East Florida and a Director of the East India Company, and this enabled him later, when he became Duke of Cannizaro, to live more in accordance with his station. His wife was a formidable contradiction of ignorance, vitality and humour, and was short and fat. She loved music, and after she and her husband came to Wimbledon round about 1817 many fine artists came to the house. She may have been a successful patron, but she was hardly a successful wife, and her husband soon left her. She let him have an allowance, and he went to live in Italy where he found himself a mistress. A few years later on, he came back again. Absence had done nothing to make his heart grow fonder. Indeed, he was soon of the opinion that he would be unable to stomach his wife at any price, and off he went back to Italy and his now aging but amply proportioned mistress. This new development did not please his wife, who decided to follow him. The sight of high seas at Dover put her off initially, but she eventually managed to cross the channel on a fine, calm day and soon afterwards turned up in Milan to trouble her erring husband and his paramour. Then the Duchess fell in love with a violinist who was working in a seedy theatre in Milan, and off back to Wimbledon she went, taking the violinist with her. He managed to run through practically all the Duchess' money before she died, an event which occurred in January 1841. What remained, she somewhat surprisingly bequeathed to her less than supportive husband.(29)

Round about 1779 the house was let to Mrs Schuster, the daughter of one of Nelson's captains, and her daughter Adela. They enlarged it, making the reception rooms bigger and building new ones. Some of their parties were attended by more than 1,000 people, and both Edward, Prince of Wales and Princess Alexandra visited Cannizaro. Perhaps the most famous events while the Schusters were at Cannizaro were the Pastoral Plays which were performed nearby on the Warren, where seats were erected in tiers, sloping upwards and backwards towards the trees. The sets and costumes were designed by E.W. Godwin who, in 1886, adapted Tennyson's *Beckett* for Cannizaro, calling it *Fair Rosamund,* and to this performance not only the Prince and Princess of Wales came, but several children too. The cost was one guinea. On this occasion, too, refreshments in the form of strawberries and clotted cream were served (a precursor of a later tradition at a very different Wimbledon event).

Adela Schuster left the house when her mother died, and on 14th October 1900, when Colonel Thomas Mitchell was living there, it caught fire and a good deal was burnt. Little was done, apparently, to ensure that the rebuilding was a faithful reproduction of the old, but it did not stop Kenneth Wilson from wanting to buy.

He loved Cannizaro, as his father had loved Tranby Croft, and he was a good master. In 1932 he was able to buy a neighbouring house to the north east. This was The Keir, and he added its gardens to his own. He moved the huge ornamental gates, elaborately monogrammed with his own initials (and difficult to decipher) from the house in Roehampton, and these were placed at the lower end of the kitchen garden, which Kenneth left, like the pond, as it was. He did, however, add great beauty to the park by introducing rare and interesting trees and shrubs. No doubt his love of gardens sprang from his early years at Tranby Croft. Kenneth became a member of the Rhododendron Society, and did much replanting. Like his father, he introduced plants and shrubs from all over the world. In spring the New Zealand Waratah would hang down its yellow fingers, and in late summer the orange flowers of the pomegranate would come into bloom. Nearby, as at Tranby Croft, magnolias grew, over 10 metres in height and, behind a group of hollies, again as at Tranby, Kenneth and Molly made space for a little graveyard for the family

Molly and Hilary at Cannizaro (from the Pressling/Woolrich bequest).

pets. Here, the gravestones are more elaborate than in Yorkshire, where they are all small, of sandstone, and have a curved top. The Kenneth Wilsons buried their pets under stepped stones, sometimes shaped like a cross and the graves themselves were surrounded by kerbs. The most imposing is a memorial to Molly's favourite dog, Spookie, who is described as "my beloved dog" and merits not only the stepped plinth, but a verse of gratitude, borrowed from Byron:

"But the poor dog in life the firmest friend
The first to welcome, foremost to defend
Whose honest heart is still his master's own
Who labours, fights, loves, breathes for him alone."(30)

Hilary was seventeen years old when she came to Cannizaro. From the capable seemingly confident little toddler who had so taken the eye when she officiated at her Uncle Clive's wedding in 1907, and who as a teenager had, with her younger cousin Thetis, acted as bridesmaid at the wedding of her Aunt Muriel, Hilary had grown into a quiet and withdrawn young woman, whose passionate and abiding love was for music. Her father adored her. Her mother dominated her. Her coming out ball took place at Dorchester House, the home of her Aunt Tottie, but Hilary was no extrovert. She seemed to reach out to people through her music. She was a talented pianist, and one of the most charming of all the Wilson portraits, by John da Costa, shows her at about, or possibly before this time, seated at a grand piano, and looking towards the artist as if she and her piano were a single identity. Hilary did not study at a music college, but as a young adult she had private lessons from Solomon who agreed that she had talent,(31) and Sir Thomas

The young Hilary Wilson. Photo by courtesy of the Guildhall, Kingston upon Hull.

Armstrong, one of the original trustees of the Munster Fund which was brought into being by Hilary later on, believes that at this time she was seriously considering a musical career.(32) This is borne out by Mr Gerald Coke, another trustee, who believes she could have earned her living as a professional pianist if she had had to do so.(33) Certainly she built up a good technical proficiency, and for the rest of her life worked to maintain that standard of performance. It seems likely, however, that such a career was regarded as unsuitable by her often ailing mother, but not even she could stop Hilary from giving her heart to music.

While at Roehampton Court during the First World War Hilary put her musical gifts to good use, playing recitals, taking part in concerts and being "at the piano" in hospitals, schools and elsewhere. She was particularly devoted to the care and well being of the war disabled at Roehampton Hospital. When peace came and her family moved out to Wimbledon she still continued with her work, although her father, with no business commitments to worry him further, preferred to play the country squire. Hilary continued to involve herself in music, and greatly admired the singer, the Hon. William Brownlow. A good marriage for her was inevitable, but when she did marry it was not to a musician. On 9th July 1928, she duly married Sir Geoffrey William Richard Hugh Fitzclarence who, that same year, had become 5th Earl of Munster. His was a family which sprang from the union between the Duke of Clarence, later William IV, with Dorothy Bland, better known as Mrs Jordan. Like Tottie's second husband he held a court appointment. He was three years Hilary's junior.

The wedding was solemnised at St Margaret's Westminster, and mounted police had to assist in keeping back the large crowd which filled all four sides of the square. Street vendors and young errand boys stood alongside "exquisitely dressed people".(34) Some of the little boys climbed the railings to get a better look, and as the car carrying Hilary and her father drew up, two girls tried to rush across the road to obtain a closer view, and had to be headed off by the police. Hilary's wedding gown, simply styled, was made of satin almost the colour of parchment. The sleeves were long and tight; the skirt was draped to one side and held with a cluster of orange blossom. The veil was once worn by Queen Adelaide, and it was surmounted by a wreath of myrtle leaves with a cluster of orange blossom at one side, and a true lover's knot in silver at the other. The long satin train was lined with silver tissue and was carried by two pages. Hilary's bouquet of orange blossom had been presented to her by Sergeant Major Rust, a limbless soldier, on behalf of her "old friends at Roehampton". There were eight bridesmaids. The guest list was very grand, and one who came was Lady Clodagh Anson who so enjoyed the Wilsons' Saturday evening parties at Grosvenor Place in the early nineties because they were so different from those of everybody else.

There were two receptions at Hilary's wedding, the first, the public one on the Saturday, was at Cannizaro and to it came patients from Roehampton Hospital, as Hilary wanted to give them the opportunity to see the wedding gifts. Prince and Princess Arthur of Connaught (whose villa lay close to that of the Wilsons on Cap Ferrat) gave the couple a set of amber crystal toilet fittings and what the local paper described ambiguously as "a garden drink equipment". This reception took place two days before the wedding itself which was on a Monday, and was followed by a reception for the family alone at Sir John and Lady Ward's residence in Park Lane. The honeymoon was spent at Sutton Park, and Hilary travelled there in an outfit of pale blue, a colour of which she, like Ethel, seems to have been very fond. Afterwards they returned to their new home in Hill Street.(35)

Hilary's Wedding with the 5th Earl of Munster on 9th July 1928 (from the Pressling/Woolrich bequest).

The early promise of a diplomatic and political career for the Earl of Munster was entirely fulfilled. Sadly, the marriage was childless. The Earl had commitments, and he had only a very limited interest in music. His wife continued to practise and to perform in public, in schools and hospitals and nearly always for some charitable purpose, and she continued to do this until as an elderly woman, she became ill. She was unfortunate enough to suffer from arthritis and from Parkinson's disease, but when she could no longer play herself, she loved to hear performances by Royal Academy students at her home at Sandhills, Blechingley. Lady Munster's friend, Mrs Faith Deller, for many years Lady Superintendent at the Royal Academy of Music, remembers her beautiful music room which contained three Steinways, two grands and an upright, and was where Hilary herself, and later the students, used to play.(36)

With such an absorbing interest in music, not able to be shared, and with no children, Lady Munster became convinced that she could and should use some of her money to enable young and talented musicians to begin to establish themselves in what was at best a difficult career, and one which, in different circumstances, she may have liked to have followed herself. Elderly and needy musicians could already be looked after through the Musicians' Benevolent Fund founded in memory of Gervase Elwes in 1931, which had the whole-hearted support of, among others, Muriel's friend Lady Maud Warrender. The idea of a musical trust that was similar, but for young people, began to grow in her mind. It would mean that the help she was prepared to give could be put on a permanent basis. On 15th December 1958 The Countess of Munster Musical Trust came into being, and wihin two years was making available almost £13,000 a year.(37)

The Trustees of the Fund were Lady Munster's friends. Sir Thomas Armstrong was Principal of the Royal Academy of Music. Mr Keith Falkner was the Director of the Royal College of Music, its opposite number in South Kensington. Sir Malcolm Sargent, conductor extraordinary and for so long so closely associated with the "Proms" also served as did the singer Miss Flora Nielsen. From the world of business came Mr Gerald Coke and Mr Leopold de Rothschild, and in addition to their ready sympathy with matters musical, they were able to advise on the Trust's investments.

It was quickly realised that in spite of the great generosity of the founder there was not sufficient money to help institutions as well as individuals, so the Trust confined itself to the latter, the recipients to be between the ages of eleven and thirty. Grants would be made for one year only, but having started such help to an individual, the Trustees would be willing to consider carrying it on until the initial difficult period was over.

There were problems. Successful applicants were not always aware of their own best interests. The administration, run to begin with on a semi-voluntary basis, had to be put on a more permanent footing. The Trustees therefore made an arrangement with the Governors of King Edward's School, Witley (one of the Royal Hospitals of the City of London) under which their Clerk to the Governors became Secretary to the Trust, and the administration could now be run from the school. In recognition of this help, Lady Munster gave to King Edward's a new Music School. This would also be a permanent base for the Trust. In addition to a small hall, suitable for recitals and for auditioning applicants for a Munster Award, the new block contained practice rooms and a small music library. Concerts could be given here by young people who had benefited from the Trust, and a very early example of this was when a new work of Alexander Goehr was performed by the King Edward's School Music Society as part of the official opening programme, along with individual items by recipients of a Munster Award. There was also a recital by

Yehudi and Hephzibah Menuhin.

During the first six years of the Trust's life almost £60,000 was given away in grants to individuals, and the last sentence of the Trust's *First Report* read "All the Arts have owed much throughout their history to the support which they have received from their lay devotees: Lady Munster will certainly take her place in the long line of those to whom music is most in debt."(38) Hundreds, perhaps thousands, of recipients will say a thankful "Amen" to that.

In 1975 the 5th Earl of Munster died, and his widow became a recluse at her home at Sandhills. Yet she kept the affection of her friends to the end and beyond. Young musicians every year are grateful for the generosity of this grandchild of Arthur and Mary Wilson. The humble efforts of music making at Tranby Croft blossomed in the skill and devotion to the welfare of music shown by Hilary, and Arthur and Mary's generosity to deserving causes found an answering response in Hilary's willingness to give financial aid to talented young musicians, no matter from whence they came. Just as Arthur Wilson built a mansion for his progeny which became an educational nursery for other people's children, so his grand-daughter, who must in her heart of hearts have wished for a career as a pianist, enabled other people's children to do for themselves what she had not been able to do. It is by no means an insignificant memorial, and her grandparents would surely have been proud of her.

Clive

Clive was a sportsman and always a convivial character. He rode as soon as he could walk, joined the Holderness Hunt at a very early age, and was soon recognised as a skilful, daring and hard rider. After Eton where, like his brothers, he was not particularly interested in the academic curriculum, he returned to the Riding and busied himself with hunting, the territorial army and, later, polo rather than with the family business. He still sang and acted, like his sister Muriel, though unlike her he confined his attentions to comedy parts. This made him a popular figure in the locality. Unlike his brothers who were known as "Mr Stanley" and "Mr Kenneth", he was always spoken of as "Clive". Like his cousins at Warter Priory he was anxious to become involved in fighting the Boers in 1899, and in mid March 1900 he had gone out to the veldt with his relative Oswald Lambert and Harold Sanderson, brother of that Oswald, who became the managing director of the Wilson Line. They were part of Paget's Corps of Imperial Yeomanry, and Clive was appointed galloper to General Bruce Hamilton. For months his family heard nothing from him, then, in the middle of October 1900, just as the excitement which accompanied Jack's entry into parliament had died down, they received the following long letter, which deserves to be quoted at length, as it does give an insight into the life of a somewhat privileged soldier out there. He began to write it in camp at Leeuw River Mills, Orange River Colony on the 7th September, and added to it as and when he could.

"We have been on the go day and night since we left Winburg, after we relieved the beleagured garrison... Well, we left Winburg in four trains at 10 a.m. on the 30th August, the general and his staff travelling in an armoured train. We expected to be attacked as we heard that the Boers were moving south and trying to cut the line. However we got to Bloemfontein at 7.30 p.m. with the first train, and the last train got in at 10.30. We unloaded our horses and just dumped our things down outside the station, the troops marching up to the camp. We (the Staff) went and stopped at the hotel. I slept in a bed that night and sheets, which were a tremendous luxury — the first time I have slept in a bed and sheets since Grosvenor Place, but we had not very much sleep, as I was not in bed till 12.30 a.m. and we were roused at 4.30 a.m. as we had to march at 6.30 a.m....

"We left Bloemfontein at 7 a.m. with our brigade. That day we marched 23 miles to the waterworks, where we arrived at 10.30 p.m. having of course, outspanned and halted for four hours at mid-day. The next morning we marched at 7.30 a.m. and did 15 miles to Thabanchu, where we arrived at 9.30 p.m., everybody dead beat. Here we halted all day, and marched off at 5 o'clock in the evening, our destination being Ladybrand, where there was the garrison being besieged by 3,000 Boers and three guns, so we had to get on as far as we could in order to arrive there in time to save them from surrendering. We had a tremendous march that night, getting into our camp at 2.30 in the morning, 17 miles march, and we have a very big convoy with us, as we are carrying 14 days' supplies for men and horses and have besides some 80 mule waggons and two traction engines, carrying three or four trucks each, in fact our column, when on the march and well closed up, is about five miles long.

"...The next morning we started at 7.30 towards Ladybrand, sending our mounted infantry ahead to get in touch with the enemy whom we could see on all the hills, but as soon as we opened fire with our guns and "pom-poms" they all fled, and could not stick it at all, so off they went, followed by our mounted infantry, who did them a good deal of harm, emptying five saddles with one volley.

"...Well, we rode seven miles into the town of Ladybrand, where we found the garrison, who had fortified themselves in the hills and caves commanding the town, and had a pretty hot time of it, too, but only had five men wounded, and didn't they cheer when the General and his staff rode up.

"We had an excellent lunch at the hotel, and then rode back to the camp, the beleaguered garrison following us. We left our camp at 2 p.m. yesterday, and after marching six miles arrived here, which is a very nice and pretty little place. The General has got a room in a house, and we have a room to dine in, and Fraser and I sleep in tents, but it is very nice as the weather is getting much better, and it is boiling hot here in the daytime, but still pretty cold at nights. We are halting here today, as there is a big move, I believe, on the go, participated in by several guns and their forces, which I hope and trust will end in a very big round up with these devils down here, and thus end the war.

"...I believe there is a wonderful future for this country in the farming line, and I expect a great number of Volunteers will stay out here. I have several times been asked if I intend to remain here, but no, thank you: I shall come home just as fast as I can get. Well, I must stop till I have anything more interesting to add.

"...I have, I believe, got an honorary lieutenant commission, but it lacks confirmation.

"...Best love to all"[39]

Clive served with distinction for 21 months until he was wounded, just before Christmas 1901. That section of Damant's horse in which he was serving was involved at Tafelkop[40] on 20th December, when fierce fighting took place. Five men were killed and eleven wounded including Col. F.H. Damant himself and Clive, who was shot in the right hand.[41] He later said it was the tightest corner he had ever been in in his life. The fighting was at close quarters, only 30 yards or less separating the two sides. The Boers had simply charged, but when they saw reinforcements approaching, they turned about and fled. The whole of the action was over within minutes. The bullet which hit Clive took off one finger and shattered another, which was removed at the field station, leaving him with no second and third finger on his right hand. Although classed as a "slight" wound, it was sufficient to get him back home again, and after hospital treatment he was honorably discharged with two mentions in dispatches, and holding the Queen's Medal with four clasps, the King's Medal with two clasps and the D.S.O.

When his second finger was amputated, Clive was allowed to keep it. He put it in a bottle and took it back to Tranby Croft, where it was placed in a "glory-hole" and forgotten. Years later, after his marriage, Clive found it again as he was rummaging in the depths of the little room. As he emerged into the corridor his young son, Raymond, was leaving the schoolroom opposite. "Look" said Clive to him, "Look what I've found" and his son vividly remembers to this day how he actually saw this gruesome relic of his father's active service.

Clive returned to Tranby Croft on Sunday, 6th March 1902. It says much for his popularity that his homecoming engendered such spontaneous excitement and goodwill. Long before his train was expected to arrive at Hessle station the local people had flocked to greet him, filling the long sloping footpaths and embankments near the station and lining the route to Tranby Croft. The train was punctual, and at five o'clock steamed into the station and Clive, eager to catch a glimpse of his family, was amazed, as he looked out of the window, to see this seething mass of enthusiasm, Union Jacks waving wildly, and to hear their cheers. As he climbed down from the carriage he was almost unnerved, for the cheering, starting at the front of the huge crowd, travelled to the back, started again — and again, like ripples blown across a lake. "Speech, speech" the cry came. Clive's bronzed face could not pale, though it would have done so if it could. The poor lad was quite overwhelmed. He raised his khaki hat, hoping that that would be sufficient, but it was not. So, in short and halting words he tried to tell these loyal friends how much he appreciated their support, and with his left hand (his right one was still bandaged) he shook the hands of a few of them, while his father, dignified and proud because of the warmth of his son's reception, thanked them also from the bottom of his full heart.

Arthur led Clive to the carriage at the top of the station rise, and on entering, Clive leaned forward to shake the hand of Mr Cutting, the coachman who had driven him to his christening in Kirkella Church nearly 25 years before; but Mr Cutting was not to be needed this evening, for Clive's friends unhitched the pair of horses, and twenty volunteers took their places between the shafts to pull him home. Another speech was demanded and given, after which Arthur, Mary and Mrs Travers joined Clive in the carriage, and the procession moved off.

It was estimated that no fewer than 30,000 people turned out to honour Clive.[42] His carriage was followed to Tranby Croft by scores of wagonettes and hundreds of cyclists. Near to the house the Wilson Line Band was waiting, and the carriage turned through the entrance gates to the sound of "See, the conquering hero comes" and "The Boys of the Old Brigade", the crowd obliging with the vocals. At the entrance to the estate a huge arch bearing the words "Welcome Home" had been erected, and here a big group of servants was waiting to change places with the "horses" and pull Clive and his family the rest of the way. There was open house at Tranby that Sunday, and the great crowd poured through the entrance gates and followed the procession up the drive. The ground staff had hung bunting on all the trees which lined the route, and the Union Jack was flying from the tower

Clive Wilson about the time of the Second Boer War, wearing the uniform of a Captain in the East Riding Imperial Yeomanry. Photo by courtesy of Dr. T. Debney.

at the south east corner of the mansion. The rest of the family who had not been to the station had placed themselves on the roof of the entrance lobby, immediately behind the balustrading, so that they had an excellent vantage point to watch the procession as it manoevred the last awkward turning of the drive. Jack, Queenie and young Arthur; Freddie, Keith and Stewart; Ethel, Edward and young Eddie and Muriel were all there. Clive's journey was completed amidst a pandemonium of cheering in which the rest of the servants, lined up along the terrace itself, joined with the populace still negotiating the drive, now, no doubt, somewhat hoarse from their protracted activities. Clive got out of the carriage and walked towards the entrance of the house. He was, however, halted yet once more by Mr Reid, the butler who, on behalf of all the staff, welcomed him home once again.

Clive was bound to reciprocate. He did so simply, and with feeling. He said "I don't know what to say. I can only thank you from the bottom of my heart for the splendid welcome you have given me. I never knew I had so many friends. I shall never, never, forget it." The crowd cheered and then euphorically demanded a word from Arthur, then Mary and Muriel, and finally Jack, the last two having, as it were, to shout their greetings from an exalted plane. Then the family were allowed to enter their own home, where hospitality had already been provided for as many of the vast crowd as cared to come in.

Even now Clive could not rest in peace. Within the house were representatives of the press, and they demanded to know how the young soldier had received the wound which brought him home. They also asked whether he had met his cousin Guy (Charles Henry's second son) out on the veldt. As it happened, Clive had done so, and he was generous in his assessment of his cousin. "He is a splendid man in the field" he said, "And he has got on exceedingly well. He is a junior subaltern in his own regiment, and a local captain, and he commanded the regiment after we were all knocked out, for about a month." He was then asked the inevitable question "What is your opinion of the behaviour of the troops?" There was great sensitivity in this country with regard to the treatment of Boer prisoners. Admittedly the weather, snow late in the year, was unusual, but the callous behaviour of the army authorities had given rise to deep concern and an outburst of indignation in the press. Clive wilfully or inadvertently side stepped the main issue. He told them:

"I can speak now as a civilian, and not as a soldier, and I say that the British soldier is absolutely the finest man in the world. You cannot beat him anywhere. He will march his 30 miles a day and never say a word. He will take whatever is given him without a grumble, and will fight like a bulldog. People have said that he behaves badly, but I have fought two years with the regulars, irregulars and colonials, and I say unhesitatingly that in my opinion he is the finest specimen of soldier living."

After the violence of war, and his unusual escapades, Clive did not find it easy to settle down again. His father attempted to arouse his interest in the business, but without success. He was far more interested in the Territorials (he continued as an officer in the East Riding Imperial Yeomanry), fox hunting, racing, and polo. His connection with the latter dated from the time of a lease of a field in Westbourne Avenue, in a suburb about a mile west of the centre of Hull, in 1896. The Avenues were a compact group of four long boulevards, built up in the late Victorian era and completed in Edwardian times. Many of the residences had coach houses, but it came to be a familiar sight to see polo ponies as well. Clive rode hard and successfully. Sometimes he was more enthusiastic than accurate, but he was always an interesting player, and many of the crowd attended because of him. His cry to his fellow players "Ride him off" was well known, and was recognised, anticipated and applauded by his supporters. Hull, however, never really warmed to polo. Eventually, Rose, Downs and Thompson took over the ground and used it for their own sports until, in 1972, the inevitable happened, and housing development occurred where Clive once spent so many dashing hours.

After his marriage to Elvira in 1907, Clive and she went to live in Beverley, at St Mary's House, on the east side of the church where their two children, Thetis and Raymond, were christened. They continued to live there until the house caught fire and was burned down, which event occurred on the night of 29th December 1912. Clive's house, in Hengate, was a three storeyed affair. Shortly after the family had retired to bed that night, the neighbour who lived opposite, Mr George Wood, happened to look out of his window and saw flames. Immediately he ran into the street yelling "Fire" at the top of his voice. Clive and his family slumbered peacefully on. Mr Wood, who had already alerted a Mr Hewson to go and fetch the fire brigade, decided that more desperate measures were called for, and he kicked the side door quite savagely, again and again, until finally the house roused, and Clive himself appeared, bare footed and in a dressing gown, he and Elvira having escaped down a staircase not normally used by them. By this time the flames could be seen throughout the house, but fortunately, that night, there was no wind, which would have fanned them to quicker destruction. The servants, now awake, made their way onto the roof. Since they slept at the top of the house, this was the only escape possible. But they were trapped, and the crowd, which had gathered as if by magic, was fearful that one of them would panic and try to jump. The firemen had not yet arrived, and even as they watched, part of the roof began to burn.

Thetis and Raymond, probably in the garden of St. Mary's House, Beverley. Photo by courtesy of Mrs. G. Mosby.

Even more dangerously situated, however, were the young Thetis and Raymond. Their night nursery was immediately above the smoking room, where the fire had originated. Fortunately their nurse, Miss Bonewell, was both courageous and resourceful. She climbed out onto the roof above the smoking room window, grabbed Thetis, and handed her down to George Wood's wife who was standing below. Then she tried to do the same for Raymond, but either smoke overwhelmed her, or she lost her footing on the narrow ledge, because the two of them pitched forward and fell — fortunately into some shrubbery in the garden, which sufficiently cushioned the fall that neither was hurt. Clive, still walking around bare footed sent them all, with Elvira, to take refuge in the Beverley Arms nearby, and this became a temporary home for the family.

Meanwhile, there was near panic because the watchers could find no ladder tall enough to reach the servants on the roof. A couple had been brought over, but they were several feet too short. Then the firemen arrived and discovered a painter's ladder which, when fully extended and placed against the wall of the house, enabled the five servants to climb down to safety. One minor casualty was the footman, Mr J. Green, who opened his bedroom window, surveyed the scene with horror, and decided that his best bet was to climb down the ivy which covered the wall at that part of the building. He had reckoned without the dense cloud of smoke, which almost suffocated him. Bewildered, no longer comprehending the difference between height and depth, he hung there until a fireman spotted him, and he was brought down to safety.

By four o'clock in the morning the fire was under control, and by this time the Hull Fire Brigade had turned up. It was immediately diverted to salvage work, and to spraying the house of Dr Munro next door as a precaution against the further spread of the fire. An upright piano was now discovered, undamaged, and was trundled out into the garden. As much furniture as possible was salvaged along with the household silver and linen. When morning came, Elvira brought round an excited Thetis and Raymond, who wanted to look at the damage; and they were photographed for the local paper, with hounds walking all round them, for these animals had also had to be rescued from the fire during the night.

Now that daylight had appeared, a full estimate of the damage was possible. It was seen that all the rooms in the north east corner were gutted, those to the west were damaged, and those to the south were partly burned out, and were also damaged by that inevitable hazard in fire-fighting — water. Kenneth offered his house at Little Tranby, just off the race course at Beverley, to his homeless brother, and to that place Clive's family shortly removed themselves.(43)

When Clive had "set up", as the local people called it, in Beverley, his mother had given him one servant from each section at Tranby Croft. A Mrs Taylor, then Miss Atkins, had been the kitchenmaid chosen, and there was also one laundrymaid, one parlourmaid and one housemaid. Mrs Taylor remembers how devoted to each other Clive and Elvira were, and not only did Clive choose red, green and white (the Italian colours) for racing, but he also had house decorations and the kitchen tiles in the same combination.(44)

The musical traditon at Tranby Croft had sunk deep into Clive's soul, and Thetis, their elder child, was taught to play the piano. Clive himself performed on the pianola. Once he put on a great favourite of the time, "Little Grey Home in the West". He had left open the door of the main hall and one of the kitchenmaids who happened to be working in that area began to sing. She had a pure, sweet voice and Clive came to stand at the open door to listen, although the performer, busy with her task, was unaware of his presence. When the song was over Clive sent for the butler, Mr Charles Bailey, and told him to bring the

Raymond and Thetis, ready for a ball. Photo by courtesy of Mr. Raymond Clive Wilson.

young singer through into the hall. A now greatly flustered Miss Atkins was produced. Clive put the cylinder on again, and listened with pleasure to a second performance.

Clive and Elvira carried on the Wilson tradition of careful supervision of staff requirements. Each member was kitted out with, as they put it, "three of everything", purchased at a local shop called Costello's. All were dressed exactly alike. They were expected to attend St Mary's Church every Sunday. Christmas had a special significance for them. On 23rd December, all the women servants received a box of chocolates, and all the material required for next year's uniforms. These were made up in the sewing room, where the seamstress spent her days. Like Mary Wilson, Elvira would come into the kitchen at ten o'clock each morning to "pass the slate" and sometimes alter it and after this, as at Tranby Croft, the kitchenmaids were sent out to put on clean uniforms before preparing the lunch.

Clive took his duties as head of a family seriously, but he remained high spirited and pleasure loving and was sometimes careless. On 13th October 1916 he had bought a new car, a Vulcan, from the Argus Motor Company in the Anlaby Road, Hull. Delighted with his purchase, he took the car straight out, only to be stopped and questioned by a Special Constable, who was on duty at Beverley Road motor halt. The car was carrying its number plate AT 805, but it soon transpired that the register of the old car had not been cancelled, and this new one had not been registered at all. This meant a summons under the Motor Car Act, and the case was heard at Hull Police Court in mid December. Clive did not appear, but it was explained on his behalf that the mistake was inadvertent, and he was dismissed with payment of costs.(45)

By the time this event occurred, Clive had taken a commission in the 3rd Volunteer Battalion East Riding Regiment as Major commanding the Beverley Company. At the beginning of the Great War he had immediately volunteered and rejoined the East Yorkshire Yeomanry as Captain, and had been stationed in a wild and desolate area north of Spurn Point. He stayed there until the first line was withdrawn in October 1914, when he was posted to the new second line and promoted Major. However, in Summer 1916, he was invalided out, and came to Beverley where he remained until the force was disbanded, still enjoying the life, and still singing with enthusiasm in the coster style at all the concerts and annual prize distributions.

He was a generous soul, thick set, spruce and still very popular. When St Mary's House had gone up in smoke he had wanted the site to be given to the borough as a public park to be maintained by him in perpetuity. The Great War had so far prevented this scheme from going ahead, but as soon as it was over Clive arranged that a memorial to the fallen should be erected in the very middle of the area. He served for many years as President of the Beverley Town Cricket Club, and the townspeople were genuinely concerned for his success as a racehorse owner. Those horses of his which were not trained by Renwick in Malton went to the new trainer at Beverley, Mr Bazley. Clive was a patron, but not a steward, of the Beverley race course. He was not particularly successful as an owner: he had horses which raced "over the sticks" with moderate success, but on 5th January 1921 "Prince Francis" was disqualified in spite of being first home at the Eglinton Steeplechase at Bogside. It seems to have been an odd race. There were only two runners, and the second horse, unhappily named "Tainted Goods", received the award because of "deviation of the course" by Clive's horse. He was furious, and immediately appealed against the local stewards to the National Hunt Committee.

The year 1921 promised to be an interesting one socially and from the point of view of sport. Family connections, Colonel and Mrs Oswald Sanderson of Hessle Mount, were the new Mayor and Mayoress of Hull. The hunting scene was alive with promise, and on Monday, 17th January Clive was out as usual, apparently in the best of health and spirits and looking forward to the next day's meet at Risby. He never made it, for the following morning he was found dead at Little Tranby at the age of only 44. The shock to family, friends and the locality was severe. The Risby meet was immediately cancelled.

The wave of sympathy from the Riding was genuine. Clive may not have been a natural businessman, but as a sportsman he was greatly admired and even loved. He did have business interests, and was a chairman of Messrs Lambert, Parker and Gaines Ltd., wine and spirit merchants, perhaps a suitable appointment, for Clive brought the same zest to his drinking as he did to life in general. He also had an interest in several other Hull companies, but although he was a large share-holder in the Wilson Line, he soon sold his interest in it after Sir John Ellerman acquired the company. But he was generous to a fault, and for that he was mourned.

Jack, who was away from home, returned at once on hearing the news. During the last year he had joined Clive in his racing programme, and he now found it impossible to comprehend that his young brother (Clive was eight years his junior), who had seemed so full of life and vigour such a short time ago, was now dead. Sadly the family drew together at Tranby Croft. Clive was to be buried with his father in the family vault at Kirkella, but before that, there would be a special service in St. Mary's Church, Beverley, to be taken by Canon Foord, his father's old friend, and Rev. J. B. Davis of Anlaby, where Clive had been taught to worship as a child. The psalm chosen was one which would bring comfort to the sorrowing family:

> "I will lift up mine eyes unto the hills, from whence cometh my help. My help cometh even from the Lord: who hath made heaven and earth . . . The Lord shall preserve thy going out and thy coming in: from this time forth for evermore."(46)

Then the congregation would sing the well loved hymns "Lead, kindly light" and "Fight the good fight" which would surely remind everybody, if any reminder was necessary, that Clive had been a fighter, and a man who could not bear to do things by halves.

On Saturday, the day of the funeral, the coffin left Little Tranby at dawn, which at that time of year was about seven o'clock. The family had not officially stated the hour of departure for this was, in a sense, their personal farewell. The coffin, of unpolished oak with oxydised steel handles and a Latin cross upon its lid, was hoisted onto a rulley drawn by two greys and the family wreaths were placed on top. The wreath from Elvira and the two children was in the shape of a broken heart and was composed of scarlet carnations. The heartbroken Mary, who had never recovered from the death of her dear husband, had now lost her "baby". She had previously sent two big bunches of violets (his and her favourite flower) and a white spray. Now she sent a big cross of Parma violets with a card which read "From mother to my dearly loved son, and the best in the world. We shall soon meet again". But the tired and sorrowing Mary had to live out six more years before her time came. Her wreath was placed next to Elvira's. The sad procession was accompanied by the huntsman, Will Scott in scarlet, by the first whipper in, Ernest Hayes, the second whipper in, Frank Short, and five couple of hounds. As Clive's coffin passed the stables several of his favourite horses were led out, every groom aware that this day was going to turn out a beautiful hunter's day of bright skies, for this funeral of a dedicated hunter. How Clive would have rejoiced to see it! The escort remained with the rulley until it was well clear of the Beverley boundary, then returned to the stables.

Kirkella Church was reached at a quarter past nine, and at the door, with Ethel and Muriel was Canon Foord, who had known Clive almost from the moment when he was born. He read the solemn words which accompany a body being brought into church "I am the resurrection and the life, saith the Lord: he that believeth in Me, though he were dead, yet shall he live: and whosoever liveth and believeth in Me shall never die".(47) A tremendous promise, and a tremendous comfort to those with faith to accept it. The coffin was placed on a catafalque in the chancel, and was then covered with a purple cloth with a Union Jack draped on top of it. On a scarlet cushion, at each corner of which a letter 'H' and a hunt button were placed, lay Clive's South African medals. His sisters and the priest now left the church, but a guard of honour remained and watched until the start of the service at a quarter past two.

The rest of the family wreaths, like those of Elvira, the children and Mary all spoke of the overwhelming sadness of the sudden parting. Muriel wrote on behalf of herself and her husband "For my brother, Clive, in remembrance of our lifelong love and happy days from his sister Muriel and his beloved Dick". His eldest sister wrote "For darling Clive, from Susan, Keith, Stewart and Ian", while from the Wimbledon family came the message "From Kenneth, his devoted brother, Molly, who loved him dearly, and Peri Hilary". A wreath came from "Gwennie" in London; Gwendoline Brogden who would have seen Clive's rumbustuous acting when she was a little girl, never forgot what she owed to the Tranby Croft family. Ethel's children sent a wreath, and were represented at the funeral by the second son, David, now a lieutenant in the Royal Navy. Members of the Hull Boys' Club, in which Clive had taken a lively interest came to the church, and also present were 40 or so of his old comrades from the A squadron of the East Yorkshire Yeomanry. Among these men were several who had been part of the guard of honour at Clive's wedding 14 years before, almost to the day.

After the service the coffin was returned to the rulley and taken to the family vault. Sailors acted as bearers. The vault was in a corner of the cemetery, and the eleven year old Raymond, saddened and bewildered as no doubt he was, still remembers clearly how, on the far side, the members of the Holderness Hunt in scarlet, with the pack lined up, stood silently; and then, as the coffin was lowered into the vault, the huntsman raised the horn to his lips and blew "Gone away".(48) There could have been no more fitting benediction.

(1) *Hull News* 20.1.1900 p.9 col.f.
(2) Ibid 17.2.1900 p.10 col.b.
(3) Ibid 24.2.1900 p.9 col.f.
(4) Ibid 17.3.1900 p.12 col.d.
(5) Ibid 12.5.1900 p.5 col.f.
(6) Ibid 21.7.1900 p.3 col.a.
(7) Ibid 1.9.1900 p.3
(8) Ibid 1.9.1900 p.9 col.b.
(9) Ibid 15.9.1900 p.5 col.b.
(10) Ibid 15.8.1903 p.3 col.g.
(11) Ibid 31.10.1903 p.3 col.g.
(12) Ibid p.10 col.c.
(13) Ibid 5.1.1907 p.6 col.c.
(14) Ibid p.12 col.b.
(15) *Hull Daily Mail* 12.4.1938 p.5 cols. c/e.

(16) Ibid 12.4.1938 p.5 cols. c/e.
(17) Ibid Friday, 10.8.1917 p.5 col.c.
(18) Ibid 17.8.1917 p.2
(19) Ibid 4.9.1917 p.5 col.f.
(20) Oswald was the son of Richard Sanderson, brother of Edward Rheam (husband of Elizabeth Gray Wilson). He opened up the New York trade for the Wilsons in the 1880s.
(21) Typescript among Ellerman's Wilson Line papers, Brynmor Jones Library, University of Hull. 4/1.
(22) Personal correspondence, E.W.L. papers 4/1.
(23) *Eastern Morning News* 14.10.1916 p.1.
(24) *Hull News* 6.8.1921 p.4 col.b and p.8.
(25) *Hull Daily Mail* Friday, 18.10.1929 p.3 col.d.
(26) Ibid 12.4.1938 p.5 cols. e/g.
(27) *William Myson and J.G. Berry: Cannizaro House Wimbledon and its park* (Darwin Press Ltd. for the John Evelyn Society 1972) p.12. I am greatly indebted to the John Evelyn Society Museum, Wimbledon for a copy of this account.
(28) Ibid p.1.
(29) Ibid pp.7-8.
(30) From a poem entitled "Inscription on the monument of a Newfoundland dog".
(31) Letter from Mrs Gwendoline Solomon to the author 8.2.1982.
(32) Letter from Sir Thomas Armstrong to the author 12.2.1982.
(33) Letter from Mr Gerald Coke to the author 1.3.1982.
(34) *Hull Daily Mail* 9.7.1928 p.5 col.c.
(35) Ibid 9.7.1928 p.5 col.c.
(36) Letter to the author 22.1.1982.
(37) et seq. *Countess of Munster Musical Trust. First Report 1958-1965.* I am indebted to Mrs Avril Mitchell, Secretary of the Trust, for a copy of this report. I should also like to acknowledge the help I have been given generally from the Royal Academy by Mrs Deller and Mr Noel Cox, Warden R.A.M. (now retired).
(38) *The Countess of Munster Musical Trust. First Report 1958-1965* p.11.
(39) *Hull News* 13.10.1900 p.10 col.d.
(40) See *H.W. Wilson: With the Flag to Pretoria (London, Harmsworth Brothers Ltd, 1901)* Vol. IV pp.794 and 884-890.
(41) *Hull News* 8.12.1901 p.7 col.c, and 12.4.1902 p.3 col.c.
(42) Ibid 12.4.1902 p.3 col.c.
(43) *Hull Weekly News* 4.1.1913 p.10 cols. a/b.
(44) I am indebted to Mrs Taylor for much of the oral evidence.
(45) Hull Weekly News 12.12.1916 p.5 col.d.
(46) Psalm 121 verses 1, 2 and 8.
(47) St. John chapter 11 verses 25 and 26.
(48) I have been greatly indebted to Mrs Thetis Malcolmson and her brother Mr Raymond Wilson, daughter and son of Clive and Elvira, for their kindness and help in the compilation of this chapter.

CHAPTER ELEVEN

Muriel

Of all Arthur and Mary's seven children, it was Muriel who received the widest recognition. A talented amateur actress, she performed on several occasions before members of the Royal Family, as well as showing a devoted interest in the well being of local and national charities. She was a well known Edwardian beauty. Her name was at various times linked with men of national importance, and for the first half of her long life she advanced steadily in social prestige and acceptance. After that, however, it was a sadder story. Marrying late, she was widowed early, and during the last thirty years of her life she was gradually forgotten by her former admirers, and had not the good fortune to become, as her friend and contemporary Winston Churchill did, a legend in her own lifetime.

Muriel was the sixth child. At the time of her birth the walls of Tranby Croft were reaching roof height, and by the time she was walking and talking her father, when he became Master of the Holderness, had already been accepted into the society of the East Riding. Muriel seemed destined for social distinction from the very beginning. She was not born in Yorkshire but, like her mother, in London, on 24th March 1875 and was christened Muriel Thetis, her second christian name being the same as that of Mary's own mother, Mary Thetis Smith, née Partridge.

She spent much of her early life at Tranby Croft, and received her education there at the hands of governesses. When she was very young she had a little French nursemaid, Marie Deschamps, very young herself, but able to ensure that Muriel would speak French and English with equal fluency. Later, her governess was Florence Isabel Brown, who coped with the necessary French grammar, with English Literature, spoken and written English and with everything else apart from art and music, for which other tutors were brought in. Muriel was receptive to literature and languages, rather than to music at which her mother and elder sisters shone. As a very small girl she was expected to entertain her mother's teatime guests, and would be brought down from the nursery, scrubbed and polished (for she was a tomboy and liked to romp around with Raymond and Clive until they went off to school), when she would declaim poem after poem to the great delight of the ladies, who were no doubt expecting a recalcitrant performer, and to the even greater delight of herself. Muriel's histrionic ability was developed at an early age.

Mary, an excellent needle-woman, wanted her daughter to become equally proficient. She could well have taught her herself, but she knew of someone who could do it even better. Mrs Wilson, the Matron of the Spring Bank Orphanage, was the one who was chosen. At first she demurred, knowing, as she did, the standard of Mary's own work, but to Mary, the matter was simple. Muriel should learn her stitches at the Orphanage, and sit on the same bench as the other girls who were under instruction. The proof that she learned well was to be found in the exquisite work she produced in later life.

At the age of ten Muriel was an attractive and lively child. We know this because of the existence of a photograph of a cricketing party at Tranby Croft in 1885. Arthur, Mary and the three youngest children sit in the middle of the throng, Muriel clutching a spaniel dog (she was passionately fond of animals) and holding it up so that it, too, should be photographed. She has an engaging grin underneath her broad brimmed straw hat which perches unsteadily upon her head, her thick, dark bushy hair flying all around it. Poor little girl! She and the nine year old Clive were to lose their adored brother Raymond before that year was out.

Muriel graduated into local society in the year in which her father was Sheriff of Hull and from that time onwards did more and more acting, but it was at Grosvenor Place that she really came to life. Beautiful and rich, she never lacked attention. The Wilson parties were lavish, but when they first acquired No. 17 they were held up, to some extent, by convention. In the early nineties Saturday evening parties were not usually good fun. They had to end early because the next day was Sunday, and Queen Victoria set the example of observing the first day of the week in a suitably dignified fashion. Lady Clodagh Anson[1] tells how the Saturday evening parties were known as "Drums" and could be truly awful. An unspectacular band on the landing and desultory conversation down below was the best that could be expected. The Wilsons, however, soon made an improvement on this. At their parties, some time after eleven o'clock, the old stagers would begin to call for their carriages and take their leave, and the band would wearily start to pack up. Muriel would then begin to move around the guests, whispering to the livelier members that they should remain where they were for a little longer. Half an hour later the drawing room, already prepared for a dance, would be opened up, the band would move into it, and "Drums" at the Wilsons' would become a thoroughly enjoyable dance which would not end until four o'clock in the morning. Perhaps, in this manner, the Yorkshire family did their bit to pave the way for the more relaxed "Jolly" which took over from "Drums" once Edward VII was well established on the throne of England.

Muriel was not the only beautiful girl in her family. Osbert Sitwell in his autobiography *Left Hand, Right Hand* mentions that when Sargent painted their family group in 1900, his mother was wearing a dress from Madame Clapham of Hull, who had made her reputation earlier when the daughters of Charlie and Arthur "had startled London... with their good looks and their dashing clothes".[2] The association between the Wilsons and Madame Clapham had been one of mutual self help. By the turn of the century this dressmaker had become very famous indeed. She occupied Nos. 1 and 2 Kingston Square but this was proving too small an area, and she was being forced to extend. Her showroom was magnificent, and she had accommodation for 150 workpeople. Just before Christmas 1901 she was reported as saying "I make dresses for most of the county and leading society ladies. Also a great many for royalty, and I send dresses out to ladies living abroad whom I have never seen — these are made from models which are kept exact to their measure."[3] The local papers invariably commented on the Wilson gowns, for Muriel's choice was always bold, and sometimes bizarre. In October 1901 there was a ceremony in Hull for the reopening of certain streets. At the entrance to King Edward Street, most suitably named during the year of his accession, two crimson covered stands had been erected to accommodate the invited guests, among whom were Mary and Muriel Wilson. Mary had chosen to wear grey, but her daughter turned out in "a crimson cloth skirt, with a short tight fitting coat of velvet to match, a black picture hat and dark sable necklet — a costume admirably chosen to show off her dark, rich type of beauty".[4] Nobody but

Muriel would have dared to wear crimson on crimson!

Muriel's clothes were noticed not only locally and in London, but also in New York. *The Times, New York City*, on 21st September 1899, wrote volubly of her arrival there the day before, for a stay of six weeks. She had arrived from Liverpool, on the White Star liner "Majestic", with her brother Kenneth, his wife Molly, and friends. Next day's *Journal, New York City* waxed more lyrical than ever.

"A girlish figure clad in a long scarlet steamer cloak that reached to her feet appeared at the gangway . . . The vivid color instantly attracted the attention of the crowd upon the pier, and friends and relatives turned their gaze momentarily from the eager happy faces of those on board whom they were there to welcome and concentrated it upon the wearer of the cloak. She hesitated a moment, mechanically brushed back with one hand a mass of wavy, brown hair that fluttered over her temples from beneath a little straw hat with heliotrope trimming, raised her skirts daintily with her other hand and descended the gang plank with as much stateliness as the steepness would permit of."(5)

The paper also sketched Muriel with a head and shoulders inset, and *The World, New York City* of the same date showed a separate sketch of her hat, and another of her beautiful eyes. Most papers said her style was unusual, one said "peculiar" and two went so far as to say "eccentric". She was described as "Great Britain's most beautiful girl . . . , Her lips are as red as the fiery cloak, her eyes are large and black and her hair wavy and dark brown". This account went on to say that she was almost an Amazon in stature, with a superb figure. It was felt to be a certainty that she would break a few hearts whilst in America, and the writer believed that "She has a way of breaking off engagements and her sisters say she is impulsive". Inevitably the papers spoke of her love affairs. Their readers were told how, some years previously, she had been engaged to the Duke of Marlborough, who had since married Consuela Vanderbilt; and had also been engaged to Lord Willougby de Eresby, but had broken this off because she thought she did not love him enough.

The beautiful visitor was not averse to talking to newspaper men who said she was "charming in conversation and when talking becomes very animated. The dark eyes flash and the beautiful white teeth show".(6) She told the reporter from the *Journal, New York City* how surprised she was that her arrival had caused such a stir, and added:

"We expect to arrange our plans so as to be in New York for the Dewey celebration. We should not care to miss that."(7)

Commodore Dewey was a war hero. The previous year, in 1898, the Americans had gone to war with Spain over Cuba. They had long had their eyes on it, first for slaves, then for sugar. The island was wretchedly governed by Spain and was rebellious, but until 1898 strong minded presidents had managed to keep out. In February of that year a United States battleship, "Maine", sent to Havana to protect American interests, was blown up in the harbour and 260 lives were lost. It might just possibly have been an accident, but press, public, and many politicians edged President McKinley into declaring war, which the Americans won with ease. Commodore Dewey, who commanded the Pacific squadron, slipped through the narrow channel of Boca Grande and blasted a Spanish fleet in Manila Bay to smithereens. The shore batteries promptly put up a white flag, and Dewey had achieved victory without the loss of a single seaman. Now he was to be honoured in New York with all the razzle-dazzle associated with such an occasion.

Many wealthy and prominent individuals had already leased boxes and windows along the route the procession would take. Some had even managed to lease vacant houses for the day. Muriel's party were staying at the Waldorf-Astoria, and boxes were being erected on the Fifth Avenue front of the hotel at first floor level, and could be acquired for 100 dollars. Kenneth secured one of these.

On her first night in America Muriel was still at the Waldorf-Astoria but the following morning her party left for Newport. The purpose of this visit was to attend the wedding of a Birdsall acquaintance, Miss Julia D. Grant, to the Russian Prince Cantacuzere. Immediately after the wedding, they returned to New York.

In the short time that she had been in America Muriel had attracted much speculation as well as attention. *The Times, New York City* reported on 26th September that the other visitors in the Waldorf-Astoria were filled with curiosity concerning her relationship with a certain young American, Robert Walter Goelet. This young man had spent every conceivable moment with the Wilson party on the journey across the Atlantic, and was proceeding to follow an identical pattern in New York. Rumours were already circulating that he and Muriel would shortly become engaged. "Mr Goelet" the paper continued "inherited an enormous fortune from his father". On 1st October *The Journal, New York City* reported:

"We are now hearing every day that Robert Goelet has become an ardent worshipper at the shrine of this fair English woman. It would be an excellent match although Miss Muriel is slightly older than her last devoted admirer. Young Goelet has been with Miss Wilson constantly since her arrival, and he looks extremely happy and unhappy by turns".

By 21st October the local paper, the *Hull News,* was on to the story but, by 4th November the same newspaper was reporting Muriel's presence at the meeting of the Holderness Hunt at Wassand. She had not, and did not, become engaged to Robert Goelet, but may have broken, at least for the time being, yet another heart.

By now Britain was at war with the Boers, and since her Warter cousins and her own brother either had gone, or were going out, to the veldt, it behoved Muriel to campaign for the war effort, as Mary, her mother, was already doing. Rudyard Kipling (whose only son was to fall, like so many others, in the next war) had written a monologue, specially for the occcasion, and had called it "The Absent Minded Beggar". In it Kipling asks his listeners to find it in their hearts to forgive the absent minded soldier who has gone off to fight for his country, leaving all kinds of personal problems at home. It was up to the civilians, he said, to look after these problems so that the "gentleman in khaki ordered south" could concentrate on winning the war. Each verse ended with a mighty plea for money, which reached its climax in the final stanza, where the reciter declaims:

"(Fifty thousand horse and foot going to Table Bay!)
Each of them doing his country's work
(And what have you got to spare?)
Pass the hat for your credit's sake,
And pay, — pay, — pay."(8)

And who would be able to resist the lovely — and determined — Miss Wilson. "The Absent Minded Beggar" was her favourite money spinner, and although Kipling once muttered that it was not poetry, it has been estimated that the poem enabled reciters and singers (for it was set to music by Sir Arthur Sullivan) to collect a total of a quarter of a million pounds before the conclusion of the war. Social life in London had not been seriously inconvenienced, but it could now, once again, proceed with a swing. One man who returned was Winston Churchill.

Muriel had known him for several years, and remembered his efforts, during an early visit to Tranby Croft, to improve his vocal delivery — essential for an aspiring politician — for in addition to his quick-fire, almost staccato manner of speaking, he was plagued by a sibilant 's'. He would walk with her up and down the main drive, reciting such immortal lines as "The Spanish ships I cannot see, for they are not in sight".(9) Later, after his return from a visit to India in 1896, he asked Muriel to marry him. She refused, perhaps surprisingly, because she was obviously very fond of him and they remained good friends. Some local people maintain that she thought him to be unambitious, which would have been an unusually imperceptive remark from a normally shrewd woman. However, they often dined together, sometimes with the addition of another of Winston's friends, Molly Hacket, who married Muriel's brother, Kenneth, in 1895.

Another survivor of the Boer war was Muriel's younger brother, Clive. In 1906 he became infatuated with her Italian tutor, Elvira Magherini, and married her on 24th January 1907, when Muriel lost a tutor and companion and gained a sister-in-law. The week before the wedding, on 16th January, an event took place which caused even more local interest than the wedding itself. Earlier in the month Muriel had travelled, as had become usual, to the Chatsworth New Year Revels, and it was now proposed to repeat her part in them to help the Anlaby Patriotic Rifle Club, which needed funds. Clive was also involved in the scheme, which was to take place in the little school room at Anlaby; but when the news got around that Muriel was bringing Viscount Duncannon with her, and that they would perform the duologue they had recently played with great success before the King and Queen, so many people demanded tickets that the venue had to be changed, and the concert eventually took place in a much bigger hall, the Parish Hall in Hessle. On the night parties turned up from all over the area in carriages and the new fangled motor car.

Muriel did not appear until after the interval. To begin with, there were a number of short items, one of which was provided by Clive, making the most of his last fortnight as a bachelor. To the accompaniment of Berkeley Mason (well known in his time as a broadcasting cinema organist) he sang "I love you in velvet", and the audience, who loved Clive and wished him well, roared their appreciation at the aptness of his choice. The duologue took up the entire second half of the programme. It was entitled "The Ninth Waltz" and was described by the local critic as "a charming trifle".(10) Muriel, wearing a ball gown resplendent in diamonds, looked just as lovely as everyone knew she would, spoke well and clearly and without any affectation. Viscount Duncannon ably supported, and the applause, when they had finished, left no one in any doubt about the success of the charitable venture.

Many of Muriel's companions belonged to the Prince of Wales' set, as it was still sometimes called, although to say the King's set would have been more accurate. One diplomat whose rise to fame had been meteoric was the Portuguese ambassador in London from 1897-1910, the Marquess Luis de Soveral. He was the confidant of Edward both as Prince of Wales and as King, and was socially supreme. Of a lively intelligence, he was circumspect but very amorous, and Muriel was one of very many young women of society who craved the favour of the "Blue Monkey". "Si tu ne viens pas au bal vendredi soir, je ne te parle plus jamais, jamais, jamais" she wrote to him, and then continued in English "Are you too busy to lunch with me tomorrow (Saturday) . . . I am quite alone, but the butler and the parrot are excellent chaperones".(11) The parrot was quite famous. Its name was Polly and it lived with the Wilsons for 23 years between 1900 and 1923, when it was buried next to the dogs in the pets' graveyard near the north east corner of the house. It travelled with the family to London and the south of France, and was reputed to bite the hand that fed it with most unchristian consistency. However, the thought of it does not seem to have deterred Soveral, or perhaps he had succumbed to Muriel's blandishments. Late in 1907 no less a person than Queen Alexandra sent him an extra invitation to Buckingham Palace with the message "I'm happy to be able to send you after all a ticket for the lovely Miss Wilson, and I hope that you and she will be very pleased."(12)

Beautiful and rich as she was, the question of Muriel's marriage was always an object of speculation. Many society mothers were willing to consider an heiress as a suitable match for their sons. Her name had already been mentioned in connection with half a dozen well known gentlemen including Prince Francis of Teck, who not only disliked Muriel's male acquaintances, but also railed against some of her women friends. Another candidate for speculation was George Cornwallis West. He was one year older than Muriel, handsome, and a Lieutenant in the Scots Guards. His father, William, was a considerable land owner in North Wales. The family was better off in land than in money, and it was important that George should marry well. Muriel was invited to Ruthin Castle for the Chester races in April 1899, just before her American debut. If, however, Mary Cornwallis West was hoping for a match, she was to be disappointed. Another guest at the house party was Jennie, widow of Lord Randolph Churchill, with whom George had fallen desperately in love, and she with him, in spite of the fact that George was only a fortnight older than Jennie's elder son, Winston.(13) Jennie, like Muriel, was often invited to parties because the Prince of Wales enjoyed her company, but on this occasion neither she nor George had eyes for anyone but the other. No doubt an extra burden of responsibility fell on Muriel as a result. The Prince of Wales *had* to be amused.

Muriel was still seeing Winston Churchill regularly, if platonically. After the villa at Cap Ferrat had been built, she spent much time there, for she loved it. It was an excellent starting point for an Italian tour, and Muriel had always been interested in the art and literature of that land. She once wrote to Winston of the villa's "lotus eating propensities" and added "Ah, it is such a divine spot — the roses and honeysuckle smell almost too strong when we sit out after dinner — it is a world of profusion of the most glorious flowers."(14) In the summer of 1906 Muriel, Winston, Lady Helen Vincent and Lionel Rothschild toured Italy from Maryland in the latter's car. The content of the tour was intellectual as well as pleasurable. Muriel carried with her a standard work on Italian art, marked off what she had seen, and also marked what she considered to be significant parts of the text.(15)

On 15th August 1908 Winston Churchill's engagement to Clementine Hosier was announced. He wired the news to Muriel at Tranby Croft, and she wrote back the same day, with generosity and warmth to congratulate him.

"I wish you every luck and happiness from all my heart. I hope I shan't lose a friend? If I thought this, I should be unhappy — but I feel we shall always like each other and remain real true friends — anyhow I shall always count you as such. Bless you dear

Winston and I can't tell you how really delighted I was to get your wire.
Yours affectionately,
Muriel"(16)

The friendship did continue, and on 16th November 1915 Muriel wrote to Winston from Charles Street, where she had lived with her mother since her father's death. Again, it was a generous and hopeful letter. Churchill had been dismissed from his post at the Admiralty because of his support of the Gallipoli plan. (The initial scheme was a good one, and the wretched fiasco which ensued was hardly his fault). Now he proposed to serve on the Western Front.

"My dear Winston,
As usual you are doing the big thing — and oh! I do congratulate you and think it quite splendid.
. . . My words are most inadequate but I just wanted to tell you how much I admired you for your courage.
God bless you dear Winston
Yours ever affectionately,
Muriel"(17)

Winston's marriage had not been the only change in relationships in that family. Since July 1900, Jennie Churchill had been married to George Cornwallis West, twenty years her junior. The marriage was not successful for very long, and Jennie's restless spirit seemed to require continual stimulus. She threw herself heart and soul into any social extravaganza, and in 1911 helped to organise a Shakespearean Ball at the Royal Albert Hall, which so attracted her that she went on to mastermind a complete Shakespearean exhibition at Earls Court. The big hall there was laid out as the courtyard of a mediaeval castle: there would be shops, sideshows, a tournament, and a club at the Mermaid Tavern. Jennie regarded it as a commercial as well as an artistic venture, but "Shakespeare's England", as she called it, was a financial disaster in spite of the fact that dukes, earls and well known members of society took part. Muriel was involved, taking the part of a "wayting lady" to Lady Curzon, who was the Queen of Beauty; and another member of the family who took part was her cousin Enid, Countess of Chesterfield, who was one of the eight excellent horsewomen in a superb Ballet de Chevaux.(18)

Muriel was not only popular because she was good company and a good actress, but because she was a highly skilled raconteur. Once, at a large country house party in Scotland she noticed that one particular evening after dinner a piper had been engaged to walk backwards and forwards along the terrace to entertain the guests, playing his music as he went. After some minutes one of the male guests, no doubt wishing to stand in favour with his host, asked if he might request the piper to play 'The Cock O' the North' as it was a favourite of his. The host looked surprised, but courteously gave his permission. The guest therefore approached the piper with this request. "The piper's face" said Muriel, when she retold the story, "was a study. 'The Cock O' the North' he exclaimed fiercely, 'Mon, do ye no ken I've been playing it for the last quarter of an hour'."(19)

But an era was coming to an end. No. 17 Grosvenor Place was left, and No. 21 Charles Street procured. Here Muriel and her mother lived when they were not at Maryland. Visits to the Riding became fewer, and the press lost interest. When her father died Muriel was 34 years of age. Most of her contemporaries had married, and her own best chances had gone. Convention now demanded moderation in her social life. When George V ascended the throne in 1910 he might well have said, as his ancestor George II did in 1754, on the death of Henry Pelham "Now I shall have no more peace". Any small disagreement in Europe might very easily become, because of tensions and German ambition, a conflagration which would envelop the whole of the continent. One of Muriel's acquaintances, Mrs Hwfa Williams, (sister-in-law of the general) may have called her memoirs *It Was Such Fun*, but Algernon Blackwood was nearer the mark when he said "Everywhere behind the fun lay the fear".

The First World War erupted for Britain on 4th August 1914. The Wilsons, like any other patriotic family, hastened to do their bit. Mary came back, for the time being, to Tranby Croft, and embarked on committee work with her energetic young niece-in-law, Lady Nunburnholme. Muriel almost certainly came with her, and was for a short period head of the ladies' organisations which provided comforts for the troops from its headquarters in Prospect Street, but she soon returned to London to work with her sister, Tottie. Several years previously Tottie had been widowed, but on 17th July 1912 she had married Lieutenant Colonel Sir George Lindsay Holford, whom she had known for a long time and who had a court appointment. His London home was Dorchester House in Park Lane, and this was now turned into a convalescent home for officers for the duration of the war. Muriel had become a Red Cross nurse, so it made sense to offer her services to her sister. She was proud of her new status, and had a portrait painted, which depicted her in uniform.

Portraits of Muriel are, incidentally, interesting and revealing. Perhaps the most famous one is the large canvas by Sir Blake Richmond R.A. (1842-1921), which was exhibited at the Royal Academy at the turn of the century, and now hangs in Hull's Guildhall. At first the artist failed to catch the colouring of his sitter, and Mary Wilson told a reporter[20] that after the portrait had been hung in the Academy Richmond had to darken both hair and eyes. The reporter had obviously found the painting very beautiful "The face is dreamy — almost wistful. No suspicion of a smile curves the Cupid's bow of the faultless mouth." Looking at the picture nearly ninety years later, one receives a rather different impression. Muriel is lovely. She wears a long, low necked dress in oyster satin, and sits turned slightly to her right, her arms hanging loosely covering the arms of her chair. But the pose is more arrogant than languid. Her upright head, with its short, fluffy hair well over her forehead, gives an impression of imperiousness. Her lively, dark eyes stare straight at the viewer, and have the same quality, as well as a certain sensuousness, which can also be seen in her full red lips. This is the arrogance of youth and beauty, of a woman who has yet to meet her match. Seven years later Sargent made a pastel head and shoulders drawing, and here again one sees the same qualities reflected by a different artist.[21] Sargent was very popular at this time. His sitters were always delighted with what he had accomplished, though Mary Clive called him "splashy".[22]

A third painting is, however, very different. Although entitled "Muriel Thetis Warde", it was painted by Philip de Laszlo in January 1916, more than a year and a half before her marriage.[23] Not much more than half the size of the Richmond portrait, this one arrests the attention through a very different emotional appeal. Muriel is much older, but still very beautiful. The artist has painted a three quarter length picture, and Muriel is looking towards her right. She wears a long and heavy rope of amber or coral beads round her neck, and holds them up in her hands. The full mouth and aquiline nose are the same, but the expression is not. The eyes are narrowed and she looks sad. This is a portrait of a woman who has had to take from life as well as to give to it. Experience seems to have cautioned

224

Muriel Wilson. The portrait by Sir Blake Richmond R.A. Photo by courtesy of the Guildhall, Kingston upon Hull.

Charcoal drawing of Muriel by John Sargent. Photo by courtesy of the Ferens Art Gallery, Hull.

her, and much of the former arrogance seems to have gone. Two portraits were painted by de Laszlo. The first one Muriel did not like and it was given to the artist's friends, the Locket Agnews, and eventually passed to Clive's daughter, Thetis, who was a god child.(24) The second one normally hangs with the Richmond portrait in the Guildhall in Hull.

It was while Muriel was nursing at Dorchester House that she met, and decided to marry, Captain Richard Edward Warde M.C. who had temporarily been invalided home. Captain Warde, at 33, was nine years younger than Muriel. Although it was not the original intention, the marriage took place at Anlaby Church just over a mile from Tranby Croft, on Saturday, 1st September 1917 at half past two in the afternoon. Not only were there to be photographs, but a film was to be made of the arrival at, and departure from the church, and this would be shown nationally. Arthur having died eight years previously, many believed that the bride would be given away by her second brother, Kenneth, since Jack was in an Austrian prison camp, but on 6th August a telegram was received with the news of his release, and a little over a week later Jack was back in England.

Madame Clapham, as usual, made the dresses. Muriel would have two bridesmaids, Hilary, Kenneth's daughter, and Thetis, daughter of Clive, who was five years Hilary's junior. Their dresses, not quite to mid-calf, were of pleated georgette in shades of pink, hanging straight from the shoulder with a loose belt and with half sleeves caught in at the elbow. Over the dresses they wore sleeveless coats of deep cream lace. Round each girl's head was a gold band with bunches of small pink lilies at either side, and each carried a sheaf of lilies. At the time of the wedding they were given pearl rings from Captain Warde, and these they wore. Muriel's dress was of cream georgette over crepe de chine, the distinctive feature being the beatiful old rose point lace which formed the front and the square train. The neckline was very low and cut square. She had a flowing veil of chiffon and this fell in deep points at the side from a Russian coronet. She carried a sheaf of tiger lilies as a bouquet.(25)

On the morning of the wedding the rain came down steadily and relentlessly, but by one o'clock it had ceased, and the sun was beginning to struggle through. This was supposed to be a quiet wedding, for Muriel had expressed a personal wish that it should be so, but the local people were determined to come and watch, and several hundred of them came out from Hull on public transport, and walked the extra mile from the terminus to the church. Only invited guests were allowed into St. Peter's and by half past two the church was packed with 200 of them. Mr Earle, now the Wilsons' head gardener, had organised the decorations here and at Tranby Croft, and much of the work had been done by women — it had taken a war to break the tradition of male gardeners at Tranby. Banks of lilies were placed on and around the altar, with hydrangeas to add colour. Their scent filled the church. Bunches of white lilies interspersed with vivid red coleus plants were at the foot of the choir stalls. Because the bridegroom was a soldier, flags of the allies hung in the chancel. Alick and Colin, the two young sons of Mr Reid the steward, who were smartly dressed in Boy Scout uniforms of the Coltman troop, stood ready to open the carriage doors as the guests arrived and keep an eye open for the arrival of the bridal party. Inside, Kenneth and Jack Travers were acting as stewards.

Captain Warde had stayed the previous night with Clive at Little Tranby. He and his best man, Sir Victor Mackenzie, arrived with nine minutes to spare. They knew that Muriel had asked for a quiet wedding and were greatly taken aback when they beheld the immense crowd, which so obviously exhibited a personal interest in what was going on.

Muriel, painted by Philip de Laszlo in 1916. Photo by courtesy of the Guildhall, Kingston upon Hull.

After smiling and nodding they entered the church, only to face another sea of curious faces. This quite unnerved them for the moment, and instead of waiting, as they were expected to do, in the pew at the front, they raised the curtain which blocked off the organ console and bolted through to join the organist.

Muriel took the bride's privilege to be late, but only by a few minutes. She made her customary dignified and graceful entrance, and looked pale but, said the local newspaper, "radiantly happy".(26) Jack carried out his duties dressed in his uniform of a staff officer. They were met at the door of the church by the choir, who moved up the central aisle singing "Summer Suns are Glowing" which, by this time, they were.

The service was taken by the Rural Dean, the Wilsons' old friend Canon Foord, assisted by the vicar, the Rev. J. B. Davis. In his address to the newly married couple Canon Foord warned them that they must not presume love. It was a gift which, if not nurtured, would wither and die. Each must be prepared to make a sacrifice of personal interests. God forbid, went on the Canon, that he should preach self sacrifice to a soldier at a time of war, but everyone had a lot to learn about giving in to other people, not just a newly married couple. After the address, and while the bride and bridegroom were kneeling, the 67th psalm was repeated. This is a psalm which asks for God's mercy and blessing, but also underlines God's judgement and His fairness, and makes the suggestion that mankind should praise His name, and live according to His pattern. "Then shall the earth bring forth her increase, and God, even our own God, shall give us His blessing". It is a psalm of thanksgiving, faith and hope.

While Muriel and her husband were signing the register in the vestry, the choir and congregation sang:

"The King of love my shepherd is
Whose goodness faileth never
I nothing lack if I am His
And He is mine for ever."

The ceremony was soon over, and they all set off down the aisle to the main door to the strains of Mendelssohn. It was now a brilliantly sunny day: good spirits abounded and the cheers were many as the bridal party re-entered the cars which would take them back to Tranby Croft. There was no reception, but friends returned to wish them well, and later in the afternoon to wave them goodbye, when they left by car for Hotham Hall, a nearby country house lent to them by Muriel's hunting friends, Colonel and Mrs Stracey Clitheroe. From there, the bride and bridegroom would leave for a short touring holiday by car, until Captain Warde had to rejoin his regiment. Mary's gift was a motor car, and perhaps this was the one used on the honeymoon — at least, until they arrived in Devonshire, when further travel had to be abandoned because of petrol restrictions.(27)

In one sense it was Goodbye. Muriel and her family would no longer visit the Riding with any regularity. Dick joined Muriel and her mother at the eighteenth century house at No. 21 Charles Street, and they only came north for Hunt Balls, charity Garden Fetes and, unhappily, funerals. Clive died very suddenly in January 1921 at the early age of 44, and another link in the family was broken. Muriel grieved for him. He had been nearest to her in age, and they had many characteristics in common — a love of people, an ability to entertain, impulsiveness and generosity. But perhaps it was to her mother that Muriel was closest, and in 1927 it was Mary's turn to go. At 84 years of age, she had long been weary of life, as her later photographs show. Her beautiful long hair, which was still given its one hundred strokes with a whale brush, night and morning,(28) was now as white as snow. Her thin face with its sad and haunted eyes peered out from the swaddling of furs which covered her as she was pushed around in her invalid carriage — she, who had been so decided, so organised, so arrogant even! It was a sad and inevitable deterioration from the days of her glory. She had sorely missed Arthur, and had never been really well after his death. Widowhood would never have suited her anyway, and she would probably have been unable to cope with it successfully, even had she had good health. Muriel had tended her devotedly, and when at last God took her tired body, Muriel remembered how, at her father's death, the gardener had cut masses of the single white dahlia, of which he was so fond, and had brought them to his room. She now went out and bought a small cross of violets, which was her mother's favourite flower, and although, later, she bought an official wreath of white lilies in the form of a cross, the violets remained in Mary's room until the coffin was taken from it, and at the funeral they were still there, so that Mary, like Arthur, was given what would have pleased her most.

She was carried to Tranby Croft by motor hearse, Dick travelling behind in his car. Muriel had had to go on ahead, but she saw to it that Mary was never deserted by the family. The hearse and Major Dick (as he now was) arrived in the darkness of Thursday evening, 24th November. The funeral service and burial was as nearly like that of Arthur as could be organised, and in due time a memorial to her was placed near Arthur's in Anlaby Church where they had both worshipped for so long, and where Mary had been churchwarden. Surely it was Muriel, with her love of Italy and her vivid imagination who thought of the epitaph, an adaptation from Stanza 39 of Shelley's Adonais:

"Peace, Peace — She is not dead,
She doth not sleep —
She hath awakened from the dream of life."

How singularly appropriate to one who, in a sense, had lived in the shadow for 20 years, and how appropriate, too, that it should have been chosen by one who was about to enter the shadows herself. There were many other tributes, but perhaps we could leave Mary by quoting from a letter written to *Truth*, that Victorian magazine which had published the best known cartoon of the baccarat game in 1891. The letter was from Lady Tatton Sykes of Sledmere, and it was printed in the issue of 21st June 1891, or a fortnight after the scandal of the court case. She had written:

"Now let me say one word of Mrs Arthur Wilson. I, as a woman who has known her intimately for eleven years, say with truth that a better and kinder person does not exist — nor a more devoted wife and mother. She is one of those rare beings whom prosperity does not spoil, and who has never forgotten or neglected a friend of former and less happy times."

After Mary's death Muriel's marriage became something of a strain. Major Warde became a greyhound race track official, and was away from home fairly often. Still, the marriage held up. On Saturday, 28th May, 1932 in the early morning, Major Warde took a telephone call from an uncle who lived at Barham Court. He was told that the house had been badly burned the previous night, and so he motored down there, to give what help he could. It was after this, that he decided to see his immediate family before returning home to London. His mother and sister, Henrietta, were living at Dene Lodge, Sevenoaks, and to get there, Major Warde had to drive across the county. At Seal, where he was

Muriel (right) with her aging mother and niece, Thetis, at Tranby Croft (from the Pressling/ Woolrich bequest).

practically on the outskirts of Sevenoaks, he ran into trouble. Leslie Alexander Price of East Court, Tatsfield, saw two cars coming towards him. One was a small Morris, the other, Warde's big Morris Isis. He saw the driver of the smaller car put out his hand to warn Warde to slow down. Warde appeared to pay no attention whatsoever, and Price, who was driving towards the two cars, realised that Warde would try to squeeze through, and so he drove his own car as far left as he could, with its nearside wheels on the grass verge. Warde got through, but Price believed that he was unable to straighten out. He had tried to do this too quickly, had got into a skid, and his car ploughed into the bank at the side of the road, turned a complete somersault and landed upside down, pinning Warde underneath the bonnet. Price had no hesitation in saying that the Isis was being driven too fast in the existing circumstances.(29) PC Westmore, the constable sent to the scene of the accident, explained how the Isis had run for 15 feet on the grass verge on the Maidstone side of the road, skidded 45 feet along the road itself, ploughed right into a bank two feet high, travelled along it for 14 feet 2 inches then got back onto the road for a further 13 feet 10 inches when it overturned. He said the total length of the skid was 88 feet.

Major Warde was taken to Foye Nursing Home, Sevenoaks. He had a fracture of the base of the skull, at least five broken ribs, and other multiple injuries. He died the next day. The verdict of the inquest was accidental death, and there was no post mortem. Warde was only 47 years old. His widow, now left alone, was 56. Thus ended Muriel's not very happy marriage.

Two years later, Ethel died and in 1938 so did Jack. His death alienated Tranby Croft from the Wilson family. During the Second World War the house was occupied by the office personnel of the Ellerman's Wilson Line, and in 1944 the building itself and 14

Muriel with greyhound at Tranby Croft (from the Pressling/Woolrich bequest).

acres of land immediately surrounding it was sold, at what by present standards seems an amazingly modest price, to the Church Schools Company Limited. By now Tottie had died, and in 1947 Kenneth followed her. Muriel became increasingly isolated. She gave up the house in Charles Street, and the rest of her life was spent, with her French companion Mademoiselle Jeanne (properly Marie Catherine) Beliac, at a lovely house she chose for herself in Hampstead. Cannon Hall stood at the east end of Cannon Place at the corner with Squires Mount, and a mere stone's throw from the Heath itself. Behind it was a beautiful garden, the retaining wall of which was some 20 feet high, since the land fell away precipitously on the east side; and an old lock up had, in earlier times, been built into it, and still remains. There was a substantial garage flat in front of the house, which at one time was occupied by Gerald du Maurier. Here Muriel lived when she and Jeanne were not at Maryland (which was left to Muriel when her mother died), and it was their permanent home after 1960 when, as Mademoiselle Beliac said, "Mrs Warde (be)came too old to travel".(30)

It was at about this time, when Muriel realised that she had outlived nearly all her contemporaries and when travelling became a burden, that she began to consider the eventual disposal of her fine collection of paintings. Many of them would go to the family, but Muriel wanted a few to return to Hull. She wrote to Vincent Galloway, then Director of the Ferens Art Gallery, inviting him to come and visit her, and view her "little collection" of pictures, some of which she was hoping to bequeath to the gallery.(31) Mr Galloway was about to retire, but his successor, Michael Compton, wrote on 9th May 1960 to say that he would like to see her Canaletto which, by this time Muriel had offered to the Ferens. The visit did not take place at once, because Muriel was ill, but the correspondence continued, and a remark of Muriel's in a letter dated 17th August shows that she had fond memories of the area. "I owe everything to Hull" she said. By November the visit had obviously taken place and on the fourth of that month Michael Compton wrote to Muriel telling her that she "must have one of the nicest houses in London" and complimenting her on her collection of pictures, all of which would be wanted by art galleries. He, himself, would very much like for the Ferens a Constable sketch and the Sargent drawing of 1907.

He must have enjoyed his visit, for Muriel's pictures were hung all over the house. There was the Constable, an oil painting by Hicks of a child with a dead canary, two Italian pictures and an oil by J.M.W. Turner (which hung over the fireplace) in the first drawing room. In the dining room she had an oil painting of herself by de Laszlo and two hunting pictures. In her garden room was the Sargent drawing. On the landing were needlework tapestries worked by the Boynton ladies. There were photographs of the Villa Maryland in the bathroom, and water-colours of the same subject elsewhere in the house; there were two drawings by Buck in her dressing room and engravings of Matlock Bath, Clivedon and Exton Park on the first flight of the secondary staircase. Elsewhere could be found the portrait of Muriel as a Red Cross nurse, which de Laszlo had painted during the First World War; a water-colour by Bunbury called "The Flower Girl"; there was a Gaudi (or could it be a Canaletto?) a picture called "Green Apples", an oil on canvas, by Lady Patricia Stanley, Queen Victoria's grand-daughter, de Laszlo's portrait of Mary Emma, Muriel's mother; and an oil by Karel du Jardin. It is possible that some of the sketches may have been the work of a member of the family, perhaps even of Muriel herself. After all, her uncle Frederick Wilson and her great uncle Bernhard Smith, were both professional painters. Art was an essential feature of a privileged young girl's education. Princess

Daisy of Pless sketched, and she hung the results of her effort in her bathrooms at Furstenstein.

Muriel died on 19th October 1964, almost to a day on the anniversary of her father's death. Her body was taken to her nephew's house at Rowley, and from there to a local crematorium, after which the ashes were interred in the family vault. In the end, five pictures were bequeathed to the gallery, "The Grand Canal at Venice" by Canaletto; a cloud study, an oil sketch on paper pasted on an oak panel, by Constable; "Green Apples", Lady Patricia Stanley's painting, a reminder of the days when the villa of her father, the Duke of Connaught, and Arthur's Villa Maryland stood next to each other; the Sargent drawing; and de Laszlo's portrait of the aging Mary Wilson. The five pictures, valued at the time by Christies at £5,447 altogether, were officially handed over to the Ferens at a ceremony in the Guildhall at lunchtime on Wednesday, 17th March 1965. Muriel's nephew, Major Ian Menzies, son of Tottie, when delivering them into the hands of the Lord Mayor, Alderman Fred Hammond, said of his aunt "She possessed extreme and unusual beauty, coupled with a dynamic personality . . . She was a friend of princes and politicians . . . I personally shall never forget her and am grateful for having known her".[32] Alderman H. Fairbotham, Chairman of the Hull Property Committee, said rather touchingly "The picture of Mrs Warde will go into what we call the Wilson Room where there are other reminders of the family which did so much for Hull in the hungry days, and did not forget Hull in the more prosperous days." Councillor Rupert Alec-Smith echoed the same sentiment when he said "We value this gift not only because of the importance of the pictures" (Alderman Fairbotham had said that the Ferens was probably the only provincial art gallery to have a Canaletto) "but because it forges another link between this city and the Wilson family".

There, with the death of the last Wilson of Tranby Croft, we must leave the family. The story has proved to be a richly woven tapestry. Again and again the same characteristics appear throughout the generations. It is even true that one of the first David Wilson's great grandsons died in 1914 — a lighterman. The descendants of the Tranby Croft family are thriving, all over the world, but there are none of them at Tranby Croft, the mansion Arthur so desperately wanted to make into a family seat. And yet, in another sense, the Wilson connection with the house has been reborn. When, in 1890, the feminist Miss C. S. Bremner, worked to secure part of the Hymers Bequest to establish a school for girls and failed to do so, the Church Schools Company stepped in, and with the help of local share-holders founded Hull High School for Girls. One of the first, and certainly the largest share-holder, was Arthur Wilson. In 1944 the school was moved from its war damaged and unsuitable buildings in Park Street to Tranby Croft itself. Subsequent alterations and new building have transformed it into a modern and successful independent school, but the heart of it is still the Victorian mansion, and enough surely remains for this extraordinary inheritance never to be forgotten. Arthur built for posterity, and generation after generation of children are being nurtured in his faith, and taught in his house. The Wilson motto was "Semper Vigilans"; the school's motto is "Fortiter". Arthur would surely have approved. His story, and the story of his house, has been a brave tale to tell.

(1) *Lady Clodagh Anson: Victorian Days* (Richards 1957) p.136.
(2) *Sir Osbert Sitwell: Left Hand, Right Hand* (Reprint Society 1946) p.234.
(3) *Hull Lady* December 1901 p.48.
(4) Ibid November 1901 p.35.
(5) 22.9.1899.

(6) *World, New York City* 22.9.1899.

(7) 22.9.1899.

(8) *Presented by Marghanita Laski: Kipling's English History* (BBC 1974) pp.88-90.

(9) *Randolph S. Churchill: Winston Spencer Churchill* (Heinemann 1969) Vol.1 'Youth' 1874-1900 p.293.

(10) *Hull News* 19.1.1907 p.5 col.c.

(11) Quoted by G. *Brook-Shepherd: Uncle of Europe* (Book Club Associates 1975) p.145 from the Soveral Family Papers.

(12) Ibid p.149.

(13) See *Peregrine Churchill and Julian Mitchell: Jennie, Lady Randolph Churchill* (Collins 1974) p.186.

(14) *Randolph Churchill: Winston Spencer Churchill* op. cit. Vol.II, pp.209-210.

(15) This was a set of eight small volumes (of which the author possesses six) of *Giorgio Vasari: The lives of the Painters, Sculptors and Architects* (Dent 1900). They are bound in dark green leather with her name in gilt capitals at the base of the front cover.

(16) *Randolph S. Churchill* op. cit. Vol.II (Companion vol. p.804).

(17) Ibid Companion Vol.III Part 2 May 1915-December 1916 by Martin Gilbert pp.1273-4.

(18) *Churchill and Mitchell: Jennie, Lady Randolph Churchill* op. cit. pp.232-233.

(19) *Hull Daily Mail* 4.9.1917 p.3 col.c.

(20) R.H.A. Curry of *The Hull Lady* (November 1901).

(21) The picture is now in the Ferens Art Gallery, Hull, and is part of the Muriel Warde bequest.

(22) *Mary Clive: The Day of Reckoning* (Reprint Society, London 1965) p.63.

(23) Both the de Laszlo and Richmond paintings are to be found in Room 80 of Hull Guildhall. The latter was presented to the City of Hull by the family of Arthur Wilson in 1939.

(24) Information supplied to the author by Mrs T. Malcolmson.

(25) *Hull Daily Mail* 1.9.1917 p.4 col.b.

(26) Ibid p.4 col.c.

(27) Ibid

(28) Verbal evidence from Mrs Taylor, once a kitchen maid at Tranby.

(29) Reported in *Hull Daily Mail* 1.6.1932 p.7 cols. b/c.

(30) Letter to the author from Jeanne Beliac January 1977.

(31) Letter to Vincent Galloway dated 14.1 (probably 1960). I am greatly indebted to Mr John Bradshaw, Director of Museums and Art Galleries, Hull for permission to see and use this correspondence.

(32) *Hull Daily Mail* 18.3.1965 p.9 cols. e/g.

INDEX

(N.B. There are only a few incidental references to Arthur and Mary Wilson, since they appear on practically every page in the book. Therefore, please consult either the event itself, or the other persons concerned.)